LIVES OF THE GREAT MAKERS

LIVES OF THE GREAT MAKERS

500 YEARS OF CREATIVE EXCELLENCE

EDITED BY REBECCA KNOTT AND JAMES ROBINSON

Thames &Hudson | V&A

CONTENTS

THE EMERGENCE OF THE CELEBRATED MAKER

ENLIGHTENMENT & EMPIRE

ART & INDUSTRY

MODERNISM & THE POST-WAR CRAFT REVIVAL

INTRODUCTION

One of the indisputable defining characteristics of the human species is our ability to create art. As creativity has evolved, so has our understanding and appreciation, and the desire to categorize different aspects of artistic endeavour – particularly in the post-Enlightenment period – has generated much debate about what constitutes art, craft or design. For the purposes of this publication, the V&A's uniquely comprehensive collection serves as a microcosm of manufacture in the broadest sense and encapsulates the various guises of the 'maker', whether they work in ceramics, glass, stained glass, woodcarving, metalwork, jewellery, furniture or textiles. The term maker has been adopted to characterize best the lives of the individuals captured in the biographies and assembled here by V&A curators. We have chosen only to feature makers who are identified by name, through their mark, signature, documentary evidence or convincing stylistic attribution, and whose name is, or was, synonymous with excellence in their field. In doing so, we reveal the design skills, technical ingenuity, aesthetic flair and artistic spirit that identifies these extraordinary objects and their makers.

The terminology used to describe makers and making has changed throughout time and differs across the globe. Making and the mastery of technique have not always been valued or prioritized in discussions around works of art, yet the physical qualities of a work, including its materials, craftsmanship and the application of tools and technology, are fundamental to our understanding of it. This book focuses on makers working within a western tradition of the decorative arts and considers how making has developed as a discipline from *c*.1500 to around the year 2000. We look at how making is impacted by the movement of people, by war, empire, trade, patronage and the development of ideas, and recognize how traditions of making are bound up in class and gender hierarchies and economic imbalances.

The focus is on makers working within the disciplines of the decorative arts, a term that was developed in the nineteenth century and used to differentiate decorative, practical or utilitarian objects and to give them the status traditionally afforded to the fine arts. Broadly speaking, the decorative arts describe objects whose design and manufacture mean that they are typically aesthetically pleasing and functional (fig. 1). This term has at times gone out of fashion but has remained in near consistent use by museums and special interest groups. Other terms that could be used to describe a similar group of makers and objects include the applied arts, industrial arts, design and craft, and each will be used where relevant throughout this book. We use decorative arts as the overarching term as it most accurately describes the output of the broad group of makers included in the scope of this publication.

Although the output of the makers featured and their methods of production differ greatly, what they have in common is that their intended outcome is an exquisitely crafted handmade object that is unique or limited in production. For all these makers, their objects were either conceived and made by the same person or were conceived by one person and made by one or many others, typically in a workshop setting. Defining the handmade is not always easy, nor is drawing a clear line between machine and tools, as few things have been made by the

Fig. 1
Teapots from the Wedgwood Shape Book, *c.*1780–90
Pencil, watercolour and ink on paper, each page 25.9 × 36.1 cm
V&A Wedgwood Collection Archive: E54-30019c

hand unaided. Industrial design sits outside the remit of this book, not for any lack of appreciation of its value but due to the differing modes of production and factors influencing its development and success. However, we do explore the great impact that industrial design and manufacturing has had on making in the nineteenth and twentieth centuries, and for some of the makers featured in the third and fourth sections of this book we look at how their practice overlaps with design for mass manufacture.

All the makers featured here are or were based in Europe and the United States of America. This is for several reasons, including the fact that the V&A collection is particularly strong in works from these areas but also that the context for making is most similar. This includes the provision of education and routes into making as well as networks of patronage and support. Our selection of makers was not made on the assumption that western traditions of making are superior or that there are no great makers from areas outside of Europe and America. Rather, the geographical limit was made on the basis that this publication was not intended to be an encyclopaedia of makers and that histories of making within a western tradition could be best represented by focusing on these areas.

Choosing 40 makers from a collection of the scope and scale of the V&A's was a difficult task and the selected list is not meant to be exhaustive. Rather, this list is intended to introduce readers to a variety of well- and lesser-known makers working across materials and in a multitude of different ways. The makers featured are some of the best in their field and their works were typically made for purchase by the most economically and socially privileged. This is because their consumers had the resources available to procure the most expensive materials and the most skilled techniques of manufacture by the very best makers. As such, the works produced will have been part of the day-to-day reality of a very small portion of society, but we also show how the makers themselves came from a range of backgrounds and how their objects have had a broad impact. To expand the creative context of those featured we have listed a small selection of related makers at the end of each biography and we hope readers might choose to seek them out independently.

Our narrative begins in the late medieval period and in the first section we explore the emergence of master craftspeople, introducing readers to some of the earliest known makers in our collection. Prior to this the names of individual makers were not commonly recorded (fig. 2), although it is sometimes possible to identify groups of works by one maker owing to similarities in technique or application of material. The identity of makers in this early period became increasingly necessary for commercial, legal and logistical reasons as much as for any desire to announce artistic brilliance. However, in time, individual makers were duly celebrated for their technical expertise and pre-eminence in their field. As new territories and markets opened up in the post-Renaissance period through colonial expansion, greater trade routes provided access to hitherto unknown materials and commodities that inspired a spirit of invention to devise the best means of enjoying them. The importation of tobacco, tea, coffee and chocolate had a transformational effect on European society, introducing new rituals of consumption with newly designed paraphernalia. However, in many instances these transformations were made possible by the exploitation of people and place through colonialism and slavery: an aspect of making explored by Simon Spier in this volume (pp. 85–6).

The Industrial Revolution was ongoing throughout the nineteenth century and necessitated that makers explore the opportunities and challenges brought by machine manufacture. Objects could be created more efficiently and cheaply by machine, resulting in the division of labour and a more consumer-led and democratized market. There was much debate about the appropriate creative response to this new modernity and the impact that this had on attitudes and markets for handmade objects. As such a series of design reforms throughout the nineteenth century sought to carve out a new path for making against the backdrop of industry (fig. 3).

The early to mid-twentieth century saw a revival of craft and the development of studio practice in the post-war period. Makers continued

to explore what it meant to create handmade objects in the context of a fully industrialized society, reimagining making and materials. Today, attempts to classify artistic activity are often challenging due to the sheer profusion of styles and materials, but the collapsing of so many artistic barriers throughout the twentieth century has also resulted in countless opportunities for new forms and processes. The ways in which objects are made continues to change dramatically, with new modes of production being steadily introduced. Objects are just as likely to be made by a large team as by one individual maker, whether through digital design and printing, or large-scale fabrication with the contribution of up to hundreds of people. Digital technologies offer newfound freedoms and possibilities for making and assist in considering what a democratized future of making could look like.

We have chosen to end our discussion of making at around 2000, with those still producing work today having practised for a good proportion of the twentieth century. The V&A is very active in acquiring and platforming the work of contemporary makers and continues to engage in the very best of global making today. However, our chosen cut-off point for this publication acknowledges the continued evolution of the landscape of

Fig. 4
John Watkins
Interior view of the V&A,
South Kensington, 1876–81
Etching
14.6 × 21.6 cm
V&A: E.366-1900

making in the twenty-first century as makers navigate the opportunities and implications of an increasingly interconnected, digitized and complicated world. Our handful of current makers were chosen because their practice was shaped by developments in the twentieth century and the makers before them, and their work continues to have a profound impact on the next generations of makers and making today.

The publication is very much in tune with the founding principles of the Victoria and Albert Museum, first conceived as the Museum of Manufactures at London's Marlborough House in 1852. Open to all and free to students, its founding purpose was to improve industrial design by educating designers, manufacturers and the public in art and design. Its creation followed the Great Exhibition of 1851, realized by a team of prominent artists, businessmen, politicians and civil servants under the patronage of Prince Albert and led by Henry Cole, the founding Director of what would become the V&A.[1]

The Museum of Manufactures was moved to Cromwell Road and renamed the South Kensington Museum in 1857. It was renamed again in 1899 as the Victoria and Albert Museum, to commemorate Prince Albert's involvement in its establishment. The foundation stone for the new building was laid by Queen Victoria in her last public appearance in 1899 and she proclaimed, 'I trust it will remain for ages a monument of discerning liberty and a source of refinement and progress'[2] – a place whose founding purpose was, in the words of Henry Cole, to serve as a 'School-room for Everyone'.[3]

The final section of the building was to be completed by the architect Aston Webb. His brief was to create a magnificent frontage and to bring coherence to the multitude of buildings making up the Museum. As the building neared completion, a Committee of Re-arrangement looked at how to fill the new galleries and decreed that the whole collection should be displayed by material type to create a magnificent three-dimensional encyclopaedia of materials and techniques (fig. 4). One of the final elements to be completed was the inscription around the archway of the Museum's main door on Cromwell Road, which was adapted from a statement by the painter Joshua Reynolds: 'The excellence of every art must consist in the complete accomplishment of its purpose.' This inscription is the unifying principle for the selection of makers represented in *Lives of the Great Makers*, which extols the artistic virtues of personalities from Léonard Limosin, Anna Maria Garthwaite, Nicholas Sprimont and Josiah Wedgwood to Émile Gallé, May Morris, Lucie Rie and Althea McNish.

Rebecca Knott and James Robinson

1

THE
EMERGENCE
OF THE
CELEBRATED
MAKER

Fig. 1
Giacomo di Tondo
Chalice, c.1360–1410
Copper-gilt, silver and enamel
21 × 15.6 cm
V&A: 237-1874

... nothing can be attempted or completed, to render it in beauty and perfection, without great and extreme labour.[1]

Historically, the identity of very many makers is swathed in obscurity or even anonymity. While the Renaissance is widely regarded as a period of recognition for artists, who appear with names, documented commissions and established reputations, it would be inaccurate to construe this as an exclusive innovation of the period. The growing recognition of artists and makers was partly dependent on the social, civic, legal and contractual conventions that were devised in the Middle Ages, whereby their names were increasingly revealed in documents detailing commissions, purchases, inventories, wills and disputes. This is not to imply that medieval makers were not also celebrated solely for the intrinsic merit of their works, but frustratingly few named makers can be attached convincingly to any surviving works from the period. Tantalizing glimpses of makers are offered by the earliest manifestations of signatures that occur on a variety of different objects surviving across Europe from as early as the eleventh century. A relatively humble inlaid tile produced at the Penn Tilery in

Buckinghamshire, England, between about 1330 and 1350 is much abraded, but the depiction of a jester's head in profile can be made out with a surrounding inscription that reads in Latin: *Ricard me fecit*, meaning 'Richard made me'.[2] In this way, the object itself is charmingly endowed with a voice and personality. The format of such a 'signature' followed an international protocol for signalling artistic ownership that originated in the classical past and persisted long after the medieval period. The use of makers' names on objects at this time may have been an attempt to show pride in a particular piece of work or simply to announce a degree of quality control and accountability.

Making was such an integral part of personal identity in the Middle Ages that the name of an individual's practice or occupation very frequently formed their surname. Among the most common names in English that illustrate this custom are 'Smith' and 'Taylor'. Other names such as 'Chandler' may appear less obviously derived from a trade, but chandlers were the sellers of candles and miscellaneous goods. So compelling is the evidence provided by a name that later commentators consider it highly unlikely for Margaret le Chaundler to be the embroiderer responsible for a cope that her name is attached to in documents detailing a dispute in 1307.[3] English women did, however, achieve great prominence because of their technical and artistic skill with a needle and are often named in commissioning documents. The products they made were known internationally as *opus anglicanum* ('English work') due to their distinctive quality and attractiveness to the deluxe trade in textiles, which the English dominated particularly in the thirteenth and fourteenth centuries. It is unquestionably a consequence of the expense of such embroideries that so many of those responsible for making them are known by name from the records. There is, however, only a single example of English medieval embroidery that survives with an inscription naming the maker. It occurs on the reverse of an embroidered linen band in the V&A's collection and reads: *JOHANNA BEVERLAI MONACA ME FECIT* ('the nun Joanna of Beverley made me').[4] Sister Joanna's signature is sewn inconspicuously on the reverse of the embroidery and would appear to be a very personal dedication rather than an advertisement of her expertise.

English medieval embroidery production also demonstrates how the craftsmen and women of the period were most usually responsible for a specific activity within a much wider workshop team. Thus, in 1396 William Sauston, embroiderer to Richard II, was given permission to enlist the effort of 'broderers, tailors, painters and other workmen of the mistery of brodery'.[5] Workshop production inevitably anonymized the contribution of individuals and recognition usually fell formally to

Fig. 2
Master of the E-Series Tarocchi of Mantegna
The Artisan, plate three from 'The Ranks and Conditions of Men', 1460–70
Engraving on paper
18 × 10.1 cm
Art Institute of Chicago, 1924.39.47

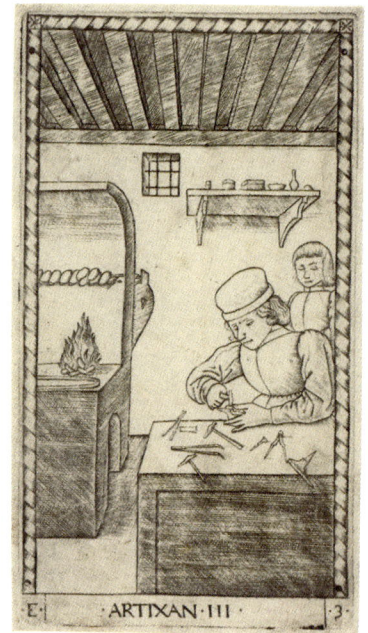

Fig. 3
Balthasar Jenichen,
Portrait of Virgil Solis, 1562
Ink on paper
10 × 7.6 cm
V&A: E.1234-1926

the master craftsman. It is fair to assume, therefore, that the 'signatures' on chalices produced in Siena in the second half of the fourteenth century were probably those of the master goldsmith. Like *opus anglicanum*, the chalices comprise a distinct body of work commonly accompanied at least by partial documentation. They are made from gold, silver and gilt copper alloy and were decorated with lustrous, translucent enamels. One such chalice, dating from between about 1360 and 1410, survives at the V&A (fig. 1). It is a composite work comprising a gilt copper-alloy foot and stem set with translucent enamels on silver with a silver-gilt bowl. The bowl, intended to receive and dispense the Eucharistic wine was most usually made from precious metals while the materials of other component parts were frequently negotiated according to cost. This example carries an inscription on the stem that reads: *FRATE IACHOMO TONDUSI DE SENA ME FECIT* ('Brother Giacomo di Tondo of Siena made me').

Goldsmiths' works were among the earliest products to acquire this type of signature in the Middle Ages and metalworkers were among the first makers to be depicted in print when the new technology became available in the fifteenth century. An early representation of a metalworker in his workshop is included in the so-called Tarocchi cards of Mantegna. Dating from the 1460s, they were probably produced in the vicinity of Ferrara for an unknown purpose, possibly as a teaching tool. The organizational principle underpinning them derives from a medieval view of the universe that is rigidly hierarchical, whereby every constituent part occupies its rightful place, from the miserable beggar to the divinity of God.[6] The card depicting the artisan is of especial interest as it represents a metalworker at his bench, surrounded by the tools of his trade (fig. 2). It shows its subject in a contemporary setting and in fashionable dress, a fitting statement of the social status commonly achieved by metalworkers and by goldsmiths in particular who enjoyed prominent roles in late medieval civic life. In London the goldsmith Sir John Shaa became Joint Master of the Mint, a Member of Parliament and Mayor of London in 1501.[7] However, despite his distinguished career and the wealth that he undoubtedly accumulated through his practice, there are sadly no surviving works known to be by his hand. Sir John Shaa had served as apprentice to his uncle Sir Edmund Shaa, a goldsmith of comparable wealth and high status. Indeed, early makers tended to work in family units and rarely departed from their chosen discipline. This familial structure continued until comparatively recent times and was undoubtedly a firm feature of the period covered in this chapter. The enameller Léonard Limosin (p. 22), for instance, probably learned his craft from the brothers Nardon and Jean Pénicaud (p. 31), while the formidable glass and ceramic decorator Ignaz Preissler (p. 52) was firmly embedded in a family tradition initiated by his father Daniel. Similarly, although the son of a Lutheran pastor, Johann Joachim Kändler (p. 76) came from a family of sculptors and was duly apprenticed to a sculptor. The advent of printmaking, however, had already disrupted this tradition somewhat as the technology of using engraved plates to produce prints, which originated in the goldsmiths' workshops of southern Germany around 1430, offered new creative possibilities.

By the time that the printmaker Virgil Solis was portrayed by Balthasar Jenichen in 1562, engraving was no longer the exclusive preserve of the goldsmith. The tools, however, that advertise Solis's craft are recognizably those also used by metalworkers to achieve surface decoration (fig. 3). Evidence provided by an epigraph that survives from other prints suggests that this representation of Solis was designed as publicity for the workshop that Jenichen himself would eventually take over upon Solis's death. The transformative role that printmaking played in design has been well documented and can be seen from works by Solis in the V&A's collection, including numerous designs for the decoration of bowls, goblets, vases, guns and ornamental panel work. Such prints were a valuable source of ideas for makers of different disciplines and were responsible for the rapid spread of stylistic influences across Europe. Solis's elaborate design for a cup and cover, with figures of Adam and Eve around the stem of the bowl and the figure of God the Father surmounting the cover, was typical of a fashion for Mannerist metalwork emanating principally from Nuremberg that proved popular throughout Germany, the Netherlands and Britain (fig. 4).

Prints, had of course, exerted an enormous influence on design practically since the invention of the printing press in the mid-fifteenth century. Arguably, the strongest impact was first felt on the ceramic production of Italy where prints were commonly used in the creation of maiolica dishes painted with narrative scenes taken from ancient mythology or the bible. Known as *istoriato*, the market for these deluxe items was well-established in the early sixteenth century in centres such as Urbino, Tuscany, Deruta, Faenza, Gubbio, Castelli and Venice.[8] Popular with a wealthy elite, these painted dishes were frequently signed and can be associated with named artists or their workshops, including Nicola da Urbino, Francesco Xanto Avelli and Guido and Francesco Durantino.[9] The status, recognition and appreciation afforded these artists is most beautifully expressed in the painting on a maiolica dish from about 1510, probably by Jacopo Maestro (fig. 5). Here, a fashionably dressed painter is seated on a throne-like bench demonstrating his skill to a wealthy couple. He is shown with pigments, brushes and examples

Fig. 4
Virgil Solis, Design for Cup and Cover, 1530–62
Ink on paper
23.9 × 14.2 cm
V&A: E.1045-1908

of his product placed casually around him. The couple may represent the artist's patrons instructing a commission. Jacopo Maestro was a supremely talented painter who worked under the patronage of the Medici from their castle at Cafaggiolo in Tuscany.

The market in the finest maiolica relied on aristocratic patronage which was frequently announced by the deployment of arms or heraldic devices that decorate many of the works, including a large number representing the Medici. Royal, aristocratic and ecclesiastic patronage was intimately connected with much of the highest-quality artistic activity throughout the sixteenth and seventeenth centuries. Patrons provided material support but they also, occasionally, provided the impetus for technological innovation. The earliest high-quality tin-glazed earthenware produced in Italy was made to meet a demand for blue and white pottery created by imports coming from Spain and China. Hugely expensive and highly revered, the mystery of manufacturing Chinese hard-paste porcelain had eluded European makers for centuries. Grand Duke Francesco I de' Medici established a pottery workshop in Florence with the express desire to discover the recipe for these bewildering and beautiful ceramics. The first successful ceramics made there, around 1574, were a technical tour de force, notwithstanding that the material

was not strictly porcelain. In fact, the recipe that achieved the closest approximation to Chinese porcelain, and was captivating enough to convince Francesco, was a fritware of white Vicenza clay mixed with glass.[10] A number of exquisitely painted Medici porcelain vessels survive. They carry the painted mark of the dome of Florence Cathedral with the letter 'F' and are decorated with trailing floral motifs in cobalt or manganese in reference to Chinese designs (fig. 6). They are exceedingly rare, with just 59 works currently known.[11] Significantly, they are remembered today by the name of the patron, Francesco I de' Medici, rather than by the undoubtedly brilliant makers who produced them. The innovative technology nurtured by Francesco did not develop after his death in 1587 and it would be almost another hundred years before an equivalent advance in the creation of European porcelain occurred.

Aristocratic patronage transcended geographical boundaries partly due to a long-established and extensive network of dynastic marriages. One of France's most influential patrons of the arts was the powerful Catherine de' Medici, wife of King Henri II. In 1562 she commissioned the highly creative ceramicist Bernard Palissy to make a grotto for her in the Tuileries gardens in Paris. Palissy had earlier gained the attention

Fig. 6
Flask, 1575–87
Soft-paste porcelain, painted in underglaze blue
17.4 cm (height)
V&A: C.137-1914

Fig. 7
Workshop of Bernard Palissy
Dish, *c.*1570–90
Earthenware, lead-glazed
26.1 cm (diam.)
V&A: C.2313-1910

Fig. 8
Thomas Toft
Dish, *c.*1670-1689
Earthenware
44 cm (diam.)
V&A: 299-1869

of Anne, duc de Montmorency, who engaged him in a similar commission, attracted by his lively figurative ceramic works. Known as 'rustiques figulines', Palissy's dishes, representing a plethora of reptiles, fish and crustaceans, were often relief-cast from life and vividly painted in naturalistic colours. He had developed his skill with enamel glazes in the town of Saintes in Charente-Maritime, where he enhanced the traditional brown and green wares with the addition of yellow and blue. Palissy's legacy is large, consisting of his prolific writings alongside archaeological assemblages and a volume of works that have been variously attributed to him or his followers who faithfully imitated his style well into the next century (fig. 7). His later influence extends to the invention of Minton's majolica in the 1850s which was greatly inspired by him.

Palissy's varied palette was symptomatic of a wider interest in the application of colour in ceramics that was also evidenced by Italian maiolica. This vibrant infusion of colour largely escaped British potters who tended to concentrate on a simpler, monochromatic utilitarian product, relying on imports to satisfy customer demand for more decorative pieces. Within these cultural constraints, however, some Staffordshire makers found a means of exuberant expression, utilizing their local rich yellow and red clays to create an outburst of controlled colour in a range of large-scale slipware dishes with bold designs. Pre-eminent among them was Thomas Toft who, between about 1670 and 1689, demonstrated considerable skill and artistry in crafting huge chargers, seemingly for display rather than use. Their precise purpose remains a mystery but their graphic designs, combined with the conspicuous signatures of the potters, have led to speculation that they were used primarily as advertising to be shown at local taverns and fairs.[12] Toft's *Mermaid* dish (fig. 8) is a prime example of his expertise in the slip-trailing technique which he employed to great effect in other works that drew on popular motifs such as 'the pelican in her piety', the English royal arms and a scene of Charles I concealed in the oak tree.[13]

Advances in technology in the seventeenth century were key not only to improving methods of ceramic production but were instrumental in significantly enlarging the range of wares available to the consumer. In the 1670s and '80s, John Dwight's Fulham pottery capitalized on the disruption to imports, caused by the periodic outbreak of wars in the Netherlands, to patent a process for the manufacture of Yixing-type red stoneware and 'the stone ware vulgarly called Cologne ware'.[14] The insatiable demand for Yixing stoneware imitations was stimulated by the trade in tea from China that was led by the Dutch from as early as the 1630s. Not surprisingly, the names of Dutch potters are associated with some of the earliest attempts at copying Chinese red stoneware to satisfy the desire for appropriate vessels for the enjoyment of tea. Arij de Milde, Samuel van Eenhorn and Lambertus Cleffius were all active in this regard throughout the 1660s and '70s. Milde and Eenhorn

Fig. 9
John Dwight
Bust of John Dwight, 1675
Salt-glazed stoneware
18.2 × 17 cm
V&A: 1053-1871

were explicitly instructed by their guild in 1679 to supply 'counterfeit East India teapots', a term generally understood to describe red teapots imported into Holland from China.[15]

Dwight was an entrepreneur, inventor and maker who revolutionized the English ceramics industry with his ambition to replace all imported wares with a domestic product. His enduring legacy is in the production of salt-glazed stoneware, which had been previously more or less the exclusive preserve of the Rhineland potteries of Raeren, Cologne and Frechen. The utilitarian, almost indestructible nature of this stoneware, combined with its impermeability, made it ubiquitous in taverns and kitchens across the country. While Dwight was keen to capitalize on the durability of stoneware, he was also determined to elevate its reception into more refined social circles. To this end, he commissioned a number of hand-modelled busts of his family, including himself (fig. 9), partly to demonstrate the possibilities of the material. In many ways, Dwight was a precursor to the potter and entrepreneur Josiah Wedgwood (p. 124), who would embrace the full power of industrialization and benefit from improved connections to global markets in the eighteenth century. He approached his craft with an understanding of science and a strong desire to improve the product, representing a different model compared with the earlier makers of ceramics by working as an entrepreneur serving a mass market.

The celebrated maker did not emerge from a prescribed route nor in a single moment in time, and questions of attribution, even concerning makers as well-documented as furniture maker André-Charles Boulle (p. 32) and silversmith Paul de Lamerie (p. 60), continue to plague scholars, connoisseurs and collectors alike. The extensive use of workshops by woodcarver Grinling Gibbons (p. 42) had, to some extent, served to obscure the excellence of his own artistic record until relatively recently. In this context, it is truly remarkable that so much material survives to testify to the unorthodox talent and remarkable success of textile designer Anna Maria Garthwaite (p. 68). While questions remain about how she learned her craft and cultivated her clients, there can be no doubt that she qualifies as a celebrated maker, not just from the body of evidence that survives from her practice but from the testimony of her contemporaries.

James Robinson

LÉONARD LIMOSIN

(c.1505– c.1576/7)

Enameller to the kings of Renaissance France

The enamelled masterpieces of Léonard Limosin are as highly esteemed
by twenty-first-century collectors as they were by his sixteenth-century
patrons. His works are held in many public and private collections around
the world. Though the son of an innkeeper, Léonard's natural talents
gained him an opportunity to train in the exacting art of enamel painting
under a skilled practitioner in Limoges. His early work caught the eye
of significant figures at the French court and, during a career of more
than 40 years, he served as enameller to four successive Valois kings.

A century after the demise of the medieval *champlevé*[1] enamelling
industry in Limoges, workshops devoted to the technique of painting
in enamels emerged from the 1460s. The earliest exponents were
anonymous. Nardon and his brother Jean Pénicaud were the first to sign
and date their work, following the practice of engravers whose published
prints provided design sources. Limosin was probably trained in their
workshop,[2] benefiting from their knowledge accrued through meticulous
experimentation. Variables in ingredients, firing times and temperatures
could ruin hours of painstaking work. Designs were built up with spatula
and brush and the enamel was manipulated with pointed tools,
particularly to reveal the contrasting colour of the layer beneath.
Successive layers were fired according to melting temperature, with
gilding added last.

Limosin established his own workshop in the enamelling quarter
of Limoges, assisted by his brother Martin and later his sons. His work
is characterized by subtlety, contour, movement and imaginative
ornamental detail, especially in delicate gilding. He was a skilled
colourist. For his *grisaille* scenes,[3] he scratched hatched lines into the
enamel paste to imitate shading in his source engravings. He was
also a skilled colourist, using dark blue or green in addition to the
more usual purplish black as grounds to his *grisaille* work. In his
polychrome enamels, he used opaque white under cobalt blue to
bring out the colour's intensity. He developed a vibrant iron red,
seen to advantage in the costume of the Cardinal of Lorraine (fig. 1),

Fig. 1
Léonard Limosin
Charles de Guise, 2nd Cardinal of Lorraine,
*c.*1556
Oval portrait plaque painted in enamels
on copper, in later gilt wood frame with
only some original plaques
46.5 × 31.2 cm (portrait plaque only)
V&A: 551-1877

and utilized red stippling to suggest flesh tones. In his later years, he experimented with pastel and citrus colours on a white ground.

Jean de Langeac, Bishop of Limoges, was a well-connected and influential art connoisseur who was quick to recognize Limosin's talents and became his first patron in the mid-1530s. De Langeac almost certainly introduced Limosin to François I's court at Fontainebleau, where the King added his enamels to his private display of treasures including cameos and goldsmiths' work. Limosin found other important patrons in the King's sister, Marguerite d'Angoulême, who was Viscountess of Limoges, and her husband Henri d'Albret. Royal patronage in turn encouraged aristocratic commissions. François I and Henri II employed Italian and French Mannerist artists to transform Fontainebleau into a fashionable Renaissance palace. Their work influenced Limosin's own designs and their drawings were made available to him as models for important enamel commissions.[4] Limosin took inspiration from Italian engravings, many after Raphael, and later used French engravings such as those by Étienne Delaune. In one rare instance, Limosin adapted his own only known etchings (scenes from the Infancy and Passion of Christ, dated 1544) for oval enamelled plaques. In 1548 Henri II appointed Limosin *peintre émailleur et valet de chambre du Roi*, a role he retained under François II and Charles IX. His wide range of enamelled vessel forms followed contemporary goldsmiths' work. He also produced unusual objects such as hunting horns, and unique works such as a reversible chess and tric-trac board (1537) and a view of the Siege of Calais (*c.*1558–60).[5] Other work includes his only known oil painting, *The Incredulity of St Thomas* (1551), which features a full-length signed self-portrait,[6] a plan of Naugeat village (1561) and decorations for the tribunes and triumphal arches for the ceremonial entry of Catherine de' Medici and her son Charles IX into Bordeaux (1564).

Limosin's first signed and dated biblical plaques (1533–4), designed to be framed together in altarpieces, were based on Albrecht Dürer's series of Genesis and Passion prints. Exposure to Italian artists at court and Italian print sources led Limosin to become increasingly fluid, colourful and Mannerist. The evolution of his Crucifixion scenes painted over the years 1536–56 demonstrates this. The V&A's plaque of 1539 (fig. 2) is less busy than the 1536 Crucifixion in the Fitzwilliam Museum, Cambridge, and introduces a striking translucent red in the scene's centre, drawing the eye to Christ above. His most celebrated Crucifixion was one of two large altarpieces commissioned by Henri II in 1552 for the Sainte-Chapelle, the other depicting the Resurrection. Limosin also enamelled a series of The Twelve Apostles[7] from cartoons by Michel Rochetel, influenced by Francesco Primaticcio. Commissioned by François I in 1545, they were

Fig. 2
Léonard Limosin
The Crucifixion, signed and dated 1539
Plaque painted in enamels and gilding on copper
21.6 × 16 cm
V&A: 2037-1855

Fig. 3
Léonard Limosin
The Feast Given by Dido in Honour of Aeneas,
signed and dated 1543
Standing dish (right) and bowl interior
(opposite), painted in *grisaille* enamels
and gilding on copper
15.5 cm (height), 21.2 cm (diam.)
V&A: C.2408-1910
Bequeathed by George Salting, Esq.

delivered after his death to Henri II at his château at Saint-Germain-en-Laye in 1547. The King later installed them in the chapel of the château of Anet built for his mistress, Diane de Poitiers.

The story of Cupid and Psyche was a favourite mythological subject of Limosin's. He first used it *en grisaille* in 1534 following engravings by the Master of the Die and Agostino Veneziano after Michiel Coxie and returned to these prints repeatedly in the 1540s and 1550s. As late as 1571 he enamelled the subject in his new pastel colours on a white ground. Seven scenes from the story feature on his elaborate table fountain of 1552; nearly 50 cm tall, it bears the cyphers of Henri II and Diane de Poitiers.[8] In 1555 Limosin enamelled a large oval dish with the 'Feast of the gods' scene[9] for Anne de Montmorency, Constable of France, whose arms and devices it bears. Portraits of the King, the Constable and their circle are flatteringly transposed onto the faces of the gods. The theme of the Trojan Wars was also popular. An engraving known as the *Quos Ego* (quoting the first book of Virgil's *Aeneid*) by Marcantonio Raimondi after Raphael published in *c.*1516 provided subject matter for enamellers. *The Feast Given by Dido in Honour of Aeneas*, lower right on the 'Quos Ego' print, is shown on the inside of a standing dish in the V&A (fig. 3). Executed subtly and skilfully *en grisaille*, Limosin embellished it top and bottom with his own design features to suit the circular format, and added turquoise and gold. Limoges enamellers also favoured the subject of Hercules, the hero of antique mythology, whose famous twelve labours often feature on the facets of pairs of hexagonal salts. His bust appears with those of Helen, Hector and Lucretia on the top of the lid of a footed bowl by Limosin dated 1536.[10] *Hercules and the Hydra of Lerne*, the hero's second labour, was painted *en grisaille* by Limosin after Rosso Fiorentino on a roundel in the V&A collections (fig. 4). Fluid and energetic, the protagonists look as if they might leap from the scene.

Portraiture is a challenge in enamel, but Limosin excelled in it. His earliest known signed and dated portrait (1533) is of the Augsburg banker Hieronymus Welser.[11] Limosin produced numerous enamel portrait plaques of the royal circle, for which he had access to drawings by the court artists, Jean and François Clouet. Many of Limosin's portraits were medium-sized and rectangular but in the late 1530s he enamelled several small medallions with intriguing portrait miniatures of ladies of the French court in white mourning dress. On the reverse are scenes in gold or blue *en camaïeu*[12] after engraved print sources. The V&A example (fig. 5) may represent Marguerite d'Autriche, Regent of the Netherlands, or Louise de Savoie, Regent of France. Others most likely commemorate Louise's daughter, Marguerite d'Angoulême, Queen of Navarre. Unsigned and undated, the medallions are ascribed to Limosin by comparison with an enamel signed 'LL 1539' showing François I in gold *en camaïeu* with, on the other side, a profile portrait *en grisaille* probably of the Dauphin (later Henri II).[13] Limosin produced some of his most mature and accomplished portraits during Henri II's reign, notably some oval enamels of exceptional size. These include portraits of Anne de Montmorency (1556), François de Lorraine, 2nd Duke of Guise (1557)[14] and his brother Charles de Guise, 2nd Cardinal of Lorraine (*c.*1556) (see fig. 1). The power of the Guise family is emphasized in Limosin's extraordinary *Triumph of the Eucharist* enamel (*c.*1561–2),[15] in which living and deceased members of the family are shown trampling Protestant reformers beneath their chariot.

Throughout his career, Léonard Limosin travelled between the French court and his family and workshop in Limoges. Apart from his large townhouse, he owned two farms and a house and garden in villages outside Limoges. His property and occupation provided a comfortable lifestyle as one of the highest taxpayers in Limoges. With Jean III Pénicaud, he served as Consul of Limoges for the Magnine canton for 1571–2. Working into his late sixties, his last extant enamels date from 1573–4. Limosin's works were avidly collected from as early as the seventeenth century and he remains admired for his originality of design, the range and novelty of his subject matter, variety of form, productivity and technical experimentation and prowess.

Judith Crouch

Fig. 4
Léonard Limosin
*Hercules and the Hydra of Lerne, c.*1570
Roundel painted in *grisaille* enamels
on copper, in later wood frame
23.3 cm (diam.) (framed)
V&A: 4875-1901
Transferred from the Museum of Practical
Geology, Jermyn Street, London

Fig. 5
Attributed to Léonard Limosin
Portrait miniature, a lady of the
French court in white mourning attire;
the counter-enamel painted in gold
with the subject of Moses receiving
the Tablets of the Law, *c.*1535–40
Painted in enamels on copper in
a gilt metal frame
8.5 × 8 cm
V&A: 7912-1862

OTHER SIGNIFICANT MAKERS

Pierre Reymond (*c.*1513–after 1584) came from an old Limousin family who may have been *champlevé* enamellers. An illuminator and designer of goldsmiths' work, his dated enamels range from 1533 to 1578. His workshop was prolific in creating *grisaille* plates and vessels, including his principal area of production, whole services with armorials for a wealthy clientele.

Pierre Courteys (*c.*1520–*c.*1581) worked for the French kings François I and Henri II. His earliest signed and dated work was from 1544. He produced accomplished *grisaille* works including large dishes deriving from print sources but specialized in polychrome caskets with Old Testament subjects, and very large embossed oval plaques.

Jean II Pénicaud (*fl. c.*1531–*c.*1549) was the son of Nardon and nephew of Jean I Pénicaud, the first Limoges enamellers whose names are recorded and to whom extant works can be matched. Jean II was a master of the *grisaille* technique. Inspired by print sources, he also devised his own designs.

Couly II Nouailher (*fl. c.*1539–*c.*1571) was the son of another Couly whose enamelled works are unidentified. Couly's painting style, in *grisaille* and coloured enamels, is particularly distinctive. Known for convex roundels with profile equestrian figures representing the heroes of antiquity after Dutch print sources, he also decorated standing cups, salts and other vessel types.

Jean de Court (*fl. c.*1555–*c.*1583) enamelled a dramatic portrait dated 1555 of Marguerite de France, daughter of François I, as the goddess Minerva. Possibly he was the same enameller as Jean Court known as Vigier, whose *grisaille* masterpieces include a covered standing cup of 1556 bearing the arms of Mary, Queen of Scots.

de Cabinet qui porte deux chan=

Ecritoire   de

toillette mònté sur son

Desseins différens de Bureaux de cabinet dans l'aspe
veus de face, Et placés à côté de leur Serre-papier.

ANDRÉ-CHARLES BOULLE

(1642–1732)

Furniture maker and master of marquetry

André-Charles Boulle has long been considered the French furniture maker par excellence, executing work of the highest sophistication and technical quality which has continued to be greatly valued, particularly in the nineteenth century. Over his long career – which substantially overlapped with the reign of the 'Sun King' Louis XIV, a period of unprecedented creative activity – Boulle's large workshop produced a wide range of spectacular luxury furnishings of striking originality. One aspect of his furniture particularly distinguishes Boulle from his competitors: his gilt-bronze mounts, 'some of the best ever made',[1] which help create the dynamic and sculptural qualities of his designs.

Boulle's great influence on furniture history is reflected in innumerable imitations and in two extraordinary tributes to his name: 'boulle marquetry' is the particularly intricate technique involving metal sheet and turtle-shell that he popularized;[2] the École Boulle (founded in 1886) is the foremost institution for the training of professional furniture makers in France.

Although we know much about Boulle's career in comparison with most furniture makers of the period, it is often extremely complicated to distinguish his work, which was not signed, from that of highly talented contemporaries. Many aspects of production remain obscure, especially before 1700, including the organization and activities of his workshop, and how his products were retailed. Dating his work is made harder by its stylistic continuity, and the practice, extended over many years, of replicating specific successful models, often with minor variations, a strategy followed by Boulle's sons after he transferred the business to them in 1715.

Boulle came from a family (originally Netherlandish) of furniture makers and trained with his father. By 1666 he was a Parisian master furniture maker ('maître menuisier en ébène') and by 1672 was granted the royal privilege of lodging in the Galeries du Louvre, having been recommended as the most adept among his profession by the statesman and administrator of the arts in France, Jean-Baptiste Colbert. As

Fig. 1
André-Charles Boulle
Detail of plate from *Nouveaux Deisseins de Meubles et Ouvrages de Bronze et de Marqueterie Inventés et gravés par André Charles Boulle*, 1708
Etching
30.4 × 68.5 cm
V&A: E.1090-1908

cabinet-maker, Bronze Chaser, Gilder and Sculptor to the King, Boulle was permitted to work in more than one profession, which was otherwise an infringement of guild rules. His outstanding technical abilities underpin his success in running a business in the period: advanced design skills, training and managing employees, organizing workshop premises and complex collaboration with other skilled makers, the cultivation of clients, and quality control to the highest levels. By 1685 Boulle employed at least 15 workmen, and by 1720 the workshop had 20 workbenches and equipment for six bronzeworkers. However, Boulle had lifelong financial problems with creditors, suppliers and clients, partly because of his avid, even obsessive, collecting of prints and drawings that provided inspiration for his designs.[3]

Boulle was also a gifted draughtsman and engraver. In 1708, at the height of his career, the leading publisher (and Boulle's friend) Jean Mariette issued eight plates of his etched designs (fig. 1), forming an invaluable record of the wide range of his products – if not their sumptuous colours.

Until then, no cabinet-maker had published such a body of work, making it a bold statement of his creative achievements and marketing abilities. These large prints demonstrate Boulle's graphic skills while tempting clients with alternative options from which to choose, as with the commode and bureau plat (writing table) illustrated here. Other plates depict curvaceous cabinets, bookcases, stands and clock cases (the mechanisms provided by others), a profitable product line which came to constitute nearly a third of production. Boulle's clientele extended to the nobility, the realms of high finance and administration and foreign courts. In particular, newly wealthy customers were drawn to his luxury materials and superlative craftsmanship. Although Boulle's work was made to commission, it was not composed of one-off pieces; rather, specific models were repeated, often with minor variations.

As made clear by the translated title of Mariette's suite – 'New Designs for Furniture and Works in Bronze and Marquetry' – Boulle also produced luxury metalwork, including andirons, wall lights and chandeliers. The eight-branch chandelier with dolphins (fig. 2) displays superb, highly expressive chasing, qualities that are characteristic of the gilt-bronze mounts on Boulle's furniture. He excelled in imbuing inanimate objects with a sense of drama and inner life, in this instance no doubt enhanced by flickering candlelight in a theatrical showpiece interior full of reflective surfaces.

Boulle's royal commissions, though prestigious, represented a small element of his production and survivals are rare. A pair of pedestals (fig. 3) are almost certainly from a set of nine made in 1684 for the

Fig. 2
Attributed to André-Charles Boulle
Chandelier, *c.*1700
Gilt bronze
78.8 (height), 80.5 cm (diam.)
V&A: 965-1882
Bequeathed by John Jones

Cabinet des Glaces ('Room of Mirrors') at the Château de Versailles, in the apartments of the Grand Dauphin, heir to the throne, and his wife, Maria Anna Christina Victoria of Bavaria. Boulle also supplied moveable furniture including upholstered seating, while the room itself incorporated wall panelling with marquetry decoration (considered a masterpiece of intricate woodwork) that he supplied for the Bâtiments du Roi, the official department in charge of the royal buildings. The nine pedestals probably supported rare vases or bronzes. Boulle's innovative architectural design features the glittering marquetry of brass, pewter and turtle-shell at which he excelled and that came to be known as boulle work, although invented some decades earlier. The craftsman would first create a stack

of sheets of turtle-shell and other materials, then cut a design through the stack with a fretsaw. Once cut, the sheets were used in different combinations: metal motifs were inlaid into a turtle-shell background, a more expensive combination known as *première partie*, and vice versa. It was costly and technically difficult to make, and over time its instability required laborious treatments to maintain a smooth surface. For the pedestals (fig. 3), *première partie* was combined with horn backed with blue pigment, alluding to the blue associated with royalty.

Metal marquetry was also used by Boulle in combination with extraordinarily naturalistic wood marquetry depicting flowers and birds among scrollwork. When it was particularly fashionable in the 1680s, Boulle made up quantities of individual wooden marquetry motifs in advance to use later when assembling his panels, but in 1715 his workshop was still well stocked with floral marquetry (and the many coloured timbers required). Boulle owned numerous flower paintings which informed his own marquetry designs. Converted into a wide range of woods, originally brightly coloured, their liveliness and finesse were achieved with expert cutting, sand-shading and engraving, as well as the staining of some woods in vivid colours. On the bureau plat (fig. 4), all four sides are covered with floral marquetry including two of Boulle's signature motifs, a foliate mask and a honeysuckle branch. The panels are combined with spectacular gilt-bronze mounts and boldly three-dimensional lambrequins in blue-backed horn, to create an effect of pulsating vitality and gorgeous luxury.

As with much of Boulle's furniture, the bureau has undergone restorations and alterations, reflecting the extraordinary esteem in which his work was held by collectors throughout the eighteenth and nineteenth centuries. Pieces often have a complicated history of (often high-quality) restorations and modifications involving structural disassembly, the replacement of missing elements and the relaying of marquetry, piece by piece.

This admiration of collectors, including John Jones from whom many of the V&A's most significant pieces of French furniture came (see figs 2, 3, 5), often focused on the sculptural qualities of his furniture and the assured crispness of its gilt-bronze mounts. These are notable features of two low tables with 'contre partie' marquetry tops (fig. 5) which were perhaps intended to flank another piece of furniture.

They are similar to tables Boulle supplied in 1701 for the Château de la Ménagerie at Versailles, the apartments of the Duchesse de Bourgogne, refurbished for her when she was just 13, as a pavilion for entertaining rather than as a residential palace. The V&A tables, with tops depicting dancing musicians, may have been made with surplus veneers created

at the time of the royal commission, using marquetry set into a brass
ground, mirroring the Ménagerie tables with a turtle-shell ground. Their
dramatic, even disconcerting, design is unified by gilt-bronze mounts
of which more than a dozen types feature (the vases are probably later
additions). Scrolling leaves on the feet and a central spiral (a favourite
Boulle motif) create a sense of sprung energy that rises through the
marquetry legs to a series of masks around a drawer front that can
be opened with a secret catch.

Fig. 4
Attributed to André-Charles Boulle
Bureau plat, 1690
Wood, veneered with boulle marquetry,
wood marquetry and horn with blue
pigment behind; gilt-bronze mounts
82 × 200 × 98.5 cm
V&A: W.19-1997
Accepted in lieu of Inheritance Tax in 1996
by HM Government from the estate of the
7th Marquess of Bath and allocated to
the Victoria and Albert Museum for display
in situ at Longleat

Boulle's meticulously chased mounts were a trademark of his work representing significant investment. In 1708 six of the twenty-six benches in his main workshop at the Louvre were dedicated to bronze working, from casting to chasing and gilding. Here too was a foundry and a store for his original plaster, wax and terracotta models. Most were destroyed when a catastrophic fire swept through Boulle's workshop in 1720. By this time Boulle had transferred the business to his sons, although he retained artistic direction. The legal documents of transfer made in 1715

provide fascinating glimpses of an elite Parisian workshop producing some of the finest luxury furniture ever made, and a maker at the height of his career.

Boulle's legacy and impact on furniture making has been profound in and beyond France, sustained in part by his enduring association with the glories of the arts during the reign of Louis XIV.[4] His work's originality, sumptuous effects and technical excellence were deeply influential on the next generation of cabinet-makers, and were uniquely prized after his death by collectors of furniture, an esteem that can be traced through the circulation of his works alongside other luxury products in the eighteenth-century art market. Notable revivals of interest in Boulle, which involved both adaptations of original pieces and new creations inspired by them, occurred in 1770s France and Regency England, paving the way for a vast range of later furniture reflecting the master's reputation and influence.

Nick Humphrey

Fig. 5
Attributed to André-Charles Boulle
Pair of tables, 1701–20
Oak with walnut, veneered with brass with boulle 'contre partie' marquetry of turtle-shell, pewter, copper and horn (back-painted in blue pigments); gilt-bronze mounts
69 × 48.5 × 54.5 cm
V&A: 1015&A-1882
Bequeathed by John Jones

OTHER SIGNIFICANT MAKERS

Jean Berain (1640–1711) was a French engraver and designer. From 1674 he was a principal artist of the court, his designs including furniture, interiors, gardens, ships and theatrical and royal events. His ornament designs, teeming with classical and 'exotic' motifs, were widely disseminated and transferred across the luxury media.

David Roentgen (1743–1807) was a German cabinet-maker working in the late eighteenth century. From his workshops in Neuwied, Germany, he sold to elite clients throughout Europe. His furniture, some of the finest ever made, was particularly celebrated for its highly pictorial 'mosaic' marquetry and inventive, precision-made mechanisms.

George Bullock (*c.*1782/3–1818) was an innovative designer of the Regency period, supplying furniture and interiors in various styles. In 1812 he moved to London from Liverpool, where he had established a business as a sculptor, modeller and cabinet-maker. His ornamental and sculptural furniture makes striking use of native woods, boulle and wood marquetry, and metal mounts.

Émile-Jacques Ruhlmann (1879–1933) was a French furniture designer and interior decorator, who was one of the most important figures in the Art Deco movement. His furniture featured historically derived forms and sleek designs, expensive and exotic materials and extremely fine craftsmanship. He considered himself heir to the great traditions of French eighteenth-century cabinet-making.

John Makepeace (b.1939) is a British furniture designer, maker and teacher. Much of his work concentrates on expensive, handmade furniture produced to commission, characterized by painstaking craftsmanship and novel forms.

GRINLING GIBBONS

(1648–1721)

Britain's greatest woodcarver

Grinling Gibbons is Britain's most celebrated woodcarver, his name synonymous with an evergreen style of decoration that transformed the interiors of many of the nation's greatest palaces, churches and institutions.[1] He was also a designer, running a flourishing business supplying carvings and sculpture in stone, marble and bronze. Gibbons's career was long, varied and unconventional and, while many of its details are unknown, written comments by contemporaries mean that we know more about him than most British makers of his day.

Gibbons was born into a prosperous English merchant family living in Rotterdam, in the Dutch Republic. His early training is unknown but he was probably apprenticed as a decorative carver in Rotterdam, where wooden shipbuilding was a significant trade. He would also have known the influential work in marble decorating the Amsterdam Town Hall, carved by the leading craftsman of his day, Artus Quellinus. Gibbons's European training helped him develop core skills such as drawing and modelling that advantaged him over English-trained carvers and sculptors. After moving to England in 1667 Gibbons spent several years in York where he worked with John Etty Senior, an architect-craftsman running a successful workshop. By 1671 Gibbons had moved to the Royal Dockyard town of Deptford, five miles downstream from London where artists and craftsmen were in high demand for refurbishing work following the Great Fire of 1666. He may well have found work producing decorative carvings for ships, an important trade at the time, while continuing to develop his artistic skills more privately. In early 1671 Gibbons's career was to take a new path. The famous diarist John Evelyn records how, while walking the streets of Deptford, he discovered the young carver working on a large panel based on an engraving of Tintoretto's painting *The Crucifixion*.[2] Evelyn was so impressed by what he saw that he presented Gibbons to King Charles II at Whitehall Palace, initiating close connections to influential figures such as the Dutch artist Peter Lely and the architect Hugh May.

Fig. 1
John Smith, after Sir Godfrey Kneller Bt
*Portrait of Grinling Gibbons, c.*1690
Mezzotint
35.5 × 26 cm
V&A: 21867
Bequeathed by John Jones

During the next two decades Gibbons's career developed extraordinarily successfully as he maintained three simultaneous professional 'strands': virtuoso limewood artworks that he himself carved; large-scale decorative carvings produced in his workshop through the well-organized division of labour under his direction; sculptures in stone and bronze. His success is reflected in two portraits of Gibbons in his prime. One (fig. 1) depicts Gibbons not as an artisan woodcarver but as someone of creative intellect and technical ability, incorporating references to mathematical proportion and Gianlorenzo Bernini (the foremost sculptor and architect in Europe). Like other successful artists, Gibbons also dealt in continental paintings and prints and had a celebrated connoisseur's 'cabinet' of artworks at home, described by Evelyn in 1679 as containing 'not onely ... his owne work, but divers excellent paintings of the best hands'.[3] A second, joint portrait with his wife Elizabeth depicted them in the grand manner of wealthy aristocracy.[4]

While contemporaries were deeply impressed by Gibbons's accomplished, sculptural works in a continental tradition – John Evelyn admired Gibbons's Crucifixion for its 'curiosity of handling, drawing & studious exactnesse, I never in my life had seen before'[5] – the artist clearly understood that virtuosity also depended on surprising the viewer. In the window of his house on Ludgate Hill, Gibbons displayed a carved flower piece of 'light wood so thin & fine that the coaches passing by made them shake surprizingly'.[6] This was just the kind of thing to enhance his reputation as someone capable of achieving the impossible.

The celebrated lace cravat (fig. 2), which has a very strong claim to be Gibbons's own work, would not have been particularly time-consuming to carve, but fulfils other criteria for virtuosity: intricacy, naturalism and the creative mastery of illusionism, the ability to represent an object more convincingly than the real thing. When Evelyn's diaries were first published in 1818, the discovery of the young genius prompted a resurgence of interest in Gibbons's work, drawn to romantic notions of the purity of the hard-working but impoverished artist.

In the 1680s Gibbons's audacious creative skills were most publicly demonstrated in two large panels which were commissioned as royal gifts for the Grand Duke of Tuscany, Cosimo III de' Medici, and Alfonso IV d'Este, Duke of Modena. The Cosimo panel of 1682 (for which Gibbons received £150 – his largest ever payment for a wood carving) is particularly rich in symbolism and compositional rhythms. Within it, Gibbons carved a conspicuous quill and scroll bearing his 'signature' 'G. Gibbons Inven[tor]', asserting that his technical skills are founded on intellectual creativity; in short, that he regarded himself as an artist, not a 'mere' woodcarver. Like the cravat, while appearing

effortless it is also technically brilliant, with subtle surface detail and radical undercutting.

Another of Gibbons's most ambitious individual works is *The Stoning of St Stephen* (fig. 3), depicting the killing in Jerusalem of the first Christian martyr, executed for defending the divinity of Christ (fig. 4). The panel, which Gibbons kept in his own Bow Street house near fashionable Covent Garden, is exceptional for its large size and an architectural setting arranged to create deep, receding perspective. The composition includes over 30 figures displaying a range of reactions from shock, through anger and grief, to indifference (fig. 5). Offsetting this intense human drama are lyrical foreground areas of plants and trees (fig. 6) and, along the palace frieze, scrolling acanthus whorls, a distinctive motif that Gibbons would develop with particular boldness in his most ambitious work of the 1690s.

Gibbons's virtuoso abilities enhanced his reputation, but to maintain a successful career spanning the reigns of five monarchs relied on his

Fig. 3
Grinling Gibbons
The Stoning of St Stephen, c.1680–90
Limewood and lancewood
185 × 121 cm
V&A: 446-1898

Fig. 4
Grinling Gibbons
Detail of *The Stoning of St Stephen*, c.1680–90
Limewood and lancewood
V&A: 446-1898

acumen and versatility as a businessman. He was skilful in developing opportunities provided by the rebuilding of London and catering to the ostentatious tastes of the wealthy English nobility. From 1673 Gibbons took on apprentices whom he could train to his exacting standards to work alongside journeymen (qualified craftsmen), and he also brought in the complementary expertise of Flemish craftsmen. Talented associates such as Jonathan Maine, Thomas Young and Samuel Watson went on to produce superb limewood carvings comparable with Gibbons's work. By the 1680s the London-based Gibbons was managing the largest carving workshop in the country, supported by a sizeable yard on the south bank of the Thames. Rigorous organization was essential to meet exacting deadlines and tight budgets on many of the most expensive building projects of the day. Gibbons's designs show that he was a talented draughtsman, and he would also have provided his carvers with full-scale drawings to follow, although none has survived. In addition to winning contracts, Gibbons also had to ensure consistency across huge volumes of work, while keeping a wary eye on competitors who had learned to produce work in his own style.

Gibbons's skills as a designer and his ability to oversee a large and organized workshop also underpinned the production of bronze and stone sculptures, which were more highly regarded and more lucrative than woodcarving. The business provided statues (including royal

commissions of Charles II and James II), funerary monuments and other decoration but this was not solo work. In 1681 Gibbons entered into a partnership with Arnold Quellin, a marble sculptor trained in Antwerp who had moved to England in 1679. In 1685 both men were involved in the largest (and most religiously controversial) building project of the day: King James II's Roman Catholic Chapel at Whitehall Palace by Christopher Wren. Two marble reliefs (fig. 7) may have formed part of the chapel's stone and marble altarpiece, dismantled after James II's deposition in 1688. In 1693 Gibbons was given the prestigious post in the Royal Office of Works: The King's 'Master Sculptor and Carver in Wood'.

For nearly 30 years until about 1700, the fashionable core of Gibbons's business lay in supplying elaborate and highly naturalistic ensemble carvings for overmantels and picture surrounds in grand, panelled interiors; his workshop also provided – at a healthy profit – great quantities of shallow carved oak cornice and mouldings. Gibbons undertook huge commissions for country houses of the nobility such as Cassiobury Park, Badminton House and Petworth House, and royal residences including Windsor Castle, Kensington Palace and Hampton Court Palace. While many of these interiors have been disfigured, dismantled or lost, his work has remained in the public eye in significant buildings such as St Paul's Cathedral and Trinity College Library, Cambridge, both by Christopher Wren.

Though carved swags and drops of flora and fauna had been seen in works designed by the architect Inigo Jones and the painter Edward Pierce, in Gibbons's workshop these motifs were transformed into something new and highly recognizable (fig. 8). He was innovative in using unpainted limewood (a pale wood that can be carved with exquisite detailing), which contrasted with darker oak panelling. In volumetric forms his hyperreal fruit, flowers and game seem to leap from the walls. The carvings are deeply undercut with sharp edges to give the impression of paper-thin forms, of a delicacy that might not withstand the touch of a human hand. In fact, his interwoven, three-dimensional forms were constructed with clever technical tricks.[7] Several layers of carving could be worked on separately then nailed together, the fully

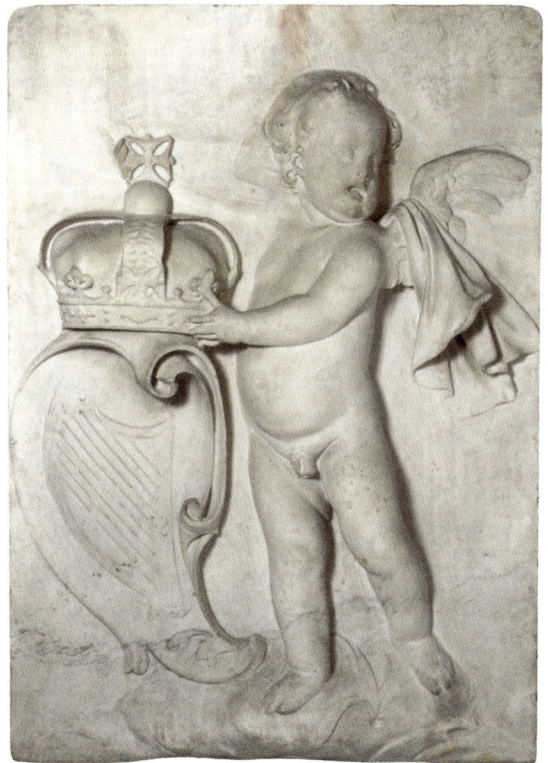

finished areas that were most visible creating the illusion of fully carved objects. Gibbons's recipe for success combined well-organized workshop production with gorgeous decorative rhythm and eye-catching detail.

Gibbons's legacy has been wide-ranging. His influence shaped a generation of English woodcarvers, some of whom worked with him and whose carvings could be equally impressive. In 1818 the publication of Evelyn's diaries stimulated the production of Victorian woodcarvings, large and small, that emulated both his compositions and his highly naturalistic style. The elevation of his reputation as the greatest British woodcarver also led to Gibbons's name being used to market derivative work in his style, obscuring his actual achievements. However, in recent decades, new scholarship and the restoration of some of his most important commissions have helped re-establish the outstanding inventiveness and rigour of Gibbons's documented work.

Nick Humphrey

Fig. 8
Workshop of Grinling Gibbons
Overdoor carving from Cassiobury Park, Hertfordshire, England, *c.*1675–7
Limewood on an oak cornice
205 × 208.5 × 19 cm
V&A: W.46 & 47-1926
Given by Harry Lloyd (the cornice given by Edwards & Sons)

OTHER SIGNIFICANT MAKERS

Edward Pierce (active from 1630, d.1658) was one of the leading British artists of the mid-seventeenth century. As a contemporary and associate of Inigo Jones, he worked particularly in the interiors of the wealthy but prints of his ornament designs helped disseminate continental Baroque styles more widely.

Daniel Marot (1661–1752) was a French architect, designer and engraver, active in France, the Netherlands and (to a lesser extent) England. At the Dutch court of William III he introduced the concept of a unified interior. His designs, published from 1703, range widely from ornament, luxury products and interiors to gardens, court festivities and funerary monuments.

Thomas Wilkinson Wallis (1822–1903) was a woodcarver working in Louth (Lincolnshire, England) from 1843. He specialized in highly realistic and detailed limewood carvings of dead birds, fruit, flowers and foliage, based on clay models. Among his awards was a prize at the Great Exhibition of 1851.

Luigi Frullini (1839–1897) was the most accomplished of the many nineteenth-century woodcarvers working in Florence. His virtuoso work in the Renaissance revival style ranges from sculpted portraits and picture frames to lavish bedroom and dining room suites. He was successful both at international exhibitions and in working for the commercial market.

IGNAZ PREISSLER

(1676–1741)

Renowned decorator of porcelain and glass

Ignaz Preissler led a successful workshop that specialized in producing
highly sophisticated and intricate decoration on glass and porcelain.
Such is the quality of this decoration that the Preissler name has become
synonymous with an entire style of decorated wares dating from the
early decades of the eighteenth century. Their work is the high point of
a tradition beginning around 1660, which saw the emergence of skilled
artisans decorating blank ceramics and glass in painted enamel colours
or gold and silver, independently from the factories in which they were
produced. The development of this industry of decoration taking place
outside of the factory occurred largely in central Europe, near to
established and sophisticated centres of art patronage and wealth,
such as Nuremberg and Augsburg in Germany. In these areas precursors
already existed in the fine painting on expensive materials by artisans
such as glass painters and goldsmiths, who had the skills and technology
to adapt their practice to decorate small items of porcelain or
earthenware in their workshops. The term *Hausmaler*, literally 'home-
painter', evolved in German-speaking areas specifically to describe such
independent decorators.[1]

Preissler was the most prominent *Hausmaler* working in eastern
Bohemia. Decoration attributed to Preissler, his family and his workshop
appears on glass manufactured locally in Bohemia or Silesia, as well as
porcelain exported from China and, most commonly, early European-
produced porcelain such as that made at the Meissen factory, near
Dresden in Saxony. The highly sophisticated work they produced is
characterized by elaborate decoration in monochrome, using mostly
black enamel, or black in combination with iron red, with some areas
of the enamel being scratched away, and some heightened with gold.
The extensive use of black enamel decoration on glass and porcelain is
known in German as *Schwarzlot* ('black lead'), a technique that developed
from stained glass painting.[2] It is widely acknowledged that this style
reached a refinement in the Preissler workshop that was rarely surpassed.
Preissler used this stripped-back palette to startling effect through

Fig. 1
Ignaz Preissler
Teapot, made *c.*1720–25,
decorated 1720–30
Made by the Meissen porcelain factory
Hard-paste porcelain decorated with
enamel colours
13.5 × 6.5 cm
V&A: C.75&A-1939

imaginative compositions that range from detailed cityscapes or fanciful and elaborate landscapes to figure scenes that were inspired by a conflation of aesthetic motifs from Asian countries such as China, Japan and India. In eighteenth-century Bohemian documents these are described as Indian figures and landscapes, and more recently as chinoiseries (fig. 1).[3]

Within a workshop that was initially started by his father Daniel, Ignaz's talents flourished and contemporary sources show that his work was in demand throughout his lifetime, but it is problematic to discern the different hands of either family member on surviving pieces of glass and porcelain which bear the distinctive 'Preissler' style of monochrome black and iron-red enamel.[4] Unlike works that were decorated in free cities such as Nuremberg, which were often signed by their decorator, the Preisslers were not able, or never felt the need, to add their name to the glass or porcelain they worked on. Consequently, no signed work by the Preisslers or their workshop appears to exist.[5]

Independent decorators often spent long periods in the service of a single wealthy patron. Much of the Preissler output was through their commissions from the Bohemian noble family of Kolowrat-Liebsteinsky whose estate encompassed the village of Kunštát (Kronstadt), now in the Czech Republic, where the Preissler workshop was based. Ignaz Preissler's father Daniel moved to this area in the last quarter of the seventeenth century with his wife and eldest son Ignaz, who

Fig. 2
Ignaz Preissler (probably)
Sweetmeat glass, 1725–35
Cut glass decorated with
enamel colours and gilt
12.6 cm (height)
V&A: C.226-1922
Given by Mr Louis C.G. Clarke

Fig. 3
Ignaz Preissler
Pair of flasks, 1720–30
Mould-blown and cut glass
decorated with enamel colours
18.4 × 9.5 × 7.3 cm (both)
V&A: C.337 & 338-1936
Wilfred Buckley Collection

had been born in Friedrichswalde in Silesia, and from then until the 1730s they are recorded as serving the Kolowrat family.[6]

From the later decades of the seventeenth century when independent decoration emerged, it primarily took place on glass vessels that were sent to artisans for embellishing. The often simple forms, such as goblets, beakers and sweetmeat glasses, were made into objects worthy of a Baroque cabinet of treasures (fig. 2). Surviving in the State District Archives in Pilsen, in the Czech Republic, is a contract involving the Preisslers that records Daniel Preissler making a number of reverse-glass paintings in the opening years of the eighteenth century.[7] These are individual panes of flat glass that are enamelled in black and red outlines and backed in gold leaf. It has been the tendency to attribute the reverse-painted glass to Daniel and the vessel glass and ceramic objects to Ignaz, but the more likely reality is that the two worked collaboratively across both, and they were ultimately produced in a workshop setting.

Letters written in the late 1720s and early 1730s by another porcelain painter on the Kolowrat estate named Tobiáš Hanuš describe Ignaz Preissler painting, as well as Chinese-inspired landscapes and figures, complex poetic subjects (*poetische Mühesame*).[8] This probably refers to allegories or scenes from classical mythology, as seen on two glass spirit flasks elaborately decorated in the black and iron-red combination of Preissler, which show extremely accomplished figurative work set in lyrical and dynamic compositions (fig. 3). Taken from engravings, one portrays an episode from Ovid's *Metamorphoses*. It depicts the moment in which the goddess Diana discovers that her maid, the nymph Callisto, has been raped by Jupiter and broken her vow of fidelity. The depiction of this scene is probably taken from an engraving after a drawing by Hendrik Goltzius. The other flask displays a bacchanalian scene that perhaps references the purpose of the flasks.

Preissler decoration is also found extensively on porcelain. Before the 1710s, when porcelain began to be commercially produced in European factories such as at Meissen and in Vienna, plain or sparsely decorated white Chinese porcelain served as a good vehicle for *Schwarzlot* embellishment. The most common type of plain white Chinese porcelain was produced in Dehua, in the province of Fujian on China's south-east coastline. However, these consisted mainly of small eating and drinking wares, and were only available to Europeans in a relatively limited range of shapes. A Preissler-decorated Chinese beaker shows how this simple form served as a blank for the addition of classical western motifs, here a scene from the story of Apollo and Coronis (fig. 4). Due to the difficulty of obtaining a diverse range of completely white Chinese porcelain, Preissler is also known to have embellished tewares with existing decoration that could be successfully worked into larger overall schemes.

Once a suitable imitation of Asian porcelain was manufactured successfully in Europe, from around 1710 at Meissen, there initially continued to be demand for decorators such as Preissler. For example, in its early years the Meissen factory did not have the capability to decorate its porcelain products in-house, so they were sent to outside artists. However, as the factory began to employ decorators and establish its own painting workshops, it was less willing to allow blank pieces to circulate on the market, taking far greater care of quality and the stylistic coherence of the porcelain produced there. Subsequently, independent decorators could only obtain Meissen pieces that were rejected due to imperfections, or shapes that were unfashionable and less saleable. For example, a sugar box produced by Meissen around 1720, and acquired and decorated shortly afterwards by Preissler, displays an exterior

Fig. 4
Ignaz Preissler
Beaker, 1720–30
Hard-paste porcelain decorated with enamel colours
7.6 cm (height)
V&A: 445-1869

scheme that relates to the original moulded relief of the porcelain, highlighting raised areas and embellishing the open reserves (fig. 5). Iron red has been used to minimal effect, simply highlighting the inside of the open mouth of the lion serving as a finial. However, the interior of the box has been dramatically filled with a scene of Chinese figures, indicating how these objects would have served to delight and surprise those who handled them. Preissler also used completely blank Meissen pieces to great effect. A teapot which he would have received completely white from his patrons has been comprehensively decorated with a scene of a bustling cathedral city in vibrant iron red, with a swirling black river bisecting the composition (see fig. 1). The scrolling handle and anthropomorphic spout of the teapot have been highlighted with black, and the lid is ornamented with Preissler's familiar 'grotesque'-style flourishes, inspired by the work of the architect and designer Jean Berain (p. 41).

It would appear that in 1731 when Preissler received a request for work in polychrome, then becoming increasingly popular, he described how he and his father considered monochrome painting in black and iron red to be the finest and most subtle form of decoration.[9] Thus the Preisslers represent the high point as well as the close of the *Schwarzlot* tradition, superseded by a greater demand for colour on fine glass, earthenware and porcelain, and the adaptation of factories to move decoration in-house.

Simon Spier

Fig. 5
Ignaz Preissler
Sugar box and cover, made *c*.1720,
decorated 1725–30
Made by the Meissen porcelain factory
Hard-paste porcelain decorated with
enamel colours
8.6 × 11.7 cm
V&A: C.121&A-1931

OTHER SIGNIFICANT MAKERS

Johann Schaper (1631–1679) was a decorator who worked in the city of Nuremberg. Schaper is the earliest and most accomplished *Schwarzlot* decorator who worked on glass and tin-glazed earthenware, and translated his training in painting stained glass into painting vessels.

Abraham (1688–1747) and **Bartolomäus Seuter** (1678–1754) were born into a family of goldsmiths. Together they ran a workshop in Augsburg which, given its prominence as a centre of fine metalwork production, also hosted a large number of decorators. The Seuters' early work is characterized by its extensive use of gilding, and they also worked in enamel colours.

Ignaz Bottengruber (d. *c.*1745) was a porcelain painter contemporary to Ignaz Preissler who worked in the Silesian city of Breslau (now Wrocław in Poland) and for a short time in Vienna. Bottengruber's work is distinguishable from the Preisslers by its greater use of polychrome enamels, utilizing colours such as green and puce.

Sabina (1706–1782) and **Anna Elisabeth Aufenwerth** (1696–after 1748) are the first documented women who carried out independent decoration. They were daughters of the goldsmith Johann Aufenwerth who worked in Augsburg. They trained in their father's workshop and maintained the business after his death in 1728.

James Giles (1718–1780) was a porcelain and glass enameller who worked in London, initially in Kentish Town and latterly on Cockspur Street in the West End. Giles's decoration can be found on objects produced by most of the main British porcelain manufactories, including Chelsea, Bow, Worcester and Derby, as well as Chinese export porcelain.

PAUL DE LAMERIE

(1688–1751)

One of the greatest silversmiths of the eighteenth century

A staggering amount of silver plate bearing the mark of Paul de Lamerie survives today (over a thousand objects, with a hefty collective weight of around 1,750 kilograms), but we have no idea what he looked like. No portrait of him survives and there is not even an extant trade card to advertise his remarkably successful workshop that produced heavy-gauge plate for English and (such was his fame) Russian royalty. Yet had it not been for the domestic and foreign policies of Louis XIV of France, his rise to prominence in London might never have happened.

Born on 9 April 1688 in Bois-le-Duc (modern 's-Hertogenbosch) in the southern Netherlands, his father, also Paul, was a member of the French minor nobility and a Huguenot. Paul Senior and his family fled France to join William of Orange in the wake of Louis XIV's revocation of the Edict of Nantes, which since 1598 had given French Protestants relative freedom of worship and some civil rights. In 1688 the de Lamerie family followed the future King William III to England and settled in London, where in 1691 they resided in a house in Berwick Street, Soho. The area was a centre for Huguenot refugees, thanks to the French Protestant chapel in Hog Lane (now part of Charing Cross Road), and by 1720 was known to be a place where an 'abundance of French people, many whereof are voluntary exiles for their Religion, live in these Streets and Lanes, following honest Trades'.[1]

In 1703 de Lamerie Senior and his fifteen-year-old son Paul applied to enjoy the same rights as a citizen of the kingdom. One of these was the right to pursue an apprenticeship. That same year, after his father had managed to scrape together the apprenticeship fee with the help of a £6 grant from a French Protestant refugee hardship fund, Paul began his seven years of training in the workshop of goldsmith Pierre Platel. The choice was a shrewd one. Platel, also a Huguenot refugee to London, was one of the most fashionable and successful goldsmiths in the city, and one who enjoyed the patronage of George I.

Paul completed his apprenticeship in 1711, but returning to France to practise his trade was not an option. Huguenot refugees were still

Fig. 1

Workshop of Paul de Lamerie or Paul Crespin
Wine cooler (one of a pair made for Philip Dormer Stanhope, 4th Earl of Chesterfield), 1727–8
Silver, raised, cast, engraved, embossed and chased
V&A: M.1-1990
25.6 cm (height)
Purchased with the assistance of the National Heritage Memorial Fund, The Art Fund, Christie's International, Pilgrim Trust, the Wolfson Foundation through The Art Fund, the Worshipful Company of Goldsmiths, Mr Jacques Koopman, Asprey Plc, Schroder Trust, John S. Cohen Foundation, Spink & Son Ltd, Sir Peter Michael, C.T. Bowring (Charities Fund) Ltd, Jocelyn and Katharine Morton Charitable Trust, Tessiers Ltd and other contributors to the Chesterfield Wine Coolers Appeal

pouring into the British Isles (over 50,000 are thought to have arrived between 1680 and 1720), and it was not until Louis XVI signed the Edict of Toleration in 1787 that French Protestants could once again worship in their own country. Moreover, from the 1660s until his death in 1715, Louis XIV was almost constantly at war with his Dutch and Spanish neighbours. To fund his armies, in 1679, 1689 and 1709 he ordered all domestic silver in the kingdom to be melted down and forbade goldsmiths to work in France. The newly qualified de Lamerie, understandably, remained in England, and on 5 February 1713 he entered his own mark at the Assay Office in the Goldsmiths' Hall (in the French fashion, with a fleur-de-lys below the first two letters of his surname) and registered his address as 'in Windmill Street near the Haymarket'.[2] The location was a good one for a business that specialized in luxury goods, as it was near the court, with its circle of wealthy potential patrons. In the eighteenth century, a silver dining or toilet service was not simply an aesthetic choice but a marker of status and a literal display of wealth that could be converted into currency, if required.

De Lamerie died a wealthy man on 1 August 1751. In a tribute, the *London Evening Post* explained that he 'was particularly famous in making fine ornamental Plate, and has been very instrumental in bringing that Branch of Trade to the Perfection it is now in'.[3] His rise had been swift: described as 'the King's Silversmith' in Goldsmiths' Company records in 1717, by 1723 his clients included members of the wealthy middle class and the nobility, and by 1728 he was supplying the Prime Minister, Sir Robert Walpole. His achievement, during a period when so many goldsmiths went bankrupt, was to maintain his business and his standing both with clients and within his profession: only his untimely death after 'a long and tedious illness' (as he recorded in his will) prevented him from becoming Prime Warden of the Goldsmiths' Company.[4]

His success was a combination of personality and circumstance. Platel recognized and developed his manual and artistic talents, while de Lamerie was unafraid to flout the law if it meant financial gain. He was fined by the Goldsmiths' Company in 1714 for failing to take his work to be hallmarked, and in 1715 and 1716 he was repeatedly charged with hallmarking as his own the work of other goldsmiths who were not registered with the Company. Meanwhile, his French Huguenot origin placed him within a world of skilful and innovative émigré French craftsmen with knowledge of French fashions at a time when France dominated European taste.

Paul de Lamerie's success made it inevitable that many of the pieces that bear his mark ('LA' for Britannia standard silver, with a higher precious metal content, and, from March 1732, 'PL' for the lower sterling

Fig. 2
Workshop of Paul de Lamerie
Candlesticks (two of a set of four), probably
made for Peter and Clara Le Heup, 1744–5
Silver, cast and chased
23.5 cm (height)
V&A: M.4-2010
Accepted by HM Government in lieu
of Inheritance Tax from the Whiteley
family and allocated to the Victoria and
Albert Museum

standard) could not have been designed and/or executed by him alone. A contemporary account of London trades observed that 'the goldsmith employs several distinct workmen, almost as many as there are different articles in his shop',[5] and the marks and manufacture of the pieces themselves point to outsourcing and collaboration. A wine cooler (fig. 1), one of a pair of 'ice-pailes' made for Philip Stanhope, 4th Earl of Chesterfield, when he became English ambassador to The Hague in 1728, bears de Lamerie's mark overstruck by the mark of his fellow Huguenot goldsmith Paul Crespin. De Lamerie's training and reputation made his workshop an obvious choice for Earl Stanhope, an early, enthusiastic follower of French fashions. The inspiration behind the coolers is undeniably French. Coolers for individual bottles of wine first appeared in the French court in the late seventeenth century, and the decoration of the Francophile Earl's examples echoes French models. The pairs of cast dolphins that form the handles, the framed, figurative scenes (in this case, representations of the four elements) and the ornamentation echo an engraving of an ice bucket by the French royal goldsmith Juste-Aurèle Meissonnier, published in 1723. The Chesterfield commission was a large one, however, and a number of other pieces are marked by Crespin alone. Were these ice pails made in de Lamerie's workshop to Crespin's design, and was Crespin moved to assert his involvement by punching his mark over de Lamerie's? No workshop records or documents survive to indicate how they collaborated, so we will probably never know.

Almost 20 years later, the finishing on a set of four candlesticks – made for the banker Peter Le Heup and his wife Clara, daughter of William Lowndes, Secretary of State to William III – offers another glimpse into collaboration in a busy workshop. The candlesticks, all cast from the same mould, incorporate the Le Heup family device of a beehive. The differences in the chasing of the twisted and coiled straw of the hives clearly show that the work for this commission was shared between two employees (figs 2 and 3).

Although de Lamerie also produced plate in the enduringly popular plain, sober forms of the early 1700s, such as a 1727 communion flagon and paten for the church of St Martin's, West Drayton, Middlesex, England (fig. 4), by the 1730s and 1740s his mark appeared on highly sculptural creations, such as this ewer made for Algernon Coote, 6th Earl of Mountrath (fig. 5). These reflect the casting skills of his workshop and de Lamerie's pioneering use of French Rococo style in English silversmithing, but also his ability to reuse and reinterpret the designs and moulds in his workshop, a practice at once convenient, economical and efficient. The year after he completed the commission for the Earl of Mountrath, de Lamerie dispatched a very similar (albeit larger) ewer and basin to the Goldsmiths' Company. Other pieces also demonstrate this reuse of workshop moulds. The largest and most expensive item in an eighteenth-century silver table service was the epergne ('machine' or 'surtout' in France), a type of centrepiece at once decorative and practical, as it acted as a stand for hot and cold dishes, condiments and even candles. The example produced by de Lamerie as a wedding gift for Sir Roger Newdigate on his marriage in 1743 (fig. 6) can be assembled in six different ways for different types of meals – and incorporates the swirling shell, flower and rock-like motifs characteristic of the Rococo style. Yet while this would have been among his most expensive orders (as was customary, de Lamerie charged separately for materials and workmanship), elements of the design, such as the lion feet or the helmeted heads of putti, are not unique to this piece but appear on other plate bearing his workshop mark.

Paul de Lamerie's business died with him: in his will he ordered all plate in hand to be finished and all stock to be auctioned. Yet he is one of a very few goldsmiths whose name has remained familiar to later writers and collectors. Partly this is thanks to the scale and artistry of his surviving output, but a mention of his name in John Nichols's much reprinted 1781 *Biographical Anecdotes* of the well-known English painter and engraver William Hogarth would also have boosted his posthumous reputation. In a list of 'prints of uncertain date', Nichols includes an 'impression from a coat of Arms engraved on a silver dish made by

Figs 3a, 3b
Detail of the beehive device on two candlesticks in the set (see also fig. 2)
V&A: M.4-2010 and M.7-2010

Fig. 4

Workshop of Paul de Lamerie
Communion flagon and paten, presented
by Rupert and Mary Billingsley to the church
of St Martin's, West Drayton, Middlesex,
England, 1727–8
Silver, raised, cast and engraved
28.6 cm (height of flagon),
16.2 cm (diam. of paten)
V&A Loan: St Martin's WD 3 and 4
Lent by the Vicar and Churchwardens of
St Martin's, West Drayton, Middlesex

Fig. 5

Workshop of Paul de Lamerie /
the 'Maynard' Master
Ewer made for Algernon Coote,
6th Earl of Mountrath, 1742–3
Silver, raised, cast, embossed and chased
46.7 cm (height)
V&A: LOAN: GILBERT. 721-2008
The Rosalinde and Arthur Gilbert Collection
on loan to the Victoria and Albert
Museum, London

Delemery'. The identification of a goldsmith by name is unusual and the link is plausible: de Lamerie was in business with Hogarth's former master Ellis Gamble in the 1720s, and a salver that de Lamerie made for Horace Walpole (now in the V&A) was probably engraved by Hogarth. Yet despite the eagerness of many nineteenth- and twentieth-century writers to take de Lamerie's maker's mark as literal proof of his personal involvement in making, this master is elusive. What evidence we have suggests a goldsmith who drew on the skills of many to run a business so successful that today his name is still synonymous with the Rococo style in English silver.

Kirstin Kennedy

Fig. 6
Workshop of Paul de Lamerie
Epergne made for Sir Roger Newdigate
of Arbury Hall, Warwickshire, England,
and his wife, Sophia Conyers, 1743–4
Silver, raised, cast, chased and engraved
23.3 cm (height)
V&A: M.149-1919
Acquired with support from Art Fund,
Goldsmiths' Company, Mr Otto Beit,
Sir John Ramsden, Mr A.S. Marsden-Smedley,
Mr Louis Clarke and Mr G.C. Bower

OTHER SIGNIFICANT MAKERS

Anthony Nelme (*fl.*1681–1722) was a successful goldsmith who ran three London shops and enjoyed royal patronage. In August 1697 he signed a petition against the work of immigrant Huguenot goldsmiths, which claimed the newcomers falsified the weight of their silver with solder, 'to the discredit of English workmen in general'.

Juste-Aurèle Meissonnier (*c.*1693–1750) was a goldsmith, sculptor and architect. Born in Turin, he moved to Paris in 1720 and became *architecte-dessinateur* to Louis XV. His designs, published between 1723 and 1725, established him as a key figure in the development of the Rococo style – although, paradoxically, few physical examples of his works survive.

George Wickes (1698–1761) was de Lamerie's business rival, who founded the company that later became the royal jewellers, Garrard. Wickes used a network of subcontractors and two ledgers survive detailing his business activities and those of his successor, John Parker. These provide a rare insight into the goldsmithing trade in eighteenth-century London.

The 'Maynard' Master (active mid-1730s to mid-1745) Some anonymous artisans employed by de Lamerie stand out thanks to their exceptional skill and use of distinctive motifs. The 'Maynard' Master – named after Grey, 5th Baron Maynard, the client for the earliest example of his work to survive today – appears to have been a chaser, using chisels and punches to work low-relief designs on the surface of metal.

ANNA MARIA GARTHWAITE

(1690-1763)

Influential designer of woven silks

Silk weaving was one of England's principal manufactures in the eighteenth century, and its chief centre was London. By 1700 silk production had grown from a long-established ribbon industry in the City and was beginning to spread to Spitalfields, the new and pleasant suburb which attracted the master weavers, many of whom were Huguenots newly arrived in the country. A thriving community established itself, focusing on dress materials and only seldom weaving furnishings. As the cut of clothes changed slowly, to be fashionable meant wearing the newest pattern of silk. By the beginning of the eighteenth century the practice of introducing new silk designs every year, or even twice yearly, had come to stay. Therefore, a successful mercer (a term nowadays closest to retailer) or master weaver had to anticipate trends and employ the best designers, whose task was not easy as they worked within three limits: fashion, cost and technique.

The first was dominant: the silks had to appeal to a fashionable clientele. However, being able to compose beautiful patterns was far from sufficient. Apart from the consumer's up-to-date taste, the designer had to consider how much he or she was willing to pay. The designer's success was thus not only measured by whether the silk sold, but also for what profit. What was essential, therefore, was understanding how the drawloom worked and how best to exploit the possibilities of this somewhat clumsy but nevertheless remarkably effective piece of machinery. Weaving is, in essence, a mechanical process where patterns are replicated along the length of the fabric. It requires considerable skill to disguise these repeats, and even greater talent to take advantage of this repetition. A designer also needed to know what would suit, for example, a damask, where the pattern is produced entirely by the contrasting surfaces, or a silk brocaded with silver or gold, where motifs should be drawn carefully so that the expensive threads are not wasted.

It is no wonder that Antoine-Nicolas Joubert de l'Hiberderie – a silk designer from Lyon, France – recommended the student designer to work as a weaver for at least a year before even starting to think of

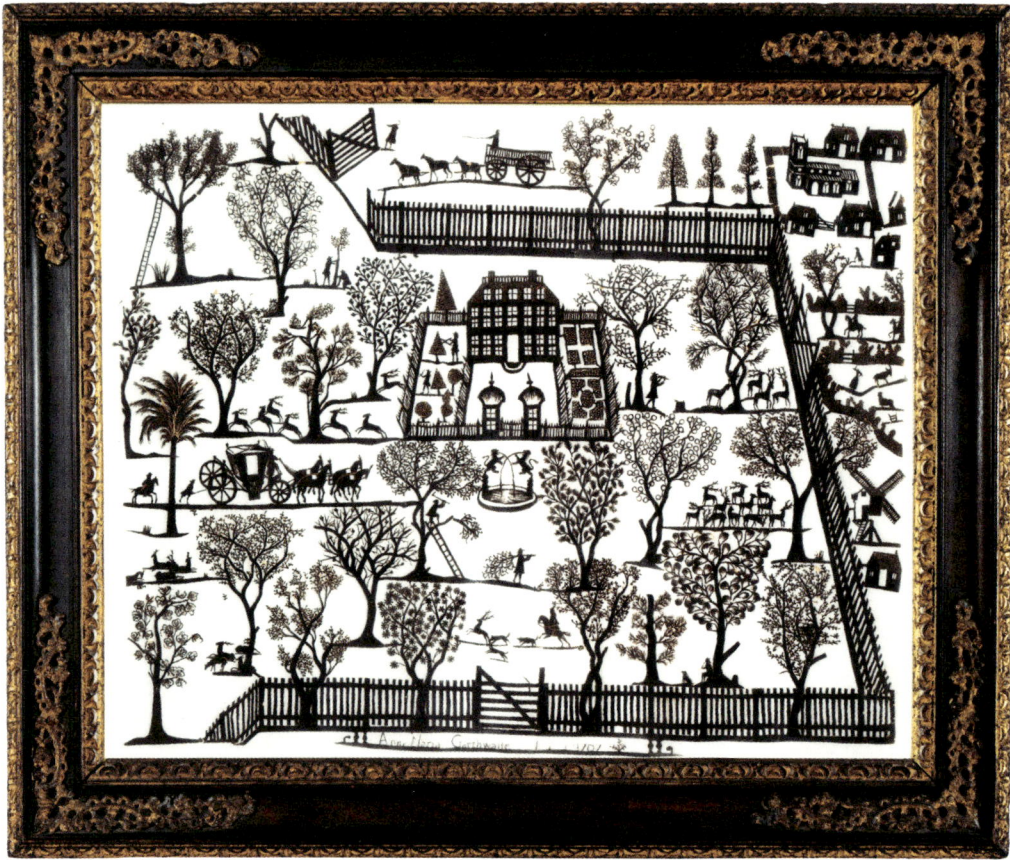

Fig. 2
Anna Maria Garthwaite
Picture of a country estate, 1707
Knife-cut cut-paper work, with pin
pricking and collage, paper and ink
on a vellum backing
32.5 × 40 cm
V&A: E.1077-1993

designing a pattern. This practice was very likely among the main
reasons why the profession in France remained out of women's reach.
However, Joubert de l'Hiberderie called this exclusion of women from
design work 'a ridiculous custom' which he believed to be 'an injustice'
to 'this delicate sex, adroit and full of taste'. While the French silk
designers were, therefore, all men, in England it was not uncommon
for women to pursue the trade. In the Spitalfields community of such
artisans, equipped with talent and specialized knowledge required
to design for 'flower'd' (drawloom-patterned) silks, how many were
women? Two are among the twelve designers mentioned in Malachy
Postlethwayt's *Universal Dictionary of Trade and Commerce* (London
1757): Phoebe Wright, who was praised as 'a pattern drawer of eminence',
and Anna Maria Garthwaite. Postlethwayt goes on to name Garthwaite
as one of the three silk designers who succeeded in introducing the
principles of painting into the loom. That alone is enough to suggest
that she was among the leading practitioners of her trade.

Anna Maria Garthwaite was born on 14 March 1690 at Harston,
Leicestershire, as the second of the three daughters of the Reverend

Ephraim Garthwaite and his wife Rejoyce. Though she and her sisters must have lived a comfortable life, we know nothing of the artistic direction they may have received. The very fine and detailed papercut image of an imaginary estate in the countryside that Anna Maria made when she was 17 (fig. 2) gives some indication of her youthful botanical knowledge and aptitude for design, symmetry and proportion. Both her sisters married parsons, and a phrase in her father's will suggests that he would have been happy to see the middle daughter do likewise. However, she never wed. Her older sister Mary married Robert Danny, Rector of Spofforth near York, and it appears that after their father died in 1719 Anna Maria joined Mary's household, where she would have enjoyed educated and intellectual company. When Robert Danny died in 1730, she and her widowed sister moved to Spitalfields where they soon took in ten-year-old Mary Bacon, the orphaned daughter of an in-law, as a ward. They settled in Princes Street (now 2 Princelet Street), known to have been in the area where the richest and most important men of the silk industry lived. Their choice of residence could not have been coincidental.

It is remarkable that a woman from an educated but provincial family, at the advanced age of 40, chose to come to a new London suburb, primarily inhabited by immigrants, to embark on a career as a freelance silk designer. By that date, had she already fulfilled enough orders for designs to be sufficiently confident about this venture? The answer lies in her work. Almost miraculously, the greater part of her impressive œuvre has survived. The V&A possesses nearly one thousand designs that make up virtually her whole output from the mid-1720s until the mid-1750s. They are almost all dated and annotated with the names of the clients who commissioned them. These inscriptions turn them from watercolours to vital documents. She subsequently annotated one series of her early designs with 'In York, before I came to London' and 'this was sent to London with the Rul'd Paper before I came up'. These confirm that she was actively producing designs for the Spitalfields clients before she moved to the capital. How and when she gained the necessary expertise to design for drawloom-woven silks remains unknown, despite considerable research. A formal apprenticeship as a weaver was not an option as she would have had to be the daughter of a weaver with no sons. No school of design was set up in Spitalfields until well into the nineteenth century. Nevertheless, her artistic skills and complete understanding of the medium made her one of the foremost English pattern-drawers who supplied the leading mercers and weavers of the day.

Garthwaite's designs from the 1730s were marked by inspiration from France, a striving for three-dimensional effects expressed by exaggerated

Fig. 3
Anna Maria Garthwaite
Design for a woven silk, 1 March 1749
Watercolour on paper
39.4 × 25.4 cm
V&A: 5987:1

floral and fruit motifs bearing only a faint resemblance to genuine naturalistic forms (fig. 1). In the 1740s there was a sudden diminution of the scale of her designs. Imaginary blooms began to give way to the flowers of the fields and hedgerows. In 1743 she introduced into her work the double 'S' or the Line of Beauty – two years before William Hogarth drew it in his *Self-Portrait with Pug*. The grace and the pronounced asymmetry of these silks with brocaded flowers set upon a white ground were considered an English speciality and are today perceived as quintessentially Garthwaite (figs 3 and 4). The 1740s were her most accomplished period when she was selling about 80 designs a year. From 1751, when her work became increasingly stylized though still inventive (fig. 5), her output changed dramatically. She was producing only 10 to 12 designs a year, with the last dated in 1756, when she was 66. Notably, this was when the manual for silk design entitled 'Of Designing and Drawing of Ornaments, Models, and Patterns, with

Fig. 4
Dress fabric woven after the design by
Anna Maria Garthwaite shown in fig. 3
Brocaded taffeta with foot-figured ground
(liseré effects of the warp), 1749
Possibly woven by the Spitalfields master
weaver Daniel Vautier
104.5 × 52 cm
V&A: T.192-1996

Foliages, Flowers, &c. for the Use of the Flowered Silk Manufactory, Embroidery, and Printing' was published, in Godfrey Smith's *The Laboratory; or, School of Arts*. Scholars have argued convincingly that Garthwaite is the author of this little but most useful essay, which offers practical and aesthetic advice to aspiring designers. It was clearly penned by an experienced silk designer in the twilight of their career, for the writer states:

> *if he [the manufacturer] is a man of note in the trade, the new pattern-drawer will soon come into vogue, and the old experienced one will be discarded. This is a great discouragement for an artist to exert his abilities, seeing he is flighted, his dependence for getting his livelihood frustrated, and himself forced to seek out for other employment to get a maintenance for himself and family. These ungenerous proceedings I have experienced myself.*[1]

By 1756 Garthwaite was having to vary her range, which included a design for a carpet and three designs for gauzes. She died in 1763, but her entrepreneurial mindset continued to live on in the memory of the English textile manufacturers. In the 1790s and the early 1800s her name was a trademark for a brand of ruled paper (point-paper). This could not have happened unless her own point-papers, and her deep understanding of weaving, had not left a lasting imprint. She was then virtually forgotten until the second half of the twentieth century when her work became the subject of intensive study and publication: more than 30 silks woven from her designs have so far been identified in the United Kingdom and abroad. Examples with an undisputed eighteenth-century provenance have survived in Norway, Denmark and Boston (Massachusetts): memorials to how the silks designed by Anna Maria Garthwaite won both admiration and captured the markets.

Silvija Banić

Fig. 5
Anna Maria Garthwaite
Design for a woven silk, 1755
Watercolour on paper
41.9 × 26.7 cm
V&A: 5990:5

OTHER SIGNIFICANT MAKERS

Christopher Baudouin (*c.*1665–before 1736) is often celebrated as the most distinguished designer of his generation. Based in Spitalfields, London, Baudouin produced imaginative work for Peter Leman and his son James, whose album includes at least two of his designs. Some of his later designs survived in Anna Maria Garthwaite's collection 'Patterns by Different Hands'.

Joseph Dandridge (1665–1746) was born in Buckinghamshire, England, before establishing himself in London as a noted silk designer and as a botanist, entomologist and ornithologist with an important collection of specimens. His work commissioned by James Leman shows professionalism rather than innovation but he was praised by his contemporaries, particularly as a teacher. He was master to John Vansommer.

Jean Revel (1684–1751) trained in Paris as a painter, before moving to Lyon where he was responsible for major innovations in silk design. His pioneering use of the shading technique of points rentrés made it possible for a woven design to be rendered with complete naturalism. Only one extant drawing is known to bear his signature.

James Leman (*c.*1688–1745) was a designer and manufacturer based in Spitalfields, London, who achieved eminence in both professions. He was apprenticed in 1702 to his father Peter Leman, whose death in 1712 gave him control of the business. While his designs were considerably sophisticated, his will shows that he had many diverse interests, including literature, mathematics and natural history.

John Vansommer (1706–1774) was a notable designer and a partner in the firm of Ogier, Vansommer and Triquet of Spital Square, London. He is said to have been the greatest rival of Anna Maria Garthwaite during the 1740s. His work is known from one silk passed down in his family and from the velvets supplied for Petworth House.

JOHANN JOACHIM KÄNDLER

(1706–1775)

Ingenious modeller of Meissen porcelain

One of the most coveted luxury goods of the eighteenth century, porcelain was a signifier of wealth, prestige and sophistication. Under the patronage of Augustus the Strong, Elector of Saxony and King of Poland, from 1710 the Meissen factory led Europe as the first manufacturer outside China to accurately reproduce strong, brilliantly white porcelain. However, it was the innovative and fanciful designs of Johann Joachim Kändler that established Meissen as makers of the most desirable European porcelain of the eighteenth century. Prior to Kändler's arrival in 1731, production at Meissen focused on emulating Chinese shapes and motifs. Kändler embraced porcelain as an art form and was a prolific modeller, producing an incredible volume of designs. Using his considerable sculptural skill and ingenuity, he created pieces for Meissen that inspired new forms and influenced tastes in porcelain across Europe.

Kändler was born into a rural middle-class family near Fischbach, Germany. His father was a Lutheran pastor from a family of stonemasons and sculptors.[1] Raised with a firm knowledge of biblical and classical mythology, Kändler was interested in artistic pursuits. At the age of 17, he began an apprenticeship under Johann Benjamin Thomae, a sculptor in Augustus the Strong's court. While studying under Thomae, Kändler assisted with work on the Green Vaults at Dresden Palace, Augustus's *Kunstkammer*, where the King displayed his porcelain and other artefacts.[2] An obsessive collector of Chinese porcelain, Augustus established the porcelain factory in the town of Meissen, near Dresden, to emulate these imported pieces on European soil. It was most likely through this fortunate assignment that Kändler's work caught the King's eye and launched his illustrious career. Kändler's skill with his hands and his sculptural aptitude were immediately apparent, resulting in his appointment as a modeller for Meissen in 1730.

Upon his arrival, Kändler quickly began work in the Saxon court creating large-scale porcelain animals alongside Master Modeller Johann Gottlieb Kirchner. These animals were intended for Augustus's Animal Menagerie at the Japanese Palace in Dresden.[3] However, as Kändler

Fig. 1
Johann Joachim Kändler
Goat, 1732
Cast-moulded hard-paste porcelain
Made by the Meissen porcelain factory
55.9 × 66 cm
V&A: C.111-1932
Purchased with the assistance of the
Captain H.B. Murray Bequest

continued to prove himself a talented sculptor and modeller, friction grew between the two artists which eventually resulted in Kirchner's resignation and Kändler's appointment as Master Modeller in 1733.[4]

In contrast to Kirchner's highly stylized and anthropomorphic animals, Kändler's deftness in porcelain is evidenced by a naturalistic quality. Rather than using printed source material to inform his designs, Kändler favoured sketching from life, which is demonstrated in the lifelike poses of his porcelain animals. Sensitively modelled, many of them were intended to be displayed as groupings, including the male goat in the V&A's collection (fig. 1). Forming part of a small family, the billy goat would have been displayed facing a female goat with her suckling kid scampering over her back.[5]

Modelling objects in porcelain was a multi-stage process. Kändler first sculpted the shape in clay, which would then be used to create sets of complex moulds allowing for multiples of one design. Many of the large porcelain animals, including the billy goat, suffer from substantial firing cracks due to their size and quick firing after modelling. The animals would have originally been cold-painted, concealing the cracks; however, these blemishes emphasize the technical difficulties Kändler faced as a modeller. Kändler first sculpted the goat in 1732 and approximately 28 were ordered for the Japanese Palace between November 1732 and March 1736.[6] However, records show that only six goats were delivered to the palace between 1732 and 1734, further highlighting the precarious nature of firing such large porcelain objects, which were prone to fatal damages.[7]

Fig. 2
Johann Joachim Kändler
Figure of a Harlequin, 1740
Cast-moulded hard-paste porcelain with enamel and gilt decoration
Made by the Meissen porcelain factory
16.5 × 12.8 cm
V&A: C.11-1984
Given by Mrs O.J. Finney in memory of Oswald James Finney

Fig. 3
Johann Joachim Kändler
Figure group in two sections of a shepherd eavesdropping on a pair of lovers, 1762 (modelled), 1765 (made)
Cast-moulded hard-paste porcelain with enamel and gilt decoration
Made by the Meissen porcelain factory
26 × 14.5 cm (left), 20 × 14 cm (right)
V&A: C.145-1931 and C.50-1962
Given by Mr W.A.J. Floersheim

Fig. 4
Johann Joachim Kändler, assisted by Johann
Frederick Eberlein and Peter Reinicke
Triumph of Amphitrite, 1745–6 (modelled),
1745–7 (made)
Cast-moulded porcelain table fountain
featuring classical motifs and figures and
mythological creatures
Made by the Meissen porcelain factory
100 × 390 × 140 cm
V&A: 246-1870
Restoration and research supported by the
Arnhold family and by the Henry Arnhold
Exchange Programme

One of Kändler's greatest and most enduring successes was his invention of small, lively figures, first produced by the factory in 1736. These figures were intended to decorate the dining table, replacing sugar sculptures as centrepieces, or were displayed in the cabinets of curiosity that were becoming increasingly popular with the eighteenth-century nobility. Using engravings as inspiration, Kändler's figures illustrated different elements of contemporary society. These include peasants, merchants and nobility, as well as classical and mythological figures and the ever-popular *commedia dell'arte* characters, such as the comic servant Harlequin. *Commedia dell'arte* was a popular form of entertainment in the seventeenth and eighteenth centuries. Entertainers would improvise much of their performance, which often relied on physical comedy. These early porcelain Harlequins appear alive with movement, their bodies playfully positioned mid-gesture (fig. 2). Kändler's *commedia dell'arte* figures became wildly popular and were often commissioned as table decorations for wealthy customers. These figures were so sought-after that they were imitated by porcelain makers across Europe.

Later figures, produced in the 1750s and 1760s, were more stylized and influenced by contemporary themes. Kändler drew inspiration from the increasingly fashionable artistic portrayals of aristocrats in bucolic settings, or *fêtes galantes*. Modelled around 1762, the figure grouping at the V&A is based on an engraving of François Boucher's *Le Pasteur Galant* (1742) and is a charming portrayal of a shepherd eavesdropping on a pair of aristocratic lovers (fig. 3).[8]

As his influence and authority at Meissen grew, Kändler became responsible for training apprentices and craftsmen, some of whom he promoted to modellers and assistants. These apprentices included Peter Reinicke, Johann Frederick Eberlein, Johann Gottlieb Ehder and Frederich Elias Meyer. In 1737 Count Heinrich von Bruhl commissioned

the elaborate Swan Service which Kändler modelled with Eberlein. Von Bruhl was Prime Minister under Augustus III and an avid collector of porcelain. Comprising more than 2,000 pieces and designed for a setting of 100 people, the service was a monumental feat and the pinnacle of Baroque porcelain, further securing Kändler's status at Meissen.

In 1740 Kändler became director of the factory's sculpture department, the *Weiss Corps*. One of the most impressive commissions he undertook during this period was the elaborate table fountain, the *Triumph of Amphitrite* in 1745 (fig. 4). Commissioned by Count von Bruhl, it was used as the grand centrepiece for a banquet to celebrate the diplomatic marriage of Louis, Dauphin of France, to Princess Maria Josepha of Saxony, which the Count had skilfully orchestrated.[9] Kändler was the principal modeller for the table fountain but was assisted by several of his protégés, including Reinicke and Eberlein. Based on a life-sized fountain sculpted by Lorenzo Mattielli located at Count von Bruhl's former summer palace in Dresden, it impressed guests by flowing with rosewater during the lavish dessert course. The focal points of the table fountain are the finely sculpted Neptune with his bride Amphitrite, possibly representing the royal marriage devised by Count von Bruhl, as well as two river gods, the Nile and Tiber.[10] Kändler's skill is also showcased in the mythical animals flanking the fountain's basin. Kändler's social status consistently increased as he continued to create new and innovative designs for Meissen. In 1748 he was appointed *Hofkomissar* or Court Comissioner to Augustus III.

The Prussian occupation of Saxony during the Seven Years War had a great impact on porcelain production at Meissen between 1757 and 1763 in particular. Prior to the invasion, Augustus III had transferred possession of Meissen to private ownership to prevent the factory's seizure as a statement of political aggression. Kändler stayed at the helm of the factory and continued creating original designs throughout the war, forming an advantageous professional relationship with Prussia's

Fig. 5
Johann Joachim Kändler
Lemon Basket from the Mollendorf Service, 1761
Cast-moulded hard-paste porcelain
with applied decoration and enamel
and gilt decoration
Made by the Meissen porcelain factory
60.1 × 24.5 × 20 cm
V&A: C.248-1921
Purchased with the assistance of the
Captain H.B. Murray Bequest

Frederick the Great, who was himself an enthusiastic collector of porcelain. In 1761 Kändler was commissioned by Frederick to make a dining service with decoration featuring classical motifs that referenced war, peace and abundance. These motifs and Kändler's modelling prowess are seen in this highly ornamented dessert basket (fig. 5). In addition to the elaborate sculptural details, the table service was painted in colours reserved for the Saxon ruler. A political statement, the service was originally made for Frederick the Great's personal use and comprised 697 pieces.

After the Seven Years War, Meissen continued to struggle financially though they never stopped manufacturing porcelain. Despite the commercial difficulties at Meissen, Kändler declined Frederick the Great's offer to work at the Berlin porcelain factory. Kändler maintained his loyalty and was active at Meissen until his death in 1775. His inventiveness not only influenced colleagues and competitors but made Meissen's porcelain the most sought-after in Europe, effectively giving rise to an entirely new and original art form.

Ashley Weaver-Paul

OTHER SIGNIFICANT MAKERS

Joseph Willems (1706–1776) was a sculptor and modeller at the Chelsea porcelain factory between 1748 and 1766 and is recognized for the sculptural figures he produced in soft-paste porcelain. Willems was directly inspired by Kändler's figures but also created original designs for Chelsea.

Étienne Maurice Falconet (1716–1791) was a well-known French sculptor who worked across media including marble, bronze and soft-paste porcelain. In 1757 Falconet was appointed director of the sculpture department at the Sèvres porcelain factory, where he pioneered the usage of unglazed porcelain, also known as biscuitware.

Agostino Carlini (1718–1790) was an Italian-English sculptor and artist who was a founding member of the Royal Academy. In addition to large-scale sculptural works in stone, Carlini also modelled small 'dry-edge' figures for the Derby porcelain factory in the 1750s.

Franz Anton Bustelli (1723–1763) was a German modeller at the Nymphenburg porcelain factory near Munich between 1754 and 1763. Trained as a sculptor, Bustelli showed great talent in modelling Rococo porcelain figures, which rivalled those produced at Meissen.

2

ENLIGHTENMENT & EMPIRE

If we consult history, we shall find, that, in most nations, foreign trade has preceded any refinement in home manufactures, and given birth to domestic luxury.[1]

The Age of Enlightenment captures a period ranging from the late seventeenth until the early nineteenth century, characterized by an acceleration in intellectual and philosophical discovery. Scientists and thinkers used reason, observation and experimentation to gain new understandings of the natural and human-made world. The fields of science, religion, politics and the arts were subject to rigorous debate, and the emergence of dictionaries and encyclopaedias reflected the new concern for a wide dissemination of knowledge.[2] This impacted making to a considerable degree. Artists, artisans and craftspeople gradually benefited from new technological advances and the publication of treatises and manuals on processes, as well as a growing consumer class that demanded objects of quality.

In this period, the relationship between people and objects changed considerably. Since the Renaissance, objects had been classified by material. The emergence of repositories where assemblages of objects

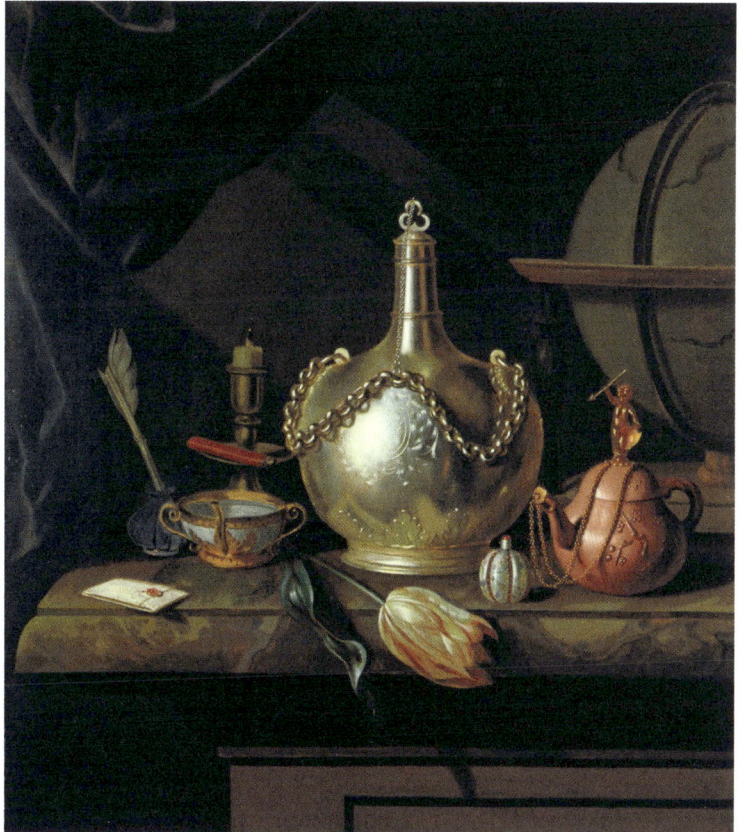

Fig. 1
Pieter van Roestraten
Still Life with Silver Wine Decanter, Tulip, Yixing Teapot and Globe, c.1690
Oil on canvas
76.2 × 63.5 cm
V&A: P.5-1939
Bequeathed by Lionel A. Crichton

could be viewed – known as *Wunderkammer* (cabinets of wonder or of curiosity) – demonstrated new attempts to understand and categorize the world and to marvel at its creations and human ingenuity.[3] Goldsmiths would mount shells with elaborately crafted supports, while the horns of animals were carved into complex and intricate forms. By the seventeenth century these could be found in most European centres, reinforcing the idea that making was a fundamental part of understanding the world. In the eighteenth century the emergence of public museums, such as the British Museum and the Louvre, introduced and reinforced hierarchies of knowledge, with the decorative arts central to this new era of understanding.

A still life executed in around 1690 by the Dutch-born artist Pieter van Roestraten illustrates a microcosm of the world that could be found in the cabinets of the elite (fig. 1). The globe emphasizes the colonial expansion that enabled these objects to be assembled. The sealed packet contains tea, one of the most widely traded products in the Early Modern world alongside luxuries such as tobacco, spices and sugar. Ceramic objects from China are demonstrative of the great influence that exports had on European makers, while the importation of rare species of flora and fauna changed the fields of medicine and horticulture (fig. 2).

Another cultural shift seen in the eighteenth century was the replacement of the court as the centre for artistic innovation by a range of spaces that were normally found in an urban setting. Clubs, societies, coffee houses, art galleries and academies became places for exchanging ideas and meeting collaborators. The culture of shopping also became a leisure pursuit, with many European capitals providing new retail spaces for makers to advertise and sell their wares (fig. 3). This kind of commodity culture relied on the expansion in global trade. The opening of new routes to Africa, the Americas and East and South-east Asia gave Europeans access to luxury items from across the world. However, this was underpinned by colonial expansion and exploitation: the amassing of considerable wealth through the seizing and appropriation of existing commercial structures, raw materials – and human life.

Global trade was by no means new in the eighteenth century: throughout the Early Modern period, trading empires dictated the widespread transportation of rare and precious materials and luxury goods, making many commonplace in the western world.[4] Rival Portuguese and Spanish empires were the first to reach across continents in the fifteenth century while the Venetian republic controlled trade with the Middle East during the Renaissance period. Exploratory and colonizing ventures followed from the Netherlands,

Fig. 2
Wolfgang Howzer
Mounted brush pot, 1630–50 (pot),
1660–70 (mounts)
China (pot), London (mounts)
Hard-paste porcelain cup, with
silver-gilt mounts and cover
33 × 16.9 cm
V&A: M.308:1,2-1962
Bequeathed by Claude D. Rotch

France and Britain from the early seventeenth century, often in direct competition with one another. With the establishment of the British and Dutch East India Companies in 1600 and 1602, respectively, and the French East India Company in 1664, monopolies on trade were concentrated in the hands of European imperial powers. Such trading routes were essential to the development of European making practices. As well as luxury items such as porcelain and lacquered furniture, or commodities like tobacco, sugar, coffee and tea, new raw materials were also transported. The availability of dyes such as indigo and cochineal, and fabrics such as cotton, would revolutionize the textile trade and allow makers to produce more vibrant, colourful designs on a material easier to work. The botanical artist William Kilburn (p. 138) was one of many makers to directly profit from newly abundant cotton, as well as the wealth of source material for designs that came in the form of collected biological specimens.

Kilburn is not a lone example, of course. The reality is that many of the creations illustrated in this book were enabled through the depredations of colonialism and slavery. Millions of human beings were transported for commercial exploitation. The global reach that the western European empires gained was only possible through the suppression of indigenous populations. The most barbarous expression of this was the Atlantic slave trade, which saw its peak during this period of putative 'enlightenment'. Between the mid-sixteenth and the

Fig. 3
Trade card for Christopher Gibson's upholstery shop, 1730–42
Ink on paper
17.2 × 21 cm
V&A: 14435:60

Fig. 4
Manufactured by George Ravenscroft
Drinking glass, *c.*1677
Lead glass, mould-blown, with ribbing
and applied raspberry prunts
16.5 × 8.6 cm
V&A: C.530-1936
Wilfred Buckley Collection

mid-nineteenth centuries, 12 million Africans were transported across the Atlantic in horrific conditions.[5] The destinations for the enslaved were plantations at which they were made to work the land, producing the raw materials that would be transported to Europe for selling or processing into new luxury manufactures. The natural resources of places such as the Caribbean, colonized by the British and French, were utilized for making. Mahogany, a tropical hardwood native to the Americas, was a staple of European furniture makers from the 1720s.[6] Its propensity to allow for crisper and more elaborate decoration and to yield a beautifully polished surface meant that craftspeople such as Thomas Chippendale (p. 102) worked in it almost exclusively. The abundant supply was only possible through the labour of enslaved people who felled the trees in Jamaica and then – once Jamaica was exhausted of this resource by the 1760s – in British Honduras (today Belize).

Throughout the period, awareness of technology and techniques of making were disseminated through texts such as François Xavier d'Entrecolles's 1712 account of porcelain making in Jingdezhen or Antonio Neri's *L'arte vetraria*, or 'The Art of Glass' (published initially in 1612 and translated into various languages from the late seventeenth century), both of which would transform European production. Meanwhile, new materials led to experimentation. The ceramic factory at Meissen, just outside Dresden, made breakthroughs in creating 'true' or 'hard-paste' porcelain in around 1709 through the financial might and personal obsession of Augustus the Strong, Elector of Saxony and King of Poland. To discover how to produce the so-called 'white gold', philosophers, chemists and alchemists such as Ehrenfried Walther von Tschirnhaus and Johann Friedrich Böttger had been persuaded – or enforced – to remain at court and painstakingly experiment.[7]

Böttger's subsequent discoveries in manufacturing hard-paste white porcelain at Meissen paved the way for many European factories to operate commercially in the same field and to receive the support of powerful sovereigns. For example, the Du Paquier factory in Vienna was bought by the Empress Maria Theresa in 1743; the factory at Sèvres, near Paris, was taken over in its entirety by Louis XV in 1756; and in 1760 Charles III of Spain moved his porcelain factory from the grounds of the Capodimonte palace in Naples to Madrid. But there were also many smaller, often short-lived, operations backed by entrepreneurs and speculators. Without institutional backing, however, the earliest factories in Britain, such as Nicholas Sprimont's (p. 94) at Chelsea (c.1745–69) or those at Bow (1747–64) or Vauxhall (1751–64), were lucky to last longer than a decade.

The impact of skilled people on the spread of artisanal knowledge can be seen in a further example of northern European dominance toward the end of the seventeenth century, in the field of glassmaking. Glassmaking had historically found its centre of excellence in the Middle East and subsequently in Venice. Though Venetian glassmakers were prohibited to travel, from about 1550 increasing numbers migrated, taking their knowledge with them. Throughout Europe, glassmakers strove to produce Venetian-style 'cristallo', a fine colourless glass developed in Renaissance Venice. From about 1660 many sought to further improve the clarity of the material. In London in 1673 a merchant named George Ravenscroft oversaw the successful manufacture of an exceptionally colourless glass by introducing large amounts of lead oxide to the recipe (fig. 4). With the successful production of clear glass, the taste shifted from thinly blown and elaborately shaped Venetian-style vessels to thicker and weightier glass that could be more easily decorated. In central Europe, specialized artists such as Johann Schaper, Abraham Helmhack and the Preissler workshop (p. 52) decorated glass in finely painted enamels. Engraving became prevalent in Germany and the Netherlands, where Jacob Sang (p. 110) and David Wolff (p. 117) worked professionally, while the amateur engraver Frans Greenwood

Fig. 5
Michael Kimmel
Bureau, 1750–55
Veneered in kingwood, with marquetry
including mother-of-pearl, ivory and brass,
on a carcase of pine and stained alder or
birch; mounts of gilt brass and gilded wood
250 × 145 × 83 cm
V&A: W.63-1977
Purchased by HM Government from the
estate of the 6th Earl of Rosebery and
allocated to the Victoria and Albert Museum

(p. 117) perfected a technique of engraving an image through a network of fine dots known as stipple engraving.

In eighteenth-century Europe, material experimentation went hand in hand with profound stylistic changes. The decorative arts from around the 1730s to the 1750s were predominantly expressions of the French Rococo style, developed initially as a reaction to the heavy grandeur of the Baroque. It is characterized by its profuse use of ornament, asymmetrical scrolls, shells and other marine-inspired forms. Makers often used the new style to imitate and even exaggerate the natural world. Major Parisian proponents of the style include the designer and goldsmith Juste-Aurèle Meissonnier (p. 67), the silversmith Thomas Germain and the carver Nicholas Pineau, who aided in the transition

Fig. 6
Jean Revel
Panel of silk brocade, around 1735
Brocaded silk
119.4 × 54.6 cm
V&A: T.187-1922
Gift of W.J. Collins

from the monumentality of late Baroque to the fluidity and inventiveness of the Rococo. The increasing availability of printed material helped the style to spread across Europe, to major cities such as Frankfurt, Leipzig, Munich and Augsburg, and there was a strong flourishing of the style in Germany (fig. 5).

Britain emerged as a central economic power between 1720 and 1770 owing to its diverse commercial activity, growth in exports and domestic production.[8] Success in various conflicts such as the Seven Years War (1756–63) and the continuation of colonial expansion, leading to sustained wealth, consolidated a feeling of national pride. By 1750 London held 11 per cent of England's population, and opportunities for patronage created communities of makers ready to cater for the new demand in luxury products. Some felt that the arts in Britain were inferior to those of France, and strong efforts were made to formulate a national style. In 1735 a group of influential artists and designers, including painters William Hogarth and Francis Hayman and sculptor Louis-François Roubiliac (p.101), formed an academy to teach drawing from life, on St Martin's Lane, London. As part of the growing artistic community around the drawing school, during the 1740s major workshops were set up in a variety of trades, including coach painting, gilding, upholstering, engraving and enamelling.[9]

This artistic circle was well populated with émigré craftspeople, many of whom were second or third generation, due to the arrival of French Protestants since the seventeenth century.[10] Silversmiths such as Paul de Lamerie (p. 60) and Paul Crespin (p. 101) were born into Huguenot families settled in London and entered a thriving trade based around Soho. Some arrived opportunistically, for instance Hubert-François Gravelot, who came to London in 1732 from France during a period of peace, becoming a central figure in the St Martin's Lane Academy owing to his skills as a draughtsman. The movement of makers had a palpable effect on trades. In textile

Fig. 7
Robert Adam (architect), David Adamson
(maker), Antonio Zucchi (painter)
Ceiling, 1771
Plaster ceiling, with painting in oil
on canvas-backed paper
1000 × 700 cm
V&A: W.43:1 to 5-1936
Given by the Adelphi Development
Company, through The Art Fund

manufacturing, for example, silks produced in Lyon had traditionally represented the epitome of fashionable design. After the arrival of Huguenot weavers from the end of the seventeenth century, silks made in Spitalfields in east London became acknowledged as equal in quality and appearance (fig. 6). By 1750 London was equal to, if not more important than, Paris as a centre of fashion and luxury production. Closely linked with Rococo – and from 1750 often found in combination with it – was the 'Chinese' style. Known usually by the French term, 'chinoiserie', it was a hybrid ornamental style conflating various motifs found in Chinese, Japanese and Korean art and architecture. Inspired by the influx of Chinese imports, it had developed in European decorative arts since the preceding century, blending with Rococo forms into a new whimsical style. Cabinet-makers such as Thomas Johnson (p. 118) and Matthias Lock (p. 123) employed this style to add flamboyance to their designs, and makers also utilized printed patterns for small-scale ornamental work. The designs of French-born, London-based painter Jean Pillement appeared on porcelain, textiles, wallpaper and silver. His book *The Ladies' Amusement, Or, The Whole Art of Japanning Made Easy*, printed in the late 1750s, became an important source text. A central part of chinoiserie decoration was the inclusion of caricatured East Asian people. Described by contemporaries as 'fantastic', 'curious' or 'grotesque', these appealed to western ideas of China as a far-off, capricious land.[11] The enthusiasm for chinoiserie survived various changes in taste throughout the eighteenth century and into the nineteenth. In Britain, the Brighton Pavilion – eccentric seaside residence of George, the Prince Regent, and designed by John Nash between 1815 and 1822 – displays a sumptuous blend of Chinese, Japanese and Indian styles.

The exuberance of the Rococo quickly drew criticism and a resurging interest in classical antiquity gave rise to a period of Neoclassicism from the 1750s.[12] Interest in Roman civilization had been prevalent in elite circles since the Renaissance; however, in this period there was greater awareness of Greece as the source of Roman culture. Johann Joachim Winckelmann, the German archaeologist, was the first to map out developments in ancient Greek art and architecture and to demonstrate their influence on subsequent stylistic movements.[13] Sites of ancient Greek culture were excavated and visited for inspiration throughout the eighteenth century. In London, the Society of Dilettanti, which comprised a group of scholars interested in the classical past, backed investigative expeditions to locations of cultural interest. The Society of Antiquaries, informally set up in 1707, received its royal charter in 1751, effectively establishing a British headquarters for the pursuit of archaeological knowledge.[14]

The allure of excavations and the high esteem in which classical antiquity was held in the late seventeenth and early eighteenth centuries gave rise to an educational rite of passage for members of European elite society, known as the Grand Tour. With formal education based on the classics, this trip was undertaken primarily by young men of means to complete their learning before entering society. Primary destinations were Florence and Rome, to study Renaissance painting and Roman sculpture, and Venice to enjoy pleasures outside of the study and appreciation of art. Makers catered for this wealthy clientele, providing expertly crafted objects that spoke to the pedagogical aims of the journey. British aristocrats brought home souvenirs, ranging from marble and bronze copies of antique sculptures, portraits by the artist Pompeo Batoni or prints by Giovanni Battista Piranesi, to glass, micromosaics and specimens of marble, sometimes neatly arranged in boxes or albums, or set into tabletops. The market for Grand Tour objects offered opportunities for craftspeople, such as the Dresden goldsmith Johann Christian Neuber (p. 132) who would skilfully set Italian micromosaics into gold boxes or, later in the nineteenth century, the Castellani family (p. 154) who produced jewellery in Rome directly inspired by ancient Etruscan treasures that had been unearthed during excavations.

As more Grand Tourists began to demand appropriate settings for their souvenirs, the architecture and interiors of grand aristocratic town and country houses required designs in the Neoclassical style. The classically trained Scottish architect Robert Adam (p. 109), himself a Grand Tourist, emphasized the need for classical ornament to be applied to all elements of architecture, from buildings to interiors to furnishings (fig. 7). The practice he established with his brother James relied on the services of independent artists such as Antonio Zucchi and craftspeople like the cabinet-making partnership of Ince and Mayhew (p. 123).

With the onset of the Industrial Revolution, makers also used a Neoclassical language to elevate the status of more humble manufactures. Josiah Wedgwood (p. 124) and Matthew Boulton (pp. 131 and 153) were entrepreneurs who transformed the mass production of ceramics and metalwork, respectively, through the reorganization of factory processes and the use of high-profile designers. Each recognized the potential appeal of their products to elite society through their strength of design. Boulton copied designs for silver from antiquity and popularized the French taste for works in gilt bronze in Britain. Wedgwood employed academically trained artists as designers, such as John Flaxman (p. 131) and George Stubbs, and translated their compositions into the ceramic form.

As the eighteenth century ended, the dominating European colonial powers began to weaken. In 1776 the Declaration of Independence freed the United States of America from British colonial rule. There were uprisings of enslaved people in France's largest colony of Saint-Domingue in response to the revolution of 1789. Due partly to this unrest, the French Republic outlawed slavery in its colonies in February 1794. The Napoleonic Wars forced Spain to relinquish its colonies in the Americas at the start of the nineteenth century. With increasing opposition to the barbarism of colonial conquest, objects were sometimes used as vehicles for political discussion. After 1776 many ceramic factories near to major port cities such as Liverpool made profits by exporting pots patriotically decorated with the American bald eagle to the newly formed United States. Josiah Wedgwood's support for the abolition of the slave trade was activated commercially in a small jasper medallion produced in 1787. Its design, taken from the seal for the Committee for the Abolition of the Slave Trade, showed a kneeling Black man in chains (fig. 8).[15] In the lead-up to and following the passing of the Slavery Abolition Act of 1833 in Britain, other manufacturers began producing objects that corresponded to popular public movements. A whole range of ceramic and glass objects signalling support for the sugar boycotts of 1825–9 was produced for use during the polite activity of taking tea (fig. 9).

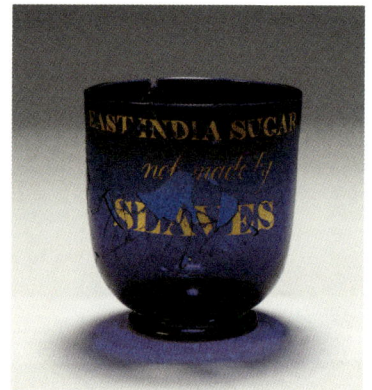

Fig. 8
Manufactured by Josiah Wedgwood & Sons;
modelled by William Hackwood
Medallion, 1787
Jasperware with metal mount
3 × 2.7 cm
V&A: 414:1304-1885
Given by Lady Charlotte Schreiber

Fig. 9
Sugar bowl, c.1820
Bristol (probably)
Blue glass with gilt inscription
10 × 10.9 cm
V&A: C.14-2023

Fig. 10
John Henry Belter
Sofa, c.1856
Carved solid and laminated rosewood,
with varnished chestnut or oak
strengthening blocks, upholstered
silk damask (not original)
148.6 × 232.4 × 114.9 cm
V&A: W.22-1983

The early nineteenth century would see yet more revivals of past styles. As Prince of Wales, Regent and King, George IV's spending on interior and furnishing projects was at odds with a country in economic uncertainty.[16] His fascination with France and his rivalry with Emperor Napoleon Bonaparte, both as statesman and arbiter of taste, encouraged the popularization of the 'Empire' style in Britain. His refurbishments of Carlton House, London, in the 1780s and 1810s adopted various French styles and made use of French craftspeople. The silversmith Paul Storr (p. 146) produced work in both the Neoclassical taste and the Rococo Revival, fashionable from the 1820s, supplying the royal family independently as well as through the firm of Rundell, Bridge and Rundell (p. 153). The French style also underwent a revival in the United States, albeit a few decades later, epitomized by the work of the cabinet-maker John Henry Belter (fig. 10). A component of nineteenth-century revivalism was based on nationalism or nostalgia for historic periods of power, such as the Rococo Revival yearning for the French *Ancien Régime*. Nevertheless, the world of making would continue to change, through rapid industrialization, further imperial expansion and political turmoil, into an age where styles and objects became more international, more eclectic and more democratic.

Simon Spier

NICHOLAS SPRIMONT

(1716–1771)

Exceptional designer in gold and porcelain

Nicholas Sprimont – designer, goldsmith, modeller and ceramic factory owner – epitomizes the quality of craftspeople who were drawn to London from the 1730s and introduced the French Rococo style to British silver and ceramics. Born into a prominent family of silversmiths in Liège, in present-day Belgium, he was baptized there in 1716. Following this family tradition, it was as a silversmith that, by 1742, Sprimont arrived in London. However, from the mid-1740s until the early 1760s, he changed career and produced some of Britain's most expensive and desirable porcelain at a manufactory established in Chelsea, west of London. As someone who could draw, model and, significantly, market his luxury products to the elite, Sprimont's success in the porcelain industry – which was brand new in Britain in the 1740s – is indicative of his artistic versatility and entrepreneurial skill.

The style of Sprimont's works in silver suggests that between his upbringing in Liège and arriving in London he had spent some time living and training in Paris, which in the 1730s was an established centre of innovation in the decorative arts and luxury trades. Evidence has been found that documents Sprimont there in 1736, when he was arrested for whistling during a performance at the Opéra-Comique.[1] The arrest papers state that Sprimont described himself to the officers as a goldsmith, indicating he was probably practising at this time. However, by 1742 he had registered his mark at Goldsmiths' Hall in London and was paying for a studio on Compton Street in Soho. Sprimont worked collaboratively in London, within a circle of Huguenot artisans, such as the silversmith Paul Crespin and the sculptor Louis-François Roubiliac, who were most likely united by their refugee status in mid-eighteenth-century England. Though perhaps not a Huguenot himself – Sprimont was born Catholic but married into a Huguenot family in London – many of the artists and craftspeople that are linked to Sprimont and his collaborators arrived in England after escaping from the persecution of Protestants in parts of Europe.

Fig. 1
Vase, *c*.1759
Manufactured at the
Chelsea porcelain factory
Soft-paste porcelain
30.8 cm (height)
V&A: C.53-2022
Purchased with the support
of Mr Masao Iketani

Fig. 2
Nicholas Sprimont
Metalwork design for a lidded
soup tureen, 1744–7
Pen and ink and brown ink wash
on laid paper
26 × 43.2 cm
V&A: E.2606-1917

Designs for silver signed by Sprimont during this period in London survive and show his competency as a draughtsman. A drawing for a soup tureen from around 1744, intended for Thomas Coke, 1st Earl of Leicester, signed by Sprimont (fig. 2), shows a playful incorporation of heavily plumed ostriches, the heraldic crest of the Coke family, into the tureen's feet. The centrality of drawing and design to high-quality decorative arts was being brought into sharp focus by a number of European artists who congregated in St Martin's Lane and established an art academy there in 1735. This group was in many ways led by Hubert-François Gravelot, the illustrator and engraver who was widely recognized as introducing his contemporaries to the virtues of inventive and sophisticated French design, and whose prints were relied upon by early porcelain manufactories.[2]

Surviving examples of Sprimont's silver were hallmarked between 1743 and 1747, overlapping with the establishment of the Chelsea porcelain factory. A number of these works, such as plates, cream jugs and sauce boats, also show a direct relationship to pieces of porcelain that were produced in the opening decades of the factory. For example, a commission for Frederick, Prince of Wales, carried out by Sprimont and Paul Crespin, was a dinner service with a marine theme. It included a pair of salts with clam-shell bowls supported on rocks – the type of

rocaille ornament that is quintessentially Rococo – and a cast crayfish. The service was completed in the early 1740s; however, the strength of the Rococo design is shown by its adaptation to porcelain by Sprimont's factory from around 1746 until the mid-1750s (fig. 3).

With the emergence of commercially viable porcelain production in Europe from the 1710s, initially in Meissen and shortly after in Vienna, factories quickly spread across the continent. Unlike state-sponsored factories such as Meissen, which was financed by Augustus the Strong, Elector of Saxony and King of Poland, or Vincennes, established near to Paris in 1740 and which received French royal patronage from 1751, British porcelain manufactories were often much more precariously funded. Their origins lay in the various ambitions and obsessions of artists, entrepreneurs, chemists and benefactors, and they were never without risk, with many factories only lasting a number of years. Such was the case with the Chelsea manufactory which was established by Sprimont and his collaborator, the Dieppe-born jeweller Charles Gouyn, possibly as early as September 1744. By the spring of 1745 the factory was already making an impact, and it was reported in the *Daily Advertiser* that 'We hear that the China made at Chelsea is arriv'd to such perfection, as to equal if not surpass the finest old Japan.'[3] Gouyn's involvement was short-lived, setting up his own rival concern around 1748, but under Sprimont's sole direction the factory at Chelsea produced some of the most desirable luxury porcelain objects in Britain and abroad, until the factory was sold in 1769 and subsumed by a rival manufactory in Derby in 1770.

It has been suggested that Sprimont modelled some of the earlier pieces of porcelain produced by the factory at Chelsea.[4] For example, several small but accomplished models of dogs are linked to Sprimont due to his technical proficiency in working silver of a comparable scale (fig. 4).[5] A large centrepiece marked by both Sprimont and Crespin, assayed in 1747–8, and bearing the arms of the Ashburnham family, displays two dynamically modelled goats supporting a large, pierced dish surmounted by realistically modelled fruits. Not only does this piece support the contention that Sprimont could depict animals with competence, but the motif of the goats acting as supports also appears on a small cream jug produced by Chelsea in the middle of the 1740s. These have been dated to the late 1740s, before or coinciding with the arrival of the Chelsea factory's principal modeller Joseph Willems (p. 81), a Brussels-born sculptor who is first recorded in the vicinity of Chelsea from 1748. Willems was known primarily for his competency in figure modelling.

Fig. 4
Modelled by Nicholas Sprimont (possibly)
Figure of a greyhound, *c.*1749
Manufactured at the
Chelsea porcelain factory
Soft-paste porcelain
19.8 × 19.8 × 8.3 cm
V&A: C.246-1976

Although the factory employed the services of accomplished modellers and painters, Sprimont obviously saw himself as responsible for the innovations implemented by the factory, and the mastermind behind the products that would shape the taste for ornamental and functional ceramics in 1750s and '60s Britain. In around 1760 a portrait of Sprimont was undertaken which shows him seated, holding a diminutive set of scales, surrounded by vases produced by the Chelsea factory in the years shortly preceding the painting (fig. 5).

The late 1750s marked the start of a period of commercial distinction for the factory. Chelsea's well-known cypher of an anchor, applied to their products as a mark of quality as well as authorship, painted in a red pigment from the year 1752, began to be added in gold from around 1758. The varied inspiration for the 'Gold Anchor'-period vases – from the French Rococo produced at the Sèvres factory, to mounted Chinese and Japanese porcelain – is evident in the forms and colours of the wares that punctuate the portrait. More intriguingly, the vases shown appear to be in differing stages of completion: a potpourri vase that directly copies a version produced by Vincennes appears in white, apparently in its fired but unglazed (biscuit) form. In the foreground a bottle-shaped vase has been glazed with its ground colour – a fashionable 'pea-green' that Chelsea invented in 1759 – but it lacks its final enamelling and gilding. We know how this vase was intended to look in its finished state from an example in the V&A's collection, complete with its finely painted birds (fig. 1).

The picture has been carefully choreographed to present Sprimont as central to the production of the factory, perhaps not the designer of the eccentric Chelsea vases, but undoubtedly their manufacturer. He is depicted with his wife Ann Sprimont, who holds a supporting hand behind him and another on one of his vases. The other figure, who is handing the only finished vase in the picture to Sprimont, is his wife's sister Susannah Protin. Both Sprimont's wife and her sister are documented as providing substantial support to Sprimont in running the factory during his period of illness and subsequent retirement in the early 1760s, and their part is acknowledged in this triple portrait. Following Sprimont's retirement, the factory lost its impetus and produced wares at a reduced rate until 1769, when a notice appeared stating the intention to sell off all stock and equipment from the Chelsea factory, signalling the end of this important centre of production.[6]

Early commercial ventures in porcelain manufacture in Britain rarely lasted as long as the Chelsea factory's two-and-a-half decades. Sprimont proved versatile as an able draughtsman and modeller who could control a skilled workforce, as well as market his novel product. The strong flourishing of the Rococo style in Britain, and the Chelsea factory's key role in this, meant that Sprimont's porcelain became an enduring symbol of luxury, being coveted by the wealthiest collectors and imitated by competing factories. Later in the nineteenth century the demand for Chelsea porcelain was still extremely high, being pursued at auction and copies made by porcelain factories during the various 'revivals' of the Rococo style.

Simon Spier

OTHER SIGNIFICANT MAKERS

Paul Crespin (1694–1760) was a Huguenot silversmith. Although he had been in London since birth, his family had fled France in the late seventeenth century, and as well as working with Sprimont, he was a frequent collaborator with other French goldsmiths such as Paul de Lamerie.

Louis-François Roubiliac (1702–1762) was a sculptor born in France who arrived in England in 1730, where he received a number of prestigious commissions, including a marble statue of the musician George Frideric Handel made for the Vauxhall Pleasure Gardens.

Thomas Frye (c.1710–1762) was an artist and mezzotint engraver, who established one of Britain's earliest and most successful porcelain factories in Bow, in east London. With the merchant Edward Heylyn, Frye applied for a patent in 1744 to manufacture porcelain that would rival imports from abroad.

Charles Gouyn (d.1785) was a jeweller who, along with Nicholas Sprimont, founded the Chelsea porcelain factory. Shortly after its establishment, in 1748 Gouyn left to set up his own concern in St James's, which was known particularly for its production of high-quality small bottles, seals and boxes known as 'toys'.

THOMAS CHIPPENDALE

(1718–1779)

Foremost Georgian furniture maker

Thomas Chippendale was an English furniture maker and designer in Georgian Britain, arguably the most influential designer beyond his own lifetime in the English-speaking world. His eclectic and substantial corpus of work spans the Gothic, Chinese, 'Modern'[1] (Rococo) and Neoclassical styles, and the techniques he employed for his furniture range from intricate woodcarving to 'japanning',[2] marquetry and gilding.

Chippendale was baptized on 5 June 1718 in the market town of Otley, West Yorkshire, the only son of Mary Drake and carpenter-joiner John Chippendale. Though very little is known of his early training, Chippendale would have had contact with country furniture crafts through his father, his second cousin William Chippendale, or other relatives working in the same trade, and it is possible he apprenticed with Richard Wood, a cabinet-maker in York.[3]

One of the first mentions of Chippendale's presence in London, aged 30, is an entry for his marriage to Catherine Redshaw at St George's Chapel, Mayfair in May 1748.[4] His arrival in London was timely; between the 1740s and '80s both the London trade and the craft of cabinet-making were marked by creative vitality and self-expression. Several moves to larger properties in more respectable and fashionable areas within London point to his growing prosperity and renown. A particularly skilled designer and draughtsman, Chippendale collaborated with engraver, designer and drawing master Matthias Darly at premises adjoining the palatial residence of the Earl of Northumberland, a wealthy and influential patron of the arts. The fruit of their collaboration was *The Gentleman and Cabinet-Maker's Director*, first published in August 1754 from this address, with an astute dedication to the Earl.[5] This was the most ambitious design book for furniture published in England, illustrating Chippendale's designs for almost every type of 'elegant and useful' furniture available in the eighteenth century in the fashionable styles of the day (fig. 1). The *Director* went through two further editions in the 1750s and '60s, disseminating Chippendale's original designs throughout Britain, setting the standard for good

Fig. 1
Thomas Chippendale
Design for a Rococo dressing table, *c.*1753–62
Pen, ink and wash on paper
34.3 × 21.4 cm
V&A: D.701-1906

taste and inspiring fellow designers to produce their own trade catalogues and pattern books.[6]

In 1754 he entered into partnership with the Scottish cabinet-maker and financier James Rannie and took up a sizeable property at St Martin's Lane, from where a notable concentration of ambitious cabinet-makers operated.[7] It is from this location that the Chippendale showrooms, workshop and firm operated for the next 60 years, with a chair as their shop sign.[8] At its height, Chippendale's workshop employed 50 specialist tradesmen, though it is almost certain that not all of Chippendale's furniture was produced there, and that he made use of the London cabinet trade's infrastructure by subcontracting work to specialist firms for brass work, marquetry, carving and gilding. Combining the skills of various practising tradesmen ensured that the production of furniture made to his designs and specifications was of exceptional quality. Once established at St Martin's Lane, it is very unlikely that any of the firm's furniture was

Fig. 2
Unknown maker to a design by
Thomas Chippendale
Breakfast table with chinoiserie fretwork
and hinged flaps on two sides, raised on
four legs, 1754–70
Mahogany and brass
72 × 58 × 57 cm
V&A: W.64:1 to 3-1950

Fig. 3
Thomas Chippendale
Armchair, designed by Robert Adam
for Sir Lawrence Dundas, 1764–5
Carved and gilded beech and walnut,
upholstery not original
106 × 77 × 77 cm
V&A: W.1-1937

by Chippendale's own hand, though he remained firmly responsible for artistic and quality control.

As well as supplying lavish state apartment furnishing for entire town and country houses for the nobility, landed gentry and illustrious clients, the firm also provided a service for more domestic and utilitarian items in native timbers for families or servants. This in turn inspired other commercially minded cabinet-makers to emulate Chippendale's work and produce their own versions of his original designs. Designed by Chippendale and made by an unknown maker, this mahogany breakfast table (fig. 2) closely matches plate 33 as published in Chippendale's *Director*. Simply decorated with chinoiserie openwork designs cut out with a fretsaw, it highlights the catalogue's importance in promoting

Fig. 4
Thomas Chippendale
Clothes press or wardrobe with four doors
(one of a pair) for the dressing room of the
Garrick villa at Hampton, England, 1775–8
Japanned (painted) pine
167 × 136 × 62 cm
V&A: W.23-1917

Chippendale's own original designs over those of his competitors. A close copy of a Chippendale design was roughly half the cost of an original.

Furniture design was closely integrated with the decoration of formal eighteenth-century interiors to create a harmonious whole, and from 1758 Chippendale began furnishing interiors in a close professional relationship with the equally significant architect and designer Robert Adam, receiving a major commission a year later for Dumfries House, a Palladian country estate in Ayrshire, Scotland. In 1764 Chippendale produced a suite of eight armchairs and four sofas to Adam's designs for the new home on Arlington Street, London of Sir Lawrence Dundas, a Scottish landowner, politician and businessman who amassed a fortune supplying weapons during the Seven Years War (1756–63). Described in Chippendale's bill as 'exceedingly Richly Carv'd in the Antick manner & Gilt in oil Gold',[9] the Neoclassical furnishings were produced for entertaining in one of the grandest rooms of the house, and remain Chippendale's only known furniture designed by an architect (fig. 3). Each item was provided with a protective leather case and cover, attesting to their great cost.[10]

Though Chippendale was influenced by Robert Adam's style and the classical sources revolutionizing design in Britain in the 1760s – then known as the 'Antique' and today as Neoclassicism – he was equally adept at freely combining features of earlier styles. Between 1768 and 1778, Chippendale provided a suite of furniture for the new Thames-side villa of actor, theatre manager and producer David Garrick and his wife Eva.[11] In contrast to Neoclassical rigour and heavily gilded finishes, the japanned furniture, painted under Eva Garrick's instructions with green chinoiserie landscapes on ivory ground, are illustrative of Chippendale's stylistic adaptability and reuse of less fashionable motifs (fig. 4).[12] Chippendale's bills from 1768 and 1769 also record refurbishing, to the Garricks' taste, furniture that his workshop may have supplied earlier.

Chippendale's career culminated with his furnishings for Harewood House, Yorkshire, his firm's largest and most valuable commission.[13] From 1769 entire suites of Neoclassical furniture, as well as frames for mirrors and paintings, were produced both to Chippendale's and Robert Adam's designs with elaborate marquetry tops, carved and gilded bases, for an eye-watering total exceeding £10,000.[14] Marquetry decoration was the perfect medium for imitating the new design vocabulary of repeating patterns and colour. Though the skill of France and Germany's marqueteurs remained unequalled, the pair of pier tables conceived by Chippendale as part of Robert Adam's plans for a Music Room (fig. 5), having never been exposed to damaging direct sunlight, represent some of the finest surviving British marquetry of the time.

Despite successive commissions from notable and wealthy patrons, Chippendale suffered several financial setbacks throughout his career which would have ultimately bankrupted the firm were it not for a restructure and injection of funds in the early 1770s. As a result, the firm became known as Chippendale, Haig & Co. until Chippendale's death in 1779, when it became Haig & Chippendale.

The enduring appeal of Chippendale's furniture is due to his ability to define and conform to the taste of his time, and his versatility left a lasting legacy well beyond his death. His designs became fashionable once more from about 1860, when many faithful Chippendale-inspired furnishings were made, and later misattributed throughout the twentieth century.[15] This has only served to further Chippendale's mythology; often described as 'the Shakespeare of English furniture makers', his name is now synonymous with a uniquely English style of eighteenth-century carved mahogany furniture. His towering effigy is one of a dozen craftsmen-designers to adorn the west façade of the V&A.[16]

Clementine Loustric

Fig. 5
Thomas Chippendale
Marquetry top from one of a pair
of pier tables, *c.*1771
Carved and gilded mahogany,
veneers of giltwood, dyed and
natural fruitwood, gilt brass
86 × 175 cm
V&A: W.6-2019

OTHER SIGNIFICANT MAKERS

John Cobb (c.1710–1778) was an English cabinet-maker and upholsterer. He formed a successful partnership with William Vile in 1751, with workshops close to Chippendale's. After their appointment as cabinet-makers to George III in 1761, Cobb and Vile became the principal suppliers of furniture to Queen Charlotte's Buckingham House (now Buckingham Palace).

Sir William Chambers (1723–1796) was an acclaimed Swedish-Scottish architect active in the later eighteenth century. He was a founder member of the Royal Academy and significantly influenced Neoclassical architecture in Britain through his designs and publications.

Robert Adam (1728¬–1792) was a significant Scottish Neoclassical architect and interior designer. Renowned for his sophisticated, symmetrical designs, he led the first phase of the classical revival in England and Scotland from around 1760 until his death, and influenced the development of architecture in Europe and in North America.

John Linnell (1729–1796) was an English cabinet-maker and designer. In 1762 he started working closely with Robert Adam and, following the death of his father a year later, he took over the family firm. His works championed marquetry and the Neoclassical ideals, and rivalled Thomas Chippendale, Ince and Mayhew, Robert Adam and John Cobb.

William Ince (1737–1804) was an English cabinet-maker. He formed a partnership with John Mayhew, producing furniture under the name of Ince and Mayhew from 1759 to 1803. Their published volume of designs, *The Universal System of Household Furniture*, was in direct emulation of Thomas Chippendale and his *Director*.

JACOB SANG

(c.1720–1786)

Amsterdam's prodigious glass engraver

Jacob Sang was the most prolific glass engraver working in the Netherlands during the eighteenth century. Around one hundred signed drinking glasses bear testimony to his exceptional skill and artistry.

Sang was born around 1720 in Erfurt, in present-day Thuringia, Germany, which was a major centre of wheel engraving on glass. His father was probably Andreas Friedrich Sang, who was also a glass engraver in Erfurt and it is likely that he taught his son. After his training, Jacob sought his fortune abroad, relocating to Amsterdam before 1748 when he became engaged there to Barbara Lolling. The Netherlands was one of the most prosperous countries at the time, with a wealthy middle class and a growing number of friendly societies and institutions. The local drinking culture involved raising toasts on all sorts of occasions, both private and public, often from specially engraved and inscribed glasses. This created great opportunities for skilled glass engravers from Germany and Bohemia who settled there to practise their art.

Sang's craft was copper-wheel engraving. With a treadle-operated lathe and small rotating copper wheels, fed with an abrasive paste, he would cut three-dimensional reliefs into the surface of the glass. This matt decoration contrasted with the smooth and reflective glass surface. Within such matt engraving, Sang often polished small details, using wheels of cork felt and soft abrasives, and these would stand out from the rest of the engraved surface. He used this technique to highlight details such as eyes and pearls on figures, windows on buildings and anchors and cannons on ships. The art of copper-wheel engraving on glass is time-consuming and requires the utmost concentration. Sang not only engraved, but also cut glass. This technique involved larger rotating wheels made of stone. He would cut and polish flat or slightly hollow areas of glass to form a geometric overall pattern. Sang's workshop would have been relatively small, and arranged so that, sitting at his lathe, he would have had all the different sizes of engraving and cutting wheels at hand.

Fig. 1
Jacob Sang
Ceremonial goblet, 1748–51
Wheel-engraved glass
24 × 11 cm
V&A: C.458-1936
Wilfred Buckley Collection

English-style lead glass was Sang's exclusive medium. This type of glass has a high lead content,[1] making it very clear, reflective, heavy and relatively soft: ideal for cutting and wheel engraving. It was first brought to perfection in England by George Ravenscroft around 1676–80. Although Sang stated that he engraved on English goblets, which were highly fashionable at the time, it is likely that at least some were made in the Netherlands. Sang often signed his work on the foot of his goblets. These signatures served as a calling card: on over 50 he adds 'Amsterdam' to his name and on at least one he gives his full address. With the addition of the Latin terms 'Inv.' for 'invenit' (designed by) and 'Fec' for 'fecit' (made by), Sang states that he both designed and executed his own work.

In March 1749 Sang enrolled in the citizens book of Amsterdam as 'Simon Jocoby of Erfurt mirror-glass cutter/engraver'. Much of what we know about his work in Amsterdam derives from an advertisement in the *Amsterdamse Courant* of 3 and 17 April 1753. He describes himself as a Saxon art-glass engraver who 'engraves and cuts English goblets; flat glass; plates for cabinets and caskets'. He claims to excel at 'large or small figures, in perspective, shallow and intaglio, on matt and hatched grounds; polished figures; coats of arms; names and all sorts of letters; emblems; busts; and other portraits; ornamentation and leaf-work after the latest fashion; Ovidian and other histories'. None of Sang's works on flat glass or mirrors are known to survive. Such plates were set into wooden frames or furniture and were prone to damage. In addition, they were not commonly signed by the maker, which makes them difficult to attribute.

Typical of Sang are his careful execution and fine detailing, including polished highlights. No other engravers working in the Netherlands at the time could rival his skill in this respect. A large goblet with allegorical engraving can be attributed to Sang based on quality and typical detailing (fig. 1). It is engraved with the arms of William IV, Prince of Orange, and his wife Anne, daughter of George II, as well as those of the seven provinces of the Dutch Republic. It shows the 'Dutch maiden' holding a lance with the 'hat of freedom', seated in an enclosed garden, a symbol of Dutch safety. Behind her is an orange tree symbolizing the House of Orange. The inscription reads 'HOLLANDS BEEDE, IS RUST EN VREEDE' (Holland's wish is peace and quiet). This dates the glass to the period of the War of the Austrian Succession, when the Netherlands were under threat from the French. The Dutch were looking for a strong leader and on 4 May 1747 the States-General of the Netherlands appointed William IV General Stadtholder of all seven of the United Provinces of the Netherlands. The war came to an end with the Peace of Aachen, concluded on 18 October 1748. It is likely that the goblet was engraved to celebrate this peace. Made in 1748, or just after, the V&A goblet is one of the very first that can be attributed to Jacob Sang.

Little is known about Sang's personal life. In 1747 he and his wife Barbara baptized their son Andreas Frederick. According to the 1753 advertisement, Sang lived in rooms in the Oudebrugsteeg on the corner of the Nieuwendijk, an address he still occupied four years later. Judging from his signed glasses, Sang was most active during the late 1750s and early 1760s. From an advertisement placed in the *Amsterdamsche Courant* of 11 April 1767 it is clear that Sang had moved to a house in the Hartestraat, located between the Heren- and Keizersgracht, where he ran 'The English Glass shop'.[2] Sang was clearly expanding his business. Alongside his own work, much of which he made to order, he dealt in all sorts of English and German cut and engraved glass as well as English mezzotint engravings.

Ships were one of his specialities and he excelled at representing different types, complete with rigging and crew. An excellent example is the goblet of about 1765 with an engraved toast to the prosperity of whaling around Greenland and the Davis Strait (fig. 2). Likely engraved

for a wealthy shipowner, this must have been an expensive goblet, showing in minute detail three different ships as well as two whaleboats with whalers busy harpooning the whale.

Sang engraved a pair of special, footed beakers, which were used to celebrate the safe birth of a child at a time when childbirth was a perilous event (fig. 3). Such 'confinement cups' were presented, often in pairs, to mothers after giving birth. They were used for serving the mother and guests with a restorative mixture of wine, egg yolks, sugar, cinnamon, cloves and lemon peel known as 'kandeel'. Both cups are signed and dated 1762; the one on the left is inscribed with a toast to the well-being of the mother, the other to the baby. On the former, the mother is shown in childbed receiving a visitor, while the latter shows the baby displayed naked on a cushion. The reverse of the former also shows a table with three chairs, prepared for visitors (fig. 4). A central dish with sweetmeats is flanked by a pair of lidded beakers just like these ones. Sang polished the beakers on the table to make them look like

Fig. 3 and 4
Jacob Sang
Pair of confinement cups, dated 1762
Wheel-engraved glass
21.6 cm (height)
V&A: C.465 and 466-1936
Wilfred Buckley Collection

Fig. 5
Jacob Sang
Confinement cup, 1778–80
Cut and wheel-engraved glass
14.4 cm (height)
V&A: C.649-1936
Wilfred Buckley Collection

glass. He also polished the eyes of all figures, adding a minute spot of black paint to indicate the pupils.

A single cup of the same shape and function is both engraved and cut (fig. 5). From 1761 Sang used cutting to decorate the foot and stem of some goblets. This is the only known beaker with elaborate, overall cutting. The style of shallow cutting on this cup was fashionable at the time in England. The engraving is confined to a cartouche with the arms of Jan George Matthes and Maria Wernier of Amsterdam whose first child was born on 28 May 1779. It is most likely that the glass was commissioned from Sang for that occasion.

During the 1770s, when Sang was in his fifties, he seems to have slowed down his production. Finally, in September 1785 Sang advertised the closing-down sale of his shop. He retired to the countryside, to the fashionable Nigtevecht on the river Vecht, where he died on 6 March 1786, leaving behind his second wife Lijsje Halveboer.

In Sang's works, the engraved subjects and figures are set off clearly against large, undecorated surface areas. Such easily readable decorations can be considered typically Dutch. In the German-speaking lands, in contrast, the entire surface of a glass would be filled with engraved ornament, sometimes incorporating figural scenes. As a German immigrant, Sang contributed vitally to the development of this typically Dutch style of wheel engraving.

Reino Liefkes

OTHER SIGNIFICANT MAKERS

Caspar Lehmann (*c*.1563–1622) was a gem and glass engraver working at the court of Emperor Rudolf II in Prague. He is thought to be the first to use wheel engraving on glass since ancient times. In 1618 Rudolf granted him an exclusive patent to engrave on glass.

Willem Mooleyser (*c*.1640–*c*.1700) was a diamond-point engraver working in Rotterdam, the Netherlands, during the last third of the seventeenth century. He worked in a free, sketchy style, often depicting drinking and merry-making country folk. He also engraved goblets with the arms of the Dutch provinces and Stadtholder Prince William III.

Hermann Schwinger (1640–1683) was a wheel engraver on glass. He worked in Nuremberg, Germany, which was the centre of this technique during the late seventeenth century, mostly on tall, ornamental standing cups.

Frans Greenwood (1680–1763) was a merchant in Dordrecht, the Netherlands, of English descent. He was an amateur poet, draughtsman and glass engraver. Most of his engravings are signed and dated by him. Greenwood pioneered stipple engraving, in which he built up the design from minute dot-shaped scratches made with a diamond point.

David Wolff (1732–1798) was a professional stipple engraver working in The Hague, the Netherlands. The over 250 known glasses by his hand show his very fine and precise way of working. Portraits were one of his specialities, as well as allegorical scenes with putti: small, often winged naked boys.

THOMAS JOHNSON

(1723–1799)

Woodcarver at the forefront of British 'Rococo' style

Thomas Johnson was one of the most influential ornament designers in eighteenth-century Britain. He had a celebrated career as a carver and gilder and published his designs from the 1750s onwards (figs 2 and 3). His work typifies what might be described as British 'Rococo', with designs that are light-hearted and fanciful in subject matter, making generous use of scrolling acanthus leaves, *rocaille* of shells and morphing natural forms.

Unusually, for a craftsman of his time, Johnson wrote an autobiography, which was discovered as recently as the early 2000s. It records not only major commissions but also the many ups and downs of his life, private and professional, including details of the progression of his training.[1] In this account he describes the challenge of establishing himself in the trade of carving and design, in particular giving fascinating insight into his determination to develop his drawing skills. He explains that his mind was so 'bent on improvement', he would stay up late into the night to practise drawing (fig. 4).

Johnson was a competent carver but, as is demonstrated by his own accounts of his career, he was also part of a new mode of production in eighteenth-century woodcarving, being a maker who could also draw and design. This meant that not only was he producing designs to print and sell, but the practice of drawing seems to have advanced his technical ability as a carver and designer. As a result, he was more ambitious in the forms that he demanded from his materials than many of his contemporaries and more adventurous in all aspects of the physical articulation of the objects he made (fig. 1).

Johnson's carved work seems to have been in limewood predominantly, which was gessoed and gilded. This medium showed off the flamboyant detail of his designs to great advantage. Limewood is relatively soft and easy to cut, making it faster and smoother to carve than harder woods, and meaning it was well suited to the type of flowing and morphing forms that Johnson wanted to produce. The applied layer of gesso – a mix of chalk and animal glue, with white pigment – that coated the carving

Fig. 1
Thomas Johnson
Candlestand, 1756–60
Carved, gessoed and painted pine with iron branches and gilt-brass nozzles
158.8 × 55.9 cm
V&A: W.9-1950

could be cut into when dry to create sharper edges, fine lines and a variety of surface types. The gilding that was applied to this gesso surface showed off the variety of finish and forms, heightening the contrast between stippled or matted surfaces and the areas of smooth or clean-cut detail.

The autobiography records how the carving of one particular 'girandole' (a wall-hung candleholder) transformed his status as a carver and designer (fig. 5). He described it as 'in a taste never before thought on; the principle of it was a ruinated building, with cattle etc.' and explained that the piece was so well received, he immediately published a small book of designs for girandoles, with other more ambitious design books following soon after.[2]

Johnson seems to have had a keen sense of how to capitalize on his successes, and his published work is notable for the high proportion of girandole and mirror designs it includes. Examples in the V&A collection offer good representative coverage of his output. It should be noted that, while contemporaries such as Chippendale (p. 102) or Ince and Mayhew included designs for large cabinet furniture and the grandest of beds, Johnson made space for smaller, more portable, possibly more attainable goods, that were highly decorative.

Fig. 2
Thomas Johnson
One Hundred & Fifty New Designs by Thos. Johnson Carver, 1761
Print on paper
28.5 × 22.5 cm
V&A: E.5699-1903

Fig. 3
Thomas Johnson
Design for a candelabra from
Designs for Picture-frames, Candelabra, Chimney pieces, etc., 1758
Print on paper
36.7 × 25 cm
V&A: E.3766-1903

Fig. 4
Thomas Johnson
Design drawing for two halves
of a Rococo pier table, 1755
Pencil, ink and wash on paper
10.8 × 18.3 cm
V&A: D.731-1906

It is also true that the furniture types Johnson focused on lent themselves to the flamboyance and frivolity of his designs, and it was with these girandoles, mirror frames, overmantels, torchieres (free-standing candlestands) and side tables that Johnson saw his greatest success and for which he is most remembered (see figs 1, 3–5). Indeed, it could be said that these were the only furniture types in which his style could have thrived: these pieces, generally positioned out of harm's reach, lent themselves to all the physically vulnerable detail of Johnson's designs, with little scenes of animals and people in romanticized miniature landscapes, wild roaming foliage and fanciful architectural structures.

Johnson's printed and drawn designs were as much about mood as they were about the reality of the specifics of the design (see fig. 2). It seems likely that part of his success in printing and selling his designs was that they sold a dream rather than a visual instruction for making an object. His design for a wall-mounted 'windmill' girandole, for example, presents a glimpse of arcadia, of a simple, rural life, full of beauty (see fig. 3). It is delicate, with fine-lined foliage that has grown without restraint, weaving itself through the structure of the windmill and the little cowshed. There are no hard or sharp lines here; there is no symmetry. This is a depiction of romanticized nature, where everything works in harmony, where there is variety, growth and movement.

When the print is compared to the small gessoed and gilded girandole that is associated with this design, the difference becomes

clear (see figs 3 and 5). While all the main subjects are present and we can recognize the windmill, the little ladder, the cow and its shed, the nature with which they are conveyed to the viewer has been altered by the medium. While in print it is possible to represent any line the mind fancies, in carved timber the constraints of the material assert themselves. The meandering lines and natural forms of the candle branches have been simplified and rely on metalwork because it would not have been possible to realize such a form and delicacy in carved timber (fig. 5). For the same reason, while wild sprouting foliage is abundant in the print, in the girandole there is very little.

What Thomas Johnson was creating and selling was a style, not necessarily an attainable style in any practical sense, but one that nonetheless had great popularity in mid-eighteenth-century Britain. Such was his success in this endeavour, Jonson's work has since come to typify that moment of mid-eighteenth-century style, because it so perfectly encapsulates the sense of freedom and fantasy that is the epitome of this mode of British 'Rococo' design. Having worked out how to make and market a dream of the fantastical, Johnson earned himself a place in the canon of great makers and designers and of his time.

Jenny Saunt

Fig. 5
Thomas Johnson
Girandole, 1760–65
Carved and gessoed pine
with water and oil gilding
86 × 59 cm
V&A: W.48-1952

OTHER SIGNIFICANT MAKERS

Giles Grendey (1693–1780) produced fashionable cabinet furniture, chairs, tables and looking glasses for the wealthy at his London workshop. He traded throughout Britain and internationally with a successful export business and is well known today for having labelled his furniture, which was not usual in British furniture production in that period.

Henry Copeland (*c*.1710–1754) was based in London and worked in partnership with Matthias Lock as a cabinet-maker and designer, also producing design prints. Copeland's 1746 publication, *A New Book of Ornaments*, was right at the start of the trend for publishing furniture designs. The V&A's 1768 edition of this book was produced in collaboration with Lock.

Matthias Lock (*c*.1710–1765) published numerous books of designs, and the V&A holds a large collection of his drawings in the Lock Album, which includes rough sketches and more highly finished drawings from across his career, which was based in London. Lock's earlier work was in a 'Rococo' style, which shifted to 'Neoclassicism' as his career progressed.

Wright and Elwick (*fl*.1745–1771) were a partnership company of Richard Wright and Edward Elwick, based in Wakefield, England, which traded variously in furniture, glass, tapestry, carpets and textiles. They were the pre-eminent cabinet-makers and upholsterers operating in Yorkshire in the second half of the eighteenth century.

Ince and Mayhew (*fl*.1759–1803) were a partnership company of William Ince and John Mayhew offering design, cabinet-making and upholstery, operating from London through the second half of the eighteenth century. From 1759 onwards they published their designs in parts under the title *The Universal System of Household Furniture*.

JOSIAH WEDGWOOD

(1730–1795)

Pioneering potter and entrepreneur

Josiah Wedgwood declared in 1769 that his ambition was to become 'Vase Maker General to the Universe'.[1] This typically bold statement captures the determination, energy and commercial awareness of one of the most noted makers of the eighteenth century, recognized for his scientific exploration and social engagement as much as for his high-quality ceramic designs. Wedgwood – both the company founded in 1759 and the man – became a shorthand for taste, knowledge, refinement and innovation. Josiah Wedgwood produced dinner services and more functional products in partnership with his cousin 'Useful' Thomas Wedgwood, while a second 'Ornamental' partnership with Liverpool merchant Thomas Bentley focused on grander and more decorative ceramics under the Wedgwood & Bentley name.

A young Josiah Wedgwood witnessed the transformation of industry in North Staffordshire. The six towns that today form the city of Stoke-on-Trent (Burslem, Fenton, Hanley, Longton, Stoke and Tunstall) were perfectly located to become a ceramic production hub, rich both in a variety of clays and coal to fire the kilns. From the 1720s to the 1760s the industry and infrastructure grew from small-scale pot-works producing wares for country markets to larger-scale factories producing finely made ceramics for a new influx of affluent global consumers. The simple earthenwares associated with the region were replaced with refined wares using innovative techniques, such as liquid lead glaze and slip-casting (which enabled detailed designs to be replicated using plaster of Paris moulds), creating a great variety of decoration in the latest styles.

Wedgwood became a master potter with an apprenticeship at age 14 to his brother Thomas at the Churchyard Works, the pottery founded by his great-grandfather. He trained for five years to learn the 'Art of Throwing and Handleing'[2] clay but was already showing an interest in experimentation rather than the factory's traditional products. On completing his apprenticeship, he entered a business partnership with John Harrison and Thomas Alders of Stoke, and in 1754 joined with respected potter Thomas Whieldon. During these early years, Wedgwood

Fig. 1
Josiah Wedgwood & Sons
First-edition copy of the
Portland Vase, 1790
Modelled by Henry Webber,
William Hackwood and William Wood
Jasperware with applied reliefs
25.5 cm (height), 19 cm (diam.)
V&A: WE.8000-2014
V&A Wedgwood Collection. Presented by
Art Fund with major support from the
National Lottery Heritage Fund, private
donations and a public appeal

worked with industry innovators including William Greatbatch, Aaron Wood and Josiah Spode. In 1759 he set up his own factory in Burslem.

Wedgwood's earliest innovations were not necessarily stylistic, but technical. Like many of his competitors, his fledgling company produced *trompe l'oeil* pots in the shape of fruits and vegetables, perfectly suited to the Rococo trends in the mid-1750s. Made from moulds and decorated in just two colours, Wedgwood manufactured fruit- and vegetable-shaped crockery which could be cheaply and quickly produced and marketed (fig. 2). Even at this early stage, Wedgwood's commercial reach went far beyond the English Midlands: he exported large quantities of 'colley-flower' wares to European merchants.

By the late 1750s cream-coloured earthenware had become the primary product of the 'Potteries', as Staffordshire was named after its primary industry. Known as creamware, this was suitable for many styles of decoration including moulded patterns and hand-painted or transfer-printed motifs. It was a more affordable answer to European or East Asian porcelain, arriving at just the moment when an explosion of aspirational middle-class consumers joined the aristocracy in seeking the latest fashionable wares. In 1765 a key commission set Wedgwood on the path to extraordinary success: St James's Palace ordered a tea set for Queen Charlotte. Along with the gilded set, Wedgwood sent a crate of samples of creamware vases. This bold strategy resulted in further

Fig. 2
Probably made by Josiah Wedgwood or Thomas Whieldon
Cauliflower ware teapot, 1764
Earthenware with cream and green glazes
12 × 18.5 cm
V&A: WE.7479:1,2-2014
V&A Wedgwood Collection. Presented by Art Fund with major support from the National Lottery Heritage Fund, private donations and a public appeal

Fig. 3
Page from Josiah Wedgwood's
Commonplace Book, *c*.1770s–1795
33.8 × 21.7 cm
V&A: E39-28408
V&A Wedgwood Collection Archive.
Presented by Art Fund with major support
from the National Lottery Heritage Fund,
private donations and a public appeal

orders, and in 1766 Wedgwood began to capitalize on his growing reputation, naming his creamware Queen's Ware and adding 'Potter to her Majesty' to bill heads and orders. Wedgwood also began stamping the base of his wares as a mark of authenticity. There were other marketing strategies: free delivery from Wedgwood's factory to London and free replacement of items broken in transit. An advertisement in the early 1770s told customers about 'Queen's Ware and Ornamental Vases, manufactured by Josiah Wedgwood, Potter to her Majesty ... he delivers the goods safe and Carriage free to London and without any danger of breaking ... and is sold at no other Place in Town'.[3] Wedgwood established a retail presence in fashionable hotspots, with showrooms in London, Bath and Dublin.

Wedgwood was an avid record keeper, recording his correspondence and experiments as well as company business transactions, production records and designs. Notes made throughout his life in his Commonplace Books – notebooks or journals – capture these details as well as his wide social circle, which encouraged his scientific and artistic interests (fig. 3). A voracious reader, Wedgwood gathered an important collection of reference books.[4] With the well-connected Bentley, Wedgwood built his network of collectors, designers, architects and patrons, affording him access to impressive art collections, which became sourcebooks. Such access and support gave his company a commercial advantage and resulted in an entirely new approach to the production of ornamental ceramics, drawing on the rich inspiration of classical antiquity. Wedgwood was also interested in modernity: he was part of a group of

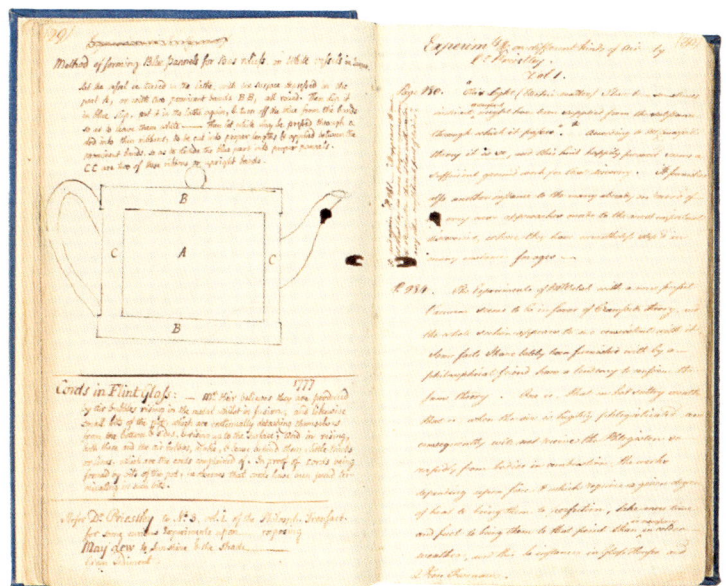

forward-thinking industrialists and thinkers based in the Midlands, including manufacturer and metal-working entrepreneur Matthew Boulton, natural philosopher and theologian Joseph Priestley, engineer James Watt and physician and poet Erasmus Darwin, who met at each full moon to discuss the scientific and political issues of the day, hence their name: the Lunar Society.

Staffordshire's ceramics were distributed via networks of turnpike roads and canals, linking the Midlands to trade routes and ports. This reduced transport costs and the losses of fragile pots on poor-quality roads. Wedgwood played a critical role in improving local transport routes, including the 'Grand Trunk' Canal (completed in 1777). The newly built canal passed directly by Wedgwood's purpose-built factory at Etruria which also featured housing for his workers and a carefully designed factory layout with a logical and efficient sequence of production.[5]

Wedgwood's Nonconformist leanings made him an avid campaigner and marked him out from both his peers and his aristocratic clientele. In 1787 he became involved with the Society for the Abolition of the Slave Trade, producing a series of medallions featuring a kneeling, enslaved man with the motto 'Am I not a Man and a Brother?' (see p. 92), for handing out at meetings in support of the cause although the abolition of the slave trade would not happen in Wedgwood's lifetime.

Having achieved major commercial success, Wedgwood continued to experiment with materials and techniques, working with skilled artists, modellers and chemists such as William Hackwood and Alexander Chisholm. He produced refined Black Basalt clays, innovative commissions such as the Frog Service (a lavish 952-piece dinner service commissioned by Empress Catherine the Great), and his most important contribution to ceramic history: the invention of jasperware (fig. 4). As with Queen's Ware, Wedgwood carried out thousands of trials to perfect this revolutionary new type of stoneware, which could be produced in an array of colours to match fashionable Neoclassical interiors – all detailed in his Experiment Books.

Uniting the arts and sciences was a particular skill of Wedgwood: he connected with the leading artists of the day to design for his company. It was in the grounds of the family home at Etruria in summer 1780 that George Stubbs painted a large conversation piece depicting the Wedgwood family – Josiah, his wife Sarah, and seven of their eight children (fig. 5). Stubbs captures something of the character of Josiah Wedgwood as an individual, his passion for his family life and for his business: seated beside his wife, quill in hand, his papers and designs laid out, and a 'Shape No. 1' vase in Black Basalt beside him, the smoke of his factory visible in the background. This painting, and the grand

Fig. 4
Josiah Wedgwood & Sons
Tray of jasper trials, 1773
Jasperware
38.5 × 30 cm
V&A: WE.7599-2014
V&A Wedgwood Collection Archive.
Presented by Art Fund with major support from the National Lottery Heritage Fund, private donations and a public appeal

2621 2523 2021 2006
TBO TBO

1605 1605 1605
Mixt Mixt Mixt
300 to 1 200 to 1 100 to 1

old 3681 old 3681 Graystis old 3681 3681
30 to 1 35 to 1 mixt 40 to 1 25 to 1 28 to

3801 3893 3894 3775 3796 3797 3798 3799 20 to 1
TTBO TTBO TTBO TTBO TTBO TTBO TTBO TTBO Ground
white fine
500

3771 3772 3774 3778+ 3776 3777 3778 3775 3780 3785
TTBO TTBO TTBO TTBO TTBO TTBO TTBO TTBO TTBO TTBO

2 133 134 135 312 313 315 318 Blue 300 to 1
2815 2817 2820 2 Cobalt
1 flux
Sugars

314 317 319 Blue 300 to 1 Blue
2704 2705 2706 2814 2816 2819 2821 2 Cobalt new Cor
1 flux Cobalt
Cobalt

304 3806 3805 3807 3808 3908 3810 3811 3812 3813 3
TBO TTBO TTBO TTBO TTBO TTBO TTBO TTBO TTBO TTBO

3809
TTBO

6 3887 3888 3889 3890 3891 3902 3903 3904 3905 3906 3
BO TTBO TTBO TTBO TTBO TTBO TTBO TTBO TTBO TTBO TTBO

portraits of Josiah and Sarah Wedgwood painted by Sir Joshua Reynolds in 1782, reflect the enormous success of the Wedgwood family, which would go on to produce many luminaries, including Charles Darwin.

Wedgwood's final major project was to create a ceramic copy of the Portland Vase in his invented material, jasper (fig. 1). The cameo glass vessel (now in the British Museum) is thought to date from around 25 CE and when it came to Britain via the ambassador at Naples, Sir William Hamilton, its reputation preceded it. Wedgwood would have been familiar with the object from prints, but it gained further prominence when Hamilton sold the vase to the Dowager Duchess of Portland, a well-known collector, and it passed to her son, the 3rd Duke of Portland, on her death. Wedgwood borrowed the vase, and after almost five years of experimentation, he celebrated the creation of his perfect copy with a ticketed exhibition, concluding, 'My great work is the Portland Vase.'[6] So associated with Wedgwood is the Portland Vase that it long featured on the company's backstamp and civic statues of Josiah Wedgwood. Wedgwood wrote in 1765: 'I scarcely know without a good deal of recollection whether I am a Landed Gentleman, an Engineer or a Potter, for indeed I am all three & many other characters by turns.'[7] His energy and creativity changed aspects of production and the world around him that can still be felt today.

Catrin Jones

Fig. 5
George Stubbs
Wedgwood Family Portrait, 1780
Oil on wooden panels
149.1 × 210.5 cm (framed)
V&A: WE.7853-2014
V&A Wedgwood Collection. Presented by Art Fund with major support from the National Lottery Heritage Fund, private donations and a public appeal

OTHER SIGNIFICANT MAKERS

Matthew Boulton (1728–1809) was an entrepreneur and fellow member of the Lunar Society. An inventive manufacturer, he developed decorative metalworking techniques including Sheffield plate and ormolu from his famous factory at Soho House in Birmingham. He collaborated with scientist and engineer James Watt in developing steam engines for use in manufacturing.

Josiah Spode (1733–1797) of Staffordshire found huge success as a potter. He is particularly associated with blue and white underglaze transfer-printed patterns, and for introducing a refined bone china formula, both of which were widely adopted in the ceramics industry.

William Adams (c.1746–1805) was a Staffordshire potter and contemporary of Wedgwood. Like Humphrey Palmer, James Neale and John Turner he built a successful ceramics business, appealing to many of the same consumers as Wedgwood with high-quality dinnerwares, teawares and vases.

John Flaxman Jr (1755–1826) is considered the foremost English sculptor of the period. Flaxman's father supplied plaster models to Wedgwood, and through this connection Flaxman Jr became one of the company's top designers of vases, plaques and sculptural medallions. He became the Royal Academy's first professor of sculpture in 1810.

JOHANN CHRISTIAN NEUBER

(1736–1808)

Goldsmith who combined science and luxury

The name of Johann Christian Neuber is synonymous with eighteenth-century Saxony's *Galanteriewaren*, small precious objects with a function. Neuber did not simply perfect some goldsmithing techniques, he created his own signature style which remained unsurpassed. His creations, widely ranging from large console tables to small snuffboxes and buttons, are distinctively composed of mosaic patterns called *Zellenmosaik*, or cell mosaics, which consist of hardstone specimens such as agates, jaspers, chalcedonies, set within gold mounts.

Neuber's stone and gold works of art have always been clearly identified and sought after. In the twentieth century, Neuber's works of art became the subject of a vivid collecting interest and can now be found in many private and public collections; the V&A holds 17 examples of Neuber's works, including eight that belong to the Rosalinde and Arthur Gilbert Collection. Recent research has shed light on Neuber and his wide array of products as well as the business challenges that such highly skilled artists encountered in the world of bespoke luxury commissions.

Johann Christian Neuber was not from a dynasty of goldsmiths. He was born in 1736 in the mining region of Neuwernsdorf, where his father had been a linen weaver. Neuber settled in Dresden where he started his goldsmithing apprenticeship at the age of 16. He became a master in 1762 and was rapidly noticed by the Prince-Elector of Saxony, Frederick Augustus III, who appointed him 'artisan maker of *Galanteriewaren* to the Court' in 1768. This title did not relate to a specific function but confirmed his role as providing the court with such specific type of objects: delightful accessories, of exquisite quality, made of rare and precious materials. In 1775 he was elevated to another honorary appointment of *Hofjuwelier*, court jeweller. Alongside the 'white gold', a term used to describe Meissen porcelain, Neuber's works reflected a Saxony that had become influential technically and artistically among European states since the seventeenth century. Two generations of Prince-Electors, Augustus II the Strong and Frederick Augustus II, had expanded their dominion by accessing the coveted title of King

Fig. 1
Johann Christian Neuber
Console, *c.*1779–80
Hardstones, Meissen porcelain,
wood, gilt bronze
81.5 × 70.5 cm
Musée du Louvre, OA 12547

of Poland. They had developed their capital, Dresden, as a magnificent city: its iconic 20 Baroque palaces included the Japanese Palace and inspired many artists such as the Venetian painter Canaletto; their treasured collections, produced mainly by Saxon artists and kept in the Green Vault, were the subject of diplomatic visits from admiring monarchs and their embassies. During Neuber's lifetime, Saxony continued to play an important role in the balance of European political alliances and artistic centres.

In contrast with France or England, the system of hallmarks for small gold objects in Saxony was barely existent, which makes it difficult to establish a clear chronology for Neuber's production. However, some rare, dated and signed examples, combined with associated archives, have helped to confirm what Neuber created during his lifetime. The goldsmith delivered his first diplomatic snuffbox in 1770, when it was presented to the Danish envoy Christian Sehestedt Juul, and at least four others in the next decade. They are all based on a similar pattern of oval form with a portrait set in the centre of the lid, following the style of diplomatic boxes designed in France. Alongside those, Neuber received some monumental commissions. These included two consoles: one presented by Marie-Amélie de Deux-Ponts to her husband the Elector, probably in 1772; another presented by the Elector to Louis Charles Auguste Le Tonnelier, Baron de Breteuil (1730–1807), envoy to King Louis XVI of France (fig. 1). He also produced a few bases for surtouts de table – ornamental centrepieces which became predominant on ceremonial dining tables during the second half of the eighteenth century. Neuber's stone masterpieces were combined with Meissen porcelain figures, and together illustrated Saxony's remarkable luxury production. One surtout was presented by the Elector to the Russian statesman Nikolai Vasilyevich Repnin. The most extravagant commission was certainly the fireplace designed for Count Marcolini,[1] signed and dated 1782, which was entirely composed of porcelain, gold and hardstones.

Meanwhile, Neuber developed his signature object: the *Steinkabinettabatiere*, literally 'snuffboxes as stone cabinets', usually referred to as 'specimen boxes' in English (fig. 2). Each specimen is numbered on its gold frame as a reference to an accompanying booklet which lists the stone identification. Of particular pride was that the stone specimens were exclusively sourced locally. While the first dated specimen box is from 1777, it is probable that some examples were in fact made earlier. That would tie in with two examples, dated 1772 and 1774, and also signed by Christian Gottlieb Stiehl. This evidence contradicts the widely held belief that Neuber was the sole inventor of such specimen boxes. Instead, he can be seen as an inventive goldsmith and astute businessman

Fig. 2
Johann Christian Neuber
Specimen snuffbox (containing
original booklet), *c.*1785–90
Hardstones, gold, silk
7.3 cm (diam.)
V&A: M.10-2017
Accepted under the Cultural Gifts Scheme
by HM Government from Nicholas Snowman
and allocated to the Victoria and Albert
Museum, 2017

who exploited a successful format that combined Saxon tradition for stone carving and new collecting interest for stone specimens.

Since medieval times, Saxony was renowned for its incredible wealth of hardstones such as amethysts, jaspers and agates, sourced from the Erzgebirge region (Ore Mountains), near the town of Freiberg. The commercial exploitation of these minerals had started quietly in the sixteenth century and became an important source of profit under the reign of Prince-Elector Augustus II the Strong. The court appointed several lapidarists, *Steinschneider*, who either kept specimens and had them mounted by goldsmiths for the princely collection or sold them outside the state. At the same time, the ruler supported scientists in their study of stones as it developed into the science of 'mineralogy'.[2] During Neuber's lifetime this fascination with stones became a fashionable collecting activity for many European amateurs who sought to emulate the most revered Electoral Cabinet of Minerals.

Neuber knew how to seize this opportunity and proudly declared that his jewels offered the perfect combination of 'luxury, taste and science'.[3] He himself was granted the concession of a mine of amethyst and jasper in the Ore Mountains in 1775 for ten years. Through archives, it is understood that Neuber was working closely with the lapidary workshops established in Freiberg, who were able to cut very thin slices of stone. These were then transported to Neuber's workshop in Dresden where they were further cut according to the desired pattern. Neuber insisted on creating unique pieces, although they tend to follow successful motifs, made exclusively of local stones. Neuber enhanced some specimens with the technique of inserting tinted cement between the slice of stone and the gold support. This is evident from a notebook (fig. 3) where intense green can be seen under the transparent agates. The goldsmith also decorated many snuffboxes with pearl borders. In reality, what look like pearls are in fact tapered rock-crystal rods which have been hollowed on the underside and poured in with a silver substance that then solidified and gave that shimmering silver effect. For further diversity, the goldsmith played with various precious and highly sought-after materials for central medallions: stone cameos, Meissen porcelain and micromosaics (fig. 4), a technique that had recently been developed by the artist Giacomo Raffaelli.

By 1782 Neuber reached the pinnacle of his career and acquired a house in Dresden. Records demonstrate that this was his home and workshop, accommodating his family as well as his apprentices,[4] a common practice in Germany until the nineteenth century. In 1785 Neuber was appointed 'inspector', or conservator looking after the condition of the royal collections kept in the Green Vault.

Fig. 3
Johann Christian Neuber
Notebook, *c*.1780–5
Hardstones, gold, later miniatures painted on ivory (exterior), silk and paper (interior)
11.9 × 8.5 cm
V&A: LOAN:GILBERT.351-2008
The Rosalinde and Arthur Gilbert Collection on loan to the V&A

Fig. 4
Johann Christian Neuber and
Giacomo Raffaelli
Snuffbox with micromosaic, 1780
Hardstones, glass micromosaics, gold
6 cm (height), 8.5 cm (diam)
V&A: LOAN:GILBERT.353-2008
The Rosalinde and Arthur Gilbert Collection
on loan to the V&A

Fig. 5
Johann Christian Neuber and
Jean-Antoine Lépine
Chatelaine, 1770–85
Hardstones, gold, watch movement,
later miniature portrait on ivory
20.5 cm (length)
V&A: M.11-2017
Accepted under the Cultural Gifts Scheme
by HM Government from Nicholas Snowman
and allocated to the Victoria and Albert
Museum, 2017

By 1786, however, commissions from the Elector had become sparse and Neuber felt the need to reach a wider clientele. In an advertisement,[5] he listed an incredible variety of delightful accessories, including chatelaines (fig. 5), boxes for men, boxes for women, watches and chains, shoe buckles, earrings, 'English wallets' – probably étuis: small decorative cases which contained personal accessories like thimble, pair of scissors, ivory note slip, earwax spoon and toothpick. He insisted that all were affordable, a sign that Neuber wanted to reach a wider clientele. Interestingly, he claimed to have invented a new technique for embellishing buttons that should please Parisian customers and specified that his creations were available at the major Leipzig trade fair with the dealer Carl Christian Heinrich Rost. No longer a courtly jeweller, Neuber was evidently placing himself among the reputed European goldsmiths, like James Cox in England or Joseph-Etienne Blerzy in Paris.

Meanwhile, Neuber requested another ten-year concession for his mine in the Ore Mountains. His efforts, however, were in vain. In October 1788 he created a lottery which offered 6,500 lots to lucky bets, probably the content of his entire stock. In 1795 he was declared bankrupt, lost his house, which he had previously mortgaged, and left Dresden. He died destitute in 1808. Yet, despite the failure of his business, Johann Christian Neuber has come to be celebrated for his visionary talent, combining Enlightenment scientific knowledge with an entrepreneurial eye for the conspicuous consumption of daily accessories. Generations of craftsmen sought to emulate Neuber's creations but failed to achieve their technical perfection.

Alice Minter

OTHER SIGNIFICANT MAKERS

Christian Gottlieb Stiehl (1708–1792) was appointed Hofsteinschneider (court lapidary) in 1753 and worked alongside Heinrich Taddel and their junior Johann Christian Neuber. His specimen boxes tend to follow a design of flowers and swirls with sometimes two of the same stone specimens, rather than being strictly a miniature mineralogy cabinet like Neuber examples.

Heinrich Taddel (1715–1794) was a leading goldsmith in Dresden, successively appointed Hofgalanteriearbeiter, court manufacturer, and director of the Green Vault where he was Neuber's supervisor. He himself was fascinated with stones and amassed a collection of 214 specimens kept in a purpose-built cabinet which is still in the Green Vault.

Joseph-Etienne Blerzy (1735–1821) was a Parisian goldsmith with a 58-year career spanning the *Ancien Régime*, the French Revolution and its aftermath. He used the typical snuffbox model of an oval shape with a central medallion to offer a large array of designs, developing extraordinary colours of translucent enamels.

James Cox (active 1749–1791) and his creations embodied the splendour of eighteenth-century British luxury accessories and his success reached as far as the Imperial Palace in Beijing. He fitted clocks and snuffboxes with automaton mechanisms and turned them into wonders intended to surprise and amaze his customers.

Giacomo Raffaelli (1753–1836) is considered the father of micromosaics, an art developed in eighteenth-century Rome. Raffaelli produced micromosaic plaques and panels of unsurpassed quality set into luxury objects, from jewellery to vases and clocks. He designed stylish furnishings for the grand residences of Europe's rulers, including Napoleon Bonaparte and Russian Tsar Alexander I.

WILLIAM KILBURN

(1745–1818)

Textile artist and copyright campaigner

Botanical artist, pattern designer and prominent London calico printer, William Kilburn is best known for his highly original textile designs featuring naturalistic floral motifs in combination with leaves, ferns, seaweeds or architectural elements. These unique patterns furnished fashionable homes and were worn by the tastemakers of the day, such as Queen Charlotte, a keen botanist to whom Kilburn presented a seaweed design. His designs circulated as part of an eighteenth-century visual and material culture influenced by imperial ambition and international trade, exploration and cross-cultural exchange and the collection and classification of the natural world. Kilburn was also an active advocate for the calico industry and played a key part in the introduction of legislation in 1787 and 1794 to protect pattern designs from imitation, in his case by rival factories such as Peel & Co in Bury, who were able to copy, print and market his designs within ten days of their first appearance, at two-thirds of the price of the original.

Kilburn was born in Dublin, the only son of Samuel Kilburn, an 'architect and builder', and Sarah Johnston, a niece of General Johnston of Tyrone. Having displayed a talent for drawing at an early age, he was apprenticed at 12 years old to Jonathan Sisson, who owned a linen- and cotton-printing factory in nearby Lucan and specialized in working from woodblocks. A diligent employee with a developing commercial acumen, it was said that 'if a new pattern caught his eye, he would take out his pocket-book and have it for his master at his return'.[1] In his free time he drew decorative patterns to sell to paper stainers (wallpaper producers).

Following his father's death in around 1776, Kilburn and his mother and two sisters settled permanently in Bermondsey, London, where he found calico printers and print shops willing to buy his designs and etchings for trade cards. In Bermondsey he became acquainted with botanist William Curtis who was so impressed with his draughtsmanship that he commissioned him to design around 28 plates for his first volume of the *Flora Londinensis* (*c.* 1777). The *Flora* was a subscription title illustrating the plants growing within a ten-mile radius of London

Fig. 1
William Kilburn
'Leontodon Taraxacum' or 'Dandelion', *c.*1777
Engraving on paper
36.5 × 27.8 cm
V&A: E.455-1996

which aimed to establish 'each species and variety on a firm basis' and be 'instructive and entertaining to the young botanist'.[2]

Kilburn's hand-coloured copperplate engraving, 'Leontodon Taraxacum' or 'Dandelion' (fig. 1), is based on his drawing held by the Botany Library in the Natural History Museum in London. The exquisitely detailed botanical illustration depicts the structural characteristics of the plant and bears the Latin inscription 'Kilburn pinxit et sculpt' (an abbreviation of 'Kilburn painted it and engraved it').

Although the *Flora* was financially unsuccessful and never completed, it was the precursor to *Curtis's Botanical Magazine* (established 1787), the

Fig. 2
William Kilburn
Furnishing fabric, *c.*1775
Printed by Talwin and Foster
Plate-printed cotton
109.2 × 72.4 cm
V&A: Circ.91-1960

world's longest-running, continually published botanical magazine, printed today by the Royal Botanic Gardens, Kew. Kilburn's association with the *Flora* ceased in around 1777 when he became manager of the calico printing works owned by James Newson and James Morison on the River Wandle in Wallington, south London; Kilburn took over the business entirely in 1784.[3]

Calico originated in Calicut, now Kozhikode, in south India, from which the name of the textile came, and denotes a plain-woven, unprinted cotton fabric. In the seventeenth and eighteenth centuries India was the primary source of printed, washable cottons which inspired the development of European calico printing. In 1676 the first English manufacturer to print textiles using madder dyes and mordants (substances to fix the dyes) was William Sherwin, who was granted a patent for 'printing broad Calico and Scots cloth with a double necked rolling press'.[4] In 1752 Francis Nixon at the Drumcondra printworks near Dublin was the first to use copper plates successfully, which allowed a fineness of detail that had not been possible in earlier block-printed textiles.

Kilburn's pattern designs are representative of the Rococo style, albeit a mild English form, characterized by their use of natural motifs in decorative configurations. His highly original polychrome designs blended identifiable flora, non-native species and marine plants to 'strike the Trade as something new, and not seen before'.[5] This sensibility can be seen in his decision to feature the passion flower in his furnishing fabric design (fig. 2), a plant introduced to Europe in the eighteenth century from Central and South America and first classified as 'Passiflora' by the Swedish taxonomist Carl Linnaeus in 1753. His design of delicate, meandering stems bearing ornamental passion flowers, peonies, berries and grasses was printed with engraved copper plates by Talwin and Foster at Bromley Hall printworks. Talwin and Foster excelled in the China Blue technique, developed in England in the 1740s, where indigo was printed directly onto cloth by plate as a finely ground paste and then the fabric fixed in lime baths.

The 'Kilburn album' provides further insights into his approach to pattern design and his desire to push the boundaries of textile printing. Containing 223 of his finished dress and furnishing watercolour designs from 1788 to 1792, this album is of crucial importance because most of the textiles have not survived, although the V&A is fortunate to have a dress in the collection (fig. 5). One design (fig. 3) features flowers and blossoms in pink, yellow and blue intertwined with delicate seaweed fronds and coral branches on an off-white background punctuated by patches of black. Kilburn produced this design for wholesale linen drapers Brown, Rogers & Co. of Cheapside who were the proprietors of most of his designs and connected by his marriage to Elizabeth Brown in 1785. This complex pattern is likely to have been printed by using a paste resist applied by a block to all areas to be white or another colour, allowing the cloth to be dyed black with only the un-pasted areas taking the colour.

In 2019 a leather-bound order book from 1799 or 1800 belonging to William Kilburn and containing 60 calico designs was offered by descendant Gabriel Sempill to the V&A. It signals a significant departure from the complexity of his earlier designs. The entries in Kilburn's hand are dated and detail quantities and colourways of fabric ordered. The book was later used as a scrapbook by Kilburn's grandson or great-grandson who contributed drawings of soldiers and animals and pasted in cartoons and illustrations from journals, which provide a unique insight into the popular culture of that period through the eyes of a child (fig. 4).

Whereas his designs of the 1780s were often printed in only one colour from their copper plates, the demand for multiple colours in the 1790s, reflected in the 'Kilburn album' designs, led to the use of sycamore

Fig. 3
William Kilburn
Design from an album of designs for printed textiles, 1788–92
Watercolour on paper (double spread)
18.8 × 25.4 cm
V&A: E.894:111/1-1978

Fig. 4
William Kilburn
Leather-bound order book belonging
to William Kilburn, 1799–1800
Watercolour, pencil and pen on paper
11.3 × 18.5 cm
V&A: E.14:1 to 60-2019

woodblocks to provide outline and solid colour combined with blocks inlaid with copper strips for detail. The woodblocks were generally of a smaller size, dictating a small repeating pattern rather than the complex interlocking branches, leaves and flowers of the late 1780s. The abstracted leaf designs illustrated in fig. 4 are examples of this new style.

The V&A holds a rare example of a dress block-printed with a Kilburn seaweed-patterned cloth dating from 1790 (fig. 5). The garment was originally made as an open-robe dress, which was worn over a skirt to create a Neoclassical silhouette. Particularly fine gowns were altered to conform to new trends or might be passed from one owner to another. This dress was reconfigured into a round gown in around 1800–5 and shows signs of minor repairs. In 2011 historian Ann Christie discovered that its seaweed design is part of the 'Kilburn album', with the fine detail of the watercolour adapted for the rudimentary lines of the woodblock. The polychromatic watercolour design was reproduced in muted tones of purple, which were cheaper to print and aligned with mainstream fashions of the time.

The dress would have made a subtle statement about the wearer's taste and sophistication. In the late eighteenth century, 'botanizing' had become a fashionable pursuit for aristocratic women who wished to engage with the natural sciences. Key among them were Margaret Bentinck, the Duchess of Portland, an important collector of natural-history specimens, and her friend and collaborator, botanical artist Mary Delany.

Kilburn was a talented botanical artist with an eye for originality whose intricate pattern designs were inspired by his observations of nature and an understanding of what would appeal to his elite customers. As one of only five 'Master Printers' in London he was at the vanguard of his field, his designs described by his employee Charles O'Brien as 'perhaps the nearest approaches to nature in drawing as far as cutting allowed'.[6] He was a powerful advocate for his industry and through social and professional connections built a network that extended to royalty. Despite his many achievements, Kilburn's business failed in 1802 and his assets were sold, including thousands of printing blocks, incorporating 'some of the most curious patterns of seaweed chintzes'.[7] His inventive and distinctive designs inspired by nature and his fine skill as a printer continue to define him as a significant maker in the history of textile production.

Sandy Jones

Fig. 5
William Kilburn
Cotton gown, 1790 (designed),
1800–5 (altered)
Block-printed cotton (maker unknown)
160 × 70 × 70 cm (when mounted)
V&A: T.84-1991

OTHER SIGNIFICANT MAKERS

Robert Peel (1723–1795) was a Lancashire cotton mill owner and calico printer who is known for his innovation in the textile industry. He first gained recognition for his parsley-leaf patterns that earned him the nickname 'Parsley Peel'. By 1795 the family business Peel & Co. was the largest company in the cotton industry with 23 mills.

Christophe-Philippe Oberkampf (1738–1815) established his printworks in 1760 in Jouy-en-Josas in northern France and produced expensive furnishing textiles for the main residences of the French court. The monochrome designs by Jean-Baptiste Huet for which the company became famous featured images of the countryside and rural industry in an idealized form.

Sydenham Teast Edwards (1768–1819) was a Welsh natural history illustrator of plants, birds and animals. Edwards contributed illustrations to the *Flora Londinensis* and *Curtis's Botanical Magazine*. In 1815 he began his own rival publication, *The Botanical Register*, subsequently known as *Edwards's Botanical Register*.

Richard Ovey (d.1931) was a linen draper based in Covent Garden who was the leading London merchant for 'furniture prints' and whose clients included the Prince of Wales. An advocate for design education, he commissioned designs from skilled pattern designers and sent them to printworks in Lancashire, Cumbria and Kent.

PAUL STORR

(1770–1844)

Goldsmith to royalty

In a corner of the churchyard of St Nicholas in Tooting, south London, is a weathered, ivy-covered grave slab with an illegible inscription marking the resting place of Paul Storr. It seems a modest memorial to the most famous silversmith in Regency Britain. Paul Storr was chief supplier to royal goldsmiths Rundell, Bridge and Rundell, and George IV was his biggest customer. His clients included British, European and North American aristocracy and government ministers and diplomats.

Storr's career spanned over 40 years, initially as a maker and later as a manager of makers. His business partnerships from 1792 to 1833 spanned 12 separate goldsmiths' maker's marks. The work for which he is remembered is a form of monumental classicism: richly ornamented silver of remarkably high quality and substantial thickness. Today, grand dinner services, presentation cups and large narrative display plates bearing his marks are in major museums all over the world.

For all his posthumous fame, Storr is something of a mystery. His historical record is sparse. He did not serve a traditional apprenticeship through the Goldsmiths' Company but became a freeman of the Vintners' Company instead, possibly through his father, Thomas, a Westminster innkeeper. Thomas had previously been a silver chaser (a specialist role doing fine decoration on silver). In 1784 Storr was apprenticed to William Rock, another member of the Vintners' Company and a harpsichord maker.[1] This cross-trade arrangement was not uncommon. Such apprenticeships were as much about learning business management as they were about craft skills.

Storr began training as a silversmith in around 1785 in Church Street, Soho, at the premises of the Swedish silversmith Andrew Fogelberg, and registered his first mark in a short-lived partnership with William Frisbee in 1792. The following year he registered an individual mark, building a reputation for quality that led to his first major commission: a gold font for the Duke of Portland in 1797,[2] followed two years later by the *Battle of the Nile Cup* for Admiral Horatio Lord Nelson.[3]

Fig. 1
Paul Storr
Soup tureen, 1807–8
Silver, raised, cast, chased and engraved
43.2 × 47 cm (diam.)
V&A: LOAN:GILBERT.784-2008
The Rosalinde and Arthur Gilbert Collection on loan to the V&A

During his early career, fashionable tables displayed dinner services inspired by the elegant classicism promoted by the architect Robert Adam. Enterprising silversmiths like Storr began adopting steam-powered factory production developed by workers in Sheffield Plate (silver fused to copper) and Britannia Metal (a tin alloy), mechanically rolling metal into thin sheets and then applying patterns using stamps and presses. The mechanical aspects should not be overstated. They complemented traditional casting and hand-finishing skills required for the finest work, adding options rather than replacing old methods. By 1800 Storr was overseeing a network of related workshops including flatting mills for rolling metal sheets, casting workshops, silver engravers and chasers. His work was renowned for its consistency, and he became the go-to silversmith for large commissions for wealthy clients requiring multiple identical pieces.

From 1807 to 1819 Storr worked primarily for Rundell, Bridge and Rundell in a workshop in Dean Street, Soho. Rundell's had a showroom on Ludgate Hill that was the centre of a goldsmithing empire.[4] The business was one of the earliest to develop a brand identity, much of it built on the reputation of its star silversmith. Prior to working formally for Rundell's, Storr had supplied them with a set of 'Egyptian' soup

Fig. 2
Edward Hodges Baily, after William Theed, after Giovanni Battista Piranesi
Design for a vase or cup, c.1820
Pen and ink on wove paper
51 × 31.4 cm
V&A: E.104-1964

Fig. 3
Paul Storr
Wine cooler, 1809–10
Silver-gilt, cast and chased with
applied ornament
34.7 cm (height), 26.8 cm (diam. at base)
V&A: M.48C-1982

tureens for the Grand Service of the Prince of Wales, later George IV, which along with similar ones made in 1806 for George's brother, Ernest Augustus, probably persuaded them to employ Storr long-term (fig. 1). The tureens are one of the boldest examples of English Neoclassical silver, which became popular after the defeat of Emperor Napoleon by Nelson in Egypt in 1798. Such was demand that when Storr began working for Rundell's they required 10,000 ounces of finished silver goods each month.[5]

Storr did not design the silver that was manufactured under his name. Like most large-scale metalworkers he produced to other people's designs: mixing, matching and adapting, free of obligation towards intellectual property. In addition to Storr's workshop, Rundell's also employed Digby Scott and Benjamin Smith in Greenwich, whose work was similar to Storr's although their output was not as great. Smith had trained with Matthew Boulton of Birmingham, a great industrial manufacturer who had a profound influence on Storr. In fact, in 1812 Rundell's bought a steam engine from Boulton, most likely to power the mills at Dean Street.[6] Both workshops shared large commissions and Rundell's sought to protect their output by employing designers in-house. The sculptor and modeller William Theed, who had previously worked for pottery entrepreneur Josiah Wedgwood (p. 124), ran the design studios supplying both.

The designer-maker relationship between Theed and Storr was so successful that in 1811 Rundell's made Storr a partner. Storr's experience as both craftsman and businessman working under the secure umbrella of Rundell's made him uniquely placed to develop high-end factory production for the aristocratic market. He understood the need not just for in-house artists but also for modellers and sculptors who could work from a designer's drawing or from existing objects to create structurally sound three-dimensional models for use in the workshop. Rundell's stock of silversmiths' models was vast.[7]

Key to this was his employment from 1815 of Edward Hodges Baily, a sculptor from Bristol who had studied under the sculptor John Flaxman (p. 131). Flaxman himself provided designs for Rundell's as did the painter Thomas Stothard. In this sense, Baily was creatively bilingual: he spoke the languages of both artists and silversmiths, becoming so valuable to Storr that he continued to work with him for the rest of his career.

Fig. 4
Paul Storr and Phillip Rundell
Inkstand, 1817–19
Gold and wood, cast, raised,
embossed, chased and engraved
20.4 × 42.9 × 24.4 cm
V&A: M.8-2003

While artists, including Baily, could work independently, their products for Rundell's belonged to the company. For expensive commissions a single design might suffice but for stock pieces Baily designed variations on a theme, altering handles, feet and lids to give customers options. Storr produced Baily's adaptations of the famous, classical Warwick Vase for years.

This organized, flexible approach can be seen in an album of Baily's designs in the V&A containing drawings based on original sketches by Theed, Flaxman and Stothard for silver to be worked up under Storr's direction. It includes a working drawing based on a design by Theed for a wine cooler derived from the so-called Medici Vase, first published by Giovanni Battista Piranesi in 1778, with a frieze on the body copied from a Roman marble relief in the Vatican depicting the Triumph of Bacchus, an appropriate motif for a wine cooler (fig. 2). Silver wine coolers made to this pattern in the workshops of Paul Storr and Scott & Smith were cast in multiples between 1808 and 1810 with subtle variations to the stands, handles and feet (fig. 3).[8] They conform fully to the prevailing London taste, described by architect Charles Heathcote Tatham, which dictated that 'massiveness' was 'the principal characteristic of good plate'.[9]

For 15 years these extravagant luxury goods produced by Storr, combining Neoclassical inspiration with Baroque monumentality, amounted to a national style in silver. Signalling the beginning of a change in taste that becomes marked during Storr's later career is a gold inkstand he produced for the statesman Viscount Castlereagh in 1817–19 (fig. 4). Twenty-one gold snuffboxes given to Castlereagh by European powers were melted and refashioned into a writing set whose design combines elements of Piranesi with sketches by Stothard and more naturalistic Baroque and Rococo-revival elements that became popular from the 1820s. The inkpot in the centre is very close to a Baily design for a larger Storr tureen of the same period whose swirling profile moves away from the fashions that made the silversmith famous.[10]

Storr sought independence from Rundell's from 1819, for several years supplying outlets including luxury retailers Green, Ward and Green, and Garrard, who later secured a royal warrant. By 1822 he was in partnership with John Mortimer, a tricky relationship as Mortimer was prone to making risky business investments. John Samuel Hunt, who later founded famous silversmiths, Hunt & Roskell, brought £5,000 of capital to the partnership in 1826 and the three partners ran a successful company until 1838, when Storr retired.

A tankard of 1834–5 still shows the characteristic Storr boldness of presence but its outlines have been blurred by asymmetrical sculptural forms (fig. 5). Whereas his earliest creations were in a light, mix-and-match form of classicism, this tankard bears an inscription protecting its neo-Baroque design from appropriation. Alongside the company's silver hallmarks is stamped, 'Published as the Act directs by STORR & MORTIMER, 156, New Bond Street London May 16, 1835', an early form of copyright later more formalized as Design Registry Marks.

Storr's career was remarkable. He was both witness to and driver of profound change in design and manufacturing in silver. He embraced technology but never abandoned craftsmanship. He oversaw the transition from production by small networks of subcontractors to large-scale factory production employing over 500 workers, where the workplace became separate from the home. The quality and quantity of his output as a silversmith over multiple business partnerships during a 40-year career can be witnessed in major collections today. The V&A has over 100 pieces by him; the Royal Collection has over 1,000.

Storr retired to Tooting Hill House and died in 1844. He only left £3,000 in his will, a surprisingly small amount considering his long history of success, and his modest grave in the local churchyard has seen better days. Given the number of designers, modellers, outworkers, contractors and retailers he used during his career it is notable that all his pieces are characteristically identifiable as by Paul Storr, unified by their quality of production and their sharp fine-detailing. The eye-watering prices they fetch at auction suggest the true lasting monument to this great silversmith is his maker's mark.

Angus Patterson

Fig. 5
Paul Storr
Tankard, 1834–5
Made by Storr and Mortimer
Silver-gilt, cast, raised, chased, embossed, tooled and engraved
35.3 cm (height)
V&A: LOAN:GILBERT.859-2008
The Rosalinde and Arthur Gilbert Collection on loan to the V&A

OTHER SIGNIFICANT MAKERS

Matthew Boulton (1728–1809) was one of the most influential metalworking entrepreneurs in Britain. He not only produced luxury goods in silver, Sheffield Plate, gilt-bronze and cut steel from his giant Soho Works in Birmingham but drove industrial change by contributing to the development of the factory system and modern ideas of flexible manufacturing and mass production.

Phillip Rundell (1743–1827) was the founding partner of royal goldsmiths, Rundell, Bridge and Rundell. He trained as a silversmith under the jeweller William Rogers of Bath. After several short-lived partnerships he teamed up with silversmith, John Bridge, and later his nephew, Edmund Waller Rundell. He was head of the most successful silver retailer in Britain.

Jean-Baptiste-Claude Odiot (1763–1850) was from a dynasty of French silversmiths leading the family company from 1785. He was the chief supplier of luxury silver and gold to Emperor Napoleon and supplied dining and tea silver in the French Empire style to courts all over Europe. His son Charles-Nicolas succeeded him as head of the company.

Digby Scott (dates unknown) and **Benjamin Smith** (1764–1823) ran a workshop in Lime Kiln Lane, Greenwich, from 1802 to 1807 supplying Rundell's with grand presentation and dining plate similar to Storr's work. Both previously worked in Birmingham for Matthew Boulton, and Smith's son Benjamin and grandson Stephen became well-known silversmiths and modellers in their own right.

James Dixon (1776–1852) was head of James Dixon & Sons, a vast factory in Sheffield producing Britannia Metal, silver, Sheffield Plate, nickel silver (an alloy of copper, nickel and zinc) and brass. He was part of a network of Sheffield and Birmingham manufacturers who adopted steam power to aid mass production – technology embraced by Paul Storr in London.

FORTUNATO PIO (1794–1865)
ALESSANDRO (1823–83)
AUGUSTO (1829–1914)
ALFREDO CASTELLANI (1856–1930)

Creators of 'archaeological style' jewellery

Fortunato Pio Castellani is known foremost as the inventor of 'Italian archaeological style' jewellery, inspired by the ancient treasures unearthed across southern Europe in the nineteenth century. From imitations of ancient gold jewellery excavated from archaeological sites to the reinvention of classical and Roman motifs, Castellani's jewellery was a stratospheric success throughout Europe for over half a century. From 1814 to 1927 the firm was run by three successive generations of the family: Fortunato Pio, succeeded by his sons Alessandro and Augusto and grandson Alfredo. During this time the Castellani's creations and their collections of ancient, medieval and Renaissance jewels captured the imagination of a wealthy clientele. The development and popularity of their jewellery in Italy and beyond is closely tied to the Castellani's involvement in politics, their networks within continental European high society and their cultural acclaim upon a global design stage.

In 1814, aged 20, Fortunato Pio opened the Castellani shop on via del Corso, Rome. Though he was from an artisan family, it is not clear who Fortunato Pio was apprenticed to for his goldsmith training and it is likely that he had assistance from financial creditors to begin trading commercially. In the first decades of the business, the majority of Fortunato Pio's activities were related to the trading of diamonds and other gems, as well as jewellery from England, France and Geneva. By 1840 he had become the foremost jeweller to the Roman aristocracy, entrusted with redesigning suites of heirloom jewels. Though the Castellani hailed from a long line of highly trained goldsmiths with links to aristocracy, they were not a noble family themselves. Therefore, making the acquaintance of Michelangelo Caetani (later Duke of Sermoneta and Prince of Teano) was pivotal to Fortunato Pio's

Fig. 1
Castellani
Necklace with heads of Io,
priestess of Juno at Argos, *c.*1820–75
Gold with filigree and glass beads
(possibly ancient)
18.5 cm (diam.)
V&A: 639-1884

fortunes. The pair shared a fascination with the art of ancient goldworking and together became the early creative and entrepreneurial force behind the advent of the archaeological style.

Fortunato Pio's access to collections of recently discovered ancient jewellery was contingent upon his success with the upper echelons of Roman society. In 1836, after the excavation of the Etruscan Regolini-Galassi tomb at Cerveteri near Rome, Fortunato Pio and his eldest son Alessandro were invited by the Papal authorities to study ancient Etruscan jewellery first-hand. Opportunities like these guided their later designs and in the Castellani archive the earliest mentions of jewellery made by the workshop that is described as 'Etruscan' or ancient Roman date to the 1830s. Caetani is credited with encouraging Fortunato Pio to pursue the making of adaptations of classical jewellery in renowned collections and may have even conceived of the design for a tiara, inspired by an Etruscan wreath (fourth century BCE), acquired by the British Museum in 1841, that features gold laurel leaves and seed pearl berries, set on a velvet band.[1] The Castellani remake is part of a set comprising a gold and pearl necklace,[2] informed by an ancient Roman model (from the second or third century CE) and gold and pearl earrings in a Byzantine style.[3] The early 1850s were an active period of practical experimentation with ancient goldworking techniques and research that resulted in the scaled-up production of copies and adaptations of Greek and Etruscan styles in the Rome workshop.

Through their relationship with Caetani and their own political connections, the Castellani were involved in the restoration and remounting of jewellery in the famous Campana collection of ancient

Fig. 2
Alessandro Castellani
Plaque with Etruscan inscription,
*c.*1870–80
Gold
2.9 × 6.2 cm
V&A: 636-1884

Fig. 3
Castellani, and possibly Luigi Podio
(mosaicist)
Bracelet with micromosaics, *c.*1855–*c.*1900
Gold, micromosaic
2.5 × 21.6 cm
V&A: M.6:1,2-2011

gold, a large quantity of which was sold to France in the 1860s (and is now in the Louvre). Only recently have jewellery historians discovered quite how many nineteenth-century 'repairs' and additions were made to these ancient jewels before they were sold. Nevertheless, they inspired a range of Castellani reproductions, such as an Etruscan diadem (300–200 BCE) thought to have been found at Cumae, a highly popular Campana imitation with gold, pearls, glass beads and enamel (fig. 4). Works like this were also the culmination of dedicated research into notoriously challenging and mysterious ancient techniques that were deemed the apex of the goldsmith's art.

The Castellani were committed to rediscovering the ancient art of 'granulation', or the bonding of minute gold spheres to a gold surface to create intricate patterns and textures, a technique for which no modern method of production had been found. Granulation was practised in Etruria (present-day Italy) from the first millennium BCE and so, for the Castellani, who claimed that they could trace their ancestral line to Etruscan goldsmiths in the seventh century BCE, the promotion of their work on ancient techniques (including filigree gold wire, and the chemistry around the colour of gold) was a vital narrative for marketing their business. A Castellani plaque from the 1870s made in Alessandro's Naples workshop has a raised inscription in granulation taken from a tomb in Tarquinia (it might be translated as 'Of the Etruscan People'), demonstrating this link between the technique and heritage (fig. 2). The marketing of the family's research around methods of ancient goldworking contributed to their international success. In the early 1860s Alessandro and Augusto gave lectures on the topic in London and Rome which resulted in publications such as *Antique Jewellery and its Revival* (1862).

While new archaeological discoveries invigorated the links between design and national identity all over Europe, Castellani's reproduction of Etruscan finds played a specific role in the societal changes taking place in Italy in the mid-nineteenth century. The waves of nationalism that resulted in the eventual unification of Italy as an independent state in 1870 were growing throughout the 1840s and '50s. Within this context, the adaptation of classical models was part of a political scheme to imagine a new identity for Italy, and the Castellani promoted the art of the goldsmith as vital to understanding the history of 'Italy' as continuous with the traditions of the ancient world. Castellani's displays in the shop in Rome and at international exhibitions promoted this idea and in a sense their jewellery became a national product. Alessandro was exiled from Rome for his support of the independence movement in 1859 and did not return until 1870. In the 1862 International Exhibition in London, therefore, Castellani's decision to exhibit in the 'Italy' section (of which Rome and the Papal States were not yet a part) was a highly political one.

An associated part of their campaign to build a continuous history of Italy through jewellery was the 'Castellani Collection of Italian Peasant Jewellery' bought by the South Kensington Museum (now the V&A) at the Paris International Exhibition in 1867. By this time the Castellani's research had extended from the study of scientific books to regional visits, including to the Marches village of Sant'Angelo in Vado, where goldsmiths were reportedly still using ancient techniques to create ceremonial jewellery and rosaries. For example, 'navicella' – crescent-shaped earrings from this village with a floral motif – are decorated using the ancient filigree technique where gold wire is fused to create a surface pattern and texture, as also used in the design of other items in the collection.[4] Whatever the agenda, the Castellani's promotion of this part of Italy's traditional craft heritage resulted in the preservation of nineteenth-century regional jewellery that would otherwise have been lost.

After their display at the 1862 International Exhibition in London, *The Times* reported that 'Every traveller who has been at Rome has seen, and everyone who has not been at Rome has heard of, Castellani's extensive and magnificent establishment.'[5] Castellani's fame with foreign visitors was at its peak and the firm catered for different tastes with their repertoire of archaeological jewellery. Those most interested in Rome's religious history may have favoured items such as a pendant with a figure of Christ, inspired by a twelfth-century mosaic in the apse of the church of San Clemente.[6] A bracelet set with six micromosaics – images made up of tiny coloured glass pieces – is replete with the symbolism to be found in early Christian churches and catacombs, including a dove representing the Holy Spirit, a ship, an anchor cross, fish and Greek characters arranged around a central Omega to make the words for 'light' and 'life' (fig. 3).

Alongside their own collecting of ancient jewellery, terracottas and bronzes, the Castellani actively traded in ancient intaglios, cameos and scarabs (carved gemstones), as well as glass beads that had been excavated from archaeological sites. The firm made use of an impressive stock of these items to recreate their successful designs with densely set necklaces, bracelets, brooches, earrings or rings. A necklace with gold

heads of the ancient Greek priestess Io has been thickly strung with glass beads (fig. 1). Henry Cole, the first director of the South Kensington Museum, bought a pair of stone scarabs set in gold mounts on a trip to Rome in 1858, very likely from Castellani.[7]

With the popularity of these styles, the Castellani had a significant influence in the revival of the ancient and Renaissance art of gem carving in Rome. They worked with specialist cameo carvers, such as Tommaso and Luigi Saulini, to introduce new types of engraved gems in a range of innovative colours and subject matter. A rare instance of a large carved sapphire in a Renaissance-style pendant shows the use of topical subject matter (fig. 5). The minutely engraved scene on the jewel, taken from a newspaper print, commemorates the loss of Italian life in the 1887 Battle of Dogali, near Massawa (in present-day Eritrea), where the defending forces successfully resisted the Italian Army's brutal attempt to colonize their lands. While the incorporation of Italian foreign policy in Castellani's output is unusual, it signals their continued desire to engage with national politics on the global stage through their jewellery as well as their savvy business strategy to expand into the wider market of revivalism of Renaissance enamels.

The three generations of the Castellani family, as goldsmiths, scholars, dealers and collectors, were influential in the establishment of Roman museum collections. Their contributions towards a historical survey of goldworking in the ancient world have had a lasting impact on the collecting and display of archaeological jewellery and antique finds in major museums and collections. The social agenda of their style, paired with their commercial activities, makes their jewellery a unique product through which to understand the nineteenth-century world.

Sophie Morris

Fig. 5
Augusto Castellani, and Giorgio Antonio Giradet (gem engraver)
'Dogali' pendant brooch, *c*.1887–8
Enamelled gold, pearls, diamond, sapphire intaglio
8.5 × 5 × 1.8 cm
V&A: M.222-1917

OTHER SIGNIFICANT MAKERS

François-Désiré Froment-Meurice (1803–1855) was a Parisian goldsmith at the forefront of the historicist movement in jewellery design. His pieces led the revival of interest in medieval and Renaissance art and architecture. He exhibited regularly at international exhibitions and was appointed *orfèvre-joaillier* (goldsmith-jeweller) to the city of Paris.

Carlo Giuliano (*c*.1831–1895) was born in Naples and learned his trade there. He is likely to have worked with Alessandro Castellani in Rome before setting up his own manufactory in London in 1860. Giuliano was hugely successful making jewellery using ancient techniques like fine filigree and granulation as well as high-quality works in opaque enamel.

Robert Phillips (1839–1900) and Phillips Brothers (firm) were revivalist jewellers represented in the English section at international exhibitions. They won medals in 1851, 1862 and 1867 for their jewellery, which was seen as historically accurate. Phillips worked for the archaeologist Henry Layard and made Assyrian-style jewellery, which was at the time an almost exclusively British phenomenon.

Giacinto Melillo (1846–1915) was a goldsmith based in Naples who worked with Alessandro Castellani during his time in exile there. His jewellery is inspired by the pieces excavated at Pompeii and Herculaneum and his workshop produced silver objects as well as jewellery.

Louis Wièse (1852–1923) was the son of the award-winning jeweller and goldsmith Jules Wièse who trained in Berlin but worked almost entirely in Paris. Louis took over the firm from his father in 1880. His jewellery follows various historicist styles such as Renaissance or Gothic Revival and Neoclassical to produce jewellery and other objects including knives and mirrors.

3

ART & INDUSTRY

There has assuredly never been since the world began an age in which people thought, talked, wrote and spent such inordinate sums of money and hours of time in cultivating and indulging their tastes.[1]

In the nineteenth century, makers were grappling with the modern world and what it meant to make in a society now dominated by industry and machine manufacture. The Industrial Revolution was ongoing, transforming daily life and economics and presenting makers with new challenges to navigate. There was much debate about the appropriate creative response to this new modernity and the impact machine manufacture had on attitudes, hierarchies and markets for handmade objects. Concerns about the quality of mass-manufactured goods, the debasement of historic styles and prevailing systems of art education ill-equipping designers for industry prompted a series of design reforms. Reacting against industrialization, makers, manufacturers and cultural leaders sought to carve out new paths for making. This increasingly interconnected world also gave makers access to wider-ranging sources of inspiration, international markets, modern materials and technologies which offered considerable new opportunities. The nineteenth century is thus characterized by a proliferation of styles and a great diversity of making.

The first decades of the century saw immense changes to the physical and political landscape in industrializing nations like Britain, France and Germany, with the diversification into capital-goods production and the transition towards a free-trade economy. The acquisition of overseas colonies by European powers and the exploitation of their resources aided the development of capitalism during the Industrial Revolution. The rise of the factory system created a division and deskilling of labour, a more consumer-led market and a new middle class, with greater social and economic disparities developing between the richest and poorest. Populations became concentrated in urban areas and a new sense of connectivity was brought by electric telegraphy, improved transportation to America and the expanding European empires. In reaction to rapid urbanization, the growth of mechanized manufacture and the political upheavals felt across Europe in the first half of the century, many makers chose to re-examine the arts of the past to escape the complicated present. Historical and archaeological studies were developing at pace and a newfound interest in antiquarianism prompted widespread revivalist styles that saw architecture and interiors imitate classical, Renaissance, Rococo or Gothic models.

The designer Augustus Welby Northmore Pugin (p. 174) was a leading proponent of the Gothic Revival in England (fig. 1). He believed that the

Gothic was the only spiritually ordained and moral aesthetic style since it pre-dated the rise of commerce and capitalism. He argued that design could only be successful aesthetically if it were the product of a good society, emphasizing the necessity of honest construction and truth to materials. These ideas found widespread support and had great impact on successive movements and makers. In France the architect and scholar Eugène-Emmanuel Viollet-le-Duc was a leading figure in the Gothic Revival and his comprehensive publications helped to sustain the movement at home and abroad.

As industrial output grew, more styles were employed as manufacturers sought to increase consumer choice for the growing middle classes. The abundance of stylistic references available meant that an array of unrelated motifs frequently decorated a single object, resulting in the fragmenting of styles and taste. In *The House Decorator and Painter's Guide* of 1840 the authors observed that 'the present age is distinguished from all others in having no style which can properly be called its own'.[2]

The eclecticism of art and design in the first half of the nineteenth century was displayed in 1851 at the Great Exhibition of the Works of Industry of all Nations, held in London's Hyde Park. This grand spectacle brought together raw materials, artworks and manufactured goods from over 30 countries and gave makers access to a global sourcebook of design and making. However, it also exposed the inferiority of British industrial design in comparison to international displays. Owen Jones, the architect, artist and design theorist, commented that one of the chief lessons was 'that we have thereby learned wherein we were deficient'.[3] Prince Albert thus decreed that the Exhibition profits should be used to 'begin the task of raising English work from the abyss of ugliness which had been so admirably disclosed' and fund a programme of reform in British design education.[4]

Concern for the quality of British-designed goods had been a topic of discussion since the 1830s. A Parliamentary Select Committee on Arts and Manufactures recommended that a School of Design inspired by European equivalents be established. The London school was founded in 1837 as the start of a nationwide network, with the aim of training designers to 'improve the patterns and designs for manufactures'.[5] Nevertheless, following the exhibition it was felt that the school was not sufficiently equipping students and so the museum was proposed as a site for education and industrial teaching, as part of a national programme to improve design standards and assist consumers in making more discerning choices. The national collection of art, craft and design was thus established as the Museum of Manufactures in 1852, renamed the South Kensington Museum in 1857 and the Victoria and Albert

Fig. 2
Owen Jones
Moresque No. 5: plate XLIII of
The Grammar of Ornament, 1856
Gouache on paper
54.1 × 36 cm
V&A: 1616

Museum in 1899. Jones helped select objects from the Great Exhibition for the school's teaching collections to instruct on proportion, harmony and utility. In 1856 he published *The Grammar of Ornament*, a visual compendium of global ornamental motifs (fig. 2). He advocated for a new contemporary style that used modern materials and suited modern society.[6] His commitment to the improvement of contemporary art manufacture dovetailed with the Museum's founding mission.

The South Kensington model was widely imitated, with 25 museums founded on the same basis in the German world before 1890 and in Hungary, Poland and the Czech countries between 1860 and 1905. These new design museums adopted South Kensington's policy of arranging their objects according to material and technique.[7] National capital museums with an applied arts department were also established in Spain, Italy, Denmark, Japan and the Russian Empire between 1871 and 1904. In America, South Kensington was an explicit reference in the founding of the Metropolitan Museum of Art in New York, the Cincinnati Art Museum and the Boston Museum of Fine Arts, among many others. These institutions fashioned themselves as arbiters of taste and, in their gathering together of 'good' examples of design from across the world, exerted enormous influence on makers.

The Great Exhibition prompted a series of international exhibitions across Europe and America that were instrumental in disseminating material culture in the industrial world, encouraging competition in the arts and sciences and demonstrating national and imperial might.[8] International exhibitions contributed significantly to an increasingly interconnected world, providing global inspiration for makers and creating international audiences for their work. They also helped revive historic techniques, such as Léonard Morel-Ladeuil's (p. 182) use of *repoussé*, while demonstrating how the same effects could also be replicated mechanically.

The process of European imperial expansion that characterized the Georgian period continued unabated throughout the nineteenth century, with Victorian Britain controlling one-quarter of the world's land surface and one-fifth of the population by its end.[9] A significant contributing factor in this expansion was the exploitation of enslaved people, with slavery only abolished in Britain in 1838.

Despite continued criticism and great expense, the pursuit of imperial expansion dominated European political life. Varied motivations, including the desire to open new markets for trade, consolidation and safeguarding of existing territories and forestalling the growth of rival empires, were fuelled by long-standing beliefs in the supremacy of white Christian civilizations over non-white communities. The East India Company was formed to trade with East and South-east Asia in 1600 and from the early eighteenth to the mid-nineteenth century acted as an agent of British imperialism in India. In the second half of the nineteenth century, seven western European powers invaded and colonized most of Africa, controlling 90 per cent of the continent by 1914.[10] The expansion of empires created new routes for trade and introduced raw materials to the western market. Makers also gained access to new sources of inspiration and decorative styles through the formation of colonial collections in European museums. Such collections were developed through diplomatic gifts or purchased via new access afforded to Europeans by empire. Some objects were illegitimately gathered through punitive expeditions, such as Asante gold regalia stolen as war loot from Ghana during the Anglo-Asante Wars in 1874.[11]

Most Europeans remained subjects of kingdoms or empires throughout the nineteenth century but the impact of the French Revolution (1789–99), calling for democratic freedoms, was felt across Europe. Few countries resisted demands for national self-expression and popular involvement in government, resulting in the widespread establishment of parliaments or similar representative bodies. The establishment of the Austro-Hungarian Empire in 1867, the reunification of Germany under the leadership of Otto von Bismarck and the temporary seizing of power by a French revolutionary government in 1871 were all consequences of industrial modernization. The American Civil War (1861–5) brought about the abolition of slavery and cemented the domination of the industrialized northern states. The war also had a significant impact on international trade networks, with global access to goods such as American cotton becoming temporarily restricted. In the decades following, the USA solidified its place as a significant industrial and agricultural power. A rapidly expanding middle class encouraged a growing market for decorative arts and American designers such as

Fig. 3
Dante Gabriel Rossetti
The Day Dream, 1880
Oil on canvas
158.7 × 92.7 cm
V&A: CAI.3
Bequeathed by Constantine
Alexander Ionides

Fig. 4
Brown-Westhead, Moore & Co.
Plate, c.1875–85
White earthenware, painted
23 cm (diam.)
V&A: C.216-1984

Fig. 5
Arthur Silver
Peacock Feathers, 1887
Manufactured by Rossendale Printing Co.
for Liberty & Co. Ltd
Roller-printed cotton
71.1 × 79 cm
V&A: T.50-1953
Given by Rex Silver, Esq.

Louis Comfort Tiffany (p. 230) looked to European makers like Edward Burne-Jones (p. 190) for design inspiration.

While reform efforts occupied the design community, from 1860 to 1900 the loose-knit Aesthetic movement aimed to create a new kind of art freed from the morality of Victorian society and the ugly materialism of the Industrial Age. It was led by a group of artists, architects and designers who were united in their search for a new beauty and producing 'art for art's sake'.[12] Originating in France as a literary movement, it came to prominence in the decorative arts in England and America. Aesthetic artists included poet and illustrator Dante Gabriel Rossetti (fig. 3), painter James McNeill Whistler and designers Christopher Dresser (p. 206) and E.W. Godwin. It was also associated with an influential group of personalities, including the writer Oscar Wilde, whose lifestyles epitomized the movement.

Aesthetic artists drew inspiration from a range of cultures and periods, including ancient Greek sculpture and East Asian art. The forced reopening of Japanese ports in 1853 resulted in a flooding of imports and a craze for Japanese art and design in Europe (fig. 4).[13] Aestheticism sought to transform the ordinary home with 'Art Furniture' and encouraged interior style as personal expression (fig. 5).[14] Although critics often derided it as self-indulgent and superficial, the movement placed value on the decorative arts by stressing their role in everyday life. It also coincided with the widespread emergence of named designers working for industry, with manufacturers employing the likes of Lewis Foreman Day and Dresser to design objects for fashionable homes. Such

Fig. 6
William Morris, Philip Webb and
John Henry Dearle
The Forest, 1887
Woven at Merton Abbey by William Knight,
John Martin and William Sleath
Tapestry of woven wool and silk on
a cotton warp
123.8 × 463 cm
V&A: T.111-1926
Purchased with Art Fund support

designers recognized the benefits brought by the Industrial Revolution and greatly improved standards of design.

Aestheticism was widely exploited commercially. A newly affluent middle class had emerged and manufacturers were quick to utilize new methods of production to create items for all consumer levels, aided by the increasing availability of design manuals, trade catalogues and pattern books. Moreover, the widespread development of the department store in the second half of the nineteenth century created new spaces for ordinary people to access and participate in trends. These 'cathedrals of consumption' dominated the retail landscape by 1900.[15] While increasing interest in furnishing the home, they also set an expectation that consumers could access a wider range of goods more readily and at lower prices. For makers this presented further challenges and the need to adapt for and retain consumers with changing priorities.

The market for decorative arts was also fuelled by the introduction of new materials and methods of manufacture. The mining of coal and other raw materials had become a crucial power source for transportation and industry, and the global trade of goods grew exponentially with many exported from British factories to the USA in the first half of the nineteenth century. New materials such as linoleum and celluloid, the first synthetic plastics, were introduced mid-century and the development of cheap steel had a transformative impact on the built environment.[16] The rapid pace of material innovation was matched by the development of new manufacturing techniques often aimed at making existing objects more cheaply or achieving greater consistency in production. The mechanization of spinning and the transition from hand to power looms in the 1830s and '40s enabled the faster production of greater quantities of cloth to higher standards, while the creation of the first synthetic dyes transformed the range of available products.[17] Industrialization also brought catastrophic social and environmental consequences, exploiting people and materials – the effects of which are still being experienced today.

The Arts and Crafts movement formed in Britain in the late nineteenth century in response to the damaging effects of industrialization on making and the relatively low status of the decorative arts. The movement did not promote a particular style and was not completely against the use of machinery. Rather, it advocated for the humane application of mechanization alongside a return to handcraftsmanship and traditional techniques. Driven by a desire for change championed by Pugin, John Ruskin and William Morris (p. 198), the movement was the first to be directed at the reform of art at every level of production and marked a gradual change in the value that society placed on how things were made.

The movement was structured around a set of ideals for living and working and took its name from the Arts and Crafts Exhibition Society, founded in London in 1887 by a group of artists, designers and craftspeople keen to assert a new public relevance for the work of decorative artists.[18] The society mounted its first annual exhibition in 1888 and for many years their exhibitions were the principal public platform for the decorative arts. Proponents looked to the medieval period for better models of living and production, calling for an end

Fig. 7
C.F.A. Voysey
Table, *c.*1905–6
Made by F.C. Nielsen
Oak
69.5 cm (height), 75 cm (diam.)
V&A: W.19-1981

to the division of labour and the reunification of artists and craftspeople. Many involved were influenced by Morris (fig. 6) who, although he only became an active participant of the society in the early 1890s, had been advocating for such an approach since the 1860s. He believed that all objects should be a source of beauty and pleasure for those who made and used them and was influenced by the cultural critic Ruskin who shared Pugin's view of the degeneracy of modern civilization and the superiority of the Gothic. Ruskin stressed the value of nature as a source of inspiration and argued that separating the act of designing from the act of making was both socially and aesthetically damaging.[19] Other prominent figures included Morris's daughter, the embroiderer and jewellery designer, May Morris (p. 246), art potter William De Morgan (p. 214), C.F.A. Voysey (fig. 7) and Philip Webb (fig. 8). The latter two trained as architects and championed the importance of designing objects for a 'total' interior. The designers John Lockwood Kipling and Bhai Ram Singh combined the British style with Indian craft and motifs.

Morris's philosophies had a great influence on making, but his own practice as a designer was at odds with his vision of a 'glorious art, made by the people and for the people as a happiness to the maker and the user'.[20] Like others, his designs were made by professional craftspeople and aimed at a wealthy clientele. Yet the Arts and Crafts movement effectively established new paths for makers that marked out handmaking from industrial manufacture and made art for the home available to the wider public. The movement evolved in the city but at its heart was a nostalgia for rural traditions and skills, and many makers left the city to establish new ways of living and working. The designer Charles Robert Ashbee (p. 254) founded the Guild of Handicraft and moved

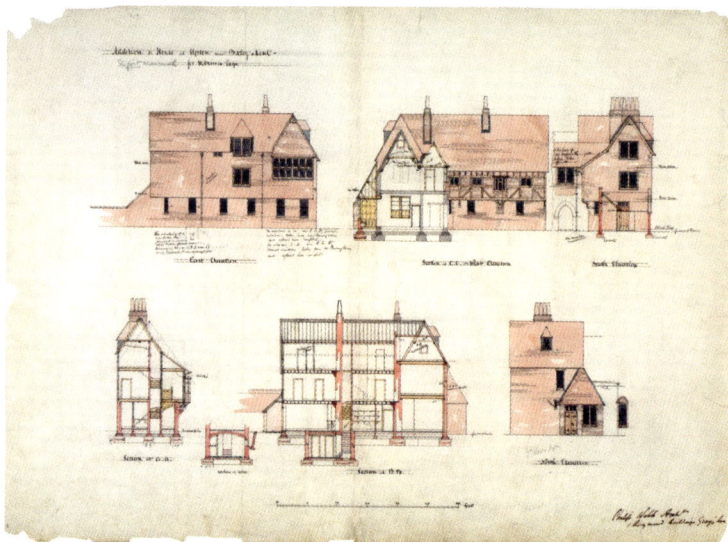

Fig. 8
Philip Webb
Elevation and section drawing showing the first arrangement of additions to Red House, c.1864
Drawing in pencil, ink and watercolour on paper
54.3 × 76 cm
V&A: E.66-1916

Fig. 9
Frank Lloyd Wright
Kindersymphony, 1912
Clear, opaque and coloured flashed glass
101.3 × 167.3 × 11.7 cm
V&A: C.115:1-3-1992
Purchased with Art Fund support

Fig. 10
Josef Hoffmann
Fruit basket, 1904
Made by the Wiener Werkstätte
Silver
27 × 23 × 23 cm
V&A: M.40-1972

the workshop to Gloucestershire to create an all-encompassing lifestyle for workers. The movement was also open to non-professional makers and encouraged amateurs and students through organizations such as the Home Arts and Industries Association. Significantly, it transformed women's lives as, for the first time, environments were created in which women as well as men could take active roles as makers and study at art schools.[21] The Arts and Crafts maker Phoebe Anna Traquair (p. 238) was one of the first women artists in Scotland to achieve professional recognition.

The ideas of the Arts and Crafts movement spread abroad to central Europe, America and Japan, with makers exploring national identity and the impact of industrialization.[22] Two well-known figures of the American movement were the designer Gustav Stickley and architect Frank Lloyd Wright (fig. 9). Stickley championed honesty, simplicity and usefulness in his popular journal *The Craftsman*.[23] In Austria the artistic movement, the Vienna Secession, was established in 1897 by Gustav Klimt, and the Wiener Werkstätte (Vienna Workshops) in 1903 by Josef Hoffmann (fig. 10) and Koloman Moser. The latter sought to use handmade goods to rescue society from industrialization by bringing art into the home. In Scandinavia greater political independence sparked nationalist feeling and debate around new cultural identities, and the movement provided a framework for new work by makers including silversmiths Georg Jensen and Evald Nielsen. In Europe the honesty of expression of Arts and Crafts was a catalyst for the radical forms of Modernism in the early twentieth century. In Britain the progressive impetus of the movement began to lose momentum after the First World War.

Throughout the nineteenth century science and art were engaged in an increasingly close dialogue, with rapid developments in the natural

Fig. 11
Philippe Wolfers
Hair ornament, 1905–7
Gold, plique-à-jour enamel,
diamonds and rubies
7.6 × 7.6 cm
V&A: M.11-1962

sciences spilling into popular culture.[24] Subjects such as biology, chemistry, zoology and botany were of particular interest, fuelled in part by the revolutionary theories of Charles Darwin, and gave makers new inspiration. A growing awareness of the need for healthy, hygienic environments also brought new priorities for domestic design. Meanwhile, the mass development of government-built national and local urban institutions, such as town halls and libraries, prompted huge growth in corporate design patronage from the public and private sectors. The rapid pace of innovation reached a crescendo in the last quarter of the century with the expansion of rail networks and inventions such as the electric-filament light bulb, motor car, moving pictures and the telephone.

   As the century ended, a new style emerged across western Europe and America. Art Nouveau was multifaceted and emerged in multiple places under different names but was characterized by its use of organic forms, geometric shapes and asymmetrical compositions.[25] The style represented an outgrowth of Aestheticism and Arts and Crafts, as makers sought a freedom to create, unburdened by the weight of artistic and historical traditions, and was expressed most fully through the decorative arts and architecture.

Fig. 12
Charles Rennie Mackintosh
Fireplace for the Willow Tea Rooms, *c.*1904
Iron, with ceramic tile surround
173.5 × 163 × 41 cm
V&A: Circ.244-1963
Given by Daly's of Sauchiehall Street,
Glasgow

The international style was to 'enrich the old patrimony with a spirit of modernness' and its epicentres were Paris, Brussels and Munich.[26] The term Art Nouveau (New Art) was made popular by the Parisian gallery Maison de l'Art Nouveau, owned by influential art dealer Siegfried Samuel Bing, but the term was first used in the Belgian journal *L'Art Moderne* in the 1880s to describe the work of Les Vingt, a group of 20 painters and sculptors who sought reform through art. Art Nouveau embraced industrial design, and different countries created their own variants, such as the Italian Stile Liberty and the German Jugendstil.

The unification of the fine and applied arts was achieved by designers including Belgium's Victor Horta and Henry van de Velde, whose architecture and interiors worked together to achieve a Gesamtkunstwerk or total work of art. International exhibitions were critical to the spread of the style, with displays of work by quintessential makers including glass designer Émile Gallé (p. 222), jeweller Philippe Wolfers (fig. 11) and the furniture designer Louis Majorelle (p. 229). Louis Comfort Tiffany championed the style in the USA with his nature-inspired works. International exhibitions created opportunities for makers to encounter the art and materials of empire while demonstrating the influence of global cultures on the development of Art Nouveau. The exhibitions also presented different exponents of the style, such as the work of Scottish designer Charles Rennie Mackintosh (fig. 12) at the Glasgow International Exhibition in 1901 and the Russian architect and graphic artist Fyodor Shekhtel at the 1902 International Exhibition of Modern Decorative Art in Turin.[27] The short-lived movement was a precursor to Modernism but, as the First World War loomed, the perception of Art Nouveau as a style of liberation shifted to being one of decadence and its popularity waned.

The profusion of styles that characterized making in the nineteenth century is evidence of a period of immense political, economic and social change, set against a backdrop of empire, industrialization and modernization. The changes brought by industrialization gained a foothold in Russia much later than elsewhere in Europe, prompting a series of revolutions in 1905 and 1917 which paved the way for the rise of communism around the world in the twentieth century. In response to a rapidly changing world and encouraged by Adolf Loos's seminal 1910 text 'Ornament and Crime', which denigrated ornament, makers increasingly moved away from the eclecticism of nineteenth-century making in favour of the emerging twentieth-century Modernism. They left behind a remarkable legacy of making and a heightened appreciation for the value of the handmade.

Rebecca Knott

AUGUSTUS WELBY NORTHMORE PUGIN

(1812–1852)

Founding father of Gothic Revival

Augustus Welby Northmore Pugin, a gifted and energetic young designer, was the pioneer of the nineteenth-century Gothic Revival. Driven by his desire to address the challenges of modernity through architectural and social reform, and ignited by his commitment to reviving Roman Catholicism, he transformed the aesthetic expression of nineteenth-century Britain. More readily thought of as a designer rather than a maker, Pugin's career highlights the importance of designing on paper as a form of making in its own right. The ideas expressed in his publications, his architectural projects and his designs for domestic and ecclesiastical furniture and fittings underpinned a widespread revival of medieval forms from the 1830s onwards. His design principles paved the way for the Arts and Crafts movement in Europe and America and his legacy is still tangible in our interiors, cities and landscapes today.

Pugin was born in 1812 in central London. His father was a French émigré draughtsman named Auguste Charles Pugin who had been employed by the architect John Nash and made his living designing furniture, engraving illustrations for journals of luxury goods and running a school of architectural draughtsmanship. The young Pugin inherited his father's artistic talent and from an early age was drawn to Gothic architecture. In his manuscript notes for an unrealized autobiography, he recalled how when he was six, his parents took him to Lincoln, York, Boston, Grantham and Peterborough where he was 'much delighted with the appearance of antient buildings though not capable of appreciating their merits'.[1] His first visit to France was made the following year, alongside his father's students. Aged 11, he 'studied different styles of Gothic' and became 'fully capable' of determining a building's date from its appearance.[2] In his father's studio in Store Street, London, he 'began to learn drawing and perspective regularly' and commenced designing buildings.[3]

Fig. 1
A.W.N. Pugin
Contrasts, or, A Parallel between the Noble Edifices of the Fourteenth and Fifteenth Centuries, and Similar Buildings of the Present Day: Shewing the Present Decay of Taste, 1836
Depiction of nineteenth-century architecture being weighed unfavourably on the scales of excellence against fourteenth-century architecture
Engraving
28.5 × 21 cm
Boston College Library collection

The elder Pugin, who was astonished by his son's precocity, gave him an exceptional opportunity when he was only 15 years old by passing him a commission for the dining room and gallery in the private apartments of George IV at Windsor Castle. The resulting Gothic furniture was positively received, even if Pugin himself looked back on it as a juvenile effort lacking proper principles. In 1829, after a brief but formative period working at the English Opera House as a stagehand managing special effects and at Covent Garden theatre as a stage carpenter, he met James Gillespie Graham, a Scottish architect, and began to work for him as a draughtsman.

During the early 1830s Pugin was occupied with a variety of projects: he set up his own business designing and making furniture and architectural details, produced designs for stage scenery, collaborated with antique dealers and designed a house for himself: St Marie's Grange in Salisbury. His business, however, failed to flourish. When he met architect Charles Barry in 1835 and began executing drawings and designing interiors for him, including for the New Palace of Westminster for which Barry won the competition, it was a welcome enhancement to Pugin's professional profile and his income.

1835 was significant for two further reasons: aware of publication as an important vehicle for disseminating ideas, Pugin published his first book, *Gothic Furniture*; and he converted to Roman Catholicism, a personal belief that had a decisive influence on his professional practice. From this point onwards, he explicitly identified Christianity, specifically the Catholic faith, with the Gothic style, and promoted it tirelessly in his designs and writings. In his opinion, the Reformation had divorced society from religion to the detriment of community and art. Pugin's critique of modern society was informed by his personal conviction but also by a period of economic recession and intense social unrest in Britain during the early 1830s. Others, including the architect-designer Owen Jones (p. 213), whose lectures Pugin may well have attended, held similar views, but Pugin's response was distinctive: to return to medieval modes and ethics.

Pugin produced publications throughout his life, but none had greater impact than *Contrasts* (1836), in which he condemned the 'present decay of taste' evident in classicism and instead praised fourteenth- and fifteenth-century architecture (fig. 1). Rejecting all developments in society and the Church since the Reformation, this polemic initiated his revival of Gothic architecture and, by extension, Gothic in the applied arts. The book employed visual comparisons between different styles, but his critique was far from superficial. Pugin's aim was nothing less than the reunification of society and God through design to create a world in

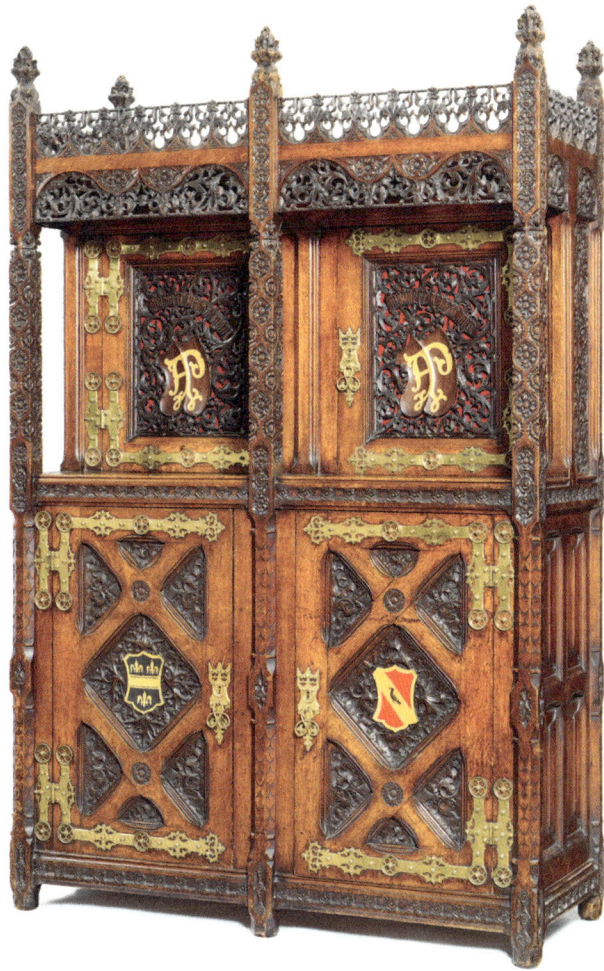

Fig. 2
A.W.N. Pugin
Dining room cabinet for Pugin's home
at The Grange, Ramsgate, about 1845
Manufactured by George Myers, hardware
by John Hardman & Co.
Oak with brass hinges
229.5 × 151.5 × 60.5 cm
V&A: W.2-2015

which there was shelter for all, provision for the poor and education for children. A biographical memoir of Pugin written by his son-in-law recorded that *Contrasts* 'startled the country' and that Pugin's 'writings and sayings were the talk of Universities, Chapters and Parsonages': the influential locations where patrons formed and developed their taste.[4] Pugin's ideas also found a receptive audience in the antiquarian associations that flourished from the 1830s onwards.

Pugin believed that architecture could be transformed through the application of certain guiding tenets, which he set forth in *True Principles of Pointed or Christian Architecture* (1841). 'The two great rules for design,' he pronounced, 'are these: first, that there should be no features of a building which are not necessary for convenience, construction or propriety; second, that all ornament should consist of enrichment of the essential construction of the building.'[5] His emphasis on necessity and truth in construction and ornament grew out of the design reform ideas that emerged in the 1830s through government-led initiatives to improve the quality of British design and manufactures and in turn shaped the tenets of the Arts and Crafts movement. Pugin professed his desire to defend the particularity of English architecture against the tidal wave of 'modernity' and foreign influences: 'England is rapidly losing its venerable garb; all places are becoming alike … national feelings and national architecture are at so low an ebb that it becomes an absolute duty in every Englishman to attempt their revival. Our ancient architecture can alone furnish us with the means of doing this successfully ….'[6] At the same time, however, he embraced modern technology, such as the railway system that facilitated the extensive travel he undertook for his work, and the modern manufacturing techniques that made the execution of his designs possible. He was also committed to designing for modern needs even where no medieval precedent existed, resulting in gas lamps and umbrella stands in a medieval mode.

In 1837 he began practising as an independent architect, working on domestic and ecclesiastical projects. His first major commission came in 1839 in the form of St Chad's, Birmingham, swiftly followed by other new designs, including his own house at The Grange in Ramsgate (fig. 2). Through St Mary's College, Oscott, the Catholic seminary in Birmingham, he established a network of patrons and developed considerable influence in the Roman Catholic Church. His most significant patron

Fig. 3
A.W.N. Pugin
Design for wallpaper for the Houses of Parliament, *c.*1847–51
Pencil, wash and bodycolour on paper
73.5 × 54.5 cm
V&A: D.741-1908

Fig. 4
A.W.N. Pugin
Chalice shown at the Great Exhibition, 1851
Manufactured by John Hardman & Co.
Silver, parcel gilt, with *champlevé* enamels and garnets
26 cm (height), 18.5 cm (diam.)
V&A: 1327-1851

was John Talbot, the 16th Earl of Shrewsbury, for whom he provided alterations and additions at Alton Towers. Shrewsbury also commissioned Pugin's masterpiece, St Giles, Cheadle. This was the first cathedral built in England since Sir Christopher Wren's St Paul's. At St Giles, Pugin created a complete ensemble of architecture and applied arts, reviving medieval techniques of encaustic tiling, alabaster sculpture, wall painting and metalwork to create a breathtakingly rich visual and spiritual experience which attracted international attention.

In September 1844 Pugin was invited by Barry to assist with the fittings and decorations of the House of Lords in the New Palace of Westminster. Pugin went on to design the interiors for the entire complex, devising furniture, wallpapers, textiles, stained glass, ceramic tiles and metalwork fittings, all in a Gothic idiom (fig. 3). His work in the applied arts reached its apogee in the Medieval Court at the Great Exhibition of 1851, an ensemble masterminded by Pugin and the only court which was dedicated to a style rather than to a country (fig. 4). It presented visitors with an array of ecclesiastical furnishings and domestic objects rich in colour and ornament. Subsequently, Pugin was involved, alongside Henry Cole, Owen Jones and Richard Redgrave, in selecting objects from the Exhibition to enhance the teaching collection of the Government School of Art and Design, which formed the nucleus of what later became the V&A.

Unlike most mid-nineteenth-century architects, Pugin did not establish an office and therefore produced all his own drawings. Despite this, he was prolific, undertaking well over 120 architectural projects as well as generating hundreds of designs for furniture, metalwork, sculpture, wallpapers, ceramics and stained glass (fig. 5). To execute his designs, he developed a close group of collaborators: George Myers, his builder based in London, John Hardman, the metalwork manufacturer based in Birmingham, John Gregory Crace, the interior decorator, and Herbert Minton, the Staffordshire pottery manufacturer. John Hardman's nephew, John Hardman Powell, effectively became Pugin's pupil but Pugin retained microscopic oversight of every commission, entailing relentless travel by railway and a steady stream of correspondence and designs that were posted up and down the country. Hardman noted that Pugin worked at an incredible pace, producing drawings without hesitation or correction to be translated into three-dimensional objects. Thousands of surviving drawings demonstrate his dynamic relationship with the makers who realized his ideas, anticipating their need for information and engaging in dialogue with them. Creating designs for items that could be produced successfully in quantity was essential for the industrialized processes that characterized nineteenth-century production.

Pugin's all-consuming vision eventually destroyed even its generator. He became overwhelmed with work and suffered a breakdown, as well as labouring under other medical conditions: thyroid problems and very probably syphilis, contracted during his time in Covent Garden. He died in 1852, aged just 41. He was critical to the establishment of the Gothic as Britain's national style in the nineteenth century and his principles shaped the next generation of designers and makers. As the architect John Dando Sedding commented, 'we should have had no Morris, no Street, no Burges, no Shaw, no Webb, no Bodley, no Rossetti, no Burne-Jones, no Crane but for Pugin.'[7]

Olivia Horsfall Turner

Fig. 5
A.W.N. Pugin
Design for an altar cross showing alternative options for cresting, 1851
Pencil and pen on paper
49.4 × 37 cm
V&A: E.536-2023
Purchased with support from Art Fund, The Rick Mather David Scrase Foundation, The Friends of the National Libraries and The Murray Family. With additional support from Bonhams

OTHER SIGNIFICANT MAKERS

Herbert Minton (1793–1858) was an entrepreneurial Stoke-based pottery manufacturer who, in 1836, inherited the company founded by his father in the 1790s. Under Herbert, Minton & Co. became celebrated for reviving various types of historic ceramics, including perfecting the modern manufacture of encaustic tiles which Pugin used throughout his projects.

Charles Barry (1795–1860) was the architect of the New Palace of Westminster, now better known as the Houses of Parliament. Although Barry chose Gothic as the most appropriate style at Westminster, in his designs for country houses, such as Highclere Castle, Hampshire, he was a leading proponent of Italianate architecture.

George Myers (1803–1875) was a mason and master builder, best known for his work with Pugin. He became Pugin's close friend, second only to John Hardman Junior. As well as undertaking construction work, he also executed woodwork, stone carving, ironwork and occasionally fitted glass.

John Gregory Crace (1809–1889), designer of furniture, stained glass and interiors, was the youngest generation of the Crace interior-decorating dynasty. He and Pugin were selected by Barry to execute the interiors at the New Palace of Westminster; they also worked together closely at the Great Exhibition.

John Hardman Powell (1827–1895) was the nephew of Pugin's confidant and collaborator, John Hardman Junior (1812–1867), the Birmingham-based manufacturer of Pugin's designs for metalwork. Powell assisted Pugin in his work with Hardman, married Pugin's daughter Anne and, after Pugin's death, became Hardman's principal designer.

LÉONARD MOREL-LADEUIL

(1820–1888)

Master of repoussé

'He succeeded in gaining a worldwide reputation as one of the greatest artists of his age,' claimed his obituary, but few people know his name today.[1] No other great maker of the nineteenth century personifies the vicissitudes of artistic fame like Léonard Morel-Ladeuil. Every work he created was a technical masterpiece in silver, steel and gold. But such was the difficulty of the sculptural technique and compositional complexity he perfected, only 42 artworks can firmly be attributed to him.[2]

Morel-Ladeuil's genius lay in chasing and *repoussé*, the laborious, highly skilled manipulation of steel and silver that involves heating and hammering metals into intricate shapes using fine steel 'punches' of various sizes. In chasing, the metal is worked from the front by repeatedly tapping the surface. In *repoussé*, the metal is 'pushed' up from the back. Sculpting a soft metal like silver requires extremely high skill levels; manipulating hard steel, the way Morel-Ladeuil did on his grand display shields, plaques, vases and centrepieces, requires breathtaking artistry.

Born in the historic French town of Clermont-Ferrand, Morel-Ladeuil's family had little connection to the arts. His prodigious talent for drawing was first noted by his art teacher, Félix Bachélery, and his classmates included the history and portrait painter Louis Devedeux, who later painted Morel-Ladeuil's portrait (fig. 2). At the age of 14 Morel-Ladeuil moved to Paris as an apprentice to his father's cousin, the bronze founder Morel, revealing a flair for manual skills that matched his drawing.

Renaissance armourers and goldsmiths such as Filippo Negroli, Jörg Sigman and Lucio Marliani had honed these techniques into a highly developed art form, but by the mid-nineteenth century they had been almost forgotten.[3] In Paris a steel-chasing revival was led by Antoine Vechte. To meet a growing demand among antiquarian collectors for historic armour, he sculpted shields in the style of the sixteenth century, decorating them with chasing and damascening, which involves inlaying patterns of gold wire into iron or steel. Vechte was technically brilliant at sculpting other people's designs, notably those of artist Jean-Jacques Feuchère. It is not known how Morel-Ladeuil came to work in

Fig. 2
Louis Devedeux
Portrait of Léonard Morel-Ladeuil, 1847
Oil on canvas
61.5 × 51 cm
Musée d'art Roger-Quilliot,
Clermont-Ferrand: 2551

Vechte's workshop but Feuchère spotted him and helped him develop his composition and modelling skills. This remarkable dual education, studying *repoussé* under Vechte and sculptural design under Feuchère, elevated Morel-Ladeuil above his contemporaries.

His first major commission, in 1852, was the *Empire Shield* for the French emperor, Napoleon III. Preparatory sketches (fig. 3) show how its composition was strongly influenced by the shields and salvers of Vechte, such as the *Italian Poets Shield* now in the V&A.[4] The central free-standing cast silver sculpture of a muscular figure kneeling astride a many-headed dragon recalls Feuchère. The *Empire Shield* represented authority overcoming anarchy and was Bonapartist propaganda in steel, silver and gold, justifying the military *coup d'état* and referendum that founded the Second French Empire. It led to Morel-Ladeuil being ostracized by many among the metalwork trade in Paris.[5]

An opportunity to restart his politically thwarted career arose in 1859 when from across the English Channel a representative from Elkington

& Co. sought his services. Elkington were based in Birmingham and London and were world leaders in the metalwork trade. Their display of electroplating and electroforming – the veneering and growing of metals from chemical solutions using an electric current – had caused a sensation at the Great Exhibition of 1851. They married historic craft skills with cutting-edge technology to pioneer stylistic revivals, nurturing a global market across the British Empire, ranging from major commissions for royal and civic patrons, to mass-market cutlery and dinnerware for middle-class households, hotels, restaurants and the new steam railway and shipping lines.

Elkington had recently employed the French industrial artist, Auguste Adolphe Willms, as head of the firm's art department. A Memorandum of Agreement of July 1859 reveals that Morel-Ladeuil was employed as a 'Designer and Chaser' for five years on an annual salary of £400.[6] His recruitment alongside Willms emulated the working relationship that the chief *dessinateur-ornemaniste*, Louis-Constant Sévin, developed with the chaser, Désiré Attarge, working for the celebrated Parisian bronze founder, Ferdinand Barbedienne. As director of the art department, A.A. Willms supervised all of Elkington's designs, while Morel-Ladeuil focused on creating awe-inspiring displays for the international exhibitions.

Almost all of Morel-Ladeuil's one-off showpieces were designed with replication in mind. Elkington's electroforming technology enabled extremely accurate reproductions, electrotype editions, of his original works to be sold to an international audience. Electrotyping was the 3D-printing of its day, allowing famous artworks to be viewed simultaneously in museums and homes all around the world.[7]

Fig. 3
Léonard Morel-Ladeuil
Study for the scene 'Empire'
on the *Empire Shield*, 1852
Ink on paper
Musée d'art Roger-Quilliot,
Clermont-Ferrand: 2005.5.155

Electrotypes of Morel-Ladeuil's artworks enable us to appreciate his genius when the whereabouts of many of his originals are unknown.

The London International Exhibition of 1862 was the first major showcase for Morel-Ladeuil and it launched his career. An eye-catching trophy, the *Modern Inventions Vase*, captured the zeitgeist of the Industrial Revolution, with winged putti holding a steam train, Jacquard's loom, a Voltaic pile and a screw propeller.[8] However, it was the allegorical beauty of *The Table of Dreams* that most captivated public attention.[9] The circular table was a swirling frieze of classical figures and putti among billowing clouds, with a free-standing female figure holding poppies representing sleep. The following year, a public subscription by the city of Birmingham raised £500 to present it as a civic wedding gift to the Prince and Princess of Wales. The press and public acclaim ensured that, when Morel-Ladeuil's contract was renewed in 1864, his annual salary was increased to £600.[10]

Morel-Ladeuil remained with Elkington for the rest of his career, winning gold medals at every world fair from 1862 to 1878. His fame during the 1860s turned his London studio into a visitor attraction:

> Around this time the company opened in the capital, amid the opulence of Regent Street, a magnificent new showroom. Above it was a vast and light workshop. It was there, over the next twenty-three years, that the artist produced a series of chased repoussé artworks, which excel, at least in quantity and importance, the work of any famous goldsmith. Always easy, accessible, and courteous, it was in this workshop that he cheerfully received the many visitors who climbed their steps: London's artists and critics, French visitors, and fashionable society figures from around the world, all desirous of meeting the artist and witnessing the creative processes behind these artworks, which at each new [International] Exhibition found such radiant acclaim.[11]

By far the most celebrated of his showpieces was the *Milton Shield* (fig. 4).[12] Its framework, a steel oval inset with silver bas-reliefs, depicts scenes from John Milton's *Paradise Lost*, the composition unified by narrow 'arabesque' panels of damascened gold. The central silver medallion shows the Archangel Raphael admonishing Adam and Eve. It has an elasticity so undercut that the foliage appears to sprout from the surface. Two more silver panels either side depict, on the left, loyal angels ascending to heaven, and, on the right, defeated rebel angels descending into hell, which gives the whole composition a sense of circular movement. The astonishingly subtle manipulation in hard steel of the sinuous figure of St Michael vanquishing the dragon and the delicate, transparent veil covering the Grim Reaper's face are bravura displays of Morel-Ladeuil's virtuosity (fig. 1).

On its return from Paris, the *Milton Shield* toured Elkington's regional showrooms. In January 1868 the *Liverpool Mercury* declared it 'one of the grandest works of its class that has been produced in any age or country'.[13] The V&A's Director, Henry Cole, acquired the *Milton Shield* for the Museum even before it debuted in Paris and persuaded the government to part with £2,000 to secure it for the nation. It was the second most expensive contemporary artwork bought by the Museum before 1900.

Electrotypes of the *Milton Shield* were bought by museums and private collectors all around the world. Elkington's visitors' book records sales at four of the international exhibitions between 1855 and 1878. It reveals that at Philadelphia in 1876, a decade after its creation, dozens of copies of the *Milton Shield* were sold to celebrities, multi-millionaires and wealthy middle-class Americans.[14] An electrotype copy was bought by Julia Dent Grant, the First Lady of America and wife of President Ulysses S. Grant, which she hung in the White House in Washington DC.[15]

For the Paris Exhibition of 1878, Elkington challenged Morel-Ladeuil to repeat the success of the *Milton Shield* with a companion *repoussé*

Fig. 4
Léonard Morel-Ladeuil.
Milton Shield, signed and dated 1866
For Elkington & Co.
Steel, inset with silver plaques and inlaid
with gold wire and partly oxidized
87.6 × 67.3 cm
V&A: 546-1868

masterpiece commemorating the bicentenary of John Bunyan's *The Pilgrim's Progress*. Although the *Pilgrim's Shield* is no longer as well-known as the *Milton Shield*, its technical brilliance and global press coverage won Morel-Ladeuil the Légion d'honneur, the highest French order of merit. The whereabouts of the original are unknown, but electrotypes are in the V&A and collections worldwide (fig. 5).

Morel-Ladeuil's reputation as one of the leading figures of French and British art seemed assured. However, the very factors that gave him global renown contributed to a rapid posthumous decline in his fame. Elkington's star French artist, who did so much to develop their creative reputation, was marginalized by the cultural hegemony of corporate industrial design and the modernist art movement of the early twentieth century.[16]

In 1890, only two years after his death, Lewis F. Day wrote in the *Magazine of Art*: 'That the name of Morel-Ladeuil is so little known beyond the circle of the silversmith and the connoisseur is another proof (were it needed) how entirely the name and fame of the craftsman allied with any modern industry is swallowed up in the reputation of the manufacturer who employs him.'[17] The march of Modernism, especially after the First World War, made his highly ornamental works seem old-fashioned. And although Elkington & Co.'s multinational success had promoted his celebrity, it also heralded a new age of multinational luxury brands in which corporate identity increasingly subsumed individual creative talent.

Angus Patterson and Alistair Grant

Fig. 5
Elkington & Co. after Léonard Morel-Ladeuil
Electrotype copy of the *Pilgrim's Shield*, 1879
Electroformed copper, electroplated
88.5 × 65.6 cm
V&A: REPRO.1879-3

OTHER SIGNIFICANT MAKERS

Filippo Negroli (*c.*1510–1579) was the best-known member of a celebrated Italian family of armourers in Renaissance Milan. He specialized in *repoussé* steel chasing, producing extraordinarily supple, Mannerist arrangements that mimicked hair, water, foliage and monsters, notably on parade helmets and shields for the Holy Roman Emperor, Charles V.

Antoine Vechte (1799–1868) was a French steel chaser who began his career making highly accomplished fakes of Renaissance-style armour for antiquarian collectors. After 1848 his talent for virtuoso *repoussé* work was spotted by Hunt & Roskell. The London silversmiths employed him on an exclusive contract to make showpieces for the Great Exhibition of 1851.

Jean-Jacques Feuchère (1807–1852) was a French sculptor and designer whose work adorns many important public monuments in Paris, notably the Arc de Triomphe. Feuchère's compositional skills were employed for an impressive variety of activities, making objects in precious metals, ivory, stained glass, enamels, tapestry, painted church decorations and prints in different media.

Louis-Constant Sévin (1821–1888) and **Désiré Attarge** (1821–1878) were recruited by the bronze founder Ferdinand Barbedienne in 1855 and became a celebrated partnership for bronze artworks. Sévin was employed as chief *ornemaniste* because of his knowledge of ancient and modern motifs. Attarge was a brilliant metalworker, who won the Crozatier Prize in 1862 and 1864 as France's best chaser.

Hugh Henry Armstead (1828–1905) was a leading English sculptor and silverware designer in the 1850s–60s. He was an early graduate of the government's School of Design before working as a designer, modeller and chaser of grand silver presentation pieces, especially sports trophies and testimonials, for the London firms of Hunt & Roskell and Charles Frederick Hancock.

EDWARD BURNE-JONES

(1833–1898)

Pre-Raphaelite visionary, artist and artisan

Edward Burne-Jones was a leading designer and painter in nineteenth-century Britain, associated with the Pre-Raphaelites, Aestheticism and the Arts and Crafts movement. He was an artist-artisan who blurred the boundaries between painting and decoration. His fascinationwith medieval legend, Christian iconography and classical mythology infused his highly pictorial designs for stained glass, tapestries, mosaics and furniture.

Born in Birmingham in August 1833, Edward Coley Burne Jones was the son of Edward Richard Jones, a framer and gilder, and Elizabeth Coley, who died a week after his birth; he would later hyphenate his last two names to become more distinctive. As a teenager he took drawing classes at the Birmingham Government School of Design from 1848 to 1852 but at this point did not intend to become an artist. Instead, he chose to study Theology at Exeter College, Oxford, where he would meet fellow first-year undergraduate William Morris (p. 198). The pair became lifelong friends and collaborators. Along with other members of their social circle at Oxford they took a great interest in both medieval literature and contemporary criticism, including the writings of John Ruskin.

Ruskin was an advocate for the Pre-Raphaelite Brotherhood, which formed at the Royal Academy of Arts in 1848. The group railed against the idolization of High Renaissance masters like Raphael, preferring the styles of his forebears in the medieval and early Renaissance periods and, under Ruskin's influence, they turned to intensive realism. After seeing the work of Pre-Raphaelite painters William Holman Hunt and Dante Gabriel Rossetti at the Royal Academy in 1854 and following a trip to northern France with Morris in 1855 to visit cathedrals and the Musée du Louvre in Paris, Burne-Jones decided to become a painter. He left Oxford without graduating and moved to London where he lived with Morris at 17 Red Lion Square and took informal painting lessons from Rossetti.

Burne-Jones's early drawings were strongly influenced by medieval manuscript painting and Northern Renaissance prints. He also worked on designs for interiors and furniture. An early surviving sideboard,

Fig. 1
Edward Burne-Jones
Ladies and animals sideboard, 1860
Pine, painted in oil paint, with gold and silver leaf
116.8 × 152.4 × 73.7 cm
V&A: W.10-1953
Given by Mrs J.W. Mackail

an item already in his possession which he painted in the week leading up to his wedding on 9 June 1860, exemplifies the close relationship between his approach to canvas and to furniture, as he treated the doors like a triptych and embellished the cabinet with gold and silver leaf (fig. 1). His wife, the painter Georgiana Macdonald, later described the three women in medieval dress on the front as 'kind and attentive', feeding pigs, parrots and fishes respectively, while on each end appear 'two cruel ones', tormenting an owl and a goldfish, and two more were assaulted by a newt and a swarm of bees.[1] This unusual wedding gift stayed in the Burne-Jones homes as they moved to Kensington Square in 1864 and then Fulham in 1867.

Burne-Jones was one of the founders of the firm Morris, Marshall, Faulkner & Co. in 1861 (from 1875, Morris & Co.), who described themselves as 'Fine Art Workmen in Painting, Carving, Furniture and the Metals'. He quickly became the company's principal designer of figure subjects for stained glass and would go on to produce 786 stained glass designs in his lifetime. In 1866, when the firm was commissioned to decorate the Green Dining Room at the South Kensington Museum (today the V&A), he designed the windows picturing young women

Fig. 2
Edward Burne-Jones
Garland Weavers, 1866
Manufactured by Morris, Marshall, Faulkner & Co.
Stained glass and lead
*c.*80 × 60 cm (each panel)
V&A: In situ in the Morris Dining Room

Fig. 3
Edward Burne-Jones
*The Mill: Girls Dancing
to Music by a River*, 1870–82
Oil on canvas
91.3 × 198.1 cm
V&A: CAI.8
Bequeathed by Constantine
Alexander Ionides

picking flowers to weave into garlands (fig. 2). The stained glass technique, with its leadwork connecting the coloured panes, particularly suited Burne-Jones's ability to unite narrative and decoration in a simple outline and he described the leads as 'part of the beauty of the work'.[2] As the designer, Burne-Jones created monochrome drawings but his awareness of the process is evident in his annotations for the glassmakers who realized his designs. His experiences with stained glass encouraged Burne-Jones the draughtsman to embrace colours from the 1860s, in both watercolour and oils.

Between 1859 and 1873 Burne-Jones repeatedly travelled to Italy, filling sketchbooks with copies of paintings, sculptures and architecture and copious notes. His debt to early Italian Renaissance painters like Botticelli, Luca Signorelli and Perugino became increasingly apparent. In *The Mill* (fig. 3), commenced in 1870 and worked on for the next 12 years, dancing figures and a musician are arranged in a linear composition in front of the water mill. The composition's 'echo of early Italianism' drew praise from American novelist Henry James who lived in London. He also appreciated its mysterious, dreamlike quality, which detached the scene from a specific time or place; James called it 'as pointless as a twilight reminiscence', adding 'I have not the least idea who the young women are, nor what period of history, what time and place, the painter has had in his mind.'[3] The dancing women were, in fact, three models dubbed the 'Three Graces' who were known to both Burne-Jones and Constantine Alexander Ionides who bought the picture. At the centre is the patron's sister, embroiderer, bookbinder and collector Aglaia Coronio, to the right is their friend the painter Marie Stillman and to the left the sculptor

Maria Zambaco, Coronio's cousin and Burne-Jones's model, pupil and lover. Burne-Jones had met Zambaco in 1866, leading to an infatuation and a tempestuous relationship which ended in a public scene.

Despite the scandal this relationship caused, the Ionides family remained important clients for Burne-Jones. His work at the Ionides home at 1 Holland Park included a grand piano for the second drawing room. Burne-Jones had long taken an interest in piano design, writing to his Morris & Co. colleague Kate Faulkner, 'they are as it were the very altar of homes, and a second hearth to people', adding 'I feel as if one might start a new industry in painting them.'[4] He preferred the harpsichord-like shaping of this example made by John Broadwood & Sons in 1883, and took inspiration from earlier musical instruments displayed at the South Kensington Museum for the decoration of lilies, birds and pomegranates. He sketched the design himself, but it was developed further and executed in gold and silver gesso by Faulkner in 1885.

Burne-Jones's election as an associate of the Royal Academy of Art in June 1885 marked the midpoint of a successful decade, one in which any distinction between his paintings and his decorative output collapsed still further. He had also been re-elected to the Old Water-Colour Society (to which he was first elected in 1864, resigning in 1870), was able to purchase a summer house in Rottingdean, Sussex, and had received numerous church commissions and exhibited widely, including at the first Arts and Crafts Exhibition Society event in 1888. There the piano was first shown, as was a watercolour and gouache design for the mosaics at St Paul's Within the Walls, the American Episcopal Church in Rome (fig. 4). The English architect George Edmund Street approached Burne-Jones about the interior decoration in 1881, a year after completing the building of the Gothic Revival church. Burne-Jones had visited mosaics in Venice in 1862, Rome in 1871 and Ravenna in 1873 and greatly admired the simplicity of form, a style which he adopted in his later work. For this design for the second chancel arch, Burne-Jones created an unusual motif of the crucified Christ between Adam and Eve, rather than St John and the Virgin Mary, and in front of a Tree of Life. He later described it in a letter to his friend Frances Graham as 'a great flowering tree growing all over the space [...] I do hope to make it beautiful'.[5] The glass mosaic tiles were made on the Venetian island of Murano and their installation in Rome was managed and completed by his studio assistant Thomas Matthews Rooke, yet Burne-Jones took pains to ensure the precision of the colour palette, through copious notes and labelling of sample tesserae.

The move of Morris & Co. to their new works at Merton Abbey in 1881 allowed greater space and the establishment of hand-weaving looms for tapestries. Burne-Jones took to this medium (which Morris called 'the

Fig. 4
Edward Burne-Jones
Tree of Life, 1888
Watercolour and gouache on paper
181 × 242 cm
V&A: 584-1898

noblest of the weaving arts') with alacrity, collaborating with Morris and with John Henry Dearle. In the same period, Morris launched the Kelmscott Press and with Burne-Jones produced a celebrated edition of Chaucer's works (fig. 5). Burne-Jones provided 87 illustrations for the publication and these were produced between 1891 and 1895. Burne-Jones quipped about the production of the book: 'I said "I like a thing perfect," and [Morris] says he likes a thing done.'[6] The process was further prolonged by the work of turning Burne-Jones's drawings into the final woodblocks. First Emery Walker made platinotype photographs of the drawings, then artist Robert Catterson-Smith made copies in pen and ink with bolder lines, and lastly engraver William Harcourt Hooper carved the woodblocks. Finally published in May 1896, the Kelmscott Chaucer was both a return to Morris and Burne-Jones's student passion for medieval literature and their last collaboration. Morris died that October and his grieving friend threw himself into his work. Two years later, on 17 June 1898, Burne-Jones died and was given a memorial at Westminster Abbey.

Obituaries as well as late texts written by friends and contemporaries record the artist's life as not only a search for beauty but one with a radical stance and an indelible impact. Art critic Julia Cartwright Ady wrote in 1894: '[T]he most original and remarkable manifestation of art during this period has been due to a painter whose aims and achievements were in marked contrast to the leading characteristics of the age. The art of Burne-Jones from first to last has been a silent and unconscious protest against the most striking tendencies of the modern world.'[7] It was this singular vision, combined with the powerful sense of line and sinuous, elegant forms that made his designs immediately recognizable, and also ensured that they were highly influential upon the international Art Nouveau. The other-worldly quality of his paintings and decorative works would see his influence continuing to both Symbolism in the late nineteenth century and Surrealism in the twentieth. His aesthetic impacted fashions during his lifetime and has been embraced by contemporary designers and photographers.

Rosalind McKever

Fig. 5
Edward Burne-Jones and William Morris
Prologue to The Works of Geoffrey Chaucer, 1896
Wood engraving on paper
39 × 27 cm
V&A: E.1255-1912

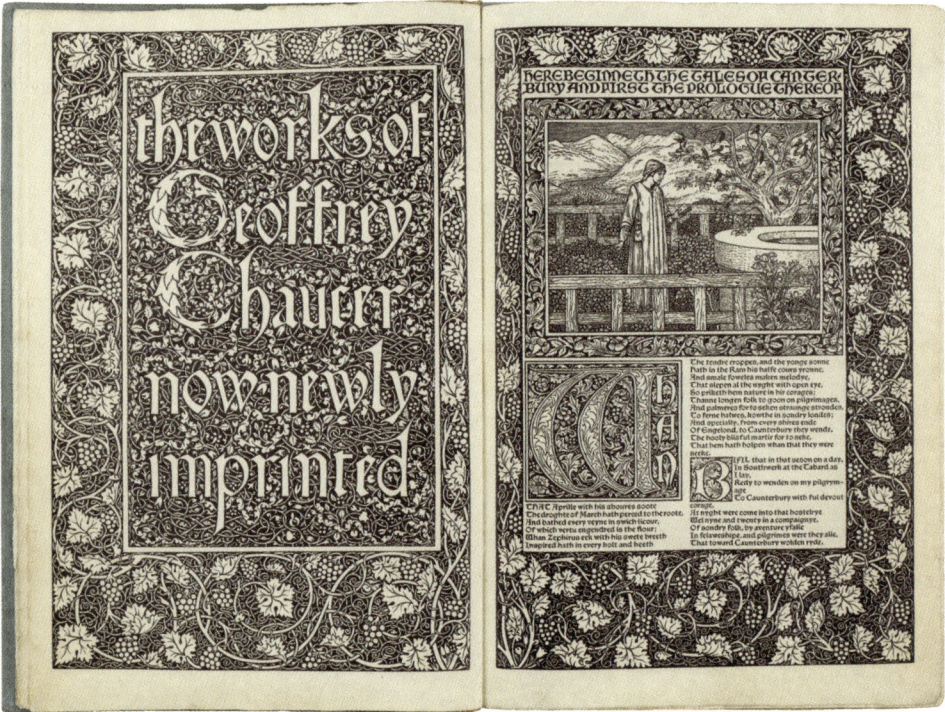

OTHER SIGNIFICANT MAKERS

Dante Gabriel Rossetti (1828–1882) was a British painter, poet and founder member of both the Pre-Raphaelite Brotherhood and Morris, Marshall, Faulkner & Co. In addition to painting religious, mythical and historical subjects, he designed stained glass windows and illustrated books for his sister, the poet Christina Rossetti.

Philip Webb (1831–1915) was a British architect and pioneer of the Arts and Crafts movement. His handcrafted and restrained furniture designs were evocative of the medieval era and later, traditional rural styles. Webb also produced designs for smaller-scale pieces including metalwork, tableware, glassware and tiles.

James Abbot McNeill Whistler (1834–1903) was an American painter, printmaker, designer and proponent of 'art for art's sake', active in London and Paris. His delicate compositions with harmonious palettes and musical titles stand in contrast to his combative personality. He had public feuds with critic John Ruskin and his patron Frederick Leyland.

Evelyn De Morgan (1855–1919, born Mary Evelyn Pickering) was a designer and painter, educated at the Royal College of Art and the Slade. Like her husband, William De Morgan (p. 214), she created pottery, tiles and narrative paintings in the Pre-Raphaelite tradition.

Charles Francis Annesley Voysey (1857–1941) was a British architect-designer best known for his wallpapers featuring stylized flora and fauna. An advocate of honest and thoughtful design, Voysey created a series of buildings whose sparsely decorated and plainly furnished interiors adhered strongly to Arts and Crafts principles.

WILLIAM MORRIS

(1834-1896)

Leading Arts and Crafts theorist

A towering figure within British art and design, William Morris channelled his creativity across the decorative arts, exploring materials and techniques with tireless dedication. Permeating nineteenth-century visual culture with his distinctive style, Morris's name is synonymous with the Arts and Crafts movement, becoming a byword for an entire aesthetic whose designs still resonate today. Underscored by firm sociopolitical beliefs, Morris's recognizable style was thoughtfully applied across a spectrum of media, from ceramics, furniture and stained glass to textiles and book design.

Born in Walthamstow, London, Morris spent his early years in middle-class comfort as the eldest son of Emma Shelton Morris and William Morris Senior, a self-made businessman who worked in finance. Upon his death in 1847, investments made by Morris Senior ensured that the family maintained their wealth, allowing William to pursue higher education and cultivate personal interests. From a young age, he was a self-proclaimed 'great devourer of books' and had a particular interest in history.[1] As an architecture student at Exeter College, Oxford, he combined his passion for the past with his love of literature and began writing medieval-inspired poetry. Morris was also fascinated by Icelandic literature and later published English translations of Old Norse sagas, whose tales of medieval chivalry enchanted him and fed his 'hatred of modern civilization.'[2]

Morris was a busy man with many self-appointed roles throughout his lifetime. A writer, designer, craftsman, businessman, conservationist and activist, each of his activities informed one another. Pivotal to his output was the critic John Ruskin, whose 1853 publication *The Nature of Gothic* had a profound effect on the young Morris. Convinced that the text 'point[ed] out a new road on which the world should travel',[3] Morris would draw heavily upon Ruskin's ideas as he developed his own ideology based on social equality and the beauty of craftsmanship. Believing that art should be accessible to all, Morris determined that people should surround themselves with well-designed and thoughtfully made objects, proclaiming 'have nothing in your houses that you do not know to be useful or believe

Fig. 1
William Morris
Wandle furnishing fabric, *c.*1884
Manufactured at Merton Abbey
for Morris & Co.
Indigo-discharged and block-printed cotton
165 × 92 cm
V&A: T.425-1934

to be beautiful'.[4] He criticized mass manufacture for valuing profit over beauty and for churning out sub-par goods made to 'supply the cravings of the public for something new, not for something pretty'.[5] Such disdain for the state of industrial production was amplified by Morris's scrutiny of the modern factory environment, whose poor working conditions, in his view, blighted how people lived and worked.[6] Believing that labour and art were integral to happiness, Morris condemned modern manufacturing for removing the maker's capacity to experience pride in one's work: the division of labour erasing the simple pleasure of making and destroying 'art, the one certain solace of labour'.[7] Morris made it his life's work to remedy this, based on the conviction that art could sustain both societal and individual harmony and that mechanization could be more considerately utilized. He called for reforms to reunite art and craft, designer and maker, to place greater value on the process of making and to be led by makers rather than by fashions or profit.

As a student, Morris befriended Dante Gabriel Rossetti (p. 197), who shared an affinity for medieval poetry and design. Under his influence,

Fig. 2
William Morris and Philip Webb
Trellis wallpaper, 1862
Manufactured by Jeffrey & Co.
for Morris, Marshall, Faulkner & Co.
Block-printed in distemper colours on paper
19 × 13.4 cm
V&A: E.452-1919
Given by Morris & Co.

Fig. 3
William Morris
Daisy tile, 1862
Decorated by Morris, Marshall,
Faulkner & Co.
Hand-painted tin-glazed earthenware
13 × 13 cm
V&A: C.58-1931
Bequeathed by J.R. Holliday

Morris abandoned an architecture apprenticeship to Philip Webb
(p. 197) and turned to painting, joining Rossetti, Edward Burne-Jones
(p. 190) and others in painting the Oxford Union's Arthurian murals, and
designing and painting furniture for his flat in Holborn, London. Soon
after, aged 25, Morris attempted to realize his design philosophy through
the decoration of Red House, his newly commissioned medieval-style
home. Disappointed to find the decorative arts 'in a state of complete
degradation', Morris and his circle of friends set about decorating the
home themselves, hand-painting tiles and murals and hand-embroidering
hangings – experimenting with a new form of 'Art Needlework' whose
free translation of designs defied the popularity of formulaic, counted-
thread embroidery such as Berlin wool work.[8] One hanging featured a
simple daisy motif sourced by Morris from a fifteenth-century manuscript.
Repeated elsewhere in the house, the motif appeared on tiles that became
one of Morris's first commercial products (fig. 3).

   In 1861 Morris, Marshall, Faulkner & Co. (later Morris & Co.) was
formed as a decorative arts enterprise of self-styled 'Fine Art Workmen',
informally known as 'the Firm'. Comprised of partners Morris, Burne-
Jones, Webb, Rossetti, Ford Madox Brown, Charles Faulkner and Peter
Paul Marshall, the group attempted to counter the creative shortcomings
of mass manufacture with workshops that stood in opposition to the
factory. Reviving traditional handicrafts – from stained glass to silk
dyeing – the Firm brought beauty into everyday spaces, designing

domestic and ecclesiastical interiors and the objects that filled them. Translating the medieval utopias of Pre-Raphaelite paintings into real-world rooms and homewares, the Firm elevated the status of the decorative arts. Foregrounding a painterly approach to colour and pattern, they sought to bring refinement and harmony to design, countering the cacophony of ornamentation cluttering fashionable homes.

For Morris, inspiration came from two enduring sources: nature and history. In his view, to study one without the other was to leave oneself vulnerable to pastiche and plagiarism. Good design functions 'in alliance with Nature' not in imitation of it and retains awareness of the past, rejecting arbitrary motifs for those with meaning.[9] Morris also believed good design could only be produced through an understanding of technical processes and materials, with designer and maker involved from the outset. Thus, throughout his life, Morris became a student of multiple disciplines and committed himself to practical learning. He sourced original materials for close study, drawing on museum collections and amassing his own collection of historical textiles and early printed books. He was also an ardent sketcher, deeming the 'art of drawing' a necessary precursor to the 'art of design'.[10]

Among the Firm's first offerings were tiles. Experimenting with various enamels and glazes, tiles were hand-painted on Dutch tin-glazed blanks with figurative and narrative designs, as well as heraldic or botanical motifs based on medieval illustrations (see fig. 3). The naïve, stylized designs of the botanical motifs demonstrated restraint and revealed the hand of their decorator, resisting the stiff architectural formality and intricate Gothic details of the era's mass-produced tiles. In 1864, following similar principles, the Firm issued their first wallpapers. Using flat, simplified designs that captured the essence of their botanical inspiration, these defied the fashion for overwrought and illusionistic wallpapers, proliferated by mass-printing technology. Against the prevailing taste for exotic imported flowers, Morris's designs took their cue from local sources. His first wallpaper, *Trellis*, is a characteristic celebration of British plant life, inspired by the rose garden at Red House (fig. 2). Within *Trellis*, as with other early wallpapers, depth is alluded to but not forced, with no integration between the foreground motifs and the plain background. Hand-printed using hand-cut blocks, Morris savoured this slower printing technique for both wallpapers and textiles. Unlike industrialized roller-printing, block-printing produced more vivid, solid colours and offered the craftsperson greater control in the translation of designs. Yet, as with other Morris & Co. goods, handmaking was expensive and so early wallpaper sales were modest, limited to those who were financially comfortable.

Fig. 4
William Morris and John H. Dearle
The Orchard tapestry, 1890
Made by Morris & Co.
Wool, silk and cotton
221 × 472 cm
V&A: 154-1898

By the 1870s Morris had refined his approach to repeat patterns in wallpapers and textiles. Depicting stylized but recognizable motifs, Morris continued to favour natural subjects, designing curling leaves and slender stems interspersed with the fruits, wildflowers and wildlife of the British countryside. His repeats were larger and denser than ever – characterized by the sophisticated interplay of background and foreground elements, balancing a sense of movement with an orderly structure. Having mastered the design of intertwining, organic arrangements, Morris concentrated his efforts on process. From 1875 he pursued the use of natural dyes in printed textiles, striving for years to perfect the processes and recipes rendered obsolete by cheaper synthetic dyes, which he considered garish. In 1881 Morris moved his workshops out of London to Merton Abbey, Surrey, cradling the River Wandle. In addition to the location's more pleasant working environment, Morris now had the space and abundance of fresh water to build huge indigo vats. There, he was able to achieve his desired shade of blue from a natural source, opening the door to experiments with indigo-discharge printing, which, combined with block-printing, resulted in some of his most celebrated designs yet, including *Strawberry Thief* and *Wandle* (fig. 1).[11] But it was the mastery of woven textiles that interested Morris the most. He experimented with the technical challenges of the loom, weaving furnishings using a hand-operated jacquard, hand-knotting carpets based on Persian rugs and reviving the ancient art of tapestry weaving, rising at dawn to practise on a loom in his bedroom (fig. 4).

In the last decade of his life, Morris returned to his original love of books. Having long collected early printed books and manuscripts, he

yearned to restore artistry to contemporary bookmaking and founded the Kelmscott Press in 1891. As exacting in his final creative endeavour as his first, Morris oversaw every element of a book's design and production, from typology and layouts to border ornamentation and illustrations. Indulging in his taste for fifteenth-century Gothic texts, Morris demanded authenticity through traditional craftsmanship and medieval aesthetics (fig. 5) with everything at Kelmscott printed on a hand-press. The perfect ink, handmade paper and bindings were sourced and silk ties were hand-dyed by Morris & Co. True to his work in other media, Morris's innovative approach at Kelmscott Press revolutionized Victorian publishing, attracting admirers and imitators.

Morris's legacy is difficult to overstate. Within his lifetime, his approach to craft stimulated a renewed interest in waning arts and triggered a wave of new schools, workshops and makers. In 1887 the Arts and Crafts Exhibition Society was formed, bestowing this movement with a name and an organizational body, steering generations of makers long after Morris's death. His appreciation of historical design would also have a lasting impact on the nation's collection of art; his decades-long relationship with the South Kensington Museum (now the V&A) included an advisory role recommending acquisitions that, to this day, constitute some of the most significant pieces within the Museum's collections. A thinker ahead of his time, Morris foresaw the difficulties associated with rampant industrial commercialism, upholding once radical values of design and ethical production that paved the way for sustainable thinking today.

Jessica Harpley

Fig. 5
William Morris
The Wood beyond the World book, 1894
Printed by Kelmscott Press
Ink on paper
21 × 15 cm (each page)
V&A NAL: 38041800870107

OTHER SIGNIFICANT MAKERS

Thomas Wardle (1831–1909) was a textile manufacturer based in Leek, Staffordshire, specializing in silk dyeing and printing. Known for his expertise in Indian wild silks and sericulture, Wardle used traditional methods to create exceptional colour. He frequently collaborated with Morris, instructing him on the use of vegetable dyes, printing Morris & Co. textiles and providing its yarns.

Kate Faulkner (1841–1898) was a Birmingham-born decorative artist and designer who worked alongside Morris in the workshops of Morris & Co., earning a reputation as a skilled craftswoman and later selling her designs independently. Faulkner produced patterns for textiles, wallpapers and tiles, and adeptly translated complex designs into embroideries and gesso-decorated furniture.

Walter Crane (1845–1915) was an English artist and designer best known for his book illustrations and paintings. As an art theorist, writer and educator, Crane co-founded the Arts and Crafts Exhibition Society, acting as its first President, became a master of the Art Workers' Guild, and later served as Principal of the Royal College of Art.

Lewis Foreman Day (1845–1910) began his career designing and painting stained glass and went on to produce designs for wallpapers, textiles, lace, embroideries, ceramics and furniture. A founding member of both the Arts and Crafts Exhibition Society and Art Workers' Guild, he also taught design and published books on pattern theory and ornamentation.

George Faulkner Armitage (1849–1937) studied woodcarving before going on to design and make furniture. He established the Stamford Studios which produced dynamically carved furniture and advocated for good craftsmanship based on material expertise. Later commissions saw Armitage employed as both architect and interior decorator, designing and furnishing spaces.

CHRISTOPHER DRESSER

(1834–1904)

Groundbreaking industrial designer

'An art object should be useful as well as beautiful', declared Christopher Dresser.[1] Advertising himself as an 'ornamentist', in 1859 he opened a London design studio which, under his direction, created thousands of designs for everything from textiles and wallpapers to metalwork and linoleum. Dresser's focus on utility and his ability to design with the properties of materials and the processes of manufacture in mind led to him being regarded in the twentieth century as Britain's first industrial designer.

Born in Glasgow to English parents, Dresser was only 13 when he enrolled at the London Government School of Design, studying design and botany. The school, established in 1837 to raise the standard of industrial design, taught students to develop designs that rejected the then fashionable illusion of depth and naturalism in favour of flat, conventionalized motifs. They were also encouraged to study historic and contemporary global cultures. Following in the footsteps of his mentor, the architect-designer Owen Jones, Dresser believed that 'we may borrow what is good from all peoples; but we must distil all that we borrow through our own minds'.[2]

Although his botanical research into plant morphology (the structure of plants) earned him a doctorate,[3] Dresser decided to follow a career as a designer, in which he sought to unite science and art. Embracing new materials and modern production methods, he traded on the theory that good design – 'art', as he termed it – could, like alchemy, transform cheaper materials like clay, cast iron or electroplated nickel (rather than solid) silver into objects of higher value. He taught his assistants that machines dictated manufacture and design, showing them machine manuals in the belief that this knowledge gave designers 'an amount of freedom and power which nothing else can supply'.[4]

Dresser's studio moved with his family homes in and around London including, at the height of his prosperity, the grand Tower Cressy in Campden Hill (1868–82). Over the decades he employed and trained numerous managers, designers and students, including his daughters. By

Fig. 1
Christopher Dresser
Chair, *c.*1880–3
Manufactured by Chubb & Co., London, or Thomas Knight, Bath, for the Art Furnishers' Alliance, London
Ebonized and gilded mahogany
81.3 × 40.6 × 45.8 cm
V&A: W.35-1992

1871 Dresser could claim that 'there is not one branch of art-manufacture that I do not regularly design patterns for'.[5] Clients included long-established companies such as Josiah Wedgwood & Sons and Minton & Co. in Stoke-on-Trent and the Coalbrookdale Company in Shropshire. In time, Dresser's studio designed for scores of manufacturers, from Dublin and Birmingham to Chicago and Rixheim (Germany, now France). A series of Dresser designs for printed cottons was produced in Lancashire for export to West Africa, an example of the imperial networks pivotal to any British designer's success.

A textile woven in Halifax (fig. 3) illustrates Dresser's use of conventionalized botanical motifs, in a characteristically energetic pattern suggestive of growth, adapted on a small scale for wallpapers and furnishing textiles. This approach became a Dresser hallmark, signifying his understanding that:

> *The requirements of manufacture are much more numerous than might be supposed, and are in some cases very restrictive. The size of the repeat, the manner in which colour can be applied, the character of surface attainable, and many other considerations have to be carefully complied with before a pattern can appear as a manufactured article.*[6]

Beyond his studio, Dresser promoted his theories and business through publications, including a series of articles in a trade journal, the *Technical Educator*, published as *Principles of Decorative Design* (1873). He addressed the book to 'working men' who had not benefited from education earlier in their lives.[7] Now they were urged to study nature, historic ornament and modern manufactures (such as Indian textiles) wherever they could, whether in museums and libraries or shop windows, to develop knowledge of the fundamentals of design such as proportion and colour harmony. He also lectured to artisans, advising jet workers in Whitby to give their products interest by introducing what he called 'poetic qualities', and to be 'bold and vigorous' with the form and treatment of their material.[8]

A tireless traveller, Dresser acted as a consultant and adviser for governments, museums and retailers and as a juror and critic at international exhibitions in Britain, Europe and the USA. From 1876 to 1877 he visited Japan, later described in a lively published account.[9] He witnessed a country which, following the Meiji Restoration of 1868, was rapidly undergoing political and economic transformations, spurred by exchanges with Europe and the USA. Dresser presented a gift of British manufactures that he had assembled on behalf of the South Kensington

Fig. 2
Christopher Dresser
Teapot, *c.*1879
Manufactured by James Dixon
& Sons, Sheffield
Electroplated nickel silver and
ebonized wood
13 × 23 cm
V&A: M.4-2006
Purchased with generous support of
the National Heritage Memorial Fund,
the Art Fund, the American Friends of the
V&A and an anonymous donor, the Friends
of the V&A, the J. Paul Getty Jr. Charitable
Trust and a private consortium led by
John S.M. Scott

Museum (now the V&A) to the National Museum in Tokyo and advised the Japanese government on the introduction of modern manufacturing methods. He visited dozens of Japanese cultural sights and workshops and collected thousands of objects and architectural elements to be sold by the London-based importing business Londos & Co. and for Tiffany & Co. in New York, as well as for his own collection, advancing the appreciation of Japanese crafts in both Britain and the USA.

One of the first European designers to visit Japan, Dresser returned to London with unrivalled knowledge of Japanese handicrafts, giving him the confidence to promote some of his most groundbreaking designs. A teapot made in Sheffield (fig. 2) demonstrates his genius in taking industrially produced sheet metal as the starting point for a design. Rather than applying additional ornamentation, he prioritized utility and considered the centre of gravity as the teapot was inclined for pouring when calculating the angles and relative positions of the handle and spout. One critic praised the 'severe design' on other pieces, 'beauty consisting rather in their outline than in the amount of labour bestowed', and noting their affordability compared with 'expensive and intricate work'.[10] Nevertheless, they required extremely skilled craftsmanship to make, with the material of this teapot accounting for only a quarter of the manufacturing cost and the remainder being the labour.

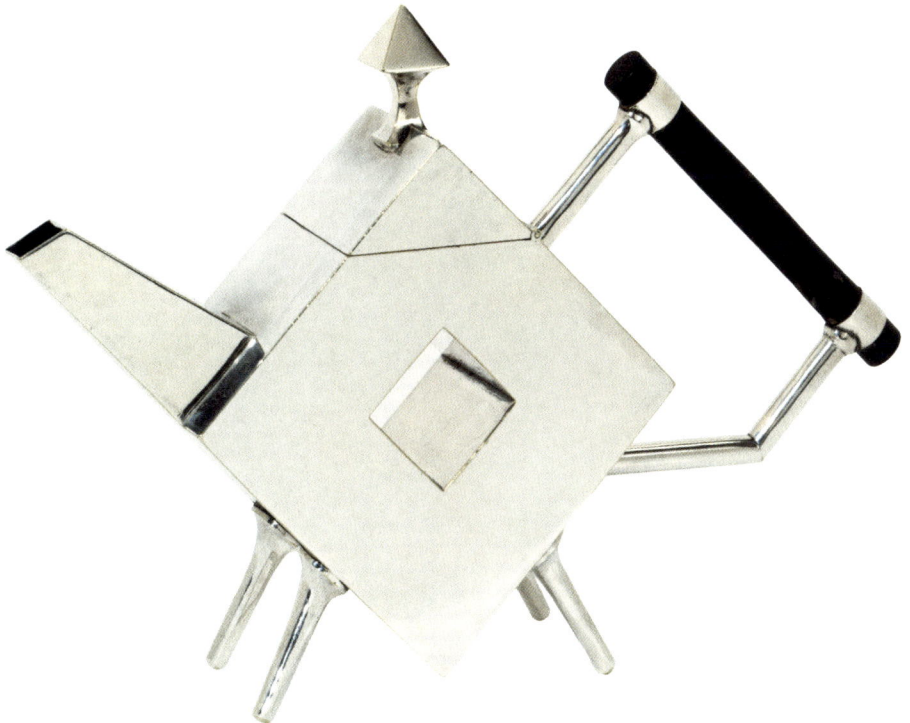

Before they left his studio, Dresser approved designs and he often took them to clients, as a salesman doubtless attempting to influence choices. Although frequently lacking control over how designs were executed, he occasionally oversaw colour trials in wallpaper factories or furniture construction in cabinet-makers' workshops. Acting as an 'Art Adviser' for manufacturers gave him even greater leverage. For example, his contract with the Ault Pottery stipulated that he would visit the pottery twice a year to discuss the production, and that his facsimile signature was to be stamped on items that he had designed. Dresser also refurbished the Halifax design studio and boardroom for the carpet manufacturer John Crossley & Sons and decorated showrooms, including that of the Manchester cotton weaver Barlow & Jones.

All aspects of interior design interested Dresser, who devised and personally superintended decorative schemes for public buildings and homes. He designed a side chair (fig. 1) for the Art Furnishers' Alliance, a business whose Mayfair shop catered to the demand stimulated by the Aesthetic movement. The chair follows the idea, traceable to A.W.N. Pugin (p. 174), of truth to materials, as Dresser believed that wood was stronger when straight and not cut against the grain. As he thought that chair backs were usually weak due to inadequate support, to remedy this Dresser designed vertical struts connecting the horizontal rails of the back to the rail between the back legs and brackets connecting the back and seat.

Dresser's role as 'Art Adviser' to the Linthorpe Art Pottery showed his interest in transforming not only modest materials but also the lives of makers. Following the failure of the iron trade, the pottery was established, in a district of Middlesbrough blighted by unemployment, on the site of clay beds used for brickmaking. He appointed manager Henry Tooth, a former butcher's apprentice whom he had talent-spotted and mentored. The fluid form of this vase (fig. 4), which Dresser based on the double-gourd shape of a contemporary, patinated copper-alloy Japanese vase, is enlivened by the glazes developed by Tooth. Although the pottery exploited new technology in the form of gas-fired kilns, Dresser understood the importance of allowing materials to express themselves, in this case the random action of running glazes. He also valued the input of the maker, a visitor to the pottery's decorating room describing how 'The designers are left considerably to their own taste, and the consequence is that a living spirit is breathed into the work.'[11]

This same 'living spirit' was, quite literally, breathed into Dresser's designs by the glassblower in Glasgow who made this vase (fig. 5). Dresser recognized the skill required for glass-blowing and admired the way in which, through manipulating the molten glass, 'the material operation of gravitation and similar forces upon plastic matter is calculated to give beauty of form'.[12] Dresser's design, inspired by Chinese vases, was enhanced by specks, bubbles and streaks introduced to the glass during the manufacturing process. *Clutha* glass designed by Dresser was retailed through Liberty & Co.'s London shop and in 1890 Couper of Glasgow exhibited examples with the Arts and Crafts Exhibition Society in London.

Many talented designers who trained in Dresser's studio, among them John Moyr Smith, Arthur Knox, Rex Silver and Frederick Burrows, proceeded to forge successful design careers. Likewise, Japanese craft and architecture, which Dresser studied and promoted, were to provide inspiration to British studio potters and architect-designers including Charles Rennie Mackintosh in Britain, Peter Behrens in Germany and Frank Lloyd Wright in the USA. More recently, Dresser's designs have inspired designers and makers such as Alessi.

Max Donnelly

Fig. 4
Christopher Dresser
Vase, designed 1879–80,
manufactured 1879–82
Manufactured at the Linthorpe Art Pottery,
Middlesbrough, North Yorkshire
Glazed earthenware
37.5 × 15.2 cm
V&A: C.237-2014
Purchased with the support of the Decorative
Arts Society and its Members

Fig. 5
Christopher Dresser
Clutha vase, *c*.1890
Manufactured by James Couper & Sons,
Glasgow
Free-blown glass
46.7 × 19.8 cm
V&A: C.146-1977

OTHER SIGNIFICANT MAKERS

Owen Jones (1809–1874), architect and design theorist, is best known for his *Grammar of Ornament* (1856), a lavish chromolithographed compendium of global ornamental motifs. Effectively a toolkit for designers, it gave them a historical overview and an analytical framework for understanding what made particular ornamental designs successful.

Edward William Godwin (1833–1886), architect and designer, pioneered the 'Anglo-Japanese' style that saw British designers assimilate Japanese motifs and design principles into their own work. Godwin's elegant furniture designs, based on his study of Japanese woodwork, were characterized by refined proportions, subtle interplays between solid and void, and ebonized finishes.

Bruce James Talbert (1838–1881) supplied designs to many manufacturers, his published designs for interiors, furniture, metalwork, wallpapers and textiles finding receptive audiences in Britain and the USA. While Talbert's interior and furniture designs deftly adapted the Reformed Gothic style to a domestic scale, his patterns encapsulated the Aesthetic movement's spirit.

John Moyr Smith (1839–1912), freelance designer of furniture, metalwork, ceramics and textiles, was an artist whose adroit figural designs were widely disseminated in the form of book illustrations and tiles. Transfer-printed by Minton China Works and Minton, Hollins & Co., Moyr Smith's tile designs included biblical, historical and literary subjects.

Arthur Silver (1853–1896) opened one of Britain's leading commercial design studios in London in 1880. Specializing in textiles, wallpapers, carpets and book jackets, the Silver Studio adapted to changing fashions, including Aestheticism and Art Nouveau. His sons Rex and Harry became designer-managers for the studio, which operated until 1963.

WILLIAM DE MORGAN

(1839–1917)

Trailblazing potter

Celebrated for his unique designs and innovative techniques, William De Morgan was the foremost art potter of the Arts and Crafts movement, producing thousands of designs for tiles, vases and dishes in a career spanning over 30 years. Inspired by the natural world, medieval motifs and the arts of the Middle East, he created a distinctive yet diverse repertoire of plants, animals, mythical creatures and ships, executed with captivating and often humorous charm. A lifelong friend of the artist and activist William Morris (p. 198), De Morgan was influenced by Morris's ideals and shared in the belief that a designer should be involved in all stages of an object's production. Committed to making high-quality art for the home, De Morgan carried out countless experiments into the technical aspects of pottery production, and was described by his business partner Halsey Ricardo as not only an imaginative designer but also an imaginative mechanic, chemist and engineer.[1] Although De Morgan worked collaboratively with a small team to produce his pottery, the designs and inventions used in its manufacture were entirely his own, including the successful revival of lustreware (ceramics decorated with an iridescent metallic glaze), a career-defining achievement.

Born in London in 1839, De Morgan was the eldest of six siblings and was raised in a liberal household. His father, Augustus De Morgan, was Chair of Mathematics at University College London, and his mother Sophia Elizabeth Frend was an advocate for women's higher education and suffrage. De Morgan attended University College School from the age of ten, joining the College six years later. Interested in art from a young age, he took art classes at Cary's Academy in Bloomsbury, a feeder school for the Royal Academy, which he joined in 1859. He was quickly disillusioned by the Royal Academy's uninspiring teaching methods and left after four years. However, his time there was formative for the students he met, including the artists Henry Holiday, Albert Moore, Simeon Solomon and William Blake Richmond, who later described De Morgan's 'commanding characteristic' as being 'unmistakably humour'.[2]

It was through Holiday that De Morgan first met Morris at his home in Red Lion Square, London, in 1863. Two years earlier, the firm of Morris, Marshall, Faulkner & Co. had been established and Morris and Edward Burne-Jones (p. 190) were gaining popularity for their revival of medieval arts and crafts, in particular their stained glass church windows. They began a long friendship with De Morgan and, with Morris's encouragement, De Morgan started to make his own stained glass and occasionally painted furniture and tiles for Morris's firm as an outside collaborator.

While making stained glass De Morgan was struck by the iridescent beauty of the silver paint used to outline his designs and attempted to produce the same lustrous effect on tiles. From 1869 he absorbed himself in experiments at his home studio at 40 Fitzroy Square, London, and following an unfortunate kiln incident, where he accidentally set fire to the roof, he moved to new premises at 30 Cheyne Row, Chelsea. Here his career as a tile designer and manufacturer started in earnest and he began to achieve success with lustre decoration, a notoriously difficult technique due to the precise calculations and firing conditions required. He remained in Chelsea from 1872 for almost a decade. In 1873 he rented larger premises further down the street to serve as a workshop and

Fig. 2
William De Morgan
Dish, 1882–8
Earthenware, painted in lustre and glazed
36.5 cm (diam.)
V&A: 832-1905
Given by Sydney Vacher

Fig. 3a
William De Morgan
Tile panel, originally designed for the
Sutlej P&O ocean liner, 1882
Earthenware, painted and glazed
59 × 31 cm
V&A: 362:1 to 8-1905

showroom, known as Orange House. Despite his Arts and Crafts ethos, he initially used industrial products to make his wares, painting onto blank tiles imported from the Netherlands or bought in from British factories such as Wedgwood, Carter's at Poole or the Architectural Pottery Company. Frank Iles managed the kiln (located at the end of the garden) and a team of painters expertly translated De Morgan's designs onto the tiles. The brothers Charles and Fred Passenger were especially gifted and worked with De Morgan for almost 30 years, eventually becoming partners in the firm.

Tiles were the mainstay of the business and De Morgan is thought to have produced over 300 different tile designs in this period, featuring inventive floral motifs and charismatic animals in vibrant colours. Many were cleverly devised to connect both horizontally and vertically, creating intricate repeating patterns which could be used to great effect. Certain designs were extremely popular and stayed in production for decades, such as the bold *BBB* flower tile, named after the Norwich firm of Barnard, Bishop and Barnard, who sold the tiles as part of their cast-iron fireplaces (fig. 1). By 1876 De Morgan was producing tiles in-house and had developed an innovative method of decoration to ensure consistent patterns. First, the design's outline was painted onto fine tissue paper and pasted onto a sheet of glass. This acted as a guide for the painter who would then fix another sheet of paper onto the reverse of the glass and paint over the design. This was subsequently placed face-down onto the slip-coated surface of the tile and covered in a transparent glaze. When fired in the kiln, the paper would burn away, leaving the design on the tile's surface.

De Morgan was greatly interested in Islamic ceramics and spent time studying the collections of the South Kensington Museum (now the V&A), taking particular inspiration from Iznik pottery of north-west

Fig. 3b
William De Morgan
Design for the Sutlej P&O ocean liner, 1882
Watercolour on paper
24.2 × 40.7 cm
V&A: E.1511-1917
Given by Mrs Evelyn De Morgan

Turkey. He developed a signature style of stylized leaves and flowers in blue, green and turquoise known as *Persian*. In 1877 he was commissioned by the artist Frederic Leighton to produce tiles for the Arab Hall at Leighton House, matching and filling the gaps of a scheme of fifteenth- and sixteenth-century tiles from Damascus. In 1882 De Morgan's growing success prompted him to move the pottery to bigger premises in Merton, Surrey, where Morris had set up textile workshops a year earlier. With more space and resources, De Morgan's focus turned towards decorating vases and dishes with elaborate yet elegant scenes in perfectly balanced compositions, appealing to followers of the new Aesthetic movement. Although he took inspiration from lustre ceramics from medieval Iran and Spain, he always gave pieces his own imaginative twist, such as a dish with an antelope set against lush foliage and expertly rendered in red lustre – a glimmering focal point in any Aesthetic interior (fig. 2). While at Merton, De Morgan was given his first commission to supply tiles for the interior of the *Sutlej*, a P&O ocean liner, using an Iznik-inspired floral scheme to evoke a feeling of exotic luxury (figs 3a and b).

Fig. 4
William De Morgan
Two-handled vase, double gourd vase, dish and vase, *c*.1888–98
Earthenware, painted and glazed; painted in lustre (two-handled vase and double gourd vase)
32.5 × 21.5 cm; 21.6 × 13.6 cm; 41.5 cm (diam.); 38.5 × 24.8 cm
V&A: C.79-1923; C.265-1915; C.261-2915; C.239-2018
Given by Miss Evelyn Brooke in memory of her father, the Rev. Stopford Brooke; Given by Mr Archibald Anderson (double gourd vase and dish); Gift of Ian and Rita Smythe

He had previously produced tiles for the Tsar of Russia's yacht, the *Livadia*, and would go on to make panels for 12 P&O ships, reflecting the appetite for fashionable design on the 'floating palaces' that were revolutionizing global travel.

In 1887 De Morgan became a founding member of the Arts and Crafts Exhibition Society, helping to organize their exhibitions, and regularly contributed his wares for display. In the same year he married Mary Evelyn Pickering (p. 197), a talented painter and niece of Roddam Spencer Stanhope, an artist associated with the Pre-Raphaelites. Evelyn would go on to play a significant role in De Morgan's life, not only as an intellectual and artistic companion, but also by providing crucial financial support to his business. In 1888 ill health and a need for larger kilns prompted De Morgan to move the pottery once more, as the daily journey to Merton proved too onerous. He entered into partnership with the architect Halsey Ricardo who, together with Evelyn, gave funding to build a new pottery at Sand's End, Fulham. De Morgan exercised his engineering and problem-solving skills to design new kilns and machinery, and the scale of production increased. The pots were now made entirely on-site to his specifications, and he began to make his most ambitious work yet, with flamboyant designs on large vases and dishes that skilfully demonstrated his talents for three-dimensional design (fig. 4). De Morgan's mastery of the lustre technique reached its pinnacle at Fulham when, after much experimentation, he used copper, silver and gold oxides to produce pots with a triple lustre effect on one piece. De Morgan's pride in these achievements is embodied in a portrait painted by Evelyn in 1909, where he is depicted with hands grasped around a magnificent lustre vase (fig. 5) with scrolling leaves and fruit inspired by Italian Renaissance motifs.

The influence of Italy became more apparent in De Morgan's work throughout the 1890s, as he and Evelyn spent their winters in Florence in an effort to improve his health. During these six-month periods Ricardo assumed full responsibility for managing the pottery. De Morgan continued to design and employed Italian painters to paint tile patterns using his glass transparency method, sending the designs to London via post. His renowned skills in the field led to an invitation from the Egyptian government to investigate how to develop the Egyptian pottery industry and he spent eight weeks in Cairo in 1893. In the years that followed, it became increasingly challenging for Ricardo to run the pottery when De Morgan was absent, and even the hiring of a general manager could not prevent the partnership from dissolving in 1898. The firm carried on in partnership with the Passenger brothers until 1907, when ongoing financial difficulties and changing tastes caused the

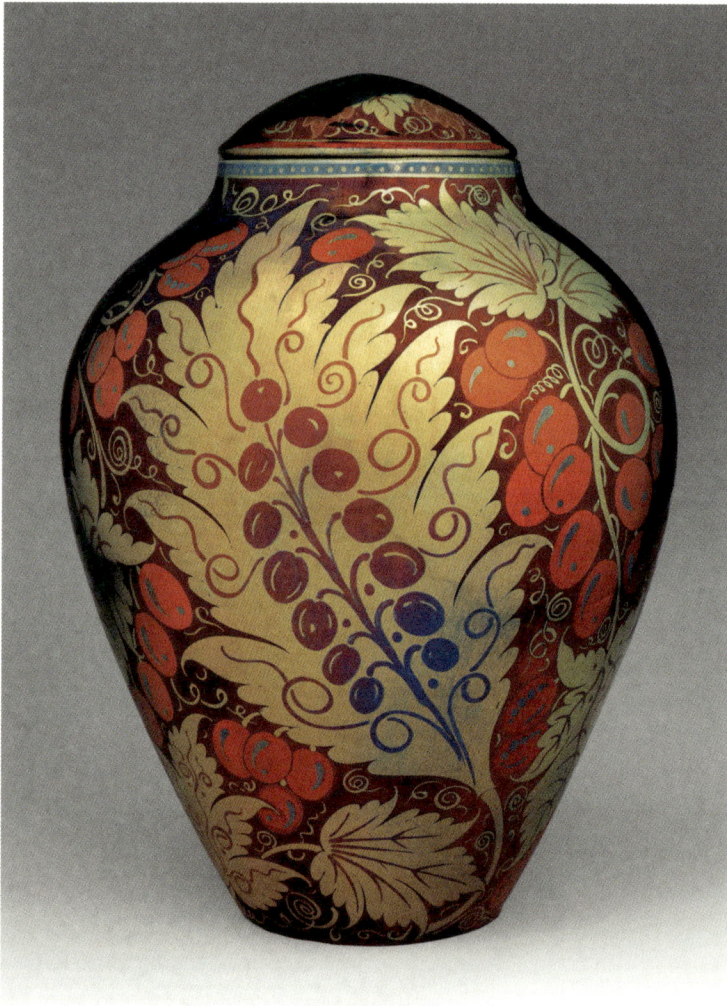

Fig. 5
William De Morgan
Vase, 1888–98
Earthenware, painted in lustre and glazed
30.4 × 23.2 cm
V&A: C.413&A-1919
Bequeathed by Mrs Evelyn De Morgan

pottery to close. In his final years De Morgan embarked on a successful second career as a novelist, publishing seven acclaimed novels before his death in 1917.

A man of diverse talents, De Morgan combined his skills as ingenious designer, determined chemist and astute inventor to make joyful pottery which brought delight and beauty to many late nineteenth-century interiors. His success with lustre and his playful designs inspired many art potters working in the late nineteenth and early twentieth centuries and continue to charm viewers to this day.

Florence Tyler

OTHER SIGNIFICANT MAKERS

Theodore Deck (1823–1891) was a French art potter who ran his own workshop in Paris from 1858. He avidly researched glaze colours and effects, and was inspired by Iznik, Japanese and Chinese ceramics. He became Director of the Manufacture nationale de Sèvres in 1887.

The Martin Brothers founded their London art pottery in 1873, making stoneware pottery and sculptures in a distinctive, singular style. Robert Wallace (1843–1923) was the principal artist and modeller, with Walter (1857–1912) and Edwin (1860–1915) supporting the manufacture and Charles (1846–1910) acting as salesman. They drew stylistic inspiration from medieval and Renaissance Europe and the arts of Japan, and were unique in that they were responsible for all aspects of production.

Hannah Barlow (1851–1916) was the first woman artist to be employed at the Doulton Lambeth pottery and is arguably the most celebrated of their artists. She decorated in a unique style, incising enchanting rural scenes and animals onto stoneware pots. She worked at Doulton for 42 years and won numerous awards throughout her career.

John Pearson (1859–1930) was an artist who worked with William De Morgan and made ceramics that were strongly influenced by De Morgan's style from the 1880s to the 1920s. He was also known for his metalwork in copper and became a founder member of the Guild of Handicraft in 1888.

William Moorcroft (1872–1945) joined the Staffordshire pottery firm of James Macintyre & Co. in 1897, forging a successful career as an artist, designer, chemist and businessman. He manufactured art pottery for a range of budgets, designing an original type of decorative slipware that was in production for over 40 years.

ÉMILE GALLÉ

(1846–1904)

Innovator of French Art Nouveau glass

An extraordinary artist, designer, botanist, writer and activist, Émile Gallé was a true visionary who developed and promoted a new style of French decorative art during the final decades of the nineteenth century. His achievements in the distinct fields of glass, ceramics and furniture reveal his natural aptitude for design and garnered him the title 'homo triplex' from the art critic Roger Marx.[1] Gallé's deep understanding of materials and technical processes enabled him to create aesthetically ambitious artworks which pushed material boundaries. He stood at the intersection of art and industry, adopting an Arts and Crafts ethos yet embracing industrial manufacturing techniques. His lifelong passion for the natural world can be seen throughout his work, reflecting his belief in nature as a proper source of inspiration for designers. This belief became a driving force in his efforts to forge a regional style, leading to the foundation of the École de Nancy, an influential group of artists who helped to define French Art Nouveau. Yet Gallé was not driven purely by aesthetic principles; his work was always imbued with symbolic meaning and often expressed political sentiments.

Born in 1846, Gallé's interests were shaped from an early age by his family and home town of Nancy, France. His father Charles Gallé-Reinemer ran a luxury glass and ceramics business, formerly owned by Gallé's maternal grandmother, buying in factory-made 'blanks' to decorate at his workshop. The products were inspired by historic French styles which appealed to a wealthy clientele, and from 1854 the firm supplied glassware to Napoleon III's palaces. Gallé started to assist his father almost a decade later, following his studies at the Lycée impérial de Nancy. In 1865 he joined the Académie de Nancy and finished his education with a year in Weimar, Germany. He spent formative periods learning the art of glassmaking at the Burgun, Schverer & Co. factory in Meisenthal, one of Gallé-Reinemer's suppliers, and on his return to Nancy in 1867 began to manage the family business. In the same year he represented his father at the Paris International Exhibition and the firm received an honourable mention for their glass display. The exhibition

Fig. 1
Émile Gallé
Vase, 1900
Glass, acid-etched, enamelled and gilded
47 × 27.2 cm
V&A: 1622-1900

exposed Gallé to art from around the world, including the arts of Japan, which had not been seen before on a world stage. Experiencing almost 2,000 Japanese works of art in person had a profound and lasting impact on the young Gallé.

Gallé's burgeoning career was briefly interrupted in 1870 when he volunteered to fight in the Franco-Prussian War. France's defeat and Germany's annexation of part of Alsace-Lorraine stirred a strong sense of patriotism within him, particularly as Meisenthal was now situated in German territory. He began to incorporate the Cross of Lorraine and thistle motifs from Nancy's coat of arms into his designs for ceramics and glass, reinforcing the importance of regional identity. Yet Gallé's outlook was both local and global, and he developed his interest in the arts of Asia and the Middle East while representing the firm at the London International Exhibition of 1871. For six months he studied historic and contemporary works at the exhibition and in the nearby collection of the South Kensington Museum (now the V&A). The following year he started to build his own collection of Japanese ceramics, paintings, lacquerware and *ukiyo-e* woodblock prints.

Fig. 2
Émile Gallé
Fire screen, 1899–1900
Ash, with applied floral decoration and marquetry in various woods; oak frame, veneered in maple on the reverse
107.5 × 56 × 35 cm
V&A: 1985-1900
Given by George Donaldson

By 1878 Gallé had taken over as director of the company and presented a display of his own designs at the Paris International Exhibition. His innovative approach to glass enamelling was highly praised and the exhibition marked a turning point for art glass in France. In the years that followed, Gallé worked tirelessly to grow the business, experimenting with decorative techniques and pushing what could be achieved with glass. Enamelling, casing, acid etching, applied decoration and wheel engraving were used in combination to give the glass sculptural qualities, with deliberate inclusions of air bubbles and metallic particles creating lively dichroic effects. Designs were executed under his supervision, but he carried out his own experiments and was determined to solve any technical issues that prevented him from realising his vision. This led to the invention of techniques such as *émaux-bijoux* (enamel jewels), where layers of enamel were fused to a metal base before being applied to the glass surface, increasing the piece's decorative potential.

Throughout the 1880s Gallé's designs were strongly influenced by Japan in both form and decoration. What began as a superficial appreciation grew into a deep affinity with Japan, seen in his use of perspective and in the belief that all plants, flowers and animals – even insects and bats – are worthy motifs in art. Chrysanthemums, a symbolic flower of Japan used on its imperial seal, were enamelled and acid etched onto vases, including a magnificent vase shown at the 1900 Paris International Exhibition (fig. 1). Gallé had referred to Japan as the 'land

of the chrysanthemum'[2] in a letter to his friend Takashima Hokkai,
a Japanese painter and forester who lived in Nancy from 1885 to 1888.
Yet the flower's French association with death also spoke to themes
of life and renewal that Gallé liked to explore in his work, imbuing
the piece with dual meaning.

Gallé's devotion to nature was stimulated from a young age by the
flower markets and botanical gardens near his family home, as well as
by his mother Fanny Reinemer, a trained gardener. Gallé once stated
that the 'love of flowers reigned in my family; it was an inherited passion,
a salvation', and Nancy – a leading centre for horticulture and botany
– was the ideal place for this passion to flourish.[3] As a young man, Gallé
studied under prominent botanists and in 1877 became a founding
member of the Société Centrale d'Horticulture de Nancy, before joining
other botanical and artistic societies throughout the 1880s and '90s.
He lectured and published widely on a range of subjects and, in a lecture
at the Académie de Stanislas, famously reflected that artists who depict
plants, landscapes and people 'produce a more vibrant work and of a
more infectious emotional quality than those whose tools are nothing
but a camera or a cold scalpel ... because the human soul is absent'.[4]
It was his scientific understanding of the natural world combined with
his skills as an artist which made Gallé's designs so uniquely compelling.

In 1884 Gallé's ambitions as a designer intensified when he began to
build a carpentry workshop on the family plot, with the aim of making
original, expressive furniture that could appropriately support his art
glass. He engaged in studies of indigenous and foreign woods and is
known to have used over 600 different types in his furniture, each one
selected for its tonal quality or symbolic relevance.[5] A prize-winning fire
screen exhibited at the 1900 Paris International Exhibition is thought to
include oak, ash, elm, burr elm, walnut, amboyna, sabicu and mahogany,
with carved tendrils and stems forming the sinuous curves of the frame
(fig. 2). Decorated with wild clematis flowers, the combination of
marquetry and carving in high and low relief gives energy and depth
to a typically flat, functional piece of furniture. These effects were made
possible by Gallé's embrace of the latest industrial technologies, using
steam-powered blades to cut finer slices of wood than would otherwise
be possible by hand. He produced tables, commodes, chests of drawers,
bed frames and trays, all united by his characteristic flowing lines and
variation of tone.

Gallé's mastery of furniture informed his approach to decoration
elsewhere, and he went on to develop the innovative technique of
'glass marquetry' around 1898 which made use of techniques usually
associated with wood. By this time the factory had expanded to

Fig. 4
Émile Gallé
Goblet, 1899–1900
Glass, painted, acid-etched,
enamelled and gilded
18.4 × 8.9 cm
V&A: 1626-1900

accommodate the making and decorating of glass and ceramics on-site, following the installation of a kiln in 1894. Gallé managed around 300 staff, encouraging them to spend time in the factory's gardens and to pursue educational courses alongside their work. In 1897 he commissioned Eugène Vallin to build a unique set of doors for the workshop, carved in oak with the inscription *ma racine est au fond des bois* (my roots lie deep in the woods). Gallé's deep affinity with the woods is embodied in his *Oakleaf* vase, a beloved design which uses layers of coloured glass to evoke the forest's dappled light (fig. 3).

The 1900 Paris International Exhibition marked a crowning achievement in Gallé's career. He was awarded two grand prizes and was appointed a commander of the Légion d'honneur. His impressive display included a large glass furnace and politically charged artworks, including a vase which referenced the injustice of the Dreyfus affair (a divisive scandal caused by the wrongful conviction of a French Army officer) and a commode made poignantly of Turkish walnut and Armenian peach wood, designed to condemn the Turkish massacre of Armenians by Sultan Abdul Hamid II in 1894–6. Gallé was also inspired by medieval literature and displayed a glass goblet enamelled with the words '*Ballade des Dames du Temps Jadis*', referencing a poem by the fifteenth-century poet François Villon (fig. 4). Gallé would often inscribe text onto his glass to enhance its meaning, referring to these pieces as *verrerie parlante* (glass that speaks).

Gallé's connection to Paris had long played an important role in his success, particularly thanks to the support he received from the art critics Roger Marx, Edmond de Goncourt and the wealthy aristocrat and collector Robert de Montesquiou, who introduced Gallé to the upper classes of Parisian society. However, following the success of the 1900 Exhibition, Gallé sought to unite his fellow Lorraine artists and industrialists to challenge Paris's dominance and promote their provincial style on a national and international level. The École de Nancy, Alliance Provinciale des Industries d'Art was founded in February 1901, with Gallé as president and the Daum brothers, Louis Majorelle and Eugène Vallin as vice-presidents. Together they organized training courses and exhibitions and began to form a museum collection. Nature remained Gallé's primary source of inspiration, apparent in a striking vase featuring a bat in flight above a dark forest canopy, set against a fiery orange sky (fig. 5). This twilight scene is thought to be one of the last designs made under Gallé's supervision before his untimely death from leukaemia in 1904.

A master of Art Nouveau, Gallé's abundant creativity and power to transform familiar materials into expressive, sculptural works of art helped to elevate the artistic status of glass and furniture and define a new modern style. His philosophical beliefs about nature and national identity, combined with his experimental approach to making, influenced the careers of many contemporary makers and left a lasting legacy on decorative arts in France and beyond.

Florence Tyler

Fig. 5
Émile Gallé
Vase, *c.*1904
Glass, cased, wheel-cut and acid-etched, with applied raised glass over silver foil in imitation of jewels
37.5 × 14.8 cm
V&A: C.53-1992

OTHER SIGNIFICANT MAKERS

François-Eugène Rousseau (1827–1891) was both a designer and retailer of glass and porcelain, who drew inspiration from Japanese art. In the 1870s–'80s his pioneering use of coloured glass overlays and decorative glass effects influenced other artists working in the medium, the result of his technical collaboration with the Appert brothers at their glassworks in Clichy near Paris.

Auguste (1853–1909) and **Antonin** (1864–1931) **Daum**, also known as Les Frères Daum, were brothers who ran an innovative glass studio in Nancy, employing a variety of decorative techniques and producing art glass initially inspired by the works of Émile Gallé. Founding members of the École de Nancy, their business flourished from the 1890s and became one of France's most celebrated glassworks.

Louis Majorelle (1859–1926) became the leading furniture designer of the French Art Nouveau movement. He inherited his father's furniture business in Nancy in 1879, following two years of study at the École des Beaux-Arts in Paris. Influenced by Émile Gallé's success, from 1894 he began to design and exhibit furniture in the Art Nouveau aesthetic and was a founding member of the École de Nancy.

Alexandre Bigot (1862–1927) was a prominent ceramicist who established a factory in Mer, France, in 1889. Influenced by ceramics from far East Asia, Bigot produced stoneware vessels with a variety of coloured and crystalline glazes, utilizing his training as a chemist. He was a leader in the field of architectural ceramics and collaborated with many Art Nouveau architects and artists from France and Belgium.

LOUIS COMFORT TIFFANY

(1848–1933)

America's leading exponent of the Art Nouveau style

A prolific designer, visionary and entrepreneur, Louis Comfort Tiffany created masterpieces across media. Adept at producing beautiful objects, Tiffany took inspiration from natural and ancient sources to generate a new style representative of the innovative spirit of turn-of-the-century America.

Tiffany was the first-born to an established New England family in 1848. His father, Charles Lewis Tiffany, was a shrewd businessman whose enduring brand, Tiffany & Co., signified elegance and quality. An emporium for all things beautiful, his father's store had a great impact on the young Tiffany's path as an artist and designer, exposing him to brilliant gems, cutting-edge design and objets d'art. Despite his father's expectations, as a young man Tiffany preferred art to business. An unenthusiastic student, he eschewed higher education in favour of an apprenticeship in 1866 under American landscape artist George Inness.

Perhaps most significant in Tiffany's artistic development were his travels to Europe and northern Africa in the 1860s and '70s. It was during these travels that Tiffany was exposed to new colours, textures and artistic techniques. While in France, Tiffany was particularly inspired by the brilliant hues of the twelfth- and thirteenth-century stained glass windows at Chartres Cathedral.[1] Tiffany's fascination with these rich colours would later manifest in many of his designs.

Upon his return to the USA, Tiffany's reputation as a skilled painter led to his election as the youngest member of New York's prestigious Century Club in 1870.[2] Tiffany travelled abroad again in late 1870, painting in the Mediterranean and northern Africa.[3] These travels exposed him to new textures and motifs that inspired both his work as a painter and designer. Tiffany never completely abandoned the canvas and continued painting nature, family and travels until the end of his career. His brilliance with colour and the ease with which he employed it across his later designs is most likely the result of his time spent applying pigment to canvas.

Fig. 1
Louis Comfort Tiffany
*Favrile bowl, c.*1900
Manufactured by Stourbridge Glass Co.,
Corona, Long Island, New York for
Tiffany Glass and Decorating Co.
Blown iridescent glass with trailed
decoration
11 × 14 cm
V&A: 1698-1900

In 1872 he married Mary Woodbridge Goddard, with whom he would have four children.[4] As the decade progressed, Tiffany became increasingly interested in the applied arts and focused particularly on stained glass. He had first become interested in the decorative arts through Edward C. Moore, the Chief Designer of silver for Tiffany & Co., who was an avid collector of Middle Eastern and Asian decorative arts. Tiffany disliked American stained glass, feeling that the prevailing technique of painting directly onto the glass obscured the natural light, resulting in dull, lifeless scenes. Tiffany admired the deeply saturated tones and imperfections found in utilitarian glass, which he sought to replicate in stained glass by infusing it with colour rather than painting its surface. Self-taught, his early glass experiments took place at his Manhattan studio and at Thill's glasshouse in Brooklyn, New York.[5] In 1878 Tiffany built his own glasshouse and trademarked his company, Louis C. Tiffany & Co. Two disastrous fires forced him to work at Louis Heidt and Company Glasshouse from 1880 until 1883 where he experimented with new ways of treating and manipulating glass to achieve new textures and effects.[6] Tiffany's chief competitor, John La Farge, also worked out of Heidt Glasshouse during this time.

While experimenting with stained glass, Tiffany explored opportunities in interior design. As a designer, Tiffany was inspired by European

Fig. 2
Louis Comfort Tiffany
Favrile vase, 1902
Manufactured by Stourbridge Glass Co.,
Corona, Long Island, New York for
Tiffany Glass and Decorating Co.
Blown iridescent glass with indented sides
7 cm × 5 cm
V&A: 1456-1902

Fig. 3
Louis Comfort Tiffany
Favrile floriform vase, *c.*1895
Manufactured by Stourbridge Glass Co.,
Corona, Long Island, New York for
Tiffany Glass and Decorating Co.
Blown iridescent glass
32 × 15 cm
V&A: C.58.1972

artistic movements and the rise of Aestheticism in the United Kingdom. In 1879, together with Samuel Colman, Candace Wheeler and Lockwood de Forest, Tiffany established Louis C. Tiffany, the Associated Artists, a firm that crafted lavish interiors for wealthy patrons.[7] The Associated Artists dissolved in 1883 but Tiffany continued to experiment with glass, eventually incorporating his business as Tiffany Glass Company in 1885.

Tiffany's first wife, Mary, died in 1884 and he married Louise Wakeman Knox in 1886, with whom he would have four more children. The work of Émile Gallé (p. 222) at the Paris International Exhibition in 1889 as well as exposure to the burgeoning Art Nouveau movement left a lasting impression on Tiffany and the development of his unique style. These motifs, characterized by graceful trailing and fluid shapes, are seen in the ornamental glass Tiffany produced in the late nineteenth and early twentieth centuries. Ornate designs were made by blowing and manipulating glass into the desired shape before threads of molten glass were trailed across the surface in a considered pattern. The surface decoration was often applied before the object's final form was realized, creating a symbiotic relationship between the decoration and the vessel itself (fig. 1).[8] In the 1890s Tiffany established the Corona Glass works on Long Island, which was supervised by Arthur J. Nash, a glassmaker from Stourbridge, England. The establishment of a dedicated glassworks allowed Tiffany to continue experimenting with stained glass. It also coincided with the 1893 World's Columbian Exposition in Chicago, in which Tiffany's Byzantian Chapel was lauded for its jewel-like interior, anchored by an ornate peacock reredos mosaic made of iridescent glass. The overwhelmingly positive reception of the chapel launched Tiffany's career into an international sphere.

One of Tiffany's greatest achievements during this period was his development of favrile glass in 1893, soon to become a signature product. It was inspired by the iridescence Roman glass developed after centuries in the ground and is characterized by radiant lustre effects on its surface, achieved by applying metallic salts to glass while still hot. An 1896 sales catalogue from Tiffany Glass & Decorating Co. described the development of favrile glass as the result of Tiffany's careful study of the natural decay of glass. Many of Tiffany's designs in favrile glass emulated the shapes of ancient Roman vessels and were blown in organic shapes, which were expertly manipulated to achieve practical yet beautiful objects (fig. 2). Favrile glass was used across his designs for domestic goods and emphasized the ethereal beauty found in the decay of man-made objects in the natural world.

In addition to his travels, Tiffany's chief inspiration for his designs came from nature. His youngest daughter, Dorothy, wrote affectionately of her father, 'To watch the flowers grow from bud to full bloom was his greatest pleasure.'[9] The popular flower-form vessels produced by Tiffany echo this observation of life with the slender stem supporting elegant budding petals made of iridescent favrile glass to form the bowl (fig. 3). This reverence for nature is seen throughout Tiffany's work, not only in the ornamental glass he produced but also in his lamps and stained glass windows. Much of Tiffany's determination to develop new techniques in stained glass were predicated on his appreciation for the natural world. His work aimed to enhance what he saw as the natural qualities of light by imbuing it with colour. After years of experimentation and with the help of technical experts such as Nash, Tiffany perfected the art of stained glass. Landscape and figural scenes were achieved by manipulating the glass, twisting and folding it to approximate movement and texture. Subtle gradations in tone to illustrate shadow and perspective could be achieved by infusing the glass with colour and texture, allowing Tiffany to effectively 'paint' in glass (fig. 4). These techniques revolutionized stained glass production and became known as 'American' glass around the world.

As his success and American industrialization soared in the 1890s, Tiffany set out to fill homes with domestic goods of the highest artistic merit. Tiffany's lamps are one of his most recognizable creations and merged his expertise in bronze and lead-fused glass. He received his first patent for a leaded glass shade in 1899 for the *Nautilus* lamp.[10] Like stained glass windows, lamps were made using templates to cut the pieces of glass before joining them together. Tiffany also pioneered the copper-foil technique, which is executed by wrapping thin sheets of copper around the edges of the glass before soldering them together, allowing for three-dimensional creations. As production increased, Tiffany engaged more artists to work at his company, including Clara Driscoll. Driscoll was one of the most talented artists Tiffany employed and is responsible for creating the recognizable *Dragonfly* motif (fig. 5). In the late 1890s Tiffany introduced a bronze foundry at his Corona site, which allowed him to produce lamp bases and other decorative objects in metal. The company also introduced pottery and enamel departments and the business continued to create new objects for the home.

At the turn of the century, Tiffany continued exhibiting his work in the United States and Europe. Admired during his lifetime, examples of his work were acquired by several European institutions, including the Victoria and Albert Museum, while his business was still in operation. In 1902 Tiffany's father died and left him a considerable inheritance, as well as the directorship of the family business. In the same year, the Stourbridge Glass Company was renamed Tiffany Furnaces and continued to produce blown and stained glass.

Fig. 4
Louis Comfort Tiffany, probably designed by Agnes Northrop for Tiffany Studios
Stained glass window depicting a landscape view, from Rochroane Castle, Irvington-on-Hudson, New York, 1905
Manufactured by Tiffany Furnaces, Corona, Long Island, New York
Leaded glass window with wooden framing
346.2 × 330.1 × 21.2 cm
Corning Glass Museum: 76.4.22

Tiffany saw great success and recognition in the first two decades of the twentieth century. Between 1902 and 1905 he designed and built his private summer estate, Laurelton Hall in Oyster Bay, New York. During its construction, Tiffany's second wife, Louise, died from cancer, leaving him with eight children. During this period he was also awarded major commissions such as the mosaic curtain in Mexico City's National Theatre, as well as numerous merit-based awards from American institutions.

In 1919 Tiffany retired from his company. Tiffany Studios and Furnaces suffered after his retirement, the latter renaming themselves after Nash's son, A. Douglas Nash, in 1924. As twentieth-century tastes changed, Tiffany's designs became unfashionable and Tiffany Studios filed for bankruptcy in 1932. In the following year Tiffany died of pneumonia, leaving behind a formidable legacy of inventiveness and perseverance. Much of Tiffany's legacy is tied to his entrepreneurial nature, which understood the importance of introducing beautiful objects into everyday life. However, it was his technological developments and artistic genius that allowed him to 'paint' in glass. His contributions to the fine and applied arts have an enduring appeal, which echoed the industrious attitude embraced by a rapidly expanding nation.

Ashley Weaver-Paul

Fig. 5
Clara Pierce Wolcott Driscoll, under the artistic supervision of Louis Comfort Tiffany
Dragonflies and Water Flowers reading lamp, 1899
Manufactured by Stourbridge Glass Co., Corona, Long Island, New York
Leaded glass lamp with blown glass and cast bronze base
46.6 × 41.3 cm
Corning Glass Museum: 2013.4.4

OTHER SIGNIFICANT MAKERS

Philippe-Joseph Brocard (1831–1896) was a French glass artist active in the late nineteenth and early twentieth centuries. He became interested in Middle Eastern and Islamic designs after seeing examples in the Musée de Cluny in Paris. Brocard emulated Islamic designs and revived the art of enamelled glass in the Islamic style.

John LaFarge (1835–1910) was an American stained glass designer and a direct competitor to L.C. Tiffany. Like Tiffany, LaFarge was inspired by medieval stained glass. Both LaFarge and Tiffany patented unique versions of opalescent glass. LaFarge's innovative stained glass won him various major commissions such as Trinity Church, Boston, in 1878.

Christopher Whall (1849–1924) was a leading British stained glass artist who is recognized for his significant contributions to the Arts and Crafts movement. Whall studied John Ruskin's writings, which inspired his conversion to Catholicism. A skilled artist and frustrated with designing windows that were made by other people, he learned how to make stained glass himself.

Clara Driscoll (1861–1944) was a designer and head of the Women's Glass Cutting Department at Tiffany Studios. She worked on and off for Tiffany Studios from 1888, as married women were not allowed to work for the company. Driscoll is responsible for designing some of Tiffany's most recognized lamps, including the *Wisteria* and *Dragonfly* patterns.

Max Ritter von Spaun (active 1879–1908) was the director of Bohemian glass manufactory Johann Loetz Witwe and grandson of the factory's namesake. Von Spaun was inspired by Tiffany's favrile glass. The Loetz company developed the iridescent Phänomen glass, which featured wavy, swirled patterns, winning the company a Grand Prix in 1900.

PHOEBE ANNA TRAQUAIR

(1852–1936)

Prolific proponent of Arts and Crafts in Scotland

Phoebe Anna Traquair was an Irish-born and educated Arts and Crafts maker who spent her adult life living and working in Edinburgh. She typically worked across several media at a time and is known for her work in enamel, embroidery, mural paintings and illuminated manuscripts. Traquair was a successful artist and celebrated figure of Scottish culture, but by the time of her death in 1936 her work had fallen out of fashion and disappeared from public view. However, thanks to large donations by Margaret Bartholomew to the Victoria and Albert Museum in the 1960s and '70s, the restoration of her murals by the Mansfield Traquair Trust, a significant exhibition of her work at the National Galleries of Scotland in 1993 and the permanent display of her work at the V&A, NGS and National Museums Scotland, today she is regarded as a highly significant maker of the Arts and Crafts period.[1]

Annie, as she was known by her family, was born in Kilternan in County Dublin on 24 May 1852, the sixth child of physician Dr William Moss and Teresa Richardson. Her father died of rheumatic fever when Traquair was eight years old and her mother brought up their seven children alone. She prioritized a good education and attending church, and together they visited many museums and churches as well as Trinity College Library. Upon finishing school in the late 1860s Traquair undertook the nationwide Department of Science and Art training with the Royal Dublin Society, which included classes in figure drawing, drawing from nature and painting in watercolours. This led to an introduction to the Scottish palaeontologist Dr Ramsay Heatley Traquair, Professor of Zoology at the Royal College of Science in Dublin, who was seeking an illustrator for his research. The couple married on 5 June 1873 at St Philip's Church in Milltown, South Dublin, and in 1874 they moved to Edinburgh upon his appointment as Keeper of Natural History at the Museum of Science and Art (today National Museums Scotland).

In the 1870s Traquair was busy caring for her family and mainly undertook domestic embroidery (fig. 1) and watercolour painting. She enjoyed visiting the museum and engaging with the city's literary culture,

Fig. 1
Phoebe Anna Traquair
Table cover, 1879
Linen embroidered with worsted wool thread
81.3 × 81.3 cm
V&A: Circ.318-1965
Given by Mrs Margaret Bartholomew

becoming good friends with the likes of John Miller Gray, the first curator of the Scottish National Portrait Gallery. In 1885 a group of academics, artists and philanthropists formed the Edinburgh Social Union. Its purpose was to provide art, music and an environment that would transform the daily lives of the working classes in the city. Traquair was the first artist appointed to provide mural art and elected to paint the walls of a new chapel for the Royal Hospital for Sick Children. This was the first of a series of large-scale murals that Traquair undertook in which she drew on her love of literature and demonstrated her ability to convey great emotional depth with vivid use of colour. Later mural commissions included an epic series for the walls of the Catholic Apostolic Church (now the Mansfield Traquair Centre) and St Mary's Cathedral in Edinburgh (fig. 2).

Literature was a pervasive intellectual source for Traquair and in the early 1880s she began composing poetry. She sought advice on the art of illumination from the writer and critic John Ruskin and they corresponded frequently over several months. She borrowed manuscripts from Ruskin's library to study and copy, and sent Ruskin her own illuminated book, *The Dream* (fig. 3). In a letter, Ruskin described 'the beautiful leaves which I could not resolve to part with' and requested

Figs. 2a (*this page*), 2b (*opposite*)
Phoebe Anna Traquair
Murals for the Song School of St Mary's Episcopal Cathedral, Edinburgh, 1888–92
View of the interior looking east; and detail of the south wall showing *The Winds of God, Fire and Heat, Summer and Winter* with (in border) *The Creation of the Firmament, Dry Land and Light*
Oil and gold leaf on plaster

to borrow it for a second time.[2] *The Dream* is a tale inspired by a visit to Dryburgh Abbey in the Scottish Borders in August 1886 and her reading of William Blake's poetry. It consists of eight handwritten and illuminated pages, bound in hand-embossed Moroccan leather, and is set with two silver clasps to her design. Bookbinding and illumination took up much of her time in the 1890s and she made illuminations of some of her favourite poems by the likes of Elizabeth Barrett Browning, Christina Rossetti and William Morris.

From 1890 she was active full-time as an artist from Dean Studio in Belford Road, Edinburgh, working on murals or manuscripts during the day and on her embroideries in the evening. Two embroidered tablecloths, a tea cosy and a painted fan from this period are in the V&A collection.[3] Between 1895 and 1902 Traquair completed *The Progress of a Soul*, a major series of four large embroidered panels loosely based on 'Denys L'Auxerrois' from *Imaginary Portraits* by the English critic and writer Walter Pater. The panels explore a theme she regularly returned to – the soul's journey from birth through life to salvation or redemption – and are now in the National Galleries of Scotland collection. She continued to develop her illuminations in the 1890s and looked to fourteenth- and fifteenth-century French and Italian manuscripts in the collection of the Museum of Science and Art for inspiration. James Caw,

Fig. 3
Phoebe Anna Traquair
The Dream, manuscript written and
illuminated by the artist, 1886
Paper, Moroccan leather binding and
silver clasps (probably made by J.M. Talbot)
12.3 × 10.9 cm
V&A: MSL/1936/1765
Phoebe Anna Traquair Bequest

Director of the National Gallery of Scotland, interviewed her at length in 1900 for the *Art Journal*. He wrote that her treatment of the 'abstract nature of the ideas, combined with the dignity or the rich sonorous rhythm and harmony of the verbal music, suggests colour schemes full and deep and rich as the rainbow'.[4] In the 1890s Traquair frequently exhibited her embroideries and illuminations, including at the Royal Scottish Academy, the Arts and Crafts Exhibition Society in 1899 and the 1900 Paris International Exhibition.

In 1899 Traquair travelled to Castle Craig Estate in Perthshire to study manuscripts in the collection of Sir Thomas and Mary Carmichael. While there, she saw the couple's enamel collection, which had inspired Mary to study the craft with Alexander Fisher, the leading enameller of the period. Enamel is crushed glass that has been fused onto a surface after repeated firings at temperatures of around 800°C. In letters to friends, Traquair wrote of happy mornings spent in Mary's small enamelling workshop developing her skill in painted enamel. She wrote of 'the pleasure I get pottering amongst ground glass, mortars, acids etc.', and went on to produce over 300 pieces of enamelwork over the next 20 years.[5]

Many of Traquair's enamels are set as jewellery and she also mounted her enamels in boxes, caskets and triptychs. She made detailed preparatory sketches for her enamels and a sketch in the V&A collection shows how she worked out her compositions by repeatedly drawing and adjusting small elements of the scene (fig. 4). The four completed designs for the two pendants of *Morning* and *Night* are finished in vivid watercolour and include drawings and instructions for the setting of the enamels. Notes such as 'This durable enamel pendant use 4 struts on each side. 8 in all' demonstrate her understanding and oversight of the mounting of her jewellery. John Maitland Talbot was an Edinburgh goldsmith with whom Traquair frequently worked to produce the silver book clasps for her manuscripts and to set her enamels. She also worked with her son Ramsay, an architect, who designed some of the enamel frames.[6]

Traquair preferred to paint with enamel and, as in *The Love Cup* pendant (fig. 5), she often used gold to edge or pick out details and metal foil beneath the enamel to increase the luminosity of the colours. The pendant depicts an angel holding the chalice of the Holy Grail painted with a red cross and surrounded by four women reminiscent of the paintings of Dante Gabriel Rossetti. The brilliant colour is typical of Traquair's enamelwork. Her enamels often represented narrative subjects and she embraced tales from classical literature, epic romances and the New Testament. A popular subject was the story of Cupid and Psyche by the second-century Roman prose writer Lucius Apuleius. She worked this narrative repeatedly, for example in a necklace of enamelled plaques that was given as a wedding present to her granddaughter. The central plaque is titled *Eros Atlas* and shows a kneeling Cupid with widespread wings holding up a green globe on a vivid blue background.[7] The careful application of layers of colour required similar skills to those she used for illumination; however, enamel quickly became her preferred small-scale craft due to the richer colours that she felt could be achieved.

Fig. 4
Phoebe Anna Traquair
Designs for *Morning* and *Night*, for the front and back views of two double enamelled pendants, *c*.1900–10
Paper, pencil and watercolour
17.8 × 25.4 cm
V&A: E.4889-1968
Given by Mrs Margaret Bartholomew

In 1906 the couple purchased a new house in the village of Colinton, south-west of Edinburgh. Traquair continued to use her enamelling kiln in the Dean Studio until she had her own kiln installed in the garden in 1917. In later life she prioritized making enamels but continued to design and work embroideries in the early morning or late evening. She received further public and private commissions and travelled widely to destinations including India, Egypt and Europe. She died in Edinburgh at the age of 84.

Traquair was a significant artist of the Arts and Crafts period and was one of the first women artists in Scotland to achieve professional recognition. Like many of her peers she worked across materials but her work on epic murals made her output unique among her contemporaries. Throughout her career she successfully blurred the boundaries between the fine and decorative arts and sought to unite art and life through her translation of great emotion and spiritual values into vibrant pictorial form.

Rebecca Knott

Fig. 5
Phoebe Anna Traquair
The Love Cup pendant, 1907
Painted enamel set in gold
8 × 5.4 × 0.7 cm
V&A: M.194-1976
Given by Mrs Margaret Bartholomew

OTHER SIGNIFICANT MAKERS

Mrs Philip (Charlotte) Newman (b.1836) worked between 1870 and 1910 and was a pupil of and assistant to the jeweller John Brogden. She made jewellery in the classical and Renaissance revival styles and after Brogden's death took over his studio and set up her own workshop.

Alexander Fisher (1864–1936) was a leading enameller and an influential teacher. He trained as a silversmith and first learned enamelling at the South Kensington Schools from 1881 to 1884. He specialized in painted enamel and became Head of Enamelling at the newly founded Central School of Arts and Crafts in 1896.

Henry Wilson (1864–1934) trained as an architect and was a distinguished sculptor, Arts and Crafts jeweller and goldsmith. His jewellery is known for innovative use of stone and enamel, rich colour combinations and sculptural qualities. He taught at the Royal College of Art and in 1903 published the practical manual *Silverwork and Jewellery*.

Jane Short (b.1954) specializes in creating enamelled silverware and uses the techniques of *champlevé* and *basse-taille*. Her often vividly coloured works are painterly, evocative explorations in enamel. She collaborates with other makers to interpret their designs in enamel and received an MBE for services to the Craft of Enamelling in 2016.

Helen Carnac (b.1968) specializes in working with enamel and metal. Her practice explores the connections between material, process and maker and responds to the changing post-industrial landscape. She enjoys developing new methods of working with enamel and metal to create innovative experimental surfaces.

MAY MORRIS

1862–1938

Multi-disciplinary designer-maker and art embroidery pioneer

May Morris was a leading Arts and Crafts embroiderer who designed, made and supervised the production of scores of embroideries for Morris & Co. and created her own exquisite pieces as an independent designer-maker. She was a key figure in the movement's lively international exhibitions scene and the Women's Guild of Arts, and had a great influence on the next generation of British textile artists through her teaching and writing. Morris also excelled in areas from wallpaper design to metalwork, designing and making numerous accomplished jewellery items.

Morris was born in England in 1862 to William and Jane Morris. Her father had just co-founded Morris, Marshall, Faulkner & Co., a decorative arts firm inspired by historical styles and a respect for the handmade. William (p. 198) was a talented designer working across disciplines and a luminary of the Arts and Crafts movement. Jane executed medieval-style embroideries for the firm alongside other women, including her sister Bessie Burden – works that signalled a rejection of the literal and vividly colourful embroidery then in fashion. May and her sister Jenny's education at Notting Hill High School was supplemented by the rich artistic education available at home. Their first home – Red House, in what was then part of Kent – must have buzzed with creative energy while being decorated with historically influenced furnishings made within the family's artistic circle, activity that led to the founding of Morris, Marshall, Faulkner & Co. In 1865 the Morrises moved to London where the flourishing business was based and by 1871 they were spending summers at Kelmscott Manor in Oxfordshire. Morris passed much of her time there outside, learning from nature, an important source of inspiration for her design work and the wider Arts and Crafts movement. She later reminisced about getting distracted from lessons in Kelmscott by blackbirds 'chuckling and feasting among the gooseberries'.[1]

Around 1880 Morris studied textile arts at the National Art Training School (later renamed the Royal College of Art). She focused partly on medieval English embroidery, with the Syon Cope at the nearby South

Fig. 1
Frederick Hollyer
Miss May Morris, 22 March 1886
Platinum print
14.5 × 10 cm
V&A: 7821-1938
Given by Eleanor M. Hollyer

Kensington Museum (now the V&A) becoming a particular favourite.[2] It would feature on the frontispiece of her *Decorative Needlework* (1893), an embroidery manual and manifesto which admires 'the most inconceivable minuteness' of this cope's stitches.[3]

These experiences laid the foundations for Morris's career as a successful Arts and Crafts designer and practitioner specializing in embroidery. In 1885, aged 23, she began managing Morris & Co.'s embroidery department (fig. 1).[4] In this role she employed artisans and apprentices and oversaw projects. The Day Book she used between 1892 and 1896 reveals the range of work that the embroiderers were carrying out for sale at the Morris & Co. shop or on commission.[5] Pieces ranged in size and purpose and were executed on ground fabric selected through Morris & Co. or provided by the customer. Clients could also purchase embroidery kits: textiles marked out with a design and sold with threads for customers to complete at home. These kits made Arts and Crafts decoration more affordable and could be ordered 'started' if clients wanted to follow pre-made stitches. In addition to overseeing the department's work, Morris also embroidered works to be sold or exhibited by the company as well as creating new Morris & Co. embroidery designs such as *Rose Bush*, which was popular as a cushion kit (fig. 2). Prior to her involvement, William had led on design for the department.

Fig. 2
May Morris
Rose Bush embroidery kit (started), designed *c.*1890, sold probably *c.*1900
Cotton with ink and silk embroidery in stem and darning stitch
62.6 × 66 cm
V&A: Circ.301-1960
Given by Miss Vere Roberts

Fig. 3

May Morris, embroidered by
Theodosia Middlemore
Fruit Garden door curtain or hanging,
designed *c.*1888, embroidered 1894
Silk with silk embroidery in darning,
stem, herringbone, buttonhole and pistil
stitch and laid work
275 × 175.5 cm
V&A: Circ.206&A-1965

Like her father, Morris loved historical stitches and as a designer celebrated natural forms while avoiding attempts to realistically represent three-dimensionality and perspective. However, she also developed her own design and making style. Many distinctive features come together in the *Fruit Garden* door curtains or hangings she designed for Morris & Co. (fig. 3). The design exemplifies her remarkable ability to capture movement and her inclusion of text in traditional script, also a facet of some of William's designs. Fruit trees, acanthus leaves and other plants appear to be swaying with the wind below poetic excerpts which vary across known examples of this embroidery. Whereas William is associated with densely stitched embroideries, these examples balance

needlework with unworked ground, a characteristic feature of May's work. The *Fruit Garden* embroidery in the V&A collection showcases a pale blue silk ground textile. Arts and Crafts may typically be associated with darker in-between shades, but Morris favoured clear, light colours. She was especially drawn to blue, which she praised highly in her book *Decorative Needlework*, and was able to capture a great luminosity through material and technique as well as her choice of colour. Her designs were usually executed using silk embroidery threads, whether by herself or others, and the completed works often include shiny satin stitches, used for some although not all *Fruit Garden* pieces. One contemporary wrote of Morris's 'great curtains covered with glowing fruit forests'.[6]

In 1896 her father died and Morris stepped back from the family firm. No longer so concerned about 'house style', her own design style evolved. She experimented with newly elongated birds and embroideries with polychrome botanical motifs and creatures against plain cream grounds, compositions inspired by pieces from around the Elizabethan era. When Morris returned to one of her father's Morris & Co. designs for a showpiece exhibited in Paris at the Exhibition of Decorative Arts of Great Britain and Ireland in 1914 – *Acanthus*, which references traditional Iranian carpets – she offered a striking reinterpretation by leaving much

Fig. 4
William Morris, embroidered by
May Morris and others
Detail of *Acanthus* bedcover or hanging,
designed *c*.1880, embroidered probably
c.1900–10
Woollen felt with silk embroidery in darning,
long and short, stem, satin and buttonhole
stitch and couching and laid work
248.8 × 200.6 cm
V&A: T.66-1939
Bequeathed by May Morris

of the blue ground fabric unworked (fig. 4). She also had more time for private commissions and teaching, and worked for London's Central School of Arts and Crafts from 1897 until 1910, alongside the embroiderer Ellen Wright whom she had taught at Morris & Co.

Between 1909 and 1910 Morris undertook a North American lecture tour on embroidery and jewellery, and a connected exhibition in New York featured her work across both disciplines. Morris recalled being enchanted by her mother's jewellery box as a child – her 'reverent adoring fingers' doing 'no damage among [its] treasures' – but she does not appear to have started working in this medium until the late 1890s.[7] She may have been inspired by her friends, the jewellers Georgie and Arthur Joseph Gaskin. It must have felt like an exciting new departure, as jewellery was not available through Morris & Co. The girdle Morris exhibited in London in 1906 through the Arts and Crafts Exhibition Society was published in *The Studio* magazine that same year (fig. 5). It demonstrates typical attributes of her jewellery in the Arts and Crafts style but also references her mother's accessories, some of which Morris later bequeathed to the V&A. Jane owned an antique girdle,[8] a form revived by Arts and Crafts jewellers, and, like similar jewellery pieces of the period, Morris's example incorporates domed stones, floral motifs and hearts.

Yet Morris never stopped stitching and her love of textiles was apparent across her work. It can be traced everywhere, from a ring she made with curling acanthus-style leaves,[9] which recalls her father's and her own designs for fabric, to imagery used in one of her introductions to *The Collected Works of William Morris* (1910–15): 'I ... marvelled to see how a thread dropped ... was unconsciously and easily picked up again ... and woven firmly into the fabric.'[10]

While Morris greatly esteemed her father's career, she must have been aware of how impressive hers was too. Her work was sought after and displayed internationally and she was invited to join the Executive Committee of the Arts and Crafts Exhibition Society in 1910. But her successes could also be overlooked in connection with gender prejudice. In 1893 she made sure to correct a newspaper which had named William as the designer of one of her sets of bed hangings. In a letter later written to the V&A, whose correspondence with Morris focused on her father's work, May appears to be reminding the Museum of her own importance to the decorative arts scene. She explained that she 'must have forgotten' to follow through with planned arrangements relating to woven hangings designed by her father while busy 'giving orders about the sending home of my Paris exhibits', a reference to the major 1914 exhibition which had featured many of her creations.[11] After she died in 1938, M.F. Vivian Lobb,

with whom the designer-maker lived during her last decades, went further still in terms of asserting Morris's talent, telling the V&A:

> William Morris could design embroideries, but he could not embroider, any way not as well as Miss Morris could, Mrs Morris could embroider but couldnt [sic] design, Miss Morris could & did both design as well as William Morris & embroider as well any one possibly could & her colour arrangements were unapproachable.[12]

Morris also paved the way for twentieth-century women embroidery designers, many of whom she influenced through her tuition, writing and artisanship. With the London-based Women's Guild of Arts – founded in 1907 in response to women's exclusion from the Art Workers' Guild – Morris and her allies established a crucial professional network for women working across disciplines, and she remained involved into the 1930s. In later life she helped girls and women locally in Kelmscott where she was based – for example, supporting the Kelmscott branch of the Women's Institute – as well as nationally and internationally. After long neglect, this influence, and Morris's other achievements, have recently been gaining considerable recognition.

Claire Allen-Johnstone

Fig. 5
May Morris
Girdle, *c.*1906
Silver with williamsite, garnets and pearls
71.1 cm (length when open)
V&A: M.17-1939
Given by M.F. Vivian Lobb

OTHER SIGNIFICANT MAKERS

Mary J. Newill (1860–1947) was part of the Women's Guild of Arts. She and Morris both taught embroidery at the Birmingham Municipal School of Art, collaborating on exhibition pieces with input from students, and Newill was also an illustrator. Her solo embroidery designs often depicted medieval scenes and have a fairytale quality.

Georgie Gaskin (1866–1934) was one of Morris's close friends and a member of the Women's Guild of Arts. Based in Birmingham, she and her husband Arthur Joseph Gaskin had successful careers as jewellers. Gaskin drew inspiration from nature and world cultures, and typically worked with silver and gemstones.

Grace Christie (1872–1953), a member of the Women's Guild of Arts, was a leading embroidery designer, practitioner, educator and writer. Her intricate depictions of plants and animals on cream grounds recall Morris's later works.

Ann Macbeth (1875–1948) helped to take the Arts and Crafts movement in a new direction in early twentieth-century Scotland. Her embroideries exemplify key features of the Glasgow Style, including the juxtaposition of curved and straight lines. A dedicated feminist, Macbeth designed women's suffrage banners which were stitched by her students.

Beryl Dean (1911–2001) advocated for embroidery in Britain in the mid-twentieth century and worked with the Needlework Development Scheme to reignite interest in the art between 1934 and 1961. She was best known for her strikingly modern yet traditionally handmade ecclesiastical pieces incorporating goldwork.

CHARLES ROBERT ASHBEE

1863-1942

Silversmith and design reformer

Charles Robert Ashbee was an English Arts and Crafts designer and founder of the Guild and School of Handicraft. Through the Guild, Ashbee merged a socialist ethos with the structure of a medieval craft guild, creating an all-encompassing lifestyle for workers that nurtured their creativity. Ashbee is known for his striking, modern designs, particularly in silverwork, that brought a pared-back aesthetic to Arts and Crafts wares.

Ashbee was born into a prosperous family in west London. His mother Elizabeth was the daughter of a Hamburg merchant and his father Henry was a senior partner in his wife's family firm. Ashbee attended school at Wellington College and studied history at Cambridge University. As an undergraduate he was exposed to new ideas and people, including Edward Carpenter, the poet and early gay rights campaigner. Carpenter was one of the founders of the Fellowship of the New Life, which promoted simplified living. Carpenter's socialism was to have a lasting impact on Ashbee.

After university Ashbee commenced training with the architectural firm Bodley and Garner. Around this time, he began living in Toynbee Hall, Whitechapel, a settlement founded by Reverend Samuel Augustus Barnett where residents ran community evening classes. Philanthropic enterprises like this were motivated by the poor living and working conditions of London's East End. Ashbee led a Ruskin reading class, exploring the work of the writer and critic John Ruskin. The reading class grew to 30 men and boys who also studied 'painting, modelling, plaster-casting, gilding and the study of heraldic forms'.[1] Under Ashbee's supervision, students created a galleon panel for the dining room at Toynbee in 1887. The ship symbol went on to become the motif for the Guild of Handicraft (a visual pun for the 'craft of the guild').

In the 1880s several craft guilds were founded, including the Century Guild and the Art Workers' Guild. These emerged in the wake of William Morris (p. 198) and John Ruskin and aimed to revive pre-industrial craft traditions, but Morris was doubtful of Ashbee's guild idea when they met

Fig. 1
C.R. Ashbee
Decanter, 1904–5
Manufactured by the Guild of Handicraft;
glass bottle made by James Powell & Sons
Silver, glass and chrysoprase
23.5 × 13 cm
V&A: M.121:1, 2-1966

in 1887. Morris believed only political action could challenge industrial capitalism and the formation of a guild under Ashbee would do little to generate real change. Ashbee was undeterred and in 1888, aged 25, he formed the Guild and School of Handicraft. Initially, it had premises close to Toynbee Hall but in 1891 it moved to Essex House in Mile End Road.

Collaboration and comradeship were the central tenets of the Guild and School. Ashbee wrote it would be for the 'advance of English Art and Handicraft; that it shall be developed not on the basis of mastership, in the ordinary sense, but co-operatively'.[2] He envisioned a symbiotic relationship between the Guild and School, with pupils of the School drafted into the Guild following their training, and teachers were craftsmen in the workshop. Ashbee was at first hesitant to hire workers with commercial experience, preferring them to develop free from the influence of the trades. Many guild workers had no prior training although some did, such as the skilled metalworker John Pearson.

On its first anniversary, the Guild had grown to eight guildsmen and 70 pupils, with classes in 'carpentry, modelling, carving, metalwork' alongside a design class.[3] The School closed in 1895 due to a lack of funding, but the Guild was able to continue. Initially, the output of the Guild was confined to metalworking, woodworking and decorative painting but after the move to Essex House the workshops expanded to incorporate enamelling, silverwork and jewellery. The Essex House Press was created in 1898 after Ashbee purchased the printing presses from William Morris's Kelmscott Press. For Ashbee the experience of his workers was central to the Guild, with supper clubs, an annual play and camping trips. In 1898, as the Guild became financially stable, it registered as a limited company and guildsmen were offered representation on the newly formed board. Workers could also gain financial interest in the Guild by investing a percentage of their wages.

Alongside the Guild, Ashbee pursued an architectural career. Following his parents' separation

Fig. 2
C.R. Ashbee
Elevation of Magpie and Stump House,
37 Cheyne Walk, 1895
Pen and ink and watercolour drawing
on vellum
82.5 × 26.9 cm
V&A: E.202-1965

in 1897, Ashbee designed a house and architectural studio in Chelsea for himself, his mother and two younger sisters on the site of an ancient pub, the Magpie and Stump, after which he named it (fig. 2). The interior showcased the Guild's wares, with beaten copper fire surrounds, enamel plaques and embossed leatherwork walls. During preparatory excavations, an Elizabethan bottle was unearthed and Ashbee likened it to bottles 'from which Falstaff and his worthies drank their sack'.[4] It inspired the design of a wine decanter which became one of the most popular of the Guild's wares (fig. 1). Throughout his career Ashbee designed a total of 23 houses and was involved in the restoration of several houses and churches. As his career progressed, his style evolved, taking on more austere forms. He was an advocate for architectural heritage and an early member on the National Trust Council. In 1894 he founded the London Survey Committee which listed buildings of historic interest.

In 1898 Ashbee married Janet Forbes, an accomplished pianist and writer. With the financial backing of Janet's father, Ashbee designed their house at 74 Cheyne Walk. Janet immersed herself in the Guild and composed the *Essex House Alphabet*, a poem dedicated to the Guild's craftsmen: 'A stands for Arthur the Cameron (19) bold, Our great Cockney Craftsmen in silver and gold.'[5] Ashbee was gay at a time when homosexuality was illegal. Following their proposal, Ashbee wrote to Janet, 'you are the first and only woman to whom I have felt I could offer the same loyal reverence of affection that I have heretofore given to my men friends.'[6] It is thought that Ashbee was a member of the Order of Chaeronea, a secret society founded by the writer and prison reformer George Ives, which advocated for homosexual liberation.

Ashbee is known for his silverwork designs and jewellery. He favoured plain planished surfaces and decorative elements such as semi-precious stones, enamelling and wirework. Ashbee looked to the past for inspiration, reworking influences in his own style. A steeple cup (fig. 3), made for the Master of the Painter-Stainers' Company, is indebted to the work of seventeenth-century English goldsmiths but has been updated with delicately embossed surfaces, cabochon turquoises and a wirework finial. As Ashbee's style evolved, his silverwork became more restrained, with simplified elements executed to the highest standard (fig. 4). Key features of his jewellery designs were naturalistic forms, the use of unusual stones and an equal focus on the metal settings and gemstones. From 1900 the Guild employed more jewellers with trade experience, bringing about a more exuberant style of jewellery, demonstrated in his design for a pendant in the form of galleon (fig. 5). Ashbee's vibrant enamel pendants were inspired by the fantastical jewels of the Renaissance. The sixteenth-century Italian goldsmith and sculptor

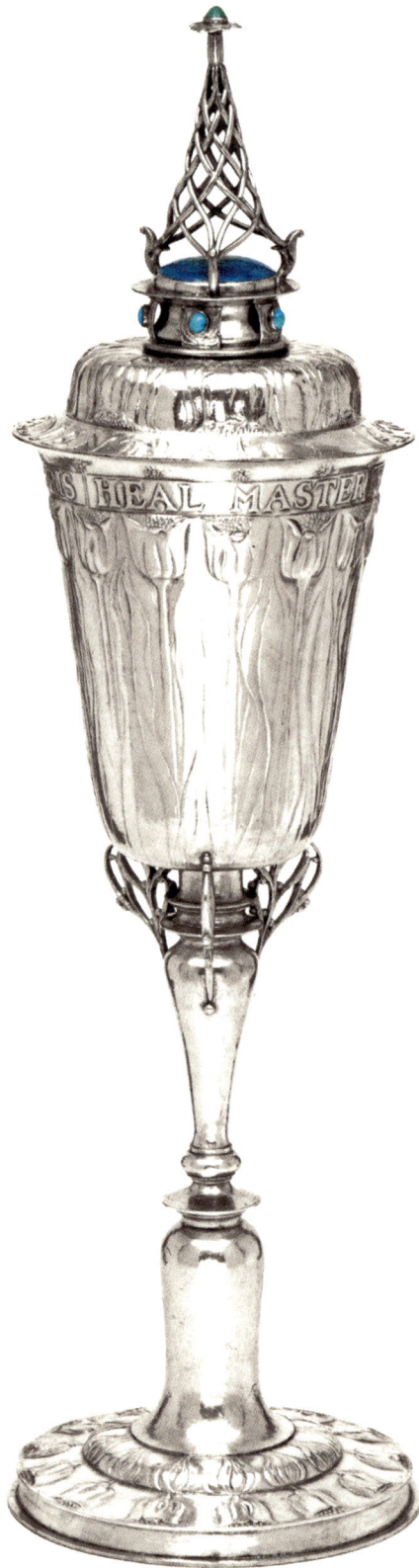

Benvenuto Cellini was a great influence and the inaugural publication of the Guild's Essex House Press was a translation of Cellini's *Treatises on Goldsmithing and Sculpture*.

In 1902 Ashbee took the bold decision to move the Guild to the Cotswolds town of Chipping Campden, moving 150 people including guildsmen and their families. The town had been an important centre for the medieval wool trade and a disused silk mill housed the Guild's workshops and empty cottages became workers' accommodation. Ashbee sought a simpler life for the workers surrounded by nature and in this respect can be seen as one of few Arts and Crafts designers who truly embodied the ideals of the movement. The move to the countryside took great courage but ultimately led to the collapse of the business. From 1905 the Guild was operating at a loss and by late 1907 it entered voluntary liquidation. The rural location isolated the Guild from London markets and alternative sources of work during quiet periods. Larger companies such as Liberty & Co. were competitors, producing cheaper Arts and Crafts-style goods with mechanized production.

The Guild was the last large-scale creative enterprise Ashbee undertook. In 1909 he published *Modern English Silverwork*, which showcased the silverwork designs for the Guild. In 1911 the Ashbees' first daughter was born, and they went on to have three more daughters between 1913 and 1917. During the First World War Ashbee undertook lecture tours in the United States and in 1917 taught English in Cairo. From 1918 to 1922 he took up a new post as civic adviser for the British military government in Jerusalem. After this he returned to England with his family and assumed a quieter pace of life in Godden Green, Kent, reading, writing and lecturing. He died in 1942.

Ashbee was a trailblazing designer who put into practice his ideas for social reform, creating a holistic experience for Guild workers. His ceaseless enthusiasm motivated him to move the Guild from London in search of a rural utopia. Although the endeavour was unsuccessful, Ashbee can be remembered for his remarkable design work that placed him at the forefront of the Arts and Crafts movement. The Guild's tenets of a community of workers lived on in Modernist design collectives such as the Wiener Werkstätte and the Bauhaus. Today, the growing crafts industry, and the desire to recover lost traditions of making, echo Ashbee's vision from 140 years ago.

Iona Farrell

Fig. 5
C.R. Ashbee
Pendant in the form of a galleon, *c.*1903
Manufactured by the Guild of Handicraft
Enamelled gold, silver, opal, diamond sparks and tourmalines
7 × 4.6 cm
V&A: M.4&A-1964
Bequeathed by Miss M.C. Annesley

OTHER SIGNIFICANT MAKERS

William Arthur Smith Benson (1854–1924) was a designer, known for his pared-back metalwork and furniture in the Arts and Crafts style. Benson was a founding member of the Art Workers' Guild as well as the Arts and Crafts Exhibition Society. He was encouraged by William Morris to pursue a career in design and following Morris's death became chairman of Morris & Co.

Arthur Stansfield Dixon (1856–1929) was a Birmingham-based architect and designer and founding member of the Birmingham Guild of Handicraft. The Guild was launched in 1890 and was strongly influenced by Ashbee's Guild and School of Handicraft in London. Dixon was the chief metalwork designer at the Birmingham Guild.

John Pearson (1859–1930) was a metalworker and ceramics artist, known for his *repoussé* metalwork. In the early years of C.R. Ashbee's Guild of Handicraft, he was the senior metalworker. In 1891 Pearson left the Guild and set up as a freelance designer. He later relocated to Cornwall and taught at the Newlyn Industrial Class.

Walter Gilbert (1871–1946) was a sculptor and designer who founded the Bromsgrove Guild of Craftsmen in 1898. The Guild was based in Worcestershire and received several important commissions, including the main gates for Buckingham Palace and the bronze doors for Freemasons' Hall in London.

Edward Spencer (1872–1938) was an artist and metalworker who became head designer at the Artificers' Guild in 1903, following the departure of founder Nelson Dawson. Spencer was influenced by medieval silversmithing and during his work at the Guild designed jewellery, church plate and domestic metalwork.

4

MODERNISM & THE POST-WAR CRAFT REVIVAL

Good craftwork can be exhilarating, tactile, reassuring, stunning, disconcerting – the whole gamut of feeling can be evoked. The response to a craft object can be physical, emotional or intellectual. The narrative, the useful and the purely formal all have a place in the crafts.[1]

A central theme of making in the twentieth century was what it meant to create handmade objects in the context of a fully industrialized society. The Arts and Crafts movement left a powerful legacy of ideas, objects and buildings that gave a public identity to making in the latter half of the nineteenth century and put in place an art education system that included an understanding of materials and techniques. Technological developments, social upheavals and the seismic political and economic crises of the first half of the twentieth century prompted significant changes in how people lived, worked and consumed. This modernity saw the term 'decorative arts' become a less useful description for objects outside the field of painting or sculpture while 'craft' and 'product' or 'industrial design' came to better express the character of making in this period. The tension between the hand and the machine remained an ever-present subject of debate throughout the twentieth century, with some makers embracing the machine age and hopes for improved standards of living by creating objects designed for multiple production. Others sought a continuation of the nineteenth-century craft revival and a modernity committed to handmaking that was often morally or ethically driven. Craft developed as a broad field of making that encompassed varied material disciplines, values and processes. An ongoing spirit of enquiry has resulted in ambitious and experimental approaches to making that continue to evolve today.

In the early decades of the twentieth century an elite international movement emerged in Europe and America, encompassing painting, architecture, literature, music and making. Modernism sought to create a radical break from the past in response to a world transformed by inventions including the automobile, aeroplane, radio broadcasting and the first moving assembly line introduced at Ford Motors in 1913. It set out to create a new alignment between the experiences and values of modern industrial life and the day-to-day reality of the home and city within modernity. More politically committed Modernists believed that excellent design should be available to everyone, with quality and mass production going hand in hand.

The roots of Modernism in making can be traced to the development of several organizations in central Europe. The architect Josef Hoffmann and artist Koloman Moser formed the Wiener Werkstätte (the Vienna Workshops) in 1902 with the goal of bringing art into the home through

well-designed domestic products. Their aim was to make the home a Gesamtkunstwerk (total work of art) and the workshops sought to create new simple, modern forms. Meanwhile, the state-sponsored Deutscher Werkbund (German Association of Craftsmen) was formed in Munich in 1907, its aim to improve the competitiveness of German products globally by creating partnerships between manufacturers, design professionals and craftsmen.[2]

Another critical development in the establishment of Modernism in design was the founding of the Bauhaus school in Weimar, Germany, in 1919 by Walter Gropius. The Bauhaus became one of the most influential design schools of the twentieth century and advocated for a harmony of formal and technical training and material mastery. Furniture such as the tubular steel *Club* chair (fig. 1), developed by architect and designer Marcel Breuer, demonstrates the Bauhaus approach to standardization, uniformity and the innovative application of industrial materials. The school fostered a cross-disciplinary approach aimed at breaking the divide between artist and craftsperson. Craft was seen as a vital tool for re-energizing design

Fig. 1
Marcel Breuer
Club chair, model 3B, designed 1925–6, manufactured 1927–8
Manufactured by Standard Möbel or Thonet Möbel
Tubular steel with red canvas
73 × 78 × 68 cm
V&A: W.2-2005
Supported by the Friends of the V&A

training through an understanding of materials and technique but not as an end in itself. The weaver Gunta Stölzl (p. 298) used her meticulous knowledge of woven structures, historic textiles and the properties of fibres to design innovative, practical textiles for modern interiors, successfully elevating the textile arts as a critical element of design to be employed in conjunction with modern architecture. The Bauhaus was closed by the Nazis in 1933 and many of its students and staff emigrated to England, North and South America and the Soviet Union, ensuring that the school's principles continued to exert enormous international influence on approaches to design and making. American designers were heavily influenced by European Modernism and its attempts to improve mass production through collaboration between designers and industry. The emerging design profession was driven by the need for cheaper, more efficient products that better suited modern life.

Meanwhile, a concurrent movement born out of modernity emerged in France, focusing on ornament rather than form. Art Deco emerged in the 1920s and developed into a major architectural and artistic style in western Europe and the United States during the 1930s.[3] After the horrors of the First World War, followed by a punitive series of peace treaties and an uncertain economic climate, wealthy consumers in flight from reality embraced luxury, valuing exotic materials and sumptuous surfaces. Art Deco borrowed key elements of Art Nouveau's visual language, such as naturalistic forms and geometric patterns, and adapted them to create an updated vision conveying the energy and excitement of the machine age. The 1925 state-sponsored International Exhibition of Modern Decorative and Industrial Arts in Paris was intended to promote France as a leader in the production of luxury goods and brought international attention to the style. Makers included the furniture designer Émile-Jacques Ruhlmann (fig. 2) and the jeweller and glass designer René Lalique (p. 276), both prominent figures of Art Deco, known for the exquisite detail and quality of their work.

As technology advanced and new materials were developed, designers also began looking for ways to bring Art Deco to the mass market. In America, designers strove to 'Americanize' Art Deco by adapting it to social habits, using cheaper materials for machine production and streamlining forms. The Wall Street stock market crash of 1929 saw the optimism of the twenties gradually decline and by the mid-1930s Art Deco was sidelined in favour of the streamlined aesthetic of Modernism.

The twentieth-century craft movement saw handmaking as the solution to the dehumanizing effects of industry, while other designers acknowledged the potential of industry for producing widely available, well-made objects. Though Modernism in design was largely accessible and rational, its ideology brought a uniformity and standardization of approach that was not as popular in Britain as it was elsewhere. In Britain, the legacy of Arts and Crafts lived on although the movement failed to re-establish itself as a modern entity.[4] An awareness of how the Werkbund had successfully taken the ideals of Arts and Crafts and adopted them for mass manufacture resulted in some disaffected designers establishing the Design and Industries Association in 1915, with the aim of raising the standards of industrial design in Britain. The Omega Workshops were another small-scale enterprise that offered a critique of the Arts and Crafts movement. Its founder Roger Fry, a painter, critic and member of the Bloomsbury Group cultural circle, set out to tackle what he saw as the false division between the fine and decorative arts by bringing artistry into interior design to satisfy 'the needs and express [...] the

Fig. 2
Émile-Jacques Ruhlmann
Dressing table, 1919–23
Oak carcase with veneers, inlaid with ivory and ebony, mahogany drawers and silvered bronze mirror frame and fittings
119 × 76 × 52.5 cm
V&A: W.14:1-6-1980

feelings of the modern cultivated man'.[5] The Workshops' output was eclectic, ranging from commercially made furniture, decorated with expressive, colourful paintwork, to painterly designs for textiles that demonstrated a flexible approach to the relationship between art, craft and design (fig. 3).

Attempts to reconcile bold design and industry in Britain in the early twentieth century had a limited impact.[6] What emerged in the inter-war period was an alternative, craft-focused 'eclectic modernism'.[7] It was spearheaded by makers who established fresh identities for their disciplines by focusing on the fundamental skills and values of handmaking, with touch, spontaneity and a freshness of material as core features of their work.[8] Important British figures included the potter Bernard Leach (fig. 4), the block-printers Phyllis Barron and Dorothy Larcher and the weaver, spinner and dyer Ethel Mairet. Leach's approach to making was greatly influenced by his experiences of Japan and acted as an ethical riposte to industry rooted in Arts and Crafts thinking that had considerable long-term impact. Studio pottery had emerged in the 1920s as a new art form that rejected the decorative eclecticism of Victorian artist-potters such as William De Morgan (p. 214) and established ceramics as a mode of formal abstraction. Hand-block and hand-woven textiles also embraced a Modernist aesthetic and the textile disciplines significantly altered the gender

balance of makers in this period. Barron and Larcher (fig. 5) first trained in fine art before turning to block printing and are credited with giving the medium a new vitality. British craft-based Modernism had, however, a limited social range, unable to answer the needs of a mass market.

The mid-century brought considerable social, political and economic changes, prompted by experiences of major global wars, the dismantling of empires, the emergence of the Atomic Age and the Civil Rights Movement in the United States. Although access to making and materials was severely limited in wartime, an influx of refugees arriving in the UK and America from Europe in the 1930s and '40s had an undoubtedly revitalizing effect. Important figures who emigrated to Britain included the Viennese potter Lucie Rie (p. 306) and the Bauhaus weaver Margarete Leischner. Other refugees from central Europe discovered handwork on their arrival, including the potters Ruth Duckworth (p. 314) and Hans Coper, the letter cutter and typographer Ralph Beyer and the jeweller Gerda Flöckinger. From 1930 to 1945 over one thousand architects and artists moved to the USA from central Europe, including Marcel Breuer and Walter Gropius, ceramicists Gertrud and Otto Natzler and Eva Zeisel, and the artist-educator Josef Albers and textile artistan and printmaker Anni Albers (fig. 6) who joined the faculty of the experimental Black Mountain College in North Carolina, bringing with them new perspectives on making and craft education.[9]

In the aftermath of war, a pressing need for inexpensive housing and furnishing created a boom in production while the introduction of commercial jet travel in 1957 and the increasing accessibility of photography brought greater cross-cultural references. Conventional approaches to domestic design were gradually abandoned and replaced by informal, adaptable solutions that made use of new materials and technologies developed during the war. Designers like Aino and Alvar Aalto (p. 292) combined their knowledge of the properties of natural materials with new technologies to create functional, modern designs for objects and buildings. In Britain the government saw the improvement of design for industry as critical to economic recovery and several major public design showcases were staged to assist in this.[10] Among the many gifted textile designers of the period in Britain, Althea McNish's (p. 328) vivid and energetic textile designs drew on her love of painting and her childhood experiences in Trinidad and Tobago, innovatively injecting much-needed colour into the industry with great commercial success. It was during this time that industrial and product design emerged as distinct disciplines and a growing public reverence for design and making assisted in creating environments receptive to post-war craft.

Fig. 4
Bernard Leach
Bottle, 1931
Stoneware, white glaze with painting in brown
34.3 × 14.2 cm
V&A: Circ.144-1931

Historically, craftspeople had been trained in apprenticeships or workshop systems whereas makers in the twentieth century pursued many forms of education, from formal academic programmes to self-instruction. The Cranbrook Academy of Art was founded in Michigan in 1925 and was the first educational institution in the USA to develop a comprehensive craft and design programme, contributing significantly to the development of American studio craft. The post-war period saw increased funding for arts and design education and new perspectives on craft education brought by émigrés prompted changes to existing models. Changes to formal education meant that many craft practitioners trained in the same academic systems as painters and sculptors and so began to draw inspiration from a much wider range of sources. This brought a heightened expressiveness to traditional hand skills and an embrace of new materials and techniques. Some makers applied their material knowledge as designers for industry whereas others chose to pursue handmaking in small workshop settings. A shift from the complex ideologies of the inter-war years meant that by the 1960s the decision to become a craftsperson was a rebellious but less 'odd' choice.[11]

Fig. 5
Phyllis Barron and Dorothy Larcher
Hanging, *c.*1935
Block-printed linen
314.6 cm (length), 85.8 cm (width)
V&A: T.297-1977
Given by Mrs M. Kostka

Fig. 6
Anni Albers
Hanging, designed 1926/7, woven 1966
Woven under the supervision of Gunta Stölzl
Triple-weave wall hanging of silk and rayon
207.6 cm (length), 121.4 cm (width)
V&A: Circ.534-1968

Fig. 7
John Piper
*Christ between Saint Peter and
Saint Paul*, 1955–60
Made by Patrick Reyntiens
Stained and painted glass
85.5 × 58.5 cm
V&A: C.77-1981

The craft practice that emerged post-war is experimental, self-reflexive and interdisciplinary, and typically involves independent makers setting up workshops dedicated to the disciplined manipulation of material to create objects with and without function. Some makers concern themselves with the principles of making whereas for others narrative or conceptual ideas take precedence, often reflecting on the global history of making. Regardless of their approach, makers of seemingly disparate craft practices are connected by links to strong traditions of making and established techniques. It is a way of thinking through practices of all kinds, 'an approach, an attitude, or a habit of action ... a way of doing things, not a classification of objects, institutions or people'.[12]

In the 1950s craft practice for some remained tied to function, with a focus on clean designs and a reverence for materials, while others explored new approaches to making and material. Lucie Rie's elegant, functional pots were rooted in a meticulous approach to making and demonstrate the influence of Modernism. The vessel has remained a crucial site of exploration in ceramics and other disciplines, both literally and metaphorically, with form and surface orchestrated in a great variety of ways. Public and private audiences for craft grew in the 1950s and '60s as the V&A's Circulation Department, the Renwick Gallery in Washington and the Museum of Arts and Design in New York actively supported contemporary making, increasing public awareness through displays and exhibitions. Opportunities to sell and exhibit works also increased with the establishment of independent outlets, specialist

galleries and membership organizations for craft. Major commissions, such as those for the interior of the new Coventry Cathedral in England, also created important platforms for craft in this period. The Baptistry window was designed by the painter John Piper and made by stained glass artist Patrick Reyntiens as 'creative translator', one of several projects by the pair (fig. 7).

Craftspeople in the 1960s built on a broader acceptance of modern craft and began to nurture the freedom to experiment. Some chose to infuse their work with humour and self-expression or sought to make works of social and political commentary, responding to events like the Vietnam War and the Civil Rights Movement. Others abandoned strict ideas about function and used materials in unconventional ways. In 1969, *Objects: USA* was a landmark exhibition in the development of American studio craft and travelled to 33 venues across the USA and Europe.[13] The exhibition demonstrated the potential of modern makers working across clay, glass, textiles, metal and wood. Though his early works, shown in the exhibition, were comparatively modest, the glass artist Dale Chihuly (p. 342) is known today for his monumental installations and sculptures, demonstrating his mastery of blown glass across scales and the evolution of his work throughout his career. Also featured in the exhibition were two early sculptures and a vessel by Peter Voulkos (p. 321), a pivotal figure in the post-war evolution of American ceramics. Voulkos and his contemporaries developed new forms of abstract expressionism in clay, repositioning ceramics as sculpture (fig. 8) and establishing highly charged environments for students to experiment freely.[14]

Studio craft continued to develop out of the experimental practice of the 1960s and, against a backdrop of a consumer boom and the burgeoning Information Age, makers increasingly drew connections from across the breadth of modern life and looked to global cultural references. The period was also one of great experimentation in form, material and technique. New thinking about the role of decorative form rather than function demonstrated the influence of Postmodernism and an anti-Modernist emphasis on surface decoration, historicism and the figurative. Makers such as the silversmith Michael Rowe (fig. 9), potter Elizabeth Fritsch and jeweller Wendy Ramshaw (fig. 10) created important works of conceptual enquiry with complex visual resonances that established new approaches to decoration.

Ceramics and furniture were particularly well suited to Postmodernism as makers juxtaposed two- and three-dimensional forms and combined materials, colours and stylistic references to create works with ambiguous functions that played wittily with histories of making. In her book *Seeing*

Fig. 9
Michael Rowe
Box, 1978
Silver and 9-carat gold
25.5 × 33 × 13 cm (max.)
V&A: M.13-2012
Purchase supported by the James
Yorke-Radleigh Bequest

Fig. 10
Wendy Ramshaw
Neckpiece for Picasso's
Portrait of a Woman, 1988
Patinated silver and Colorcore
36 × 33 × 1.1 cm
V&A: M.29-1998
Purchase supported by the James
Yorke-Radleigh Bequest

Things, the celebrated ceramicist Alison Britton (p. 364) describes how it is the breadth and ambiguity of craft that make it so interesting.[15] The fluid categories and blurred edges mean that objects and experiments are open to different readings as ideas and disciplines cross over. Asking why the crafts are still necessary when the requirements of modern life can so quickly and cheaply be made in factories, she writes that they are wanted and needed for a complicated variety of reasons including 'nostalgia, aesthetic accessibility, notions of individuality and – what is more surprising – an ideology of opposition' against the development of an industrialized society.[16] In an era that celebrated the rational functionality of Modernism and mass manufacture, craft practice carved out a space for makers to assert their individuality, and the heightened experimentation of the post-war years resulted in objects of great aesthetic variety.

The establishment of new organizations, such as the American Craft Council and the World Craft Council, and publications dedicated to craft helped foster dialogue between communities of making, garnered broader public interest and demonstrated the heightened professionalism of craft. In Britain the Crafts Council was first formed as the Crafts Advisory Committee in 1971.[17] Its remit was to 'advance and encourage the creation and conservation of works of fine craftsmanship and to foster and promote those works to the public in England and Wales', and comparable organizations were established in many countries.[18] Over the years the Crafts Council has hosted numerous important exhibitions, including *The Craftsman's Art* at the V&A in 1973 and *The Maker's Eye* in 1982.[19] The contents of the latter were selected by an intergenerational group of makers, including potter Michael Cardew, textile designer Enid Marx and furniture maker John Makepeace (fig. 11), who were asked 'to define the idea of craft in terms of his or her personal experience'.[20] The 500 works exhibited demonstrated the broad array of approaches and disciplines encompassed within craft, and included works by potter William Staite Murray, furniture designer Eileen Gray (p. 284) and the product designer Nobuo Nakamura, alongside a carpenter's plane, a Triumph Bonneville motorcycle and a leather saddle. The curator Ralph Turner wrote of his aspiration that the exhibition '... points the way to a broader definition whereby we recognise craftsmen and craftswomen in factories, drawing offices, street markets, studios and shops'.[21] Though it received mixed reviews, the generous and inclusive exhibition demonstrated the multiplicity of views on what craft could be and has had great long-term impact.[22]

In the late twentieth century, makers established new material and technical methodologies and a hybridity of approach that altered the expectations of their craft. The studio glass movement had developed principally in America and central Europe, with makers like Erwin Eisch (fig. 12) and Stanislav Libenský and Jaroslava Brychtová (p. 322) developing bold, highly political languages for glass through material and technical experimentation. They were successful in elevating the medium from its decorative background to become a material of great artistic expression, with installation as well as large sculptural works commanding increasing attention. In eastern Europe the relatively low status of 'craft' made it possible for artists to experiment with forbidden areas such as abstraction in ceramics, glass and textiles. The New Jewellery movement, spearheaded in the Netherlands, saw jewellers abandoning jewellery as an expensive one-off status symbol and moving to prioritize ideas and form over material and techniques to radically expand the field. Marjorie Schick (p. 336) and Peter Chang utilized vivid colour, non-precious materials and ingenious construction methods to create works that could function as sculpture on or off the body. Others, like Charlotte de Syllas (p. 356), David Watkins and Arline Fisch, mixed traditional and novel materials and techniques to explore interactions with the human form. Many makers across disciplines have also played with scale to create new modes of sculpture, such as the ironworker Albert Paley

Fig. 11
John Makepeace
Column of Drawers, 1977–8
Birch plywood, acrylic and stainless steel
130 × 50 × 50 cm
V&A: W.56-1978

(p. 348), whose practice ranges from jewellery to monumental public works. Installation and performance craft also emerged, as makers continued to interrogate and expand their field of making in myriad unprecedented and ambitious ways.

This publication draws to a close around the turn of the century and, despite ever increasing commercialism, new technologies and continued upheaval, making remains a thriving and exciting global field of endeavour. Today, craft continues to evolve and encapsulates a wide range of making with qualities from the traditional and functional to the most abstract. Many of the themes discussed in this book – such as material, technology and explorations of the personal, the conceptual, form and ornament – continue to preoccupy makers. However, makers are also increasingly using their work to explore narrative, identity and place, to challenge social and political norms and to confront or bear witness to humanitarian and environmental issues. Meanwhile, new tools for creating with and within the digital realm present both opportunities and challenges for the handmade, and the ever-growing field of craft practice signals an expansive, materials-driven and socially engaged future for making. Craft is a 'dynamic phenomenon, open to debate and dissent as well as affirmation',[23] and the spectrum of making, material and purpose is today broader than ever.

Rebecca Knott

RENÉ JULES LALIQUE

1860–1945

Art Nouveau glassmaker and jeweller

René Jules Lalique was among the foremost designers and makers of jewellery in the Art Nouveau style and is celebrated as an exceptional glassmaker in the Art Deco style. His innovative approach to the use of materials, colour and form and his championing of the natural world and human form as sources of artistic inspiration are evident in the numerous examples of jewellery and glass designed and made by Lalique during his lifetime. The continued operation of the Lalique glassworks at Wingen-sur-Moder, Alsace-Lorraine, is testament to the success of his venture into commercial artistic production.

Lalique was born in Aÿ-en-Champagne, in the rural Marne region of north-eastern France, on 6 April 1860. Following the death of his father in 1876, Lalique undertook an apprenticeship with one of the leading Parisian jewellers and goldsmiths, Louis Aucoc, and attended evening classes at the École des Arts Décoratifs. These first forays into formal study and the decorative arts left an impression on the young Lalique. He went on to spend the period 1878 to 1880 as a student in graphic design at Sydenham College in London, the art school attached to the Crystal Palace, and later took classes with the sculptor Justin Lequien at the École Bernard Palissy back in Paris. At Sydenham, Lalique would have encountered the ideas and values of the Arts and Crafts movement and it is possible that his fascination with the beauties and complexities of the natural world in the midst of the Industrial Age was at least partly nurtured during his time in London.

Lalique returned to Paris in the 1880s and by 1885 had set up his own workshop on Place Gaillon. He began designing and making jewellery for private clients and leading firms, including Cartier, Boucheron and Vever. While many of these early pieces were unsigned and have now been lost, Lalique's association with prominent jewellery retailers would continue throughout his career. In 1895, for example, he produced a spectacular three-leaf brooch made of platinum and gold and set entirely in diamonds for Tiffany & Co., now in the V&A collection.[1]

Fig. 1
René Jules Lalique
Tiara comb (top) and bodice ornament (bottom), 1903–4
Horn, cast glass, enamelled gold and fire opals (tiara comb); cast glass, enamelled gold and fire opals (bodice ornament)
15.9 cm (width) (tiara comb); 13.3 × 5.8 cm (bodice ornament)
V&A: M.116-1966 (tiara comb) and M.116A-1966 (bodice ornament)

In 1887 Lalique opened his first retail premises on the rue du Quatre Septembre, in the heart of Paris. The following year he registered his makers mark – RL – and in 1890 he opened a second shop in the Opéra area. It was around this time that Lalique began experimenting with materials and forms. He undertook a series of technical investigations into the possible uses and visual effects of different non- and semi-precious materials such as glass, horn, enamel and ivory and, in so doing, created a new style which transfixed the public. His designs came to be considered a fresh new approach in a jewellery market that had traditionally placed high financial and aesthetic value on precious gems and metals. Informed by his knowledge of organic materials and rooted in his love of nature and the fluid sensuality of the human form – perhaps inspired by his early childhood in rural France and his sculptural studies with Lequien – Lalique crafted a new aesthetic for jewellery, which took the world by storm.

Fig. 2
René Jules Lalique
Winter Woodland pendant, *c*.1899
Glass, gold and enamel
8.9 × 6.3 cm
V&A: LOAN:MET ANON.8:1-2007
Lent through the generosity of William & Judith, Douglas and James Bollinger

The materials used in this tiara comb and bodice ornament are typical of Lalique's creations from around 1900 (fig. 1). This was a period of astonishing artistic innovation often now referred to as *fin de siècle*, during which the Art Nouveau aesthetic – with its focus on virtuosic design, simplicity of form and innovative use of materials – reached its zenith. In these works, cast glass, enamelled gold, fire opals and horn are brought together to form a set of jewellery of understated sensuality, full of iridescent movement and subtle undulations of form. Inspired by sweet pea flowers, Lalique's use of finely cast glass to depict the delicate petals lends an air of touching fragility to these two pieces, in great contrast to the fiery sun evoked by the blazing orange of the fire opals.

The winter landscape pendants created by Lalique around 1900 display a similar mastery of materials and forms and showcase his continued command of Art Nouveau naturalism. *Winter Woodland* is one of the most beautiful and vivid of Lalique's many winter scenes (fig. 2). The opalescent central glass panel depicts four bare tree trunks standing in front of an icy lake and the entire pendant is bordered by another tree, this one made of exquisitely executed enamel in frosty greens, greys and blues. The branches, roots and matt lilac leaves envelop the scene with a sense of the quiet stillness of winter.

Harking back to his formative apprenticeship with Louis Aucoc, Lalique's skill as a silversmith is on full display in this buckle from c.1895 (fig. 3). Made of partially gilded silver, the allure lies in the simple yet striking design and the sensual yet serene aesthetic of the piece. A row of irises is depicted growing out of a shimmering pool of water, with the long, curling leaves reaching above the flowers and forming the continuous outline of the buckle itself. The asymmetrical profile of the buckle and the choice of subject matter signal Lalique's interest in Japanese art, and indeed the influence of Japanese art and design on the wider Art Nouveau movement.

Lalique's extraordinary artistic vision and technical brilliance as a designer and maker of jewellery led to great acclaim and considerable commercial success. He was a star exhibitor at the 1900 Paris International Exhibition, was awarded the Croix de la Légion d'Honneur at the World Fair in Brussels and developed a high-society client list including the actress Sarah Bernhardt, who wore his jewellery both on- and offstage. He also had several solo exhibitions across the globe, including two in London: at the Grafton Gallery in 1903 and at Agnew & Sons in 1905.

From around 1910 Lalique became increasingly interested in glass and by the end of the First World War he had largely abandoned jewellery design in favour of glassmaking. He combined his virtuosic understanding and handling of the material – honed during decades of using glass to such stunning effect in his jewellery – with his astute business acumen. In 1905 he formed a successful business partnership with the perfumier François Coty and then in 1912 he took over a glass factory at Combs-la-Ville, south-east of Paris. In 1922 Lalique opened his glassworks at Wingen-sur-Moder with around 50 glassmakers.

Lalique was swiftly recognized as an exceptional glassmaker, with his creations triumphing at the 1925 International Exhibition of Modern Decorative and Industrial Arts in Paris: a showstopping 15-metre-high fountain featuring 17 layers of luminescent glass supported by 128 caryatids (female sculptural figures) astonished and delighted the public. Such was the demand for his glass creations that by 1929 Lalique employed over 300 glassmakers at his Wingen-sur-Moder factory. Indeed, it was through the medium of glass that Lalique was able to bring his designs to the wider public: the innovative mechanical techniques used at his factory meant that the Lalique glassworks could

Fig. 4
René Jules Lalique
Thistles vase, 1926 (designed),
1928–1947 (made)
Press-moulded,
opalescent glass with blue staining
21.3 × 19.6 (max) cm
V&A: Circ.381-1970
Bequeathed by Mrs G.M. Spear

mass-produce beautiful works of art at more affordable prices than his
jewellery commanded.

He carried his trademark opalescent aesthetic, seen to such stunning
effect in the *Winter Woodland* pendant, into his glass design and making.
The *Thistles* vase, designed by Lalique in 1926, shimmers with opalescent
glass, giving light and life to the thistles depicted (fig. 4).

The themes that had so inspired Lalique as a jeweller also continued
to develop in his glassmaking. His fascination with the human form, and
particularly the curves and contours of the female body, can be seen in
his *Bacchantes* vase (fig. 5). Designed by Lalique in 1927 and made by the
Lalique glassworks *c.*1970, this vase demonstrates Lalique's seamless
transformation from Art Nouveau jeweller to Art Deco glassmaker at
the forefront of commercial production, and the transition from the
uninhibited natural forms of his jewellery to this stylized, classically
inspired Art Deco vase. The use of the vibrant amber yellow colour is

particularly arresting and was achieved by the inclusion of iron oxides in the glass body.

By the time of his death in 1945, Lalique had become one of the most acclaimed European makers of the Industrial Age. With a career spanning the two world wars, Lalique's remarkable corpus of work moves from the highly individual, often avant-garde, *fin de siècle* jewels that so delighted and revitalized the world of jewellery, to the perfume bottles, vases and carafes in the Art Deco style that adorned fashionable homes, restaurants and cafés throughout Europe and America. Towards the end of his career, Lalique took on several large public glass commissions for diverse bodies such as commercial ocean liners, churches and the luxurious Paris to Ventimiglia Côte d'Azur Pullman Express train, for which he designed a series of relief-moulded decorative glass panels featuring his trademark naturalistic motifs.

Lalique's instantly recognizable visual aesthetic with its focus on natural forms and movement, and his championing of non- or semi-precious organic materials, endure today. He is, without doubt, one of the best known and most loved of the great makers, with his creations delighting visitors to museums and galleries around the world, and the Lalique brand continues to produce jewellery and glass out of the Wingen-sur-Moder factory. Lalique's work speaks to what it is to be alive – to be moved by the joys of nature, the sensuality of the body, and the fragile beauty of organic materials and luminescent colours in the midst of an ever-changing world: 'la variété qui donne le mouvement, le mouvement, c'est à dire, la vie.'[2]

Jessica Rosenthal McGrath

Fig. 5
René Jules Lalique
Bacchantes vase, 1927 (designed),
c.1970 (made)
Press-moulded glass
26 cm (height)
V&A: Circ.379-1970
Bequeathed by Mrs G.M. Spear

OTHER SIGNIFICANT MAKERS

Alexis Falize (1832–1898) founded Maison Falize, Paris, in 1838. The firm quickly became renowned for its expertise in cloisonné enamelling and its Japanese- and Chinese-inspired jewellery designs. Falize's partnership with French enameller Antoine Tard resulted in an instantly recognizable and hugely popular style of colourful, vibrant jewellery.

Philippe Wolfers (1858–1929) was the son of the Belgian jeweller Louis Wolfers. After joining the family jewellery business at age 16, Wolfers rapidly became one of the most respected Art Nouveau jewellers in Brussels. Specializing in *plique-à-jour* enamel work, Wolfers was greatly influenced by the forms and movement of the natural world.

Georges Fouquet (1862–1957) took over the already hugely successful Parisisan family jewellery firm, Maison Fouquet, in 1895. Known for his expert spanning of the Art Nouveau and Art Deco aesthetics, Fouquet's designs moved from naturalism into the highly stylized motifs of his later work, while many of his pieces are large in scale and hold a certain theatrical or dramatic quality.

Henri Bergé (1870–1937) was the chief decorator and illustrator at the Daum Frères glass factory in Nancy, France, during the 1890s. Specializing in delicate plant and flower motifs and heavily influenced by Japanese naturalism, Bergé's floral and pastoral designs for Daum glassware were hugely popular.

Maurice Marinot (1882–1960) is one of the most significant glassmakers of the twentieth century; his designs are bold, experimental, and often contain natural flaws (such as bubbles) as part of the finished glasswork. In 1944 much of Marinot's work was destroyed following an explosion outside of his factory; as a result, surviving examples of his work are extremely rare.

EILEEN GRAY

1878–1976

Trailblazing lacquer artist, designer and architect

Eileen Gray was one of the most exceptional designers and architects of her generation. Her career spanned painting, lacquerware, furniture design, interior decoration, architecture and photography – and yet she had no formal training in most of these disciplines. While she became best known for her inter-war furniture and the celebrated E.1027 house, it was the art of lacquerware that she was first drawn to.

Born into a wealthy aristocratic Scots-Irish family in Enniscorthy, Ireland, Gray enjoyed regular travels abroad, a second family home in South Kensington, London, and an education in fine art at the Slade School of Art in London, followed by the Colarossi and Julian academies in Paris. Caring for her sick mother settled her back in London in 1905. There, Gray remembered early visits to the South Kensington Museum (now the V&A), where she was struck by the lacquerware on display. Keen to learn how to make such objects, she approached Dean Charles, the owner of a lacquer repair workshop on Oxford Street, to resume the apprenticeship she had started with him in 1901. What followed was a 25-year mentorship. Charles supported and advised Gray while she stubbornly attempted to achieve shades and colours in lacquer previously thought to be practically impossible to obtain.[1]

The process of lacquering involves layering around 20 thin coats of natural resin onto a prepared substrate such as wood, metal or leather. It requires meticulous work as every mistake or change in environment can alter the surface and lead to failure. It was Gray's inherited wealth that enabled her to pursue this expensive and time-consuming practice. In 1907 she moved back to Paris, where she met the Japanese master Seizo Sugawara. Under his tutelage, Gray mastered East Asian lacquering techniques and gained the confidence to pursue this activity professionally. Together, they created Gray's first exhibited piece, *Le Magicien de la Nuit*, and formalized their collaboration by setting up a series of workshops: first in Paris (1910–30), then in London after fleeing the war (1915–17) and finally in Samois-sur-Seine (*c.*1921–4) once the war had ended.

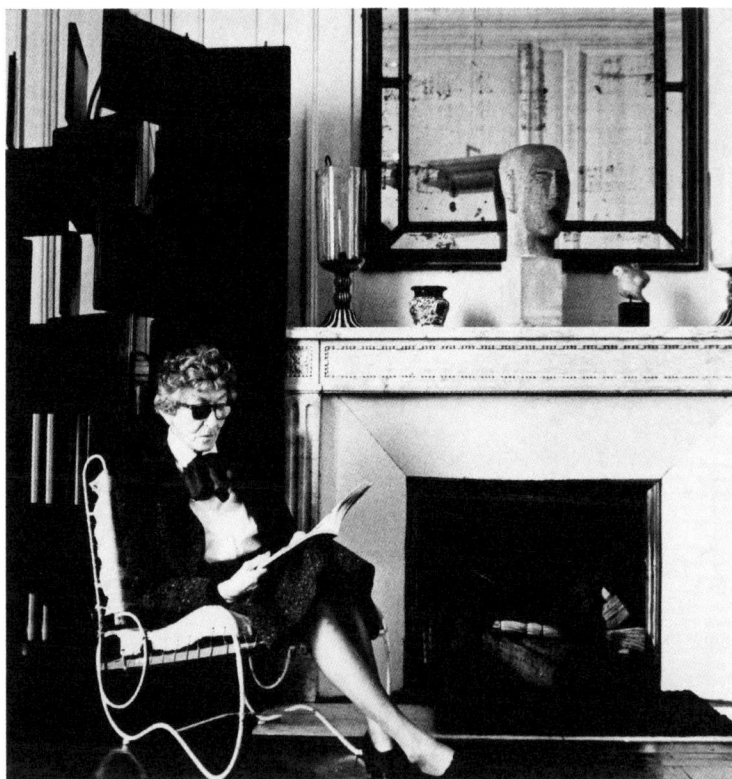

Fig. 2
Photographer unknown
Eileen Gray in her apartment on
rue Bonaparte, Paris, 1971 (detail)
(chair and screen designed by Gray)
Photograph
22.5 × 34.6 cm
National Museum of Ireland:
NMIEG 2003.543

Gray's lacquers included panels, screens and furniture. Her early work often exoticized and amalgamated multiple cultures, with pieces referring to Buddhist mantras, African art or featuring Asian motifs such as lotus flowers. While Gray became known for her prowess with traditional lacquering processes (fig. 3), she is also recognized for her technical innovations. *Le Destin*, a screen she made for couturier Jacques Doucet in 1914, features extremely rare blue hues whose recipe still puzzles makers and historians today.

Throughout this period, Gray expanded her practice beyond lacquer and towards textiles. Building upon her training as a painter, she remained committed to producing decorative flat works. Together with her friend Evelyn Wyld, she visited the Moroccan Atlas Mountains to learn weaving and natural wool dyeing. Following their visit, the pair set up a workshop on the rue Visconti in Paris with looms, wool and a teacher from the National School of Weavers that Wyld brought from the UK. Led by Wyld, the workshop produced rugs designed by Gray. The hand-knotted rug (fig. 1) in the V&A collection is typical of Gray's 1920s production. Abstract and geometric, her designs were often inspired by collage work and, here, the composition of the rug suggests that Gray was playing with cut-out paper shapes. The incomplete lettering in the lower shape might even indicate the use of magazines in her collages.

Following the success of her work for Doucet, Gray was well placed to decorate the apartment belonging to wealthy milliner Suzanne Talbot (also known as Juliette Lévy) on the rue de Lota, Paris (1918–22). While Gray's early love of screens already demonstrated her ability to create rhythm and intimacy in a room, this commission enabled her to conceive of an entire interior and marked the beginning of her engagement with architecture. Talbot's entrance hall with its 450 mobile lacquered panels and the screen design directly inspired by it (see fig. 2) illustrate the designer's shift towards a three-dimensional approach and a pursuit of a simpler, more geometric style.

While working on the apartment, Gray opened a gallery called Jean Désert in spring 1922. Although the origin of the name is unknown, it may have been used as a strategy to penetrate a male-dominated field. Correspondence was often addressed to the fictitious 'Mr. Jean Désert'.[2] The gallery allowed her to promote her interior design, as well as presenting her rugs, lighting, lacquer objects and furniture alongside works by other artists, to a fashionable middle-class market increasingly interested in interior decoration. Although never financially thriving, the gallery counted international and prestigious clients such as Elsa Schiaparelli, Romaine Brooks and the Maharaja of Indore.

Fig. 3
Eileen Gray
Screen, *c.*1923
Wood with red and black lacquer,
silver leaf and composite decoration,
brass hinges
207 × 435 × 1.7 cm
V&A: W.40:1 to 8-1977
Given by Prunella Clough

Fig. 4
Eileen Gray
Fauteuil transat, c.1925–30
Sycamore, chromium-plated metal,
faux leather upholstery made from
a kaolin-filled polyacrylate resin
79 × 55 × 98.3 cm
V&A: Circ.578-1971
Given by the designer

After opening Jean Désert, Gray's production increasingly focused on furniture sets that offered a visual unity to interiors and demonstrated her growing interest in spatial design. Gray progressively stepped away from making one-offs in lacquer, which were time-consuming and not profitable enough, and moved toward making easily adaptable and reproducible prototypes. Instead of being mainly chosen for their decorative properties, materials became the means through which Gray could answer users' needs. Her experimentations with tubular steel, glass, celluloid, slate and cork led her to expand the number of collaborators she entrusted to produce her objects and shifted her focus from making to designing.

When conceiving furniture, Gray was obsessed with comfort and practicality. She often designed pieces to serve multiple functions and to be easily moveable. The *Fauteuil transat* (*Transat* chair) (fig. 4) was intended for indoor and outdoor use. Its slung seat and pivoting headpiece offer the sitter a comfortable and adjustable reclining position. Although the sycamore joints required careful handcrafting, the chromed joints and connecting rods of the frame demonstrate her interest in simplifying manufacture and in modern ways of making. Other chairs of Gray's design – such as the plump *Bibendum* and the one-armed *Fauteuil non conformiste* (*Nonconformist* chair) – present names and unusual forms showcasing her unique wit and humour.

The *Transat*, *Bibendum* and *Nonconformist* chairs furnished E.1027, a house conceived by Gray from 1925 to 1929 with support from her then partner, the Romanian architect and editor Jean Badovici. Built for them to stay in Roquebrune-Cap-Martin, southern France, the house was Gray's first architectural project and yet is still regarded as one of the great examples of Modernist architecture. The design of E.1027 was influenced by the work of contemporary architects such as Le Corbusier and Theo van Doesburg, but it also showcased a high degree of independence by the self-taught architect. A founding member of the Union des Artistes Modernes, Gray shared other Modernists' interests in open-plan interiors and questions of hygiene, health and light. She developed these ideas by claiming that 'hygiene [is] poorly understood. Because hygiene doesn't exclude either comfort or activity.'[3] Her nuanced views are visible in a plan for E.1027 (fig. 5) which studies the distribution of natural light in relation to the projected use of the space by inhabitants and their staff. In this way Gray demonstrated her belief that the main object of architecture is 'the living human being'.[4]

Gray's interiors can also be viewed through a queer lens, connecting the architect's work to her sexuality (Gray engaged in relationships with women and men) and principles of homosociality.[5] Recent studies suggest that she created interiors for a 'sexually dissident modernity' by offering safe spaces to dwell in, away from normative environments.[6] E.1027's sliding walls and screens, for example, create partially obstructed views and provide feelings of privacy and intimacy. The attention to colours, textures or even the reflective or cooling properties of the materials selected for furnishings participate in creating a sensuous experience and an erotically charged environment. Together, these elements can enable different ways of socializing.

Gray went on to conceive other (mostly unbuilt) architectural projects, including two houses for herself on the French Riviera: Tempe a Pailla (1932–4) and Lou Perou (1954–8). Much of this later work was increasingly linked to socialist political values and concerned with offering low-cost housing as well as public and cultural spaces.

In her later years Gray returned to Paris to live in the apartment she had bought in 1907 on rue Bonaparte (see fig. 2) and continued creating art and designing furnishings and buildings. In the late 1960s she became conscious that her work had become increasingly marginalized or credited to others. This was partly due to her lack of interest in self-promotion, but mostly to the ease with which women's legacies can be erased from history. She actively sought to remedy the situation by organizing her papers, commercializing designs and taking part in exhibitions with the support of her niece, the artist Prunella Clough. In 1968 a *Domus* article written by Joseph Rykwert paid homage to her work, and the *Modern Chairs* exhibition (1970) organized by the V&A and the Whitechapel Gallery, as well as the *Eileen Gray: Pioneer of Design* exhibition (1973) organized by the Royal Institute of British Architects, brought her work to a new and wider audience. The former show led to the acquisition of her *Transat* and so-called *Fold-up* chairs by the V&A. In 1973 Zeev Aram in London began to manufacture and distribute Gray's designs, finally meeting her ambition to scale up the production of furniture which had existed as prototypes for most of her life. Today, her furniture is still in production.

Eileen Gray died in 1976 having finally obtained the recognition she was due. Her furniture now fetches record prices – something she would have disapproved of – with her so-called *Dragon* or *Serpent* armchair being the most expensive piece of twentieth-century furniture sold to date (£19.4 million in 2009). Gray's work is collected by the most prestigious museums in the world and is the topic of numerous exhibitions, books, films and research projects. In the words of Rykwert, Gray will remain 'a remarkably humane and sensitive artist who has had the courage and the force to break new ground'.[7]

Maude Willaerts

Fig. 5
Eileen Gray
E.1027 (Maison en Bord de Mer), diagram
showing the path of the sun and circulation
routes within the principal plan, *c.*1929
Pen and ink on paper
36.5 × 56 cm
V&A: AAD/1980/9/188/29
Given by Prunella Clough

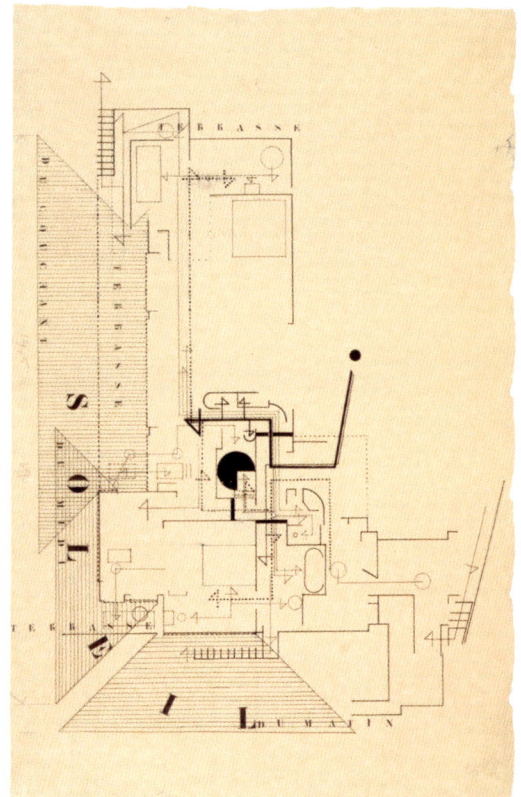

OTHER SIGNIFICANT MAKERS

Kichizo Inagaki (1876–1951) was a woodworker and lacquer artist who lived with Seizo Sugawara and other Japanese artists in Paris. Especially skilled with lacquering on oak and tropical woods, he collaborated with Gray on the production of lacquer panels for the rue de Lota apartment and furniture including lanterns with ostrich eggs.

Evelyn Wyld (1882–1972) was a rugmaker and designer with a keenness for floral motifs. After leaving the workshop on rue Visconti where she managed a staff of up to eight women, she moved to the south of France to establish an interior design shop that sold lacquer furniture with her partner Eyre de Lanux.

Seizo Sugawara (1884–1937) was born in Jahoji, Japan, and came to Paris to restore lacquerware presented by his native country at the 1900 Paris Exposition. An accomplished artist and teacher, he trained some of the best lacquerers of the time and is credited for much of the success of lacquer in Paris then.

Jean Badovici (1893–1956) was born in Bucharest, Romania. A well-connected architect, he also founded and edited the influential magazine *L'Architecture Vivante* (1923–32), to which Gray contributed. Badovici encouraged Gray to pursue architecture and dedicated a whole issue of his magazine to E.1027. The pair became life and work partners.

Prunella Clough (1919–1999) was a prominent British artist known for her paintings, prints and assemblages of found objects. She collaborated on paintings with her aunt Eileen Gray. Clough supported Gray's career recovery, assisting with organizing her archival material, museum acquisitions and retrospectives, at the V&A for example.

AINO MARSIO-AALTO 1894–1949
ALVAR AALTO 1898–1976

Visionary product and furniture designers

Aino Marsio-Aalto and Alvar Aalto are often referred to as the most important couple in the history of modern architecture and product design. Over the course of their careers, the Finnish couple built a creative legacy that gave rise to the notion of a Scandinavian modern design language, and the furniture for which they are known can be found today in homes and museum collections alike. The creative production of the Aaltos has generally been discussed in relation to architecture and design but their deep interest in understanding the physical properties of materials and their experimental approach to making are key characteristics of great makers. The technological optimism brought about by European post-war rebuilding undoubtedly informed the Aaltos' practice. But most importantly, their utilitarian approach to making always responded to human needs.

Marsio-Aalto was born in Helsinki on 24 January 1894. Her parents owned a small apartment, where she grew up with nine siblings. Both parents were public sector workers and, together with a small group of railway workers, they established the first working-class housing association in Finland. Though Marsio-Aalto initially considered pursuing a career in engineering, as an accomplished draughtsperson she eventually chose to study architecture. She was one of three women to graduate from the architecture course at Helsinki's Polytechnical Institute in 1920. Marsio-Aalto took part in many work placements during her studies and, as a result, her excellence as an architect was equalled by her skill as a bricklayer, interior designer, furniture maker and photographer. In addition, from early on Marsio-Aalto's projects demonstrated a concern with social issues. A state nursery school formed the case study for her diploma project and later in her career she was involved with the development of social housing projects. This breadth of creative practice proved vital to the success of the Aaltos' Gesamtkunstwerk (total work of art) approach whereby all elements of a space are conceived as an aesthetically coherent whole.

Fig. 1
Alvar Aalto
Armchair 41 (Paimio armchair), *c.*1935
Manufactured by Huonekalu-ja
Rakennustyötehdas Oy
Birch plywood and solid birch, painted seat
63.5 × 61 × 89 cm
V&A: W.41-1987

Alvar Aalto was four years Marsio-Aalto's junior and was born on 3 February 1898. He grew up in the small town of Kuortane in the Finnish countryside. Like Marsio-Aalto, he studied architecture at Helsinki's Polytechnic Institute, where the couple met despite being in different year groups. After graduating, Aalto moved to Jyväskylä and opened an office named Alvar Aalto Architecture and Monumental Art. Marsio-Aalto joined the practice as an assistant in 1924 and they married a few months later.

From this point in their careers, the work produced by the Aaltos should be approached as a shared creative entity owing to the collaborative nature of their personal and professional lives. Aalto's life and work has enjoyed greater study than Marsio-Aalto's and many shared projects have been discussed exclusively in relation to him. Gender and class difference have influenced this disparity, together with the media's interest in promoting him as the greatest Finnish architect. Only recently has there been a revision in approach, to look jointly at the couple's creative output.[1] One of the Aaltos' most significant achievements was the design of a sanatorium for tuberculosis patients built in the rural Finnish town of Paimio. The Paimio Sanatorium was completed in 1933 and is generally seen as the epitome of Finnish functionalist architecture. The building uses simple and assertive organic lines, both in its structure and interior furnishings, in keeping with the surrounding nature and topography, and its design follows the principles of a Gesamtkunstwerk. In 'Rationalism and Man', a lecture Aalto delivered at the Swedish Society of Industrial Design in 1935, he spoke about the need to go beyond the practical concerns of modernist rationalism in design and to respond instead to human needs.[2] The 'humanization' of design was a central idea in the Aaltos' creative ethos, and they sought to create spaces that holistically promoted mental and physical well-being. This is made manifest in the way light, colours and sounds were kept at unobtrusive levels throughout the sanatorium owing to the heightened sensory sensitivity of tuberculosis patients.

The *Armchair 41* (or Paimio armchair) exemplifies their humanist approach to furniture making (fig. 1). The armchair was made with wood instead of tubular metal, which would have been a more usual choice of material for hospital furniture. In contrast with the coldness and rigidity of metal, wood's flexibility and warmth acknowledged the access needs of patients experiencing pain and discomfort from physical contact with cold surfaces or from sitting down for long periods. In terms of aesthetic innovation, the chair's single-piece moulded plywood seat is suspended in a wooden frame, showing soft curves. This flowing construction

demonstrates a desire to move towards organic forms, away from the hard-edged geometric furniture designs from the previous decade.[3]

Although the Aaltos are primarily known as designers, their practice developed through careful understanding and hands-on exploration of material properties. The pioneering 'L-bend' technique emerged from experimentations with wood in the early 1930s. By making several cuts along the grain of a piece of wood and then filling the cut slots with thin sheets of wood, Aalto was able to steam-bend the piece to a 90-degree angle. This breakthrough technique created an effective clean curve and improved the material's strength.

Aalto applied the L-bend to the construction of the stackable *Stool no. 60*, made for the Viipuri Library (fig. 2). Each of the stool's three L-bent legs was attached to a circular seat made with plywood and solid birch. Although experiments in bentwood furniture had been taking place for over a century – notably through the work of Michael Thonet – Aalto's approach to using the bentwood simultaneously as leg and seat support makes a feature of its innovative construction. This technique shows truthfulness to the wood's properties and modern visual potential, an idea that became important in modernist thinking.[4] The Paimio project was well received by the Finnish media and, soon after its completion, the *Architectural Review* published an article on Aalto, helping to project his name internationally.

The limited literature on Marsio-Aalto makes it difficult to ascertain the level of her involvement with projects that came out of Aalto's office in Jyväskylä (and later Turku). However, as more material comes to light, it is becoming clearer that she played a central role in establishing the success of the practice.[5] The collaborative nature of the Aaltos' practice became more explicit with the founding of Artek (a fusion of the words 'art' and 'technology') in 1935 with both their names appearing on the company's letterhead. They founded Artek in Helsinki, with arts patron Marie Gullichsen and Finnish bohemian Nils-Gustav Hahl, as a furniture shop and creative hub where works by avant-garde artists including Edgar Degas, Fernand Léger, Alexander Calder and Henri Matisse were shown. Aalto was responsible for managing the company's international affairs while Marsio-Aalto held the post of Head of Design and, later, Managing Director. Marsio-Aalto was instrumental in shaping the company's aesthetic language and her study of the relationship between objects and the properties of materials was the foundation of furniture design at Artek. Marsio-Aalto's *Side Table 606* was first designed for the Paimio project and, like many furniture objects made for the sanatorium, it was later relaunched as an Artek product. The small table was made by attaching a circular birch plywood seat to a tubular steel frame base. Its tubular steel base in a three-quarter-moon shape allowed the table to neatly fit the edge of armchairs, beds or sofas. Its relationship with Aalto's *Stool no. 60* is entirely intentional. The two objects have a similar visual language and, by being slightly taller and wider, *Side Table 606* can be slotted together with the stool, in what looks like a snug embrace. This exemplifies the simple and affective functionality for which Artek came to be recognized.

In 1931 the Prohibition Act was repelled in Finland and alcoholic drinks started to be sold there again. At the same time, the country was going through fast urbanization and there was a demand for compact houseware. It quickly became clear that Finnish glassware needed a new, modern look. The Aaltos started working with glass in 1932 and their approach to the material carried the principles of rationality and standardization seen in their furniture designs. Marsio-Aalto's glassworks brought her international recognition as a creative innovator in her own right. The *Bölgeblick* range was designed in 1932 for Karhula Glassworks, as Marsio-Aalto's entry in a competition for affordable glassware (fig. 3).

Bölgeblick won second place in the competition, and it was awarded a gold medal at the Milan Triennale. Marsio-Aalto drew inspiration from the ripples on the surface of water to design pieces that could be made from molten glass pressed into custom-built moulds. The concentric rings of the thick and durable glass hid imperfections in the material, which simplified the industrial making process and made it an affordable product. Aalto's early glassworks followed similar principles of

standardization but, from around 1936, his glassworks started to show asymmetrical shapes, as can be seen in Aalto's vase designed for Helsinki's Savoy Restaurant (fig. 3). The expressive shape of this vase proved technically challenging for glassblowers, suggesting that Aalto's later glassworks show a desire to experiment beyond functionalist design.

Like the Paimio armchair, *Stool no. 60* and *Side Table 606*, the Aaltos' glasswork captures the modern Scandinavian feel. As key figures in the history of design, the Aaltos' exploration of the properties and industrial capabilities of materials resulted in objects that continue to be manufactured, studied and admired today. The Aaltos' visionary work consistently sought to resolve human needs and, as a result, they engaged with questions of sustainability and disability, decades before these two topics entered the public arena. Major exhibitions on their life and work have taken place in institutions such as MoMA in New York and the Vitra Design Museum in Germany, crystallizing the Aaltos' legacy and main role in the formation of a modern Scandinavian cultural identity.

Danilo Marques dos Reis

OTHER SIGNIFICANT MAKERS

Otto Korhonen (1884–1935) was a Finnish woodworker who worked on various architectural projects, including the iconic Viipuri Library. He was a close collaborator of Alvar Aalto and his expertise in woodworking contributed to the legacy of Scandinavian Modern.

Charles Eames (1907–1978) and **Ray Eames** (1913–1988) were an American couple renowned for the work they produced at the Eames Office, making historic contributions to industrial design and modern architecture and furniture. They also worked in the fields of graphic design, fine art and film.

Maija Heikinheimo (1908–1963) was a Finnish interior architect. She worked at Artek for most of her career, collaborating closely with the Aaltos. Her work significantly influenced Finnish interior design aesthetics.

Florence Knoll (1917–2019) was an American architect and furniture designer. As a pivotal figure in mid-century Modern design, she co-founded furniture company Knoll Associates. Knoll's minimalist and functional approach to furniture design helped shaped the aesthetic of modern interiors.

GUNTA STÖLZL

1897–1983

Influential Bauhaus weaver

As the sole female workshop master at the Bauhaus art school, Gunta Stölzl cultivated a creative and prolific weaving studio with a distinct design identity and enduring influence. Although weaving was not her initial medium of choice, she mastered the practice and developed an approach that combined her artistic creativity with the technicalities and materiality of weaving.[1] Within the collaborative environment of the Bauhaus Weaving Workshop, Stölzl was both maker and teacher and influenced the early development of other significant makers, including Anni Albers and Otti Berger.[2]

Gunta Stölzl was born in Munich in 1897. She attended the Munich School of Applied Arts and took classes in drawing, painting, glass, ceramics and art history. She interrupted her studies to volunteer as a nurse for the Red Cross in 1917. Returning to her studies in 1919, Stölzl encountered Walter Gropius's Bauhaus manifesto and transferred to the Bauhaus Weimar. Operating from 1919 to 1933, the Bauhaus became one of the most influential design schools of the twentieth century. Advocating for a harmony of formal and technical training and a mastering of material, the Bauhaus fostered a cross-disciplinary approach aimed at breaking the divide between artist and craftsperson. Initially attending classes across multiple disciplines, Stölzl was accepted on Johannes Itten's foundation course on a full scholarship in 1920. Despite Gropius's declaration of gender equality when establishing the Bauhaus, he promptly reneged on this commitment and established a Women's Department, excluding most female students from all workshops other than Pottery, Bookbinding and Weaving (subsequently, almost all female students were directed towards the Weaving Workshop). Georg Muche was *Formmeister* (form master, director) of the Weaving Workshop, providing formal training but never undertaking weaving himself.

From the outset Stölzl demonstrated an innate talent for weaving and began applying to the loom the compositional techniques and colour theory taught in the classes of Itten, Paul Klee, Muche and others. Her quickly established ability made Stölzl a de facto technical teacher

Fig. 1
Gunta Stölzl
Red-Green Tapestry, 1927–8
Cotton, wool, silk and linen
15 × 11 cm
Bauhaus-Archiv, Berlin

in the workshop. Stölzl developed her understanding of different structures and weaving techniques and applied her artistic training to handwoven compositions, later describing her works from this early period as *Bilder aus Wolle* (pictures made of wool). This approach is illustrated in her first formal textile work, *Kühe in Landschaft* (cows in a landscape), from 1920.[3] Expressive and pictorial, the tapestry intersperses different shades of yarn to create colour gradients. As Stölzl gained experience, she explored the inherent properties of woven structures, experimenting with weave patterns, yarn weights, types and fibres to explore the creative potential of loom-woven textiles. As she leant into the structural possibilities of weaving, her designs became more abstracted. Stölzl continued to develop her expertise through external training courses in weaving and fibre technology. In 1922 she and fellow student Benita Otte travelled to the city of Krefeld to attend a course on dyeing, which resulted in the creation of a dye laboratory for the Weaving Workshop.

Alongside the development of her technical knowledge and experimentation, Stölzl began to consider the purpose and context of textiles and how their intended use informed the design. In 1921 she designed her first textile for a three-dimensional object when fellow Bauhaus student, architect and furniture designer Marcel Breuer, asked her to design the textiles for a chair (later named the *African Chair*). She wove directly onto the chair back with a freehand design that complemented the expressionistic style of Breuer's frame.[4] She later created textile seats and backs for Breuer's renowned tubular steel chairs. In line with Gropius's aim to apply the concept of Gesamtkunstwerk (total work of art) to design practice, Stölzl and her fellow weavers regularly worked closely with other Bauhaus workshops to design and produce furnishing textiles for large commissions such as schools, lecture halls and private houses.

In 1923 Stölzl passed her journeyman's examination as a weaver, which involved producing an exemplary piece of work demonstrating the necessary level of skill (although, unlike other disciplines in the school, this was not an official qualification, rather an internal certificate, as the local *Handwerkskammer*, or crafts council, did not include weaving in their list of accredited crafts).[5] Her examination piece, a 6-metre-long knotted runner, was displayed and sold alongside other examples of her work at the Bauhaus *Werkschau* exhibition the same year. In recognition of her expertise, Stölzl was appointed *Werkmeister* (craft master) of the Weaving Workshop in 1925 and given greater responsibility for coordinating the practical and theoretical teaching curriculum, while continuing to design and create her own works.[6] Following Muche's

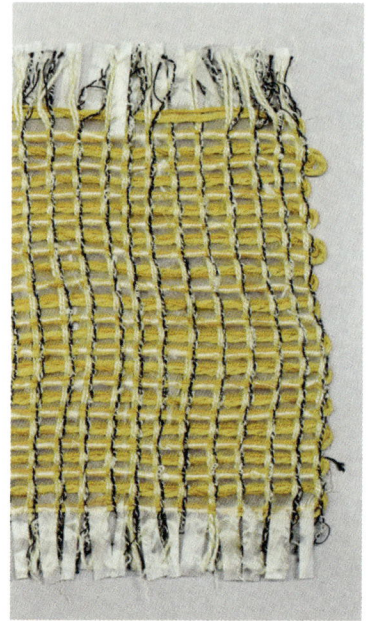

Fig. 2
Gunta Stölzl
Handwoven textile sample, 1929–31
Cellophane, wool and cotton
V&A: Circ.403-1969

Fig. 3
Gunta Stölzl
Design for a tapestry, 1927
Watercolour on paper
28.8 × 21.8 cm
V&A: Circ.708-1967

departure, in 1927 Stölzl was promoted to *Jungmeister* (young master) and director of the Weaving Workshop, becoming the only female master at the Bauhaus.

For both teaching and designing, Stölzl championed handweaving. This was not out of romantic nostalgia: she asserted that handweaving offered 'the clearest and simplest way of developing the possibilities of weaving'.[7] When trialling the 'aesthetic implications' of different fibres and structures, Stölzl designed directly on the loom rather than draughting on paper, arguing that the tactile qualities of yarn could never be truly represented on the page.[8] A result of this careful trialling is demonstrated by a reference sample in which strips of cellophane are interspersed with yarns of various weights and colours to create a rhythmic three-dimensional surface that would give a striking effect against a window or other light source (fig. 2). Playing with the transparency of the cellophane and pairing lighter yarns alongside dark, Stölzl creates depth by mimicking shadow.

As Stölzl developed her aesthetic style, she also established a theoretical design approach that sat within the wider Bauhaus rhetoric but advocated for weaving as a distinct practice.[9] She contributed to the burgeoning theory of her craft, championing weaving as 'an aesthetic whole, a unity of composition, form, colour and substance'.[10] When the Bauhaus moved to Dessau it cemented a shift in the school's focus to designing for industry, which Stölzl embraced. She thought critically about material qualities, durability, practicality and the suitability of a textile for a particular purpose. As she explained in 1926, 'a woven piece is always a serviceable object, which is equally determined by its function as well as its means of production.'[11] However, Stölzl did not believe that a focus on function should be at the expense of experimentation or broader art education. She arranged research trips to mills and museums as part of her teaching and later described the curriculum as 'a living thing that was always changing', built upon the premise of simultaneous artistic and technical education, with neither being placed above the other.[12] An advocate of learning through doing, she stressed the importance of knowing one's materials intimately and argued that a balance between the artistic and the practical gave students a valuable insight into the feasibility of production, better equipping them as effective designers for industry. This was demonstrated in 1930 when the Weaving Workshop entered a partnership with the large textile manufacturer Polytex. The Bauhaus workshop provided samples of 'reasonably priced, artistically and technically exceptional' furnishing fabrics that Polytex would mass-produce under the label 'bauhaus-dessau'.[13]

For Stölzl, tapestries and wall hangings were distinct from functional furnishing textiles, more closely aligned with fine art and 'in the area of free artistic expression'.[14] Warranting a different approach, Stölzl trialled her compositions first on paper. For handwoven tapestries, she produced freehand watercolour designs that would later be used as a prompt or guide to be elaborated on in the weaving process (fig. 3). A finished piece embodies much more complexity: through intersecting shapes, contrasting colours and patterns Stölzl creates a balanced division of surface with a lively sense of perspective (fig. 1). Jacquard-woven hangings required exact drafted designs and here she cultivated an exploration of rhythmic colour and shape combined with graphic precision (fig. 4).[15]

In 1928 Gunta Stölzl married Bauhaus architect Arieh Sharon and they had a daughter. They divorced in 1936 and in 1942 she married Swiss author Willy Stadler and had another daughter. In the spring of 1931 she was forced to resign from the Bauhaus following politically motivated

Fig. 4
Gunta Stölzl
Design for a jacquard wall hanging, 1928
Watercolour and pencil on paper
26.7 × 27.3 cm
V&A: Circ.703-1967

complaints against alleged improprieties in her private life.[16] At the instigation of several of her students, the 1931–2 issue of *Bauhaus* magazine was dedicated to her accomplishments. Stölzl's wider impact was recognized in 1939 when British weaver Ethel Mairet invited Stölzl to write a contribution to her book *Handweaving Today: Traditions and Changes*.

A focus on designing for industry and architectural spaces remained with Stölzl in the next stage of her career. She relocated to Switzerland and founded a handweaving company, S-P-H Stoffe, with fellow former Bauhaus members Gertrud Preiswerk and Heinrich Otto Hürlimann. In 1933 this company closed and Stölzl and Hurlimann established another venture, S-H-Stoffe, producing fine apparel fabrics, upholstery fabrics and bespoke commissions for architectural projects.[17] When Hürlimann left the company in 1937, Stölzl continued independently under the name *Handweberei Flora* (Flora handweaving studio). Stölzl maintained the design approach established at the Bauhaus, combining formal colour and pattern theory with an intimate knowledge of woven structures to design innovative, appealing and practical textiles that suited the modern, functional objects and spaces produced in the post-war period. Her designs won several prizes at international exhibitions, including a *diplôme commémoratif* at the Paris World Exhibition in 1937 and the Grand Prix at the Paris International Exhibition of Urbanism and Housing in 1947.

The 1960s and '70s saw renewed interest in Stölzl's earlier work and she featured in several exhibitions that spotlighted the radical innovation and experimentation of the Bauhaus Weaving Workshop. Original and commisioned reproductions of Bauhaus textiles were acquired by several museums in Europe and the USA. These retrospectives cemented the Weaving Workshop's significance and influence on subsequent generations of textile designers. In 1967 Stölzl dissolved *Handweberei Flora* and turned her full attention to weaving pictorial tapestries and wall hangings. Stölzl died in 1983, having contributed to the re-evaluation and rising status of textile work and weaving theory within the wider realm of modern art and design.

Connie Karol Burks

OTHER SIGNIFICANT MAKERS

Ethel Mairet (1872–1952) played an important role in a revival of handweaving in Britain in the early twentieth century. Originally inspired by the handcraft she saw when visiting Sri Lanka and India, Mairet was self-taught. She published instructional books on handweaving and dyeing and hosted several influential weavers in her workshop, Gospels, including Marianne Straub and Peter Collingwood.

Marianne Brandt (1893–1983) studied painting before enrolling at the Bauhaus in 1924. She went on to be the only woman admitted to the Metalwork studio where she designed several homewares of lasting popularity. In 1929 she became head of the design department at the Ruppelwerk hardware factory in Gotha and later taught at Dresden Academy of Fine Arts and the Academy of Applied Art in Berlin.

Otti Berger (1898–1944) was born in Zmajevac in the Austro-Hungarian Empire, present-day Croatia, and studied at the Bauhaus Weaving Workshop from 1927. She went on to establish her own studio in Berlin, designing innovative modernist textiles for a number of manufacturers. Berger was murdered in Auschwitz in 1944.

Anni Albers (1899–1994) studied in the Weaving Workshop at the Bauhaus before moving to the USA with her husband Josef Albers in 1933. She became one of the most influential textile artists and designers of the twentieth century and was instrumental in repositioning textiles as an art form.

Marcel Breuer (1902–1981), architect and designer, led the Bauhaus Carpentry Workshop where his experiments in metal furniture led to the design of his renowned *Wassily* chair. He briefly worked for the Isokon Company in London before emigrating to the USA in 1937. While a professor at Harvard University, he collaborated with Walter Gropius on a number of architectural projects, and later designed the Whitney Museum of American Art in New York.

LUCIE RIE

1902–1995

Iconic modern studio potter

Subtle, considered and resolutely modern, Lucie Rie's pots are some of the most recognizable and admired in the field of twentieth-century studio ceramics. Over a long life, which spanned two world wars and seismic shifts in fashion and society, Rie's work pushed at the edges of conventionality. She embraced Modernist ideals while remaining anchored by deeply personal influences and her scrupulous, almost scientific approach to making. The enduring appeal of her work is perhaps best explained by its ability to reconcile contradictions: robust yet delicate, meticulous yet vital, modern yet timeless.

Lucie Rie was born in Vienna in 1902 into a middle-class, liberal and secular Jewish family. She was the youngest child and only daughter of Benjamin and Gisela Gomperz, and the family lived in one of the city's most attractive neighbourhoods. Vienna was the prosperous capital of a large empire and in its coffee shops new ideas were discussed and debated. Visionaries of the era crossed paths with the Gomperz family; Benjamin was a doctor who knew Sigmund Freud, and the painter Oskar Kokoschka had been a teacher at Rie's progressive girls' school. Rie's childhood was punctuated by frequent visits to her maternal family's property in rural Eisenstadt and it was here that she received some of her earliest and most abiding inspiration. Her uncle Sándor excavated several Roman pots from the grounds, objects which she later recalled seemed to float.[1]

Despite relatively comfortable beginnings, two personal tragedies coloured Rie's teenage years. First, the death of her brother Paul, killed on the Italian Front at the infamous battle of Caporetto in 1917 and, just four years later, the loss of her close friend Ernst Rie in a skiing accident. Paul's own artistic interests may have played a role in Rie's decision to attend art school (she had previously considered medicine) and the loss of Ernst brought her closer to his brother Hans, whom she would later marry.

In 1922 Rie enrolled at the Kunstgewerbeschule, the School of Applied Arts, which was attached to the Museum of Art and Industry in Vienna.

Fig. 1
Lucie Rie
Bowl, *c.*1976
Porcelain, bronze rim and foot, incised lines with pink inlay under a white glaze
12 × 23.8 cm
V&A: C.43-1982

It was here, under the influence of Modernist designers like Josef Hoffmann and Adolf Loos and the tutelage of ceramicist Michael Powolny, that Rie would begin to develop the distinctive, restrained aesthetic for which she is now known. She initially enrolled to study sculpture but an opportunity to try throwing on the wheel seduced the young art student. Rie gained valuable experience not only in the technical aspects of making, but in the diligent and methodological ethos of the training. She threw her pots on a continental kick-wheel without a splash pan, a set-up which required – in stark contrast to American and British methods – the very frugal use of water. Those who knew her would often remark on the astonishing cleanliness of her throwing practice. In a later interview she said, 'The wheel is a perfect machine and it makes perfect pots.'[2]

The period in which Rie attended art school was an exciting one for the applied arts. Influenced in part by the Arts and Crafts movement in Britain, organizations such as the Wiener Werkstätte and the Österreichischer Werkbund, both co-founded by Hoffmann, promoted the artistic production of utilitarian items and the breaking down of barriers between high and low art. Hoffmann was an early supporter of Rie's, even buying one of her early works, and in 1923, while she was still a student, he invited her to exhibit her pots at the Palais Stoclet in Brussels. However, her work perhaps had more in common with that

Fig. 2
Lucie Rie and Hans Coper
Coffee pot and pouring vessel with side handles, *c.*1955–8
Stoneware, manganese glaze with *sgraffito* lines; stoneware, white glaze exterior
20.7 × 21 × 11 cm; 11.9 × 16 × 9.9 cm
V&A: C.63:1,2-2022; C.65-2022
Given by Heather James

of Hoffmann's rival, the architect Adolf Loos. Both men held competing ideas on Modernism and, while Hoffmann's works often had a highly ornamented splendour, Loos famously abhorred decoration and prized spare, clean lines. Rie's approach to decoration was never to adorn her works and rather she let the marks, colours and textures of her surfaces enhance rather than compete with her forms.

On leaving the school, she married Hans Rie and they moved into an apartment in Vienna. It was furnished by the young modernist architect Ernst Plischke, with whom Rie went on to have a long and close relationship. There she set up her studio and began fulfilling orders, positioning her work at the higher end of the market. Hers were domestic objects made to be used and admired aesthetically, but they were also upmarket pieces for a relatively affluent consumer.

The pots she created in Vienna testify to experiments with richly coloured glazes and have neat, compact forms. A small, thinly thrown, lobed pot with splashes of orange and blue (fig. 4) speaks to the more exuberant tastes of the day, while a teapot of burnished earthenware made for Plischke is more in keeping with her evolving style, referencing the efficiency and line of Modernist architecture. Both were a contrast to the work of her art school peers and teacher, Powolny, whose output tended towards the more decorative and figurative styles.

In 1938 the dominance of the Nazi Party forced the couple to leave Vienna for Britain and they separated shortly after, with Hans ultimately settling in the United States. In moving to London, Rie had left behind her home and her status, as she was virtually unknown in British circles. This, together with the outbreak of war, forced her practice in new directions and for a time she made buttons for the fashion industry, an undertaking which, though far from ideal, allowed her space to experiment with glazes. She employed other Jewish refugees in the enterprise, including the young German émigré Hans Coper, who would become her collaborator and lifelong friend.

At this time, British studio ceramics was dominated by Bernard Leach who, at his studio in Cornwall, produced weightier, robust pieces, heavily influenced by East Asian traditions. For a period Rie followed his steer, producing pots with thicker walls and a more grounded feel but, encouraged by Coper, she gradually returned to the light, balanced shapes which characterized her earlier work. She also differed from Leach in her choice of environment, choosing to remain in a large city with a home-based studio. Though far from the first urban studio potter, Rie's metropolitan life has often informed later interpretations of her work.

Between 1946 and 1958 she and Coper shared her small studio at Albion Mews near Hyde Park. The compact building had been converted by Rie

from a garage, and she had Plischke's furniture brought over and adapted
for the space. For a period, the pair produced functional items together
including tea and coffee sets, often with dark manganese glazes, some
of which were sold through fashionable London stores like Heal's and
Liberty's (fig. 2).

Having previously worked with earthenware clays, it was in this
period that she began to use more durable stoneware, employing an
electric kiln to fire at the required high temperatures and achieving
wonderful results. She raw-glazed and single-fired her pots, a high-risk
strategy forgoing the lower temperature biscuit firing which permanently
changes the clay to a more durable but porous material onto which a
glaze can be easily applied. By omitting this step, Rie's practice was
vulnerable to a host of potential problems, from glazes adhering badly,
to explosions in the kiln. She mastered the technique and developed an
enticing range of glazes and surface effects, from pitted volcanic textures
achieved by layering up glazes, sometimes thickened with gum Arabic
(fig. 3), to fine *sgraffito* striations in vertical, diagonal or cross-hatched
lines. Applied freehand with a steel knitting needle, these scratches were
sometimes inlaid with coloured slip (see fig. 2). Rie smoothed away rings
from throwing and other more conspicuous evidence of making, which
potters like Leach tended to retain, presenting a different kind of
handmade aesthetic in her work.

By the 1950s Rie was becoming more established in Britain. She
and Coper both exhibited at the Festival of Britain in 1951 and at the
important Dartington Hall pottery and textiles show and conference

Fig. 3
Lucie Rie
Oval bowl on conical foot and cylindrical
vase, 1967
Stoneware, grey glaze over blue body
14 × 14.6 cm (bowl); 15.6 × 11.6 cm (vase)
V&A: C.1229-1967 & C.1228-1967

Fig. 4
Lucie Rie
Pot, *c.*1926
Earthenware with blue, orange,
white and brown glaze splashes
7.8 × 10.5 cm
V&A: C.35-1982
Given by the potter

organized by Leach the following year. One critic singled out the duo as a pleasing contrast to the 'rural quietism' he saw manifest elsewhere at the event.[3] In 1959 Rie began teaching at the Camberwell School of Art and several high-profile exhibitions followed, organized by the Arts Council in 1967, the Sainsbury Centre, Norwich, and V&A in 1981–2, and the Metropolitan Museum of Art, New York, in 1994. The latter showed her work alongside Coper's more sculptural ceramics.

Rie worked with a remarkable energy and focus into her later years, even after the death of Coper, which impacted her greatly. She produced an array of shapes and designs that have become quintessential to her output. She made tapered, footed bowls, in a variety of often jewel-like colours, which were decorated with bands of bronze pigment frequently left to trickle down the rims (fig. 1), and her famous sweeping flared-rim bottles displayed spiralling colours – the result of stains in the clay body – which recalled the spin of the wheel (fig. 5). Throughout her work there are echoes of her roots in Vienna's Modernist design milieu together with the earlier influences of her uncle's Roman excavations and other ancient Mediterranean and Neolithic forms.

Rie died in 1995, having suffered a series of strokes. Her legacy is that of a formidable potter and, to those who knew her, an attentive and hospitable friend. She changed the landscape of British studio pottery, influencing countless other potters, artists and designers, who found inspiration in her refined forms and experimental approaches. A famously private person, Rie spoke little publicly of her practice or ethos and divulged still less of her inner life. Coper once described her evocatively as a 'steel hand in a velvet glove',[4] but the last word is best left to Rie. Laconic, self-effacing and as pleasingly efficient as her work: 'I make pots, it's my profession.'[5]

Kate Devine

OTHER SIGNIFICANT MAKERS

Bernard Leach (1887–1979) was arguably the most influential figure in the history of British studio pottery. Trained as a potter in Japan after attending art school in London, Leach's work and writings sought to reconcile East and West. In 1920 he founded the Leach Pottery in St Ives, Cornwall with Hamada Shōji, which remains an important centre of production and training today.

Katharine Pleydell-Bouverie (1895–1985) was among the most accomplished studio potters to emerge in the 1920s and '30s. Following evening classes in London, she trained at the Leach Pottery in St Ives. She established her own workshop in 1925, pioneering the use of ash glazes made from vegetation on her family's estate.

Marguerite Wildenhain (1896–1985) was born in France (as Marguerite Friedlaender) and trained in ceramics at the Bauhaus in Germany. She designed Modernist porcelain before moving to the Netherlands and then the USA. She founded Pond Farm in California, an artists' colony and workshop where she taught ceramics following the Bauhaus model and was an inspirational mentor to many.

Gertrud Natzler (1908–1971) was an Austrian ceramicist who worked in partnership with her husband Otto. She made the clay forms and he glazed them. The couple fled Nazi-occupied Vienna for Los Angeles where they set up a successful studio and went on to be influential in the emergence of American studio pottery.

Hans Coper (1920–1981) is among the most internationally important ceramic artists of the twentieth century. Born in Germany, he went to Britain as an émigré in 1939. He began working with Lucie Rie in London, initially as her assistant, but soon developed the sculptural vessel forms for which he is most remembered.

RUTH DUCKWORTH

1919–2009

Pioneer of handbuilt ceramic sculpture

Ruth Duckworth stands among the most important and influential ceramicists of the twentieth century. A pioneer of handbuilt sculptural forms, she changed the course of ceramic art through her innovative work and her teaching. By the 1970s her standing was such that 'exhibitions in Europe and America gain in status if her work is included, as if Callas had come to sing'.[1]

Born in 1919, Ruth Windmüller was the youngest of five children in a prosperous family living in the Hamburg suburb of Eppendorf. Her Jewish father Edgar, a successful lawyer, was born in Manchester, the son of a German cotton trader. Less academic than her siblings, Ruth as a teenager harboured artistic ambitions and showed a determined spirit and an unwillingness to conform. Confronted with the rise of Nazism, life was becoming increasingly oppressive for Jewish families in Germany, and Edgar, as a dual-national, applied for British passports and nationality for his wife and children. In April 1936, aged 17, Ruth followed her older sister Renate to Liverpool.

There she enrolled at the Liverpool School of Art but found the teaching restrictive. Expected to choose between sculpture, drawing and painting as a course of study, Ruth refused and pursued all three. Moreover, she found her sculpture teacher out of touch, observing that 'Jacob Epstein was too modern for him'.[2] Ruth left Liverpool in 1940, and for two years worked for a travelling puppet theatre before taking up work in a munitions factory in support of the war effort. However, her mental health was suffering and so, released from her wartime occupation on medical grounds, she moved to join friends in London in 1944, where her parents were also living.

Close to her parents' home was the workshop of the Austrian-born potter and fellow émigré Lucie Rie (p. 306). Following an introduction by her father, Ruth gained some work making plaster moulds for Rie's ceramic button-making. She also enrolled at the Kennington School of Art, where she learned stone carving skills and put these to use as a monumental mason working on headstones and memorials. Still

Fig. 1
Ruth Duckworth
Pot, 1959
Stoneware, coil-built, green glaze at lip
24.5 × 23.8 cm
V&A: Circ.242-1959

Fig. 2
Ruth Duckworth
Tile Mask, 1962
Stoneware, matt black mask on a
mottled-green glazed tile
15 × 15 cm
V&A: Circ.617-1962

suffering from depression, she began undergoing regular psychoanalysis in the later 1940s, a transformative experience that came to play a significant positive role in her life and work.

It was during this period that Ruth gained her first major commission for a series of sculptural relief carvings for a church in New Malden, Surrey. She also met her husband-to-be, the designer and sculptor Aidron Duckworth, who assisted her in carrying it out. Ruth and Aidron married in 1949, and with parental support bought a house at Kew Bridge and established a studio. Working as a sculptor in stone, bronze and wood, Duckworth gained her first solo exhibition at the Apollinaire Gallery in Chelsea in 1953. However, by 1955 her interests were shifting to ceramics and an approach to Rie for glaze recipes led first – at Rie's suggestion – to her attending classes at Hammersmith School of Art, and then to study ceramics at the Central School of Arts and Crafts the following year.

The Central School had at that time the most progressive pottery department in London. Led by Dora Billington and Gilbert Harding-Green, it instilled in its students core skills such as throwing but was not doctrinaire and encouraged a broad range of technical approaches and styles. Teaching at the Central School was a succession of avant-garde potters with contemporary outlooks, among them William Newland, Gordon Baldwin, Nicholas Vergette, Ian Auld and Dan Arbeid. These artists were notable for their interest in sculptural form and handbuilding techniques, including coiling and slab-building. In this environment of material-focused exploration, Duckworth flourished and her work was quick to gain recognition. In 1959, the year after she left the Central School as a student, the V&A acquired two examples of her work: a stoneware dish decorated with abstracted figures, and a coil-built stoneware pot with a marked asymmetry that suggested a naturally occurring yet sculptural form (fig. 1). The following year she was awarded her first solo exhibition of ceramics at Primavera, the influential London gallery of Henry Rothschild, a champion of contemporary craft. Further exhibitions would follow there in 1962, shared with Aidron, and in 1967, when she showed alongside studio-glass pioneer Sam Herman (p. 347). Meanwhile, Ruth and Aidron acquired a plot of land at Kew Gardens in 1959 and built a new home, Ruth House, designed by Aidron and the architect Christopher Reid. She also soon returned to the Central School as a part-time teacher, a typical pattern whereby the school's most promising students were kept within its creative orbit.

The innovative and radical nature of Duckworth's practice in this period can hardly be overstated. Writing of her impact in his 1967 survey *The Art of the Modern Potter*, Tony Birks noted: 'more than any other potter who has worked in England, [she] is responsible for the

Fig. 3
Ruth Duckworth
Weed Pot (will not hold water), 1966
Stoneware, handbuilt, spattered black and green glaze
31.4 × 34 cm
V&A: Circ.764-1967

explosive charge which blew up traditional thinking about pottery at the end of the 1950s.'[3] While she was in the early years an accomplished thrower and a maker of much-admired coffee sets – which sat well alongside Aidron's design-led practice – it was as a sculptural handbuilder that she truly excelled, and this broadly took two forms. The first was in large coiled or soft-slabbed stoneware pot forms, weighty but poised and well-balanced, growing as if by forces of nature from typically small bases. The second were small-scale, delicate organic forms modelled in porcelain, other-worldly and strange, often set on single stems like mushrooms. Both groups of works were in essence forms of sculpture; neither purported to be useful in any practical sense. Suggestive of natural or organic forms, they were also essentially abstract. Yet more overtly figurative elements occasionally appeared, as in her *Tile Mask* of 1962 (fig. 2), foreshadowing the figural sculpture she produced late in life.

An article by Ruth and Aidron entitled 'Potting in a Vacuum', published in *Pottery Quarterly* in 1961, noted the wealth of talent among contemporary British potters, but detailed some of the challenges they faced. Among the opportunities that they sought was collaboration with

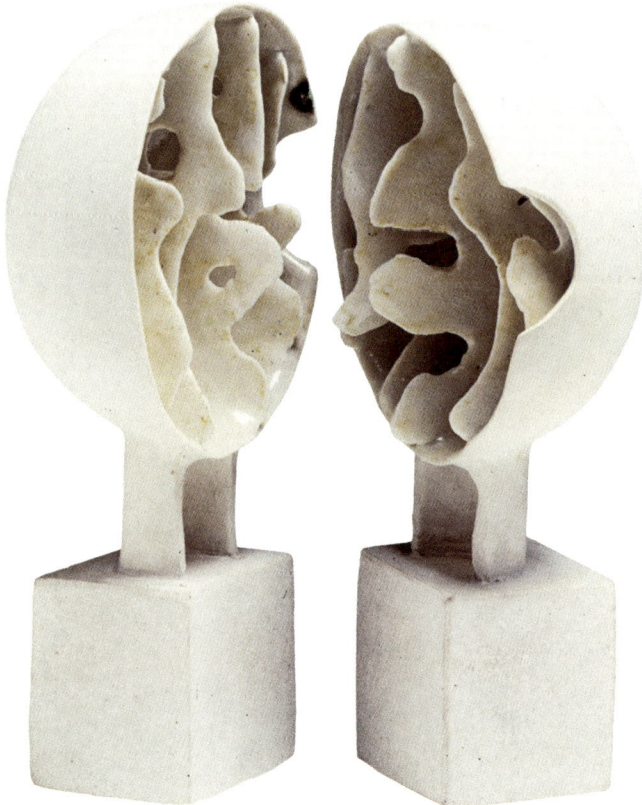

Fig. 4
Ruth Duckworth
Untitled (sphere with interior sculptural forms), 1979
Porcelain, handbuilt
17.4 × 6.7 cm
V&A: C.118&A-1980

architects and interior designers, and perhaps such a desire lay behind their decision to seize an unexpected offer that came their way. In 1964 Ruth was invited to go to the Midway Studios, University of Chicago, as a visiting artist and ceramics teacher. It would be, if nothing else, an opportunity to travel and to see the USA and Mexico, and Ruth accepted. Initially, the post was for a year, and she returned to England in 1965–6, working again at Kew, making pots for what would be her final show at Primavera the following year. These included her *Weed Pot (will not hold water)*, as it was titled at the exhibition (fig. 3). However, in 1966 she returned permanently to Chicago to continue teaching, believing that America offered greater opportunities, particularly for working at scale. Aidron also moved to the USA, but the couple separated shortly after.

An opportunity for Ruth to work on a grand scale soon came in the form of a mural commission for the entrance hall of the University of Chicago's newly built Geophysical Sciences Building. Completed in 1968, *Earth, Water and Sky* covered all four walls and the ceiling with stoneware panels modelled in relief, reflecting celestial and terrestrial themes. It was the first of many mural commissions, the next at scale being her *Clouds Over Lake Michigan* for the Dresdner Bank's Board of Trade Building in Chicago, which she worked on from 1976. A further major mural, on the subject of *The Creation*, was completed in 1984 for the Congregation Beth Israel of Hammond, Indiana. By this time, Duckworth had realized another substantial ambition and had converted a former pickle factory on the north side of Chicago to form an extensive studio and living space.

Duckworth's individual sculptural ceramics, meanwhile, continued to evolve. Working still in both stoneware and porcelain, she increasingly explored themes and ideas in distinct series. Emerging in the later 1960s and continuing through the 1970s is a varied series of smaller porcelain sculptures, loosely conceived as 'reveal/conceal' or 'open and shut' pieces (fig. 4). In these works, there is a heightened sense of exterior and interior space, with elements partially hidden. These sensuous works often take the form of a bisected, stemmed sphere with interior flanges and openings, set upon a single or sometimes separate pedestal bases. With comparable psychological intensity, and rendered in stone-like porcelain, are Duckworth's 'cup and blade' forms – perhaps her most celebrated sculpture series (fig. 5). Begun in the late 1970s and made through to the 2000s, these works typically comprise an open cup or bowl-like vessel, within which a blade form is suspended, the blade supported on the cup's rim, creating a sharp meeting point that quite literally gives edge to the sculptures. Duckworth's 'mama pots' – large, rounded stoneware vessels with pronounced fissures, so called because

of a young child's warm response on seeing one – were made during
the same extended period as the 'cup and blade' forms and stand as the
descendants of earlier rugged forms like *Weed Pot*.

Ruth Duckworth's six-decade career as a potter and sculptor was
celebrated in a major retrospective that toured six venues in the USA
in 2005–7. Following a further retrospective at the Ruthin Craft Centre,
Wales, in 2009, she is said to have been moved to return permanently
to the UK but died in Chicago later that year. Throughout her working
life, Duckworth thought 'as a sculptor', making ceramics that defied
expectations of the medium and which ultimately changed the way
it is perceived.[4]

Alun Graves

Fig. 5
Ruth Duckworth
Untitled (two cup and blade forms), 1985
Porcelain, handbuilt
14.6 × 18.5 cm (left), 11 × 11.4 cm (right)
V&A: Circ.67&A, 68&A-1986
Given by Helen Drutt and Ruth Duckworth

OTHER SIGNIFICANT MAKERS

Peter Voulkos (1924–2002) was a prodigious talent whose example and teaching transformed ceramics into an expressionist sculptural medium. In 1954 he was appointed Head of Ceramics at Otis Art Institute, Los Angeles, moving then to the University of California at Berkeley in 1959. He is renowned for his large, muscular stoneware sculptures constructed from thrown elements.

Karen Karnes (1925–2016) was an iconic figure in American craft. She studied ceramics at Alfred University, New York, and in 1952 took up a residency at the progressive Black Mountain College, North Carolina. Subsequently working at Stony Point, New York, and later Vermont, Karnes made functional stoneware pottery of individual expressive character.

Gordon Baldwin (b.1932) is among the most significant ceramic sculptors in Britain. A pioneer of handbuilding techniques, he concentrated on abstract vessels and forms. Baldwin was also an influential teacher at the Central School of Arts and Crafts and Goldsmiths' College, both in London, and at Eton College.

Gwyn Hanssen Pigott (1935–2013) was Australia's most acclaimed studio potter, and an artist of international significance and influence. Trained in Australia and England, she established workshops in London and rural France before returning to Australia in 1973. A maker of refined domestic forms, she broke new ground through her development of still-life groupings of her work.

Gillian Lowndes (1936–2010) was a radical and innovative ceramic artist who explored materials in daring new ways in the creation of sculptural forms. Part of a progressive generation of post-war artist-potters, Lowndes was a contemporary of Ruth Duckworth at the Central School of Arts and Crafts, London, both as a student and as a teacher.

STANISLAV LIBENSKÝ 1921–2002
JAROSLAVA BRYCHTOVÁ 1924–2020

Masters of modern glass sculpture

The Czech artist couple Stanislav Libenský and Jaroslava Brychtová are among the most influential glassmakers of the twentieth century. They spent most of their lives in northern Bohemia in the Czech Republic, an area with a centuries-old glassmaking tradition. Libenský and Brychtová married in 1963 and are best known for their large-scale abstract glass sculptures, for which they developed a new technique of mould-melting. In these works, glass and shape interact with light to create an interplay between colour and space and the couple's artistic endeavours have influenced generations of glassmakers worldwide.

Libenský and Brychtová's careers are interwoven with the glassmaking vocational schools of northern Bohemia and a system of education which emphasized the integration of the fine and applied arts. Jaroslava Brychtová's father, Jaroslav Brychta, was a sculptor teaching at the Specialized School of Glassmaking in Železný Brod and specialized in small glass figures. Jaroslava Brychtová carried out her first experiments with mould-melting glass with her father, during the 1940s. Stanislav Libenský, trained at the Department of Applied Painting and Glass Art at the School of Applied Arts in Prague from 1939 until it was closed during the Second World War in 1944.

The war caused great harm to the glass industry in Bohemia. There was a shortage of materials, and many skilled German glassmakers and decorators left the area. After 1945 the glass schools at Nový Bor, Kamenický Šenov and Železný Brod were restarted with a new vigour. Many of the teachers had a fine-art background which encouraged a break with the traditional and conservative aesthetics of glass. Libenský was appointed Head of the Department of Painting on Glass and Stained Glass at the specialized glass school in Nový Bor. There he focused primarily on the decoration of glass. Between the years 1945 and 1948 he produced designs for decorated vases, many with fantastical and impressionistic compositions using motifs ranging from African art to fairy tales and dreams. The decoration combined acid

Fig. 1
Stanislav Libenský and Jaroslava Brychtová
Winged Head I, 1962
Mould-melted glass
33 × 49 cm
V&A: C.19-1996
Given, in exchange, by the Museum
of Decorative Arts, Prague

Fig. 2
Stanislav Libenský
Preparatory drawing for *1001 Nights* vase, 1946
Graphite on paper
43.9 × 59.9 cm
V&A: E.34-1987
Presented by Rainer Zietz

etching, applied by technicians, and enamel painting, executed by the
students as part of their training (figs 2 and 3).

Jaroslava Brychtová went on to study sculpture and applied sculpture
at the Academy of Fine Arts in Prague until she returned to Železný Brod
in 1950. Building on her experiments with cast glass, she established a
workshop at her family home, which served as the Glass in Architecture
Department of the Železnobrodské sklo glassworks. The workshop later
moved to larger premises and grew into a venture equipped to create
glassworks on a monumental scale, with a production team of up to
ten glassworkers and technicians.

The year 1948 heralded a substantial change for the production of
Czech glass. The industry was nationalized, with small workshops being
amalgamated into larger production enterprises and the artistic
departments of the Specialized Schools of Glassmaking in Nový Bor
and Kamenický Šenov were closed. However, the Czechoslovak state
recognized the importance of its national heritage in glass and Brychtová's
Glass in Architecture Centre was allowed to continue working as part of
a group of cultural enterprises aimed at preserving folk artistic production
and artistic crafts. The school at Železný Brod was also allowed to
continue and Stanislav Libenský joined the teaching staff in 1953. He was
made Director a year later, a post which he held until 1963 when he became
Head of the Glass Department of the Academy of Applied Arts in Prague.

Around 1955 Libenský made a sketch of an oval bowl in the shape of
a woman's head with a classical profile and long, flowing hair. His fellow
teacher Jaroslava Brychtová asked him if she could use it for the design
of a three-dimensional model for glass melting. This first object set the

tone for their lengthy and fruitful collaboration in which they exploited the casting technique that Brychtová had developed with her father to its full sculptural potential. Libenský would start the creative process with sketched designs that Brychtová would translate into a three-dimensional model in clay. From this, she created a negative plaster mould which would remain open at the top. The mould was filled with small chunks of coloured glass, between 3 and 15 centimetres in diameter, and placed in a kiln. This was heated until the glass had melted completely and filled the entire space of the mould. A lengthy period of annealing, in which the temperature was gradually brought down, was required to avoid internal stress in the glass which could cause breakages. For the larger pieces, this could take up to a month. The piece was then excavated from the plaster mould and cleaned. The top surface, where the mould was open, would have a rough, uneven surface, which was subsequently ground flat and polished smooth. This surface is usually the side from which the sculpture should be viewed. When the sculpture is lit from behind, a negative relief becomes visible, in which the different thicknesses in the glass make the colour of the work seem more or less intense. In this entirely new type of work, it seemed that Libenský and Brychtová were able to sculpt, as it were, directly with light, space and colour.

Their shallow, negative reliefs were ideally suited for architectural application. From 1957 onwards the Czechoslovak state repeatedly commissioned Libenský and Brychtová to produce works for integration into architectural settings. Between 1964 and 1969 they created new windows for the St Wenceslas Chapel in Prague's St Vitus Cathedral. Their abstract design responds, through its tonal subtlety, to the early sixteenth-century decoration of the chapel.

Though Communist Czechoslovakia was somewhat closed off from the western world, Libenský and Brychtová were still able to present their work at major international exhibitions. The Czechoslovak pavilion at the Expo '58 in Brussels (also known as the 1958 Brussels World Fair) included a series of glass *Animal Reliefs*, for which Libenský and Brychtová were awarded a Grand Prix. The reliefs were set into a concrete wall and lit from behind. Through their smooth outside surface, they revealed three-dimensional, negative reliefs of animals inspired by the cave paintings of Altamira, Spain, and Lascaux, France. For this work, the couple took advantage of new colours developed for the paste jewellery industry in the Czech city of Jablonec nad Nisou. They selected brilliant colours, which showed high contrasts through variations in the thickness of the glass.

Expo '58 also provided Libenský and Brychtová with the opportunity to visit the exhibition *Fifty Years of Modern Art*. Here they saw the works of pioneers of Modernism for the first time which previously they had

Fig. 3
Stanislav Libenský
1001 Nights vase, 1946
Decorated at the Specialized School of Glassmaking in Nový Bor, Czechoslovakia
Blown glass, etched and enamelled
24.5 × 17 cm
V&A: C.104-1984

Fig. 4
Stanislav Libenský and Jaroslava Brychtová
Arcus 1, 1991
Mould-melted glass
75 × 98.5 × 11 cm
V&A: C.4-1993

only known through books and reproductions. The profound impact this had on the couple can be seen in their first major abstract sculpture, *Winged Head I* of 1962 (fig. 1). This powerful expressionist sculpture was first shown in the 1964 exhibition *Glass: Czechoslovakia and Italy*, at the Museum of Contemporary Craft in New York.

At Expo '67 in Montreal, Canada, Libenský and Brychtová created three large sculptures for the Czechoslovak pavilion. These multi-part sculptures, modelled in high relief and mounted on metal supports, were on a scale and of an ambition not previously seen in art glass and had a great impact internationally. Even more ambitious was their contribution to Expo '70 in Osaka, Japan, for which Libenský and Brychtová designed a huge glass and steel sculpture 22 metres long. It is interesting to reflect that the Communist regime in Czechoslovakia suppressed contemporary art because it might have conveyed subversive messages. However, glass art, with its centuries-old national tradition, was deemed 'safe' and so makers could continue working. At the same time, it was state sponsorship that allowed artists such as Libenský and Brychtová to work on a scale that western artists could only dream of. However, in Osaka, the couple had gone too far. The iconography of their large sculpture *River of Life* contained references to the Soviet-led occupation of Czechoslovakia since 1968 that were understood by the public as well as the Czechoslovak authorities. As a result, Libenský and Brychtová were expelled from the Party and forbidden to travel abroad together for a time. However, their fame was such that they continued to receive state commissions. Their work of that period avoided political messages and concentrated on pure, abstract sculpture, making use of the optic qualities of glass.

Libenský and Brychtová created *Arcus I* in 1991 (fig. 4), not long after the Velvet Revolution. It is a large and simple geometric shape in clear blue glass, which is pierced through the middle with a diagonal channel. The front side is cut smooth and polished as usual, while the reverse is untreated and slightly rough. This mature work shows the couple's complete mastery and control of the interplay between space, light and colour. The V&A was able to acquire this work in 1991–3 directly from the makers, selected from a small display of works in their studio in Železný Brod, where they continued to work until Libenský's death in 2002.

It is hard to overestimate Libenský and Brychtová's artistic legacy. Through their teaching at the Prague Academy and the glass school at Železný Brod they directly influenced and inspired many young glass artists. But more importantly, they were the first to create monumental abstract sculptures in glass. They devised a new artistic language which elevated the medium of glass from its largely decorative background to something capable of conveying purely artistic ideas and feelings. They also developed a technique for this which has been adopted by several generations of glass artists, not only in the Czech Republic and Slovakia but all over the world.

Reino Liefkes

OTHER SIGNIFICANT MAKERS

René Roubíček (1922–2018) was one of the leading glass artists working in Czechoslovakia under the Communist regime during the 1950s and '60s. His works in blown glass are exuberant, playful and colourful. After the Communist regime barred Roubíček from major or international exhibitions in 1970 his works became darker and more reflective.

Erwin Eisch (1927–2022) was one of the founders of the studio glass movement. In 1965 he set up Europe's first studio glass furnace, within the Eisch family glassworks in Germany. More than anyone, Eisch was responsible for developing blown glass as a material for artistic expression, liberating the material from its previous, almost exclusively decorative use.

Jiří Harcuba (1928–2013) is probably the best-known Czech glass engraver of the twentieth century. He taught glass engraving at the Prague Academy and worked there as an assistant to Libenský. During 1965–6 he was a visiting professor at the Royal College of Art in London. Harcuba made abstract work and later specialized in portraiture.

Colin Reid (b.1953) is one of Britain's foremost artists working with cast glass. Using the lost wax casting method, he often takes moulds from naturally occurring materials as a starting point for his dynamic sculptures in optical glass. By taking on apprentices, Reid has taught many younger glass artists.

ALTHEA MCNISH

1924–2020

Internationally renowned textile designer

> *My work is my statement. I am a citizen of the world and
> I am multi-cultural. My ancestry is carib, native American,
> African, Ethiopian and European. My world is the world of
> colour and nature.*[1]

Althea McNish was thought to be the first designer of African Caribbean heritage to gain international recognition in the textile world. Her instantly recognizable designs for fashion, the home and business and transport environments inserted much-needed colour and life into a British fashion and textiles industry still recovering from the after-effects of Second World War austerity. Her dazzling colours and energetic brushwork are synonymous with Modernism in textiles of this period. Britain was at the forefront of innovative textile design and McNish led the way with her experimental approach to colour, form and technique. She is responsible for some of the most memorable textile designs of the twentieth century.

McNish was born in Port of Spain, the capital of Trinidad and Tobago, in 1924. She moved to London with her mother in 1951 to join her father who was already working there. Her mother was a respected designer and dressmaker in her own right and McNish grew up spending time in her mother's Trinidad sewing room, often sketching out her mother's ideas. McNish displayed a love of painting and drawing from an early age and her parents encouraged her creativity. Her desire to paint was stimulated by winning a set of paints as a child and she soon became a junior member of the Trinidad and Tobago Arts Society, presenting her first exhibition in Port of Spain at the age of 16. Although self-taught, through the Society McNish's obvious painting skills were nurtured by renowned Trinidadian artists Geoffrey and Boscoe Holder, Carlisle Change, Andrew Carr, Sybil Atteck, M.P. Alladin and Pierre Lelong. Upon leaving school she served as an apprentice at a private architect's practice and then in the civil service as a cartographer and entomological illustrator.

Fig. 1
Althea McNish
Golden Harvest furnishing fabric, 1960s
Designed for Hull Traders Ltd
Printed cotton satin
126.5 × 138 cm
V&A: T.178-1989
Given by the makers

Fig. 2
Althea McNish
Tropic dress fabric, 1959
Made by Ascher Ltd
Printed silk
96 × 93 cm
V&A: T.192-1988
Given by Zika Ascher

On arrival in London, McNish's intention was to study architecture. Before she left Trinidad, she had won a scholarship to attend the Architectural Association. However, once in London McNish chose instead to take a course at the London School of Printing and Graphic Arts (now the London College of Communication). This change in direction was partly aided by the Colonial Office, which allowed her to take a secondment from her work as a cartographer. It was during this period of study that McNish happened upon the inspirational textile design work of students studying at the Central School of Arts and Crafts, under the tutelage of artist and Independent Group (IG) member Sir Eduardo Paolozzi. Founded in 1952, the IG is regarded as the forerunner of the Pop Art movement in Britain. The radical painters, sculptors, architects, writers and critics who made up this influential group challenged the then elitist approaches to art appreciation, introducing popular and commercial culture into the debate. McNish took evening classes with Paolozzi while completing her undergraduate

Fig. 3
Althea McNish
Trinidad furnishing fabric, 1960
Made by Heal & Son Ltd
Printed cotton
274 × 123 cm
V&A: T.444-1999
Given by Heal & Son Ltd

studies. With his encouragement, she concluded her design education in 1957 with a postgraduate degree in textiles at the Royal College of Art (RCA), then part of the V&A. McNish and her peers studied with influential tutors, including designer John Drummond, photographer Humphrey Spender and painter Roger Nicholson in textiles, and architect Hugh Casson in architecture.

At the RCA, McNish was given freedom and autonomy to develop her practice. She recalled visiting many galleries in London and was drawn to Modernism, admiring the work of artists including Henri Matisse, Pablo Picasso, Georges Braque, Vincent van Gogh and Paul Gauguin. This long-standing interest in painting informed her approach to designing textiles. She was less concerned with scale and repeat and indeed saw no separation between the artistic works she produced. During her final year at the RCA, she visited the Essex home of her tutor, painter and graphic artist Edward Bawden, and his wife Charlotte, a ceramicist. This trip, and her encounters with the English landscape, proved to be a significant turning point in McNish's career. Walking in the nearby countryside, she saw a wheat field for the first time and it reminded her of the sugar cane fields in Trinidad. Two years later, in 1959, she developed a wheat motif for the furnishing fabric *Golden Harvest* (fig. 1). The textile is screen-printed onto heavy cotton satin. Produced in four colourways, *Golden Harvest* went on to be her most celebrated design for the textile manufacturer Hull Traders Ltd, remaining in production for over ten years after its release in 1960.

Prior to this, McNish had already found commercial success through London's Liberty department store. On seeing her graduation show, the chairman Arthur Stewart-Liberty commissioned McNish to deploy her already distinctive aesthetic to create unique designs for Liberty fashion and furnishing fabrics. Stewart-Liberty rightly intuited that British consumers were ready for colour and that McNish could be the designer to supply it. McNish was introduced to Zika Ascher whose eponymous brand, Ascher Ltd, produced high-end experimental woven and printed fabrics for use in Parisian haute couture. Ascher collaborated with contemporary artists, such as the sculptor Henry Moore, who designed prints for the company in the 1940s. Ascher was drawn to McNish's free brushstrokes and confident use of unexpected colour combinations. He commissioned her to work on exclusive designs like *Tropic* (fig. 2) for production on silk, and such designs were chosen by Ascher's couture clients, most notably Christian Dior.

McNish's work was in great demand and many more commissions followed. For example, a 1960 Heal & Son Ltd commission yielded *Trinidad* (fig. 3), a lively foliage design rendered in green, purple and blue on a deep indigo ground. Damasco Fabrics and Hull Traders followed suit, helping to establish McNish as a designer at the forefront of British textiles. Her designs also appealed to young customers and found their way into new high street fashion collections such as Mary Quant's Bazaar and Barbara Hulaniki's Biba, which were making cutting-edge fashions available to the mass market for the first time. From the 1950s onwards McNish's exuberant designs made full use of scientific developments in dyeing techniques, printing and fabrication. Manufacturers like Imperial Chemical Industries (ICI) developed new synthetic dyes and synthetic fibres that could achieve long-lasting vibrant colours. They sought out McNish's designs since her colourful palette allowed them to show off the properties of Terylene, a polyester cloth that did not fade as easily as natural fibres such as silk.

A skilled print technician, McNish pushed the boundaries of what was achievable with silkscreen printing. It is technically difficult and costly to produce designs that incorporate painterly brushstrokes, ombre textures and multiple layers of colour through this technique. McNish challenged those technicians who suggested that what she wanted to achieve could not be done, using her grounding in and experimentation within the practicalities of printing to find solutions to printing complex layered designs: 'I challenged them in their own ground and then they wanted to prove to me that they could do it.'[2] She also applied her energetic brushstrokes and riotous colour palette to designs destined for architectural murals and wallpapers, such as *Zircon* (fig. 4), a yellow and mustard swirling pattern created for Sanderson-Rigg Ltd in 1968. Here, as in McNish's other signature designs, the process of painting is deliberately made visible. In the 1950s she was commissioned by the Design Research Unit, whose clients included British Rail and the Orient Steam Navigation Company. McNish produced mural designs for restaurants on-board ocean liner SS *Oriana* in 1959, velvet drapes for British Rail's London offices in 1969 and a banner for London's Design Centre in 1981. In 1966 McNish designed and dressed a 'Bachelor Girl's Room' for London's influential and popular Ideal Home Exhibition: a lively modern space clearly designed for an independent girl-about-town.

McNish continued to paint while working as a freelance designer. She was also an active member of the Caribbean Arts Movement (CAM), founded in London in 1966 by creative writers, artists and critics from the newly independent English-speaking Caribbean. CAM aimed to promote the work of creatives from across the spectrum of art and design practices. Its members sought to rediscover Caribbean aesthetics and histories emerging from Amerindian and African roots to inform new directions for the arts. McNish was one of a small group of women attached to CAM that

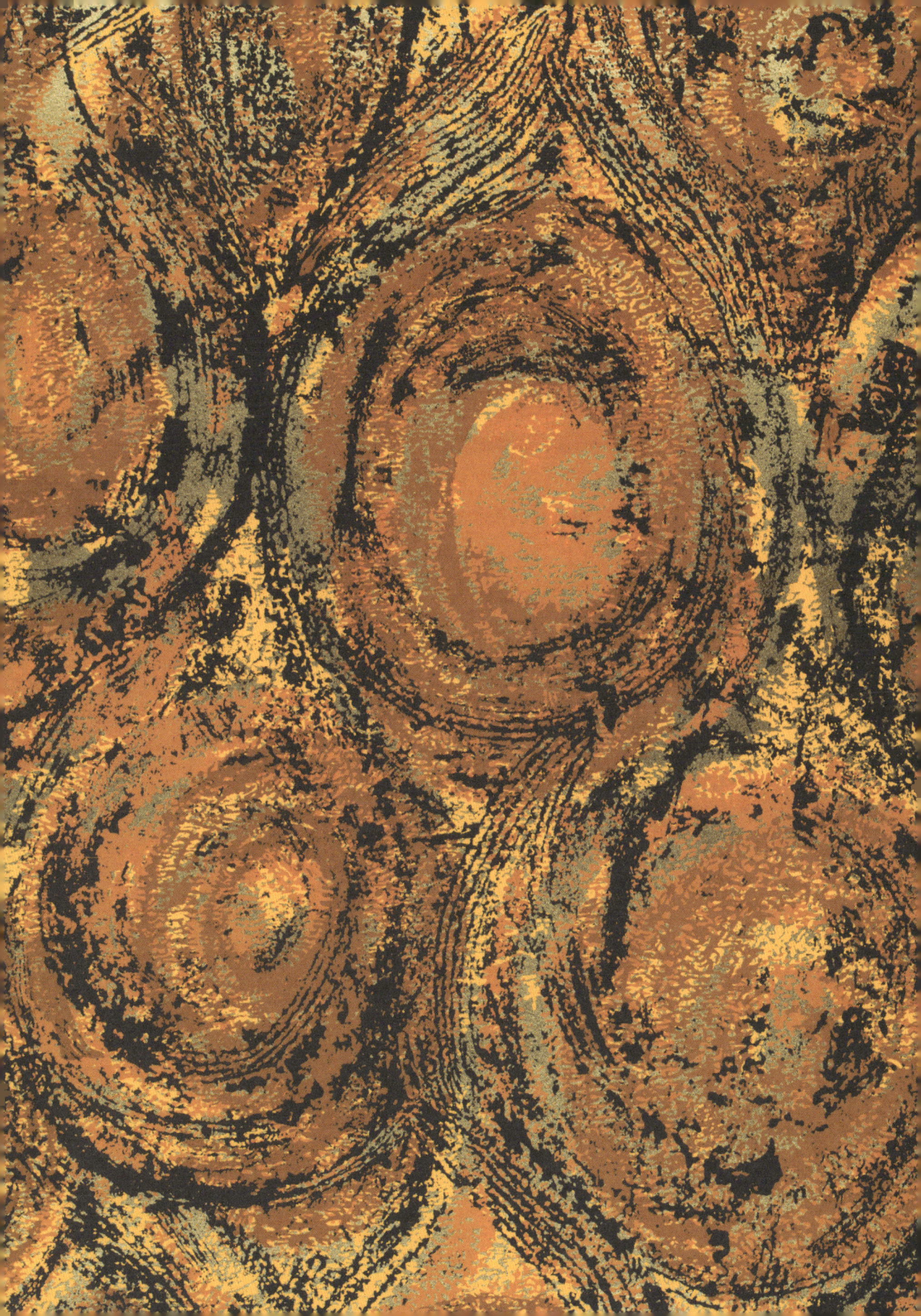

included Marina Maxwell, Elsa Goveia, Jean Franco, Pearl Connor, Yvonne Brewster and Doris Harper-Wills. McNish's print designs on laminated plastics were shown in the first of their exhibitions in 1967, alongside works by Karl 'Jerry' Craig, Aubrey Williams, Ronald Moody and Errol Lloyd, and her work was included in all but two of the CAM exhibitions between 1967 and 1971. CAM gave artists a platform and a sense of unity which, in an often hostile London, was more important than artistic differences. In 1973 McNish designed the set for the BBC television programme *Full House* which filmed a special edition on Caribbean arts, produced by John La Rose, the writer and founder of CAM.

The creative vision of Althea McNish – her effervescent designs in dazzling colours (fig. 5) – shifted the character of British Modernism, overthrowing sterile rules of taste and drab palettes that previously shaped mass-produced design. She continued to paint and draw throughout her later life. At the age of 90, when asked if she still made work, McNish replied 'Yes', adding 'it's in my blood'.[3] She remained committed to the world of design, sitting on the board of the UK Design Council, mentoring fledgling creatives in the Caribbean and the UK. She received an honorary doctorate in fine arts from the University of Trinidad and Tobago in 2006. Exhibitions such as *Althea McNish: Colour is Mine* at London's William Morris Gallery and the Whitworth Art Gallery, Manchester (2022–3), alongside her inclusion in *Get Up, Stand Up Now* at Somerset House, London, in 2019, bear witness to McNish's enduring appeal and relevance.

Christine Checinska

OTHER SIGNIFICANT MAKERS

Marian Mahler (1911–1983) was an Austrian textile designer. She studied at the Kunstgewerbeschule, Vienna, moving to Britain in 1937. During the 1950s she designed for Allan Walton, Edinburgh Weavers and Donald Brothers. She created sophisticated designs that used a new roller-printed manufacturing process, generating affordable textiles that appealed to young customers.

Lucienne Day (1917–2010) was a highly influential British textile designer of the 1950s and 1960s. She graduated from the Royal College of Art in 1940, but her breakthrough came later with her textile design *Calyx* for the Festival of Britain in 1951. She created over 70 designs for Heal Fabrics, London. Her designs became dress and furnishing fabrics, tea towels, wallpapers and carpets.

Eddie Pond (1929–2012) was a designer of textiles, wallpapers and ceramics. He studied at Dagenham Art School and then at the RCA from 1955 to 1958. Before attending college, Pond set up his own business, painting and selling head scarves. He became Chief Designer at Bernard Wardle's Everflex coated fabric works in Wales from 1958.

Barbara Brown (b.1932) attended Canterbury College of Art and enrolled at the Royal College of Art in 1953. Brown sold her first fabric to Heal Fabrics, London, before graduating from the RCA and subsequently designed for them for 20 years, creating unique geometric designs and often adopting optical patterns characteristic of 1960s Pop Art.

Shirley Craven (b.1934) studied painting, sculpture, and textile design at Hull College of Art and the Royal College of Art, London, between 1955 and 1958. From 1960 she freelanced for Hull Traders Ltd, creating vibrant abstract designs for screen-printing. In 1963 she became Chief Designer and Director, steering the business through its most innovative period and dictating the style of the swinging '60s through textiles.

MARJORIE SCHICK

1941–2017

Pre-eminent American jewellery artist

The revolutionary jewellery artist Marjorie Schick created colourful, extravagant and voluminous sculptures for the body. Renowned for her use of unusual materials and techniques, her approach to jewellery was atypical. She constructed unapologetically bold structures for the human form featuring materials such as metal, cardboard, wire mesh, wooden dowels, canvas, steel rods and papier mâché. Defying convention, Schick danced to the beat of a drum which she fashioned herself.

Born on 29 August 1941, in Taylorville, Illinois, her mother was an art educator and she was introduced to art from an early age, surrounded by an abundance of publications and materials. She was encouraged to take up sewing, painting and collage making, skills which would prove to be pivotal in her future creations. Schick's early aspiration was to become a Hollywood costume designer and building on her solid foundation in art at home, she made good use of a high school curriculum rich with inspiring artistic subjects. Saturdays were spent travelling from Evanston, a suburb of Chicago, to study a plethora of courses exploring subjects such as illustration, fashion design and watercolour painting at the Art Institute of Chicago's School of Art. In 1963 she received a bachelor's degree in art education at the University of Wisconsin. Under the tutelage of the celebrated American jewellery designer and silversmith Alma Eikerman, Schick subsequently received a Master of Fine Art in Jewellery Design and Metalsmithing at Indiana University. In 1983 she undertook an extended study programme at the Sir John Cass School of Art in London. Upon completing her studies, Schick taught at Pittsburgh University for half a century.[1]

It is impossible to find articles or interviews about Schick which fail to mention how requisite her close relationships were for her, with her life and career very much intertwined. The bonds she shared with her mother, husband and Eikerman fostered a fertile environment for Schick's growth, fuelling boundless freedom of exploration and self-expression. Her husband, James Schick, was instrumental

Fig. 1
Marjorie Schick
Ring of Fire, 1995
Corrugated cardboard, steel rods
and painted papier mâché
48.5 × 50.5 × 10 cm
V&A: M.58-1997

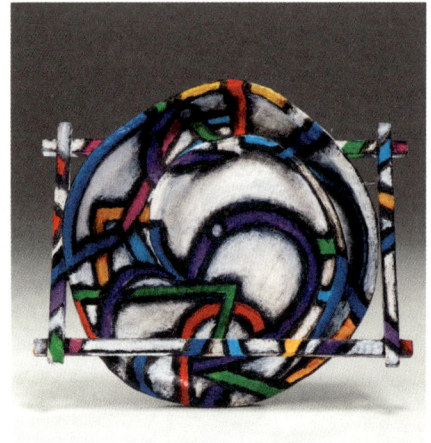

throughout her career. In this message to her mother, she credits him with her choice to study jewellery design at a critical stage:

> Mother, I met a man, Jim Schick. He plans to be a history professor. After marriage, he would begin a PH.D. program that fall, so I applied for an advanced degree. The question on the application for graduate school proved difficult. For which degree would I apply? I chose M.F.A because it had three letters of the alphabet while the other degree had only two. Next was to select an emphasis. Not knowing which of the art subjects in school I preferred, I asked Jim, the person who has guided my life. Watching me through four years of college, he thought I liked jewelry best so I chose jewelry design and metalsmithing. Simple as that, he decided my future. I am forever grateful.[2]

Her career commenced during the late 1960s, at a time of profound social change and a period of great transformation in jewellery design. Across Europe and America, artist-jewellers had begun confronting traditional concepts of jewellery and categorizations of what was deemed 'precious'. Art jewellery was intended to be purchased by the wearer, as an expression of their personality and creativity. From the 1940s through to the 1960s, artists such as Alexander Calder, Margaret De Patta and Art Smith moved away from traditional jewellery, creating Modernist, abstract, kinetic, organic and avant-garde works of art with a variety of unusual materials and processes. Along with other contemporaries of that era, their continued influence on future generations cannot be underestimated and had a great impact on the development of Schick's work.[3]

Schick trained as a traditional metalsmith and between 1961 and 1966 produced works made predominantly from metal. In 1966 she read an article on David Smith, an artist she admired. Smith was regarded as the

Fig. 2
Marjorie Schick
Basic Geometry, 2008 (part of a set)
Painted wood
6.5 × 12 × 8.5 cm
V&A: M.19:1-2-2018
Given by Robert A. Hiller

Fig. 3
Marjorie Schick
The Colours of London: Tube Map brooch, 1998
Painted papier mâché, wood and stainless steel wire
11 × 12.3 cm
V&A: M.24-2024
Given by Dr James B.M. Schick and Robert M Schick in honour of the artist

greatest sculptor of his generation and this article, along with the images of his sculptures, inspired a new direction in her work. While reading, she began to wonder what it would feel like to put his sculptures on the human body. Schick often stated that there was something about the constructivist nature of his work that ignited a curiosity within her, marking the beginning of her exploration. Her mission was to make jewellery a fine art form and the body a mobile plinth, from which her work could be viewed from different perspectives.[4]

The dedication to her work and the energy captured within her pieces generated excitement beyond the USA. Exhibiting locally and internationally, her work was well received across Britain and Europe – a long way from her classroom at Pittsburgh University, where she created most of her pieces. Although her creations, exploding with colour and texture, are standalone sculptures, they are best appreciated on the body as they become even more alive when worn. Her one-of-a-kind masterpieces attracted a great deal of interest and were collected widely across continents, including by institutions such as the Victoria and Albert Museum in London, Renwick Gallery of the Smithsonian American Art Museum in New York and the Nelson-Atkins Museum of Art in Kansas City.

Schick did not sketch her ideas but worked with a freedom that allowed her pieces to evolve as they took form. She laboriously constructed them, layer on layer, until she was satisfied. By her own account, 'jewellery making was magic, albeit hard work magic'.[5] Her three-dimensional forms pushed the boundaries of the radical jewellery expressions of the time. Her works, which she described as 'wearable paintings', were intentionally confrontational, challenging scale, space and comfortability.[6] They spread far beyond the wearer's body and fill the space around them while invading that of others close by.

Her combined use of lightweight materials and the methods she mastered during her early developmental years enabled the creation of her signature avant-garde sculptures. Among her vast body of work are iconic pieces such as the *Ring of Fire*, named by her husband (fig. 1). In a letter to Clare Phillips, Curator of Jewellery at the V&A, Schick states that the neckpiece 'took over a year and approximately 150 to 200 hours to construct', using corrugated cardboard, steel rods, heavy thread, glue, newspaper and paint.[7]

Other works in the V&A collection include her *Basic Geometry* rings (fig. 2) and *Colours of London*, a series of four large sculptural brooches acquired in 2024. These lightweight yet robust brooches were expertly crafted from papier mâché with wooden dowels and steel pins and finished with a spectrum of colours and texture. As with all her pieces, the more you look, the more you see. The aptly named series encapsulates her memories of the city during her time in London in 1998. *Tube Map* (fig. 3) features the multi-coloured flowing lines of the Piccadilly, Circle and District lines, while *Shopping Harrods* is painted with the instantly recognizable and iconic green shade of one of London's oldest department stores. The *A–Z Guide* (fig. 4) gives an insight into how Schick might have travelled through the city during her stay. *Patchy Drizzle* (fig. 5) combines swirling colours in the form of multiple umbrellas to capture the atmosphere of a typical grey and rainy day in London.

These pieces together exemplify Schick's ability to create paintings for the body as well as her creative use of materials. Although non-precious, each material was carefully considered. Her work was labour-intensive and she used traditional metalsmithing techniques in her finishing. At first glance the untrained eye might easily dismiss them as vibrant paper or wooden costumes; however, this is work which deserves a second and third glance. It is work which encourages the onlooker to delve deeper into the construction, materials, techniques and unquantifiable amount of time invested in their creation. They are more than colourful works of art; they are an amalgamation of layers of thoughts and processes, housing within them the courageous spirit of a woman from the Midwest of America who dared to dream big.

During an era in which originality and freedom of self-expression reigned, artists such as Schick worked from a place of authenticity, using unconventional materials and processes. Along with other great makers of the period, Schick successfully challenged the preconceived notions of jewellery, forever changing the landscape and future of the discipline.

Emefa Cole

Fig. 4
Marjorie Schick
The Colours of London: A–Z Guide
brooch, 1998
Painted papier mâché, wood and stainless steel wire
14.5 × 13 cm
V&A: M.26-2024
Given by Dr James B.M. Schick and Robert M. Schick in honour of the artist

Fig. 5
Marjorie Schick
The Colours of London: Patchy Drizzle
brooch, 1998
Painted papier mâché, wood and stainless steel wire
13.5 × 18.3 cm
V&A: M.23-2024
Given by Dr James B.M. Schick and Robert M. Schick in honour of the artist

OTHER SIGNIFICANT MAKERS

Arline Fisch (b.1931) is an American jewellery artist, known for her billowing metal textile pieces. She blends textile techniques such as knitting, weaving, plaiting and crochet with jewellery-making skills to create large-scale, soft and flexible wearable sculptures. She founded the jewellery programme at San Diego State University in 1961 where she taught until her retirement in 2000.

Gijs Bakker (b.1942), a celebrated industrial and multidisciplinary designer, is regarded as a pioneer in non-precious material exploration and a leader of the radical jewellery movement in the Netherlands. He is known for fashioning materials such as stainless steel, aluminium, paper, laminated plastic alongside gold and precious stones to create sublime and minimalistic yet monumental works of wearable art.

Peter Chang (1944–2017) worked from his Glasgow studio where he created other-worldly, extravagant and exuberant works of art from unorthodox materials such as polyester, epoxy resin, polyurethane, fibreglass and acrylic salvaged from worn toothbrushes, old felt-tip pens, broken razors and discarded plastics to create the most exquisite and surreal works of art. His use of found plastics reflects the throwaway culture of the modern day.

Otto Künzli (b.1948), based in Munich, is widely known as an iconoclast and one of the most respected conceptual jewellers of our era. Throughout a career spanning over 50 years, he has created works using materials ranging from nylon, acrylic, rubber, steel and gold. His work challenges preconceived notions of value, power and vanity.

DALE CHIHULY

b.1941

Celebrated glass artist

Dale Chihuly is known for his creation of fluid colourful forms and hugely ambitious installations. Working predominantly with blown glass, his ethos of embracing the inherent qualities of his material has helped him create some of the largest blown-glass pieces ever seen. He is credited with propelling the American studio glass movement of the 1970s and '80s, and the broad appeal of his work has widened the audience for glass as an art form.

Chihuly was born in Tacoma, Washington, in 1941 to George, a butcher and union leader, and Viola, a homemaker. In his teenage years two tragedies struck the family, when first his older brother died in a Navy flying accident and the following year he lost his father to a heart attack. Despite these difficult times, Chihuly remembers his childhood fondly, including his mother's beloved garden and the colourful blooms that have influenced his creative work.

Chihuly studied interior design and architecture at University of Washington in Seattle, during which time he travelled to Italy and the Middle East. Following a weaving project in which he incorporated glass shards, he experimented with melting stained glass in his basement and blowing his first glass bubble in 1965.[1] The experience was transformative and the following year Chihuly began a postgraduate degree in glassblowing at the University of Wisconsin–Madison, the first programme of its kind in the country. The course was taught by Harvey Littleton, a ceramicist turned glassblower, who pioneered the practice of studio glass in the United States. It had previously been held that glassblowing required industrial infrastructure and staffing but Littleton's experiences in Spain and Italy showed him how studio production – the making of objects by a designer-maker with perhaps one or two assistants – was possible in glass.

Chihuly continued his studies at Rhode Island School of Design (RISD) where he received a Fulbright scholarship to spend nine months at the prestigious Venini Glass factory on Murano, the first American apprenticed to a Venetian master. Glass has been produced in Venice

Fig. 1a and b
Dale Chihuly
V&A Chandelier, 1999–2001
Blown glass, mould-blown glass, steel
823 × 365.8 cm
V&A: LOAN:CHIHULY.1-1999
On loan from Chihuly Studio, Seattle, Washington, USA

since the seventh century, with the city, and particularly its constituent island of Murano, becoming globally famed for the quality and creativity of its glasswares. Throughout his career, Venice has remained a constant presence and is the artist's favourite city. Many of his works bear Italian names, a reminder of the lagoon's centuries-old significance to the craft.

In 1969 he became head of the glass programme at RISD where he taught for 11 years. In this period he began work on the *Navajo Blanket Cylinder* series and later the *Baskets* series, both of which were inspired by Native American objects. In 1977, while visiting the Tacoma Historical Society, he recalled seeing 'Indian baskets that were stacked one inside the other … dented and misshapen'.[2] They initiated a period of works which recall the squashed baskets through their fluid, sometimes puckered forms and are often cradled one inside the other. He returned to nested compositions in his *Seaforms* series, which evoke ocean worlds with their scalloped shells and rippling textures and speak to the artist's love of water (fig. 1). These works represent a shift from culture to nature, the latter being undoubtedly Chihuly's most abiding source of inspiration.

From early in his career Chihuly has always worked collaboratively, either with fellow artists to realize a dual vision or with his team. In the early 1970s he produced installations using neon and ice with the artist James Carpenter and, once established as a glassblower, has maintained a talented team in his studio, inspired by his experiences as part of efficient team environments in Venetian workshops. Glassblowing is a physically demanding craft and nearly always requires the assistance of one or more helpers. However, this need became more pronounced when, in 1976, during a visit to the UK, Chihuly was involved in a serious car accident, resulting in the loss of an eye. From that point on he became a director or conductor for his team of glassblowers, overseeing and instructing the creation of his artistic visions. Artists in their own right, his team has included glassblowers like William Morris, with whom he had a close eight-year working relationship from the late 1970s, and Flora Mace, who met her long-term artistic collaborator Joey Kirkpatrick through working with Chihuly.

By the time of his accident Chihuly had already embarked on his most enduring project, the cofounding of Pilchuck Glass School on a farm in Washington State. In keeping with the countercultural, communally minded spirit of the day, he and fellow glassblower Ruth Tamura, with support of landowners John Hauberg and Anne Gould Hauberg, organized an annual summer season of glassblowing workshops. They often brought illustrious masters from abroad, such as the Venetian maestro Lino Tagliapietra, known for his glassblowing prowess, and

Fig. 2
Dale Chihuly
Kyoto Orange Macchia with Tar Lip Wrap, from the *Macchia* series, 1982
Glass, gathered with layers and patches of colour, blown into an optic mould, free-blown and hand-worked
33 × 23 cm
V&A: C.107-2001
Purchased with support from Art Fund and Paul Bedford

Pino Signoretto, who is unmatched in his skill in hot-sculpting. Both taught at Pilchuck and worked with Chihuly to produce the *Venetians*, *Putti* and *Ikebana* series of works.

Chihuly began his first Italian-named series, the *Macchia*, in the early 1980s. Using up to 300 colours of glass, these bright, freckled vessel forms were named by the artist's friend Italo Scanga after their spotted decoration ('macchia' meaning spot or stain in Italian), though his mother apparently referred to them unflatteringly as the 'uglies' (fig. 2).[3] Later that decade came the enduring *Persians* series. Beginning as an experimental 'search for forms', glassblowers Robbie Miller and Martin Blank worked from Chihuly's exuberant sketches and developed vivid organic shapes.[4] The series evolved into a spectrum of large undulating forms that surround clusters of smaller blown parts. Chihuly was inspired by a wide variety of objects and motifs: the patterns and colours of early core-formed Egyptian vessels combined with the shapes of Venetian goblets, the bird-like mouths of Persian scent bottles and sweeping arabesque tendrils. These works are typically striped with waves of different coloured glass, which Chihuly refers to as 'body wraps', and are sometimes enhanced with fine trailed glass and lips or rims of contrasting hues (fig. 3).

This series formed part of Chihuly's first large-scale installation at the Seattle Art Museum in 1992. The exhibition showcased new works, including walls of undulating *Persians* and his new *Ikebana* series which was inspired by the Japanese art of flower arranging. Perhaps most spectacular of all was the *Seattle Art Museum Chandelier*, the first of

Fig. 3
Dale Chihuly
Deep Blue and Bronze Persian Set, 1999
Glass, with threading and twisted canes, blown into an optic mould, free-blown and hand-worked
89 cm (depth; other dimensions depending on arrangement)
V&A: C.108:1 to 8-2001
Purchased with support from Art Fund and Paul Bedford

many Chihuly would go on to produce. It was assembled from a multitude of hand-blown balloon-like forms, all delicately attached to a central armature. Dropping down from the ceiling to approximately eye height, the installation gave visitors a close-up view not generally afforded by conventional chandeliers.

Chihuly took the chandelier to new extremes when he created a multi-site installation *Chihuly over Venice* for the Venezia Aperto Vetro biennial for contemporary glass in 1996. The audacious project saw 14 *Chandeliers* installed in different locations around the city and involved a global team, with parts blown in Finland, Mexico, Ireland and Italy. In 1999 the V&A received its own Chihuly *Chandelier* of multiple green, blue and yellow bulbous and serpentine elements. The work was originally more modest in size but Chihuly continued to add to it, altering the overall shape for his exhibition *Chihuly at the V&A* in 2001. It has since gone on to become an icon of the Museum (fig. 1).

The artist's taste for the epic continued and in 1999 an even larger installation-based exhibition, *Chihuly in the Light of Jerusalem 2000*, opened at the Tower of David Museum in Israel and was visited by more than one million people. Since then, Chihuly has completed a host of indoor and outdoor installations, often architectural in scope, sometimes on water and typically making innovative use of light and space. These include garden exhibitions in Singapore, and Kew Gardens in London, as well as huge towers and sun-like orbs installed across the United States and beyond.

Chihuly continues to work with a dedicated team of assistants at his studio in Seattle and since 2019 has been developing a new technique of *merletto* glass (the Italian for lace). A Venetian cane-working method, *merletto* glass is made by forming a clear glass bubble on the end of a

Fig. 4
Dale Chihuly
Davy's Gray Seaform Set with Black Lip Wraps, 1985
Free-blown clear greyish-tinted glass with trails of grey, mauve and multicoloured inclusions
66 cm (length), 56.4 cm (width)
V&A: C.111 to G-1987
Given by the artist

blowpipe before rolling the molten bubble across a series of clear glass rods which themselves contain twists of opaque white glass. The glass is then further manipulatcd by rolling, stretching and blowing to form lace-like patterns. Chihuly employs a particularly loose approach, achieving extremely delicate meshes of white threads in his transparent glass vessels.

Dale Chihuly's unabated energy is matched by his fascination and reverence for glass which, after more than 50 years, remains undimmed. His achievements in scale and technique have broadened the horizons of the art form, and his pioneering installations have created a daring new category of glass art. He has described himself as an 'explorer [...] searching for new ways to use glass and glassblowing to make forms and colours and installations that no one has ever created before – that's what I love to do'.[5]

Kate Devine

OTHER SIGNIFICANT MAKERS

Harvey Littleton (1922–2013) grew up near Corning industrial glassworks in New York State where his father worked. He went on to study art, becoming first a ceramicist and then a glassblower. Through his work as a glassblower and educator, he was instrumental in founding the American studio glass movement.

Lino Tagliapietra (b.1934) was born on the island of Murano in Venice. He is a world-renowned glassblower and Venetian maestro known for his mastery of colour and form. He was apprenticed to Venetian master Archimede Seguso and has gone on to teach future generations, both in Venice and in the United States.

Sam Herman (1936–2020) was a glass artist, painter and sculptor and a leading figure in the studio glass movement in Britain. He established glass studios in the UK and Australia. His work is known for its innovative expression of colour and texture.

Richard Meitner (b.1949) is a glass artist, designer and teacher. Born in Philadelphia, he later settled in the Netherlands where he ran the glass department at the Gerrit Rietveld Academy for nearly 20 years. His work is often informed by his interest in the relationship between art and science.

Anna Dickinson (b.1961) received her MA in Glass from the Royal College of Art in 1985 and her sculptures are often made from cast glass and frequently incorporate metal. She also employs a range of cold-working methods including carving to achieve her characteristically clean, geometric forms.

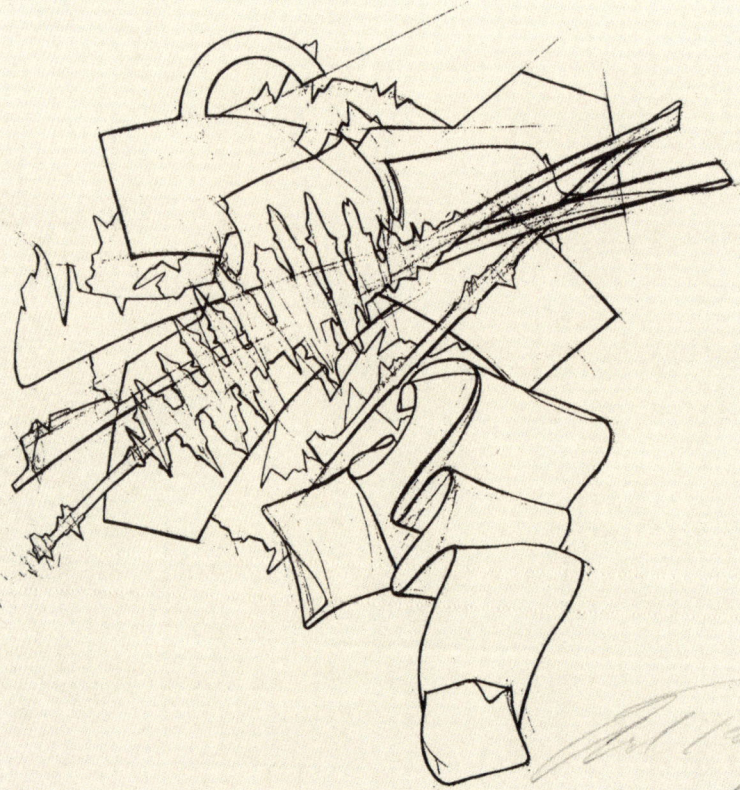

#2

(1991)

ALBERT PALEY

b.1944

American modernist metal sculptor

Albert Paley is an American metalsmith and sculptor who is regarded as one of the foremost ironworkers of the modern era. Making objects from jewellery to gates and monumental public sculpture, his work stresses the materiality and vitality of iron and has significantly expanded modern metalworking. Few other makers have worked so successfully across scales and consistently demonstrate such a clear aesthetic vocabulary.

Paley was born in Philadelphia in 1944. He did not have much interest in school and preferred being outside, 'building things' and learning about the natural world.[1] Upon leaving school, a friend went to Tyler School of Art in Philadelphia and Paley was amazed at the opportunities available there. He decided to enrol, majoring in sculpture and minoring in metalwork, and has since described how attending the school transformed his life. He began making jewellery, and his teacher, the jeweller Stanley Lechtzin, had a profound influence on his artistic and intellectual development. Lechtzin was part of the New Jewellery movement in America, which argued that jewellery must work with one's body and that its ornamental quality should have a significant meaning. Paley's early jewellery is made from precious metals and stones and is typically highly ornamented with heavily interlaced forms.

As a graduate student, Paley specialized in goldsmithing and continued making jewellery and vessels. He also began working in iron and found that he was drawn to the plasticity of the metal and the immediacy of forging. Lechtzin was by then a great friend and together they scoured local junkyards for a forge and anvil and set up a blacksmith's shop in Lechtzin's garage. From the late 1960s Lechtzin encouraged him to experiment with forged ironwork and Paley began making domestic furniture as well as increasingly large items of jewellery. He was fascinated by the Art Nouveau period and the naturalism of urban metalwork developed by architects including Hector Guimard and Antoni Gaudí. He continued to develop his own language of organic naturalism, drawing inspiration from the natural world and the extreme

Fig. 1
Albert Paley
Design for a fabricated steel
wall sculpture, 1997
Photostatic print
21.7 × 28 cm
V&A: E.2949-2016
Given by Paley Studios

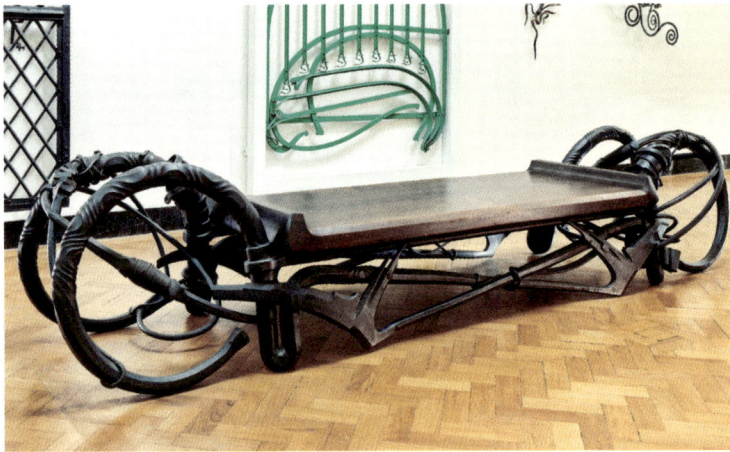

Fig. 2
Albert Paley
Bench, 1994
Mild steel, with Honduran mahogany seat
ingrained with gold dust
76.2 × 350.5 × 93 cm
V&A:M.11-1995
Purchased with assistance from the
United States Information Service

fluidity and malleability of hot iron during the forging process, establishing a distinctive style of modern ornamental metalwork.

A decisive moment came when he received his first major commission in 1973 for a pair of gates for the Renwick Gallery in Washington. He had recently moved to Rochester to teach goldsmithing at the School for American Craftsmen at Rochester Institute of Technology and was working in a small garage forge. Paley had not previously made anything on this scale and so the commission necessitated a change in his way of working. He moved to a bigger workshop, upscaled his tools and equipment and hired a student to work alongside him. The *Portal Gates* took over a year to complete and are made of forged and fabricated steel, brass, bronze and copper. The richly detailed design drew on his experience as a jeweller and helped to establish his aesthetic vocabulary at scale. Their production greatly improved his forging skills and, before he had even finished the gates, he began receiving requests for future projects. The commission significantly elevated his work, establishing him as a high-profile international artist and propelling his practice towards monumental metalwork.

By the late 1970s he had stopped making jewellery and, in between commissions, continued to develop his designs for domestic furniture. It was during this period that he refined the decorative vocabulary that he has since become so well known for. Characteristic features emerged such as encircling loops of iron as structural supports for lights, vigorously twisted table legs and flowing ribbons of iron as decoration. These distinctive features are clearly demonstrated in a bench of forged and fabricated steel made by Paley to celebrate the reopening of the west wing of the Ironwork Gallery at the V&A in 1994 (fig. 2). In a letter to the Museum that year, Paley described how his proposed design had a linear

Fig. 3
Albert Paley
Victoria and Albert Gate, 1982
Forged and fabricated mild steel with
a black patina
209.6 × 270.5 × 34.3 cm
V&A: M.17-2018
Purchased with assistance from the
James Yorke-Radleigh Bequest Fund

lyricism which 'stresses the forged aesthetic' and included a variety
of forms that he had been developing over the previous 25 years.[2]
He wrote, 'The bench, therefore, could function as a lexicon of my
understanding of decorative ironwork. The bench will include tapering,
splitting, upsetting, twisting, wrapping, coiling, bending, forming,
riveting, swaging, punching, welding, and white smithing.' The seat
is made from Honduran mahogany ingrained with gold dust and is
supported by a framework of forged and decorated steel. The main
structure is made of four faceted, tapering steel bars which have been
forged into a hoop at each corner of the seat to form the legs of the
bench, and the upper section of each hoop has been decorated with
sinuous, rippling patterns in low relief. Steel is well known for its great
strength and rigidity, yet the bench somehow both celebrates and
subverts this by the seeming effortlessness of its forms. The bench is
more than just a comfortable seat for a tired visitor to the Museum; it
has a great theatricality that is a pervading feature of Paley's furniture.

Many of Paley's commissioned works in the 1980s and '90s were for
site-specific locations and include the *University Centre Gate* at Florida
State University, the *Portal Gates* for the New York Senate Chamber and
the *Entrance Gate* to Boston Milk Street Station. Gates, portals and
entranceways have been central to his practice and are important to
Paley as they enhance the boundaries of our built environment and
are markers of transitional spaces. In 1982 he created the *Rectilinear
Gate* (later renamed the *Victoria and Albert Gate*) for the V&A and Crafts

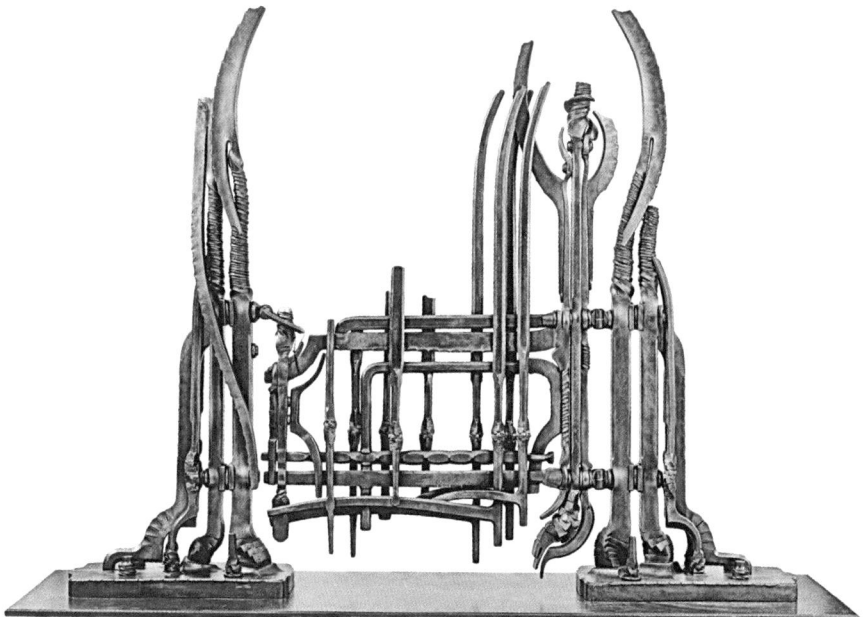

Council exhibition *Towards a New Iron Age*.[3] This exhibition sought to re-establish ironwork as a valid, contemporary medium and brought together a broad range of makers. The gate (fig. 3) is a remarkable exercise in forging steel and clearly encapsulates Paley's formal vocabulary of the period. The basic material retains its integrity but is made to do an astonishing variety of things, incorporating techniques such as tapering, twisting, incising, upsetting (the shortening and thickening of metal), riveting and welding. Every detail demonstrates exemplary craftmanship, from the elegant curves of the gate posts to the brass details and invisible joinery. The spontaneity of the steel forms belies the enormous effort required to make the gates and demonstrates Paley's extraordinary command of material. A central theme of Paley's work is the bringing together of structure and ornament in this way, so that they coexist naturally.

Drawing is a crucial part of Paley's practice. Most of his sculptures begin with a series of quick sketches on paper which emerge as flurries of line and texture and ultimately get refined into the final form. He says that 'drawings enable me to experience and completely understand the form before going into metal'.[4] In the 1990s and early 2000s the V&A's Development team periodically commissioned an edition of work by a contemporary maker for the Museum's high-level patrons and one would be acquired for the collection. In 1997 Paley was selected for the commission and he sent five design drawings to the Museum for consideration. Each design employs a typically heavy use of interlocking abstract forms and sinuous ribbons of metal. Two of the designs are for small free-standing sculptures which draw clear parallels with the monumental public sculptures that Paley had begun to develop. In correspondence, he described how he would like the wall or free-standing sculpture to function 'in a symbolic context for the V&A and the relationship to the metalwork gallery'.[5] He provides detailed descriptions about the design of each object, and for the selected design for a wall-mounted sculpture (fig. 1) he stresses the importance of the interlaced structure and organic ornament. Together, the design drawing and the finished wall sculpture show how effectively he is able to translate a two-dimensional design into a three-dimensional form (fig. 4).

Paley began making public sculpture from the late 1980s and an early example includes *Synergy*, two 25-foot pylons for the entrance to an apartment complex in Philadelphia in 1987. Notable commissions include *Animals Always*, a large-scale exterior gateway sculpture at the entrance to St Louis Zoo, Missouri, in 2006, *The Beckoning* for the National Harbor development in Maryland in 2008 (fig. 5) and a series of 13 sculptures for display along Park Avenue in New York in 2013, with each of the works

Fig. 4
Albert Paley
Wall sculpture, 1997
Formed and fabricated steel with
an oxidized surface, clear-coated
38.5 × 34 × 4 cm
V&A: M.75-1997

being fully integrated into their architectural context. These monumental polychrome assemblage-like sculptures include many of the distinctive forms of his smaller works but, in addition to the forging of iron and steel, also make use of other materials, techniques and colour. To make work on this scale, the Paley Studios expanded to encompass three independent studios for design, development and fabrication. In the fabrication studio the team combines modern fabrication with historic metalworking processes to create these complex forms. They are also active in exploring the behaviours of different metals and materials as well as developing new processes to realize Paley's designs. The studio has now made over 50 monumental works of public sculpture and together they demonstrate Paley's clear vision and understanding of scale and materiality. In the summer of 2014 a major retrospective exhibition of Paley's career, *American Metal: The Art of Albert Paley*, was held at the Corcoran Gallery of Art in Washington.[6]

Iron and steel have long served as significant materials of the modern world and Paley has successfully imbued them with a great vitality for contemporary life. With a career spanning more than five decades, Paley has consistently demonstrated high-quality craftmanship and has made a profound contribution to modern metalwork in jewellery, architecture, ornamental art and sculpture.

Rebecca Knott

Fig. 5
Albert Paley
The Beckoning, 2008
Formed and fabricated steel with a polychromed finish
259 × 100.6 × 100.6 cm
National Harbor Complex, National Harbor, Maryland

OTHER SIGNIFICANT MAKERS

Alfred Gilbert (1854–1934) was one of Britain's most prominent sculptors. His most famous public work is the statue of *Eros* in Piccadilly Circus, London. Gilbert's interest in metal also led him to design highly distinctive pieces of jewellery, using iron wire and set with inexpensive materials such as glass, shell or semi-precious stones.

Louis Henry Sullivan (1856–1924) was an American architect who is well known for his groundbreaking tall buildings and theories on architectural ornament. Many of his buildings were among the first skyscrapers that made use of steel structures to achieve unprecedented heights. He also used iron and botanically inspired ornament for features such as elevator grilles.

Hector Guimard (1867–1942) was a leading exponent of the French Art Nouveau style. Strongly influenced by Victor Horta, his work is characterized by flowing scrolls and fluid aqueous and vegetal ornament. His best-known works include the Castel Béranger in Paris (1894–8) and the entrances to the Paris Métro (1900). He also designed furniture and interior fittings.

Wendy Ramshaw (1939–2018) was a leading, internationally renowned artist-jeweller. Her early jewellery used screen-printed acrylic and paper before she turned to gold and silver in 1970 to create ring sets and brooches in a distinctive Modernist style. She also designed several notable architectural commissions in iron, such as the *Double Screen* in the V&A collection.

Junko Mori (b.1974) is a Japanese metalsmith based in Wales. She makes sculptures from the assembly of forged and cast metal, working in mild steel or pure silver. She is inspired by tree and plant matter and her work ranges from small-scale objects in precious metal to enormous welded-steel works.

CHARLOTTE DE SYLLAS

b.1946

Foremost hardstone carver

The flowing contours of Charlotte de Syllas's jewellery make gemstones malleable in bespoke creations from rings to necklaces. The carved forms set into jewellery that she is renowned for are both stylized and organic. They recall sedimentary layers and undulating ridges on a sandy shore. Certain dynamic motifs appear throughout her œuvre, including figures (faces and eyes), birds in flight and aquatic life.

De Syllas was brought up in the post-war period in England within a creative family environment. Her father, Leo de Syllas, was an architect and her mother, Phoebe de Syllas, was a trained illustrator who made a career as an interior designer. In 1963 de Syllas was inspired to seek jewellery training after seeing an exhibition of Georges Braque's art jewellery in Paris. From 1964 to 1966 she was enrolled on a new experimental jewellery degree course at the Hornsey College of Art in north London, led by avant-garde jeweller Gerda Flöckinger. Courses at art schools were unusual because at this time most jewellers completed their training working in the trade as studio apprentices. While she was a student, the Worshipful Company of Goldsmiths acquired 20 pieces of de Syllas's work for their collection. The beginnings of what would later become her distinctive style can be glimpsed in a piece from this period. It is a brooch with slices of watermelon tourmaline seamlessly inlaid into silver (fig. 2). Here de Syllas's early interest in the form, colour and structure of gemstones is clear.

Working independently since 1966, de Syllas has dedicated significant time to researching innovative materials for jewellery. As a student she soaked lace in porcelain to create beads and since then has developed methods for the fiendishly tricky casting of hollow fine glass forms, as well as the cutting of synthetic rubies and sapphires. However, it is the art of stone carving combined with sophisticated metalworking that she has made her life's work, now widely recognized as the foremost gemstone carver in Britain. Flöckinger taught de Syllas to carve stones for jewellery in cabochon form (shaped and polished rather than cut) and this early introduction prompted her to continue teaching herself

Fig. 1
Charlotte de Syllas
Coffee Bean choker, 1970
Iolite, emerald, blued steel, gold, silver
38.8 cm (length, choker open)
V&A: M.30:1-2022

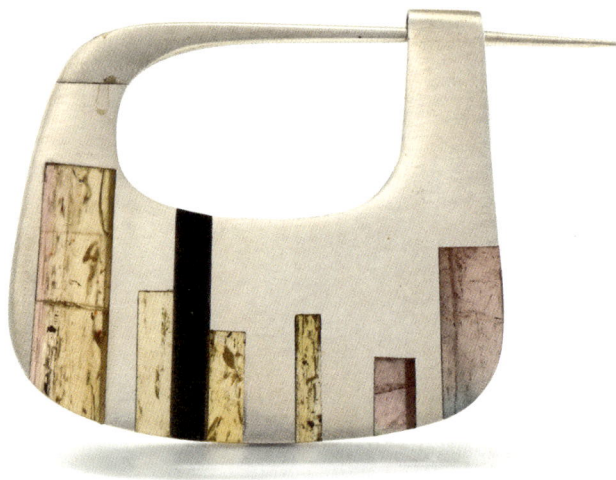

Fig. 2
Charlotte de Syllas
Tourmaline and silver brooch, *c.*1965
Silver, tourmaline
5.1 cm × 7.4 cm
The Goldsmiths' Company Collection

basic gem-carving skills from a book on the subject. De Syllas credits her jewellery training for her ability to work precisely at a small scale and to design three-dimensional jigsaws in stone that piece contrasting colours together. The black and white nephrite *Millennium* bracelet (2000), a commission in the Goldsmiths' Company collection, is an excellent example of the perfectionism her tessellation in stone entails.

Gemstone carving requires great technical skill as well as an experienced understanding of the way that different stones behave under pressure, and de Syllas incorporates years of tacit knowledge into her creations. The relative hardness of stones dictates their resilience to abrading and cutting. Nephrites and jadeites are some of de Syllas's favourite stones to carve because their structure feels more fluid when worked with tools. Black nephrite jade from Wyoming, USA, was the first type of jade de Syllas ever carved, later noting that this mineral 'will cut paper thin, does not chip or craze and can carve as fine as one likes'.[1] Stones, like rock crystal, have different qualities to jade. Rock crystal's fractious, macrocrystalline structure can cause the piece to splinter or break more easily. Sourcing the stones is also very important and de Syllas takes time finding the right colours and the right quality, selecting stones without internal flaws that make them unpredictable to carve. Modelling the shapes for her jewels in soft boxwood and briar root wood before tackling the stone is vital to the design process.[2] The sophisticated treatment of stones in de Syllas's work is telling of an important objective for the maker: that her jewellery is designed to be lived in. In many pieces, the smooth stone elements are excavated from within so that finished articles are ergonomic and surprisingly light to wear and she often repeatedly uses spirals and arcs in her designs, forms that are weightless but strong.

The sheer amount of time it takes to carve hardstones has meant that, throughout her career, de Syllas has predominantly worked on bespoke commissions. After graduating, her first commissions came from the architects within her family's network. Her first major commission, *Bobby's Ring*, is a carved human head in creamy chalcedony (fig. 3). Looking back, de Syllas has noted that, after this commission, 'combining the technical, the aesthetic and the personal in an original design came to be my aim in all future work'.[3] She went on to complete her first necklace in 1974.

Sometimes, a design idea sets de Syllas on the hunt for the exact stone while other creations are the result of living with a gem on the workbench for many years, getting to know it and waiting for the right pairing of personality to material. Though the inclusion of faceted gems in her jewellery is extremely rare, she has occasionally incorporated stones with sentimental significance for the client. A 'diamond eye' ring made of rock crystal cut into the shape of an eye in the V&A's collection includes a cut diamond that once belonged to the original owner's mother.[4] Some stones that de Syllas has turned into jewels also come with a more personal provenance. An aquamarine from the estate of the London jeweller Moshe Oved, for example, was gifted to her by the British jeweller Jacqueline Mina. Likewise, a star sapphire that was given to de Syllas by the family of the British jeweller, sculptor and architect Henry Wilson was set into a ring. In a note to its new owner, de Syllas wrote, 'I hope you enjoy this tiny piece of history in the life of the stone that has come to you after unimaginable years that it has been on this earth.'[5]

Fig. 4
Charlotte de Syllas
Magpie necklace, 1988
Silk braid made by Catherine Martin;
catch mechanics by Paul Nicol
Carved jade and labradorite, silver
and braided silk
12.4 cm (width)
V&A: M.29-2022

De Syllas's jewels are always paired with a bespoke case. Some she makes herself and some are crafted by other makers, including Stephen Gottlieb. A copper case made by de Syllas has a swirling design and depiction of a coffee-bean in enamel that reflects the form of the necklace it was made to protect. The close-fitting *Coffee Bean* choker is made of fine blued steel interlinked to form a chain band (fig. 1). The chain, consisting of small steel rings knitted together was inspired by nineteenth-century steel mesh purses made using the 'mail' (or 'chainmail') technique developed for medieval armour. The central pendant of the necklace features pieces of iolite, a blue-brown gem, held together with silver inlay between the joins. Here each composite iolite dome has a soft fold like a coffee bean which allows light to enter and amplify the unique colour of the gemstone.

De Syllas's jewellery is inspired by the people destined to wear it and she intends each piece to reflect the wearer's personality, lifestyle and complexion. The original owner of the *Magpie* necklace liked to wear blue, black and white (fig. 4). The two magpies of the old folk rhyme – 'one for sorrow, two for joy' – meet at the centre of this winged necklace, flying in opposite directions. The tail feathers and wings are black nephrite jade with shimmering blue-green labradorite veneers that catch the light. There are flashes of white jadeite too, notably at the tip of the tail feather which falls below the nape of the wearer's neck. Flexible joints between the elements allow the wings to shift against the chest, following the natural movement of the breath. The stone pieces are assembled with silk *kumihimo* braids made by Catherine Martin, a British jeweller and specialist in this ancient Japanese art of braiding. Necklaces allow the most space for carving and the joyful *Magpie* necklace is a masterpiece which took over four years to complete. The donor who commissioned the necklace later requested de Syllas to make her the accompanying *Black Hoopoe Ring*, also in the V&A collection.[6] Even the V&A-commissioned 'shell necklace' was created for an imaginary person. When the Museum requested de Syllas to make a necklace for the collection in 1989, she carved cockle and snail shells from green nephrite jade, white jadeite and coral, interspersed between threads of tiny seed pearls (fig. 5). Catherine Martin hand-dyed the silk strings for this necklace so that the seed pearls appear subtly different shades: on the left a slight pink, on the right a hint of green. The clasp for fastening the necklace around the neck is revealed when the central green nephrite shell is separated into two pieces.

To date, de Syllas continues to work on bespoke commissions in her studio where she now lives in Norfolk. She is passionate about bringing gemstones to life, carving them into complex organic forms to become

wearable sculptures. She has delivered lectures on the subject to
academic audiences and taught carving workshops throughout her
career, continuing to share her deep knowledge of gemstone carving
with a new generation of makers in short residential courses each year.
In a career spanning more than six decades she has produced distinctive
jewels that are characteristically sculptural and timeless.

Sophie Morris

Fig. 5
Charlotte de Syllas
Necklace of carved shells and
seed pearls, 1989
Silk braid made by Catherine Martin
Green nephrite jade, white jadeite,
silver lacquer, coral, silk, seed pearls
35.5 cm (length)
V&A: M.4-1990

OTHER SIGNIFICANT MAKERS

Gerda Flöckinger (b.1927) was born in Austria but emigrated to England as child. By the 1960s she became a leading figure in British art jewellery. In 1962 she established the pioneering course in experimental jewellery at Hornsey College of Art. Flöckinger was the first contemporary jeweller to have a solo exhibition at the V&A (1971).

Jacqueline Mina (b.1942) is renowned for her use of precious metals, particularly the invention of a fusion inlay technique with platinum and gold that creates a unique pattern each time it is used. She has had exhibitions at the V&A (1986) and Goldsmiths' Hall (2011).

Catherine Martin (b.1949) is a British designer-goldsmith who learned the classical textile art of braiding, or *kumihimo*, in Japan where she lived for some time working as a classical musician. When she later transferred the art from silk to precious metals in the 1990s, it was a groundbreaking technical feat.

Kevin Coates (b.1950) is a goldsmith who makes jewellery, tableware and sculptures that are carved and modelled from a range of precious materials. His work is renowned for its distinctive colourful style, figurative forms and symbolism. He has had exhibitions at the Wallace Collection (2011) and the Ashmolean Museum (2014).

Lin Cheung (b.1971) is a jewellery artist and a Reader in Jewellery at Central Saint Martins, London. Her work responds to everyday experiences and strives to disrupt the traditional meanings and uses of jewellery. She has won several prestigious awards and in 2017 was shortlisted for the Woman's Hour Crafts Prize exhibited at the V&A.

ALISON BRITTON

b.1948

Innovative ceramicist of the Postmodern era

Alison Britton is very much an artist of her time. One of the leading ceramicists of her generation and a central figure in the development of new approaches to craft practice in the later 1970s and '80s, Britton embraces a contemporary spirit and sensibility in her work and her ideas. Postmodern and reflexive, her work draws upon sources from within and beyond the world of ceramics, provokes questions about the nature of pottery and revels in a sense of ambiguity. It is bold, colourful, often a little uncomfortable and almost always joyous.

Born in 1948, Alison Britton grew up in the north-west London suburbs of Harrow Weald and Hatch End. At the North London Collegiate School in Edgware, she was taught art by the muralist Philippa Threlfall and there had her first encounters with clay. Britton's mother was herself an art teacher, while her father taught would-be English teachers at the University of London's Institute of Education. Also teaching at the Institute was the potter and family friend William Newland. Britton, encouraged by Newland, began visiting the Institute and exploring pottery aged 14, triggering a deeper interest. An art foundation course at Leeds College of Art provided an escape from suburbia but proved too orientated towards fine art for Britton's broad-minded tastes, and she returned to the capital in 1967 to study Ceramics at the Central School of Art and Design. There she was taught by Gordon Baldwin (p. 321), among others, and was a contemporary of Andrew Lord and Richard Slee.

Progressing to the Royal College of Art, London, in 1970 for three years of postgraduate study in Ceramics, Britton admits to having at first been completely stuck. After briefly deviating into photography, she found a way out of her impasse by working with clay in two-dimensional form as tiles for architectural settings – a mode of practice that continued in the years immediately following her study. At the College, Britton was taught by Hans Coper (p. 313), whose ideas would increasingly play a part in her thinking. Coper's recognition of studio pottery as a craft of ambiguous purpose and function in the context of the twentieth century, but one given meaning through the discipline of making, resonated with

Fig. 1
Alison Britton
Jar with Handles, 1998
High-fired earthenware, handbuilt, painted with slips and underglaze pigments under a clear matt glaze
48.3 × 38.7 cm
V&A: C.10-1999

Britton, and in effect provided the philosophical basis of her practice. The College also afforded Britton a remarkable peer group of direct or close contemporaries, including Elizabeth Fritsch, Jacqueline Poncelet, Carol McNicoll and Jill Crowley. These women potters formed a loosely affiliated group, whose work – though distinct – shared certain approaches and ideas. Bonds between them were also strengthened through the sharing of studios. In the years following the Royal College of Art, Britton shared space with McNicoll at 401½ Workshops, a large complex where Crowley also worked, and then moved to a studio at King's Cross in 1975, sharing this initially with Poncelet.

It was at this new studio that Britton began reasserting herself in three dimensions, and she showed jugs and dishes alongside tiles at her first solo exhibition, held at Amalgam in Barnes, London, in 1976. Significant exhibitions followed in 1979 at Aberdeen Art Gallery – where her *Flat-backed Jug with Stork, red version* (1978) was first exhibited (fig. 3) – and at the Crafts Council, London. The latter reflected the still-young organization's promotion and support for the new, progressive generation of craft makers of which Britton was part. Her work of the time consisted of jugs and occasionally bowls built from flat slabs of clay, their forms asymmetrical, twisted and leaning, but also planar, angular and sharp-edged. These were usually made in high-fired buff earthenware and painted with figurative drawings and decorative patterns, both before and after the slabs were assembled into pots. The figurative elements – birds, humans, human-animal hybrids, flora and fauna – appear as if from classical antiquity but hold perhaps some more personal and contemporary symbolic value.

Writing in the catalogue for her Crafts Council exhibition, Britton noted that she was drawn to making jugs 'because of the stronger

Fig. 2
Alison Britton
Yellow Pot, 1990–1
High-fired earthenware, handbuilt, painted with slips and underglaze pigments under a clear matt glaze
19.8 × 57.5 cm
V&A: C.254-2014
Gift of Ed Wolf

Fig. 3
Alison Britton
Flat-backed Jug with Stork, red version, 1978
High-fired earthenware, slab-built, painted and sprayed underglaze pigments and crayon under a clear matt glaze
27.5 × 28.3 cm
V&A: C.100-1979

implication of usefulness'.[1] But as she would soon after go on to observe, such works operated at 'the outer limits of function', where an object's possible use became as much an idea as a practical consideration.[2] This later statement comes from Britton's essay for the 1982 Crafts Council exhibition, *The Maker's Eye*, for which she had been invited to be one of 14 selectors. Her text – one of the most noteworthy pieces of writing in late-twentieth-century craft – identified common threads in the work of her peer group. This included the idea of possible function, a self-referential aspect and a relationship with modern still-life painting, such that a pot might seem to be both the representation of a pot as well as an actual one. For the exhibition, Britton selected work by contemporaries such as McNicoll, Poncelet, Fritsch and Lord, along with others who worked in different craft disciplines including the glassmaker Steven Newell, her then partner. In identifying this group of makers and defining something about their shared preoccupations, Britton – in effect – placed herself at the centre of a movement that shifted the agenda for craft practice and came to dominate the field throughout the 1980s – the 'new ceramics', and more widely, the 'new crafts'. Britton's text

Fig. 4
Alison Britton
Outpour (left), *Ruse* (right) 2012
High-fired red earthenware, handbuilt, with poured and painted slips and glazes
51 × 33.5cm (left); 12.5 × 46.5 cm (right)
V&A: C.132-2013; C.27-2016
Given by the artist (*Outpour*);
acquired through the generosity of
Gerard and Sarah Griffin (*Ruse*)

for *The Maker's Eye* marked the start of her parallel strand of activity as a writer on – and sometimes curator of – the crafts. Building up a formidable body of critical writing over more than four decades, Britton has approached this as an 'insider', someone who understands things 'with head and hands', and who senses that 'a different reading of art objects may come from a person who makes them'.[3] A further important long-term strand of activity came in 1984 in the form of a teaching post at the Royal College of Art, which she held until 2018.

As she was commencing her work as a writer in the early 1980s, Britton brought to bear a significant shift in her own practice and abandoned figurative imagery. This move from the pictorial to the abstract allowed a more complete integration of form and surface and demonstrated a greater level of engagement with three-dimensionality. By the late 1980s she had moved to a new studio in Stamford Hill, London – where she continues to work – and her pots were characterized by angular, sculptural forms and bold, gestural painting. Reflecting the experience of 'someone urban, with a life composed of a mixture of intersecting fragments', they were, as Britton observed, 'composed of disparate parts that relate to each other with tension and, I hope, interest. [...] I am aiming for a sort of poise or resolution, but after a bit of a struggle.'[4] Her *Yellow Pot* (1990–1) is an eye-catching example of this type (fig. 2). Britton calls it 'both bridge and container, a bowl and long beak spanning the table surface and resting on its point'.[5] This allusory aspect of her forms would become increasingly important. Often a pot might suggest a body, the clothing of a body, an architectural element or a domestic object. As the 1990s progressed, her pots became more contoured, with fewer flat planes, occupying space with a kind of assured uncertainty (fig. 1). Bold, spare brushwork and intense colours predominated.

In the early 2000s a new theme emerged in Britton's work: that of flow. The form of pots, which incorporated elements such as pipes, suggested the movement of water between interconnected parts or into or out of the vessel. Her titles, which had previously been resolutely descriptive, echoed the new theme. The idea of liquidity extended to Britton's treatment of surfaces, bringing with it risk and improvisation. From 2007 she began to pour rather than spray glazes and from 2010 she experimented with poured rather than painted clay slips. These strategies were brought together in her 2012 exhibition *Standing and Running* at Marsden Woo Gallery, London, in which *Outpour* (2012) was shown (fig. 4). Writing of the work and the changes it represented in her making, Britton observed:

For me fluidity and speed are linked ideas, the gravity of splashing liquid, reminders of the glorious rush conveyed by these gestures; uncontrolled verve responding to the instant. I stuck for a long time to the paintbrush, seeing the slow 'painterly' application and layering as important in the gradual bringing into being of an improvised object. Now I need to speed up.[6]

This sense of movement and rapidity of gesture have continued into more recent work. *Outcrop* (2015) – one of a group of new pieces shown in Britton's retrospective *Content and Form*, held at the V&A in 2016 – has gently fluted sides made by running wet fingers through the original soft slab of clay, perhaps evocative of pleated fabric (fig. 5). This in turn offers Britton 'new reaches of un-control', as a line of liquid clay slip thrown across the ridges forms a stuttering arc.[7]

After more than five decades of professional practice, Alison Britton continues to innovate. For almost as long, she has been committed to the ceramic container, exploring both its formal possibilities and its capacity to hold and communicate thoughts and ideas. It is a self-imposed constraint that Britton has found endlessly stimulating, enjoying the possibility that objects can slip between categories and be read in different ways. As she has written: 'The breadth and ambiguity of the craft field is what has always attracted me to it. You can be concerned with basic practicalities or with elusive ideas, feet on the ground or head in the clouds, or both.'[8]

Alun Graves

Fig. 5
Alison Britton
Outcrop, 2015
High-fired earthenware, handbuilt,
with poured and painted slips and glazes
46.8 × 36.8 cm
V&A: C.28-2016
Acquired through the generosity
of Gerard and Sarah Griffin

OTHER SIGNIFICANT MAKERS

Betty Woodman (1930–2018) was a groundbreaking American artist known for her vibrant and exuberant painterly works that positioned ceramics in the realm of fine art. Dividing her time between studios in New York and Tuscany, she increasingly deconstructed and reimagined her vessel forms as sculptures, wall-pieces and mixed-media installations.

Elizabeth Fritsch (b.1940) was the first of the progressive generation of women potters that emerged from the Royal College of Art, London, in the 1970s, having been taught by Hans Coper. A highly influential artist, Fritsch produced meticulously painted handbuilt vessels that explore spatial characteristics, responding in particular to musical themes.

Richard Slee (b.1946) is an important and highly influential British artist whose finely honed ceramics have increasingly been recognized by the world of contemporary art. Colourful and highly glazed, his work employs Postmodern strategies of quotation and subversion to offer pithy and witty commentaries on art and society.

Jacqueline Poncelet (b.1947) is an enormously inventive artist who has radically reimagined her practice at different stages of her career. A contemporary of Alison Britton at the Royal College of Art, London, she worked primarily in ceramics until 1986, during which time she significantly advanced the potential of clay as a sculptural medium.

Magdalene Odundo (b.1950) is one of the most distinguished ceramic artists of our times. Born in Kenya, she came to the UK in 1971 and studied ceramics at Farnham and the Royal College of Art, London. Her fine, burnished, handbuilt vessels embody human characteristics and reflect multiple cultural and historic sources, including Nigerian and Kenyan pottery and Modernist sculpture.

NOTES

Introduction

1 Julius Bryant, *Creating the V&A: Victoria and Albert's Museum (1851–1861)* (London 2019), p. 11
2 *London Gazette*, 19 May 1899, p. 3186
3 Henry Cole, First Report of the Department of Practical Art (London 1853), p. 30

1: The Emergence of the Celebrated Maker

1 Pallisey 1957, p. 192
2 V&A: 1072-1892
3 Davies 2016, p. 43
4 V&A: T.70-1923
5 Davies 2016, pp. 45–6
6 Hind 1910, pp. 217–35
7 Cherry 1992, p. 26
8 Hildyard 1999, pp. 28–9
9 Ibid., p. 29
10 Ibid., p. 46
11 www.metmuseum.org/art/collection/search/211368
12 Hildyard 2005, pp. 16–17
13 British Museum D.49;1916,0506.1; 1935,0716.1; V&A: 2079-1901
14 Hildyard 1999, p. 46; Hildyard 2005, pp. 29–30
15 Hildyard 2005, p. 54

Léonard Limosin (c.1505–c.1576/7)

1 Coloured enamels fired solid within small cells gouged from the surface of copper plaques or vessels.
2 Some plaques backstamped with the Pénicaud punchmark bear Limosin's enamelled monogram. Both Limosin and the Pénicauds used Albrecht Dürer's prints as design sources for plaques. Both used clear, colourless enamel on plaque backs, as well as allowing copper to show as part of the design on the front. They used translucent coloured enamels backed by large foils. They made lavish use of gold decoration and intricate painting in gold *en camaïeu*. They were early exponents of painting *en grisaille*. They painted enamelled portrait miniatures, a novel art. A later Pénicaud worked with Limosin and his sons on decorations for the royal entry to Bordeaux in 1564.
3 Monochrome painting with the dark ground showing through varying thicknesses of white enamel to create tonality.
4 He is said, for example, to have enamelled plaques, now vanished, after cartoons by Rosso Fiorentino for the ceiling and panelling of the gallery at Fontainebleau.
5 Both Musée du Louvre, Paris
6 Musée des Beaux-Arts, Limoges
7 Musée des Beaux-Arts, Chartres
8 Formerly in the collection of Sir Andrew Fountaine, now Waddesdon Manor, Buckinghamshire, England
9 Under negotiation for acquisition to the French national collections
10 V&A: C.2452-1910
11 Landesmuseum für Kunst und Kulturgeschichte, Oldenburg
12 A scene or portrait painted entirely in any single colour.
13 British Museum, London
14 Both Louvre Museum
15 Frick Collection, New York

André-Charles Boulle (1642–1732)

1 Koeppe and Rieder (eds) 2006, p. 66
2 Ramond 2011
3 On Boulle's collecting of prints, see Jackson 2014
4 Dassas 2014

Grinling Gibbons (1648–1721)

1 This essay was informed by discussions with my colleagues Dr Jenny Saunt and Dr Kira d'Alburquerque, with whom the online Gibbons collection pages were written in 2021, on the 300th anniversary of his death: www.vam.ac.uk/collections/grinling-gibbons

2 De Beer (ed.) 1955, pp. 567–8
3 Ibid., p. 179
4 The portrait, by John Closterman, is lost, but recorded in John Smith's contemporary mezzotint: https://collections.vam.ac.uk/item/O646813/print-smith-j/
5 De Beer (ed.) 1955, p. 567
6 The account is recorded by the engraver and antiquary George Vertue (1684–1756). Vertue 1936, p. 11
7 For an account of Gibbons's carving techniques, see Esterly 1998, pp. 174–205

Ignaz Preissler (1676–1741)

1 The most comprehensive overview of this subject remains Pazaurek 1925
2 Liefkes (ed.) 1997, p. 64
3 Quoted in von Strasser 1973, pp. 135–42
4 Brožková (ed.) 2020, p. 33
5 A number of glasses that are securely linked to the Preissler workshop were published by the glass scholar Professor Rudolf von Strasser and provide a group from which to base further attribution: von Strasser 1973
6 Brožková (ed.) 2020, p. 33
7 Brožková (ed.) 2009, p. 99
8 Von Strasser 1973, p. 138
9 Quoted in Cassidy-Geiger 1987, p. 52. The letter was originally transcribed in Jiřík 1924, p. 31

Paul de Lamerie (1688–1751)

1 John Stowe, rev. John Strype, *A Survey of the Cities of London and Westminster*, vol. II (London 1720), Book VI, p. 85
2 Goldsmiths' Company Mark Book for Large Workers, vol. A, no. 1 (unpaged), 5 February 1713. Cited in Susan Hare, 'Paul de Lamerie 1688–1751', in Hare et al. 1990, p. 8 and note 11
3 Hare et al. 1990, p. 15
4 Ibid., p. 13
5 R. Campbell, *The London Tradesman* (London 1747), chapter XXIX, p. 142

Anna Maria Garthwaite (1690–1763)

1 Anon. 1756

Johann Joachim Kändler (1706–1775)

1 Sigalas and Chilton 2023, p. 27
2 Von Wallwitz 2006, p. 15
3 Andres-Acevedo and Ottomeyer 2016, p. 224
4 Von Wallwitz 2006, p. 17
5 Ibid.
6 Wittwer 2006, p. 309
7 Ibid.
8 This figure grouping in two parts may have been made at different times. However, it is apparent, based on printed source material, that they were intended as a grouping. See the engraving: https://collections.louvre.fr/ark:/53355/cl020549381
9 See the V&A Explore the Collections page for further information: www.vam.ac.uk
10 While parts of the fountain are original, including Amphitrite, the two river gods and Triton blowing his horn, there are a number of pieces that were remade in the late eighteenth or early nineteenth centuries using original moulds. There are also several replacement parts that were commissioned by the V&A in 2013–14 in collaboration with the Royal College of Art.

2: Enlightenment & Empire

1 Hume 1985 (from 'Of Commerce', 1752)
2 For instance, the French philosopher Denis Diderot published his *Encyclopédie* between 1751 and 1772
3 Impey and MacGregor 1985, pp. xvii–xx
4 See Berg 2005
5 Lovejoy 2004
6 On this subject, see Anderson 2012 and Walvin 2017
7 Gleeson 1998
8 Snodin 1984, pp. 10–17

9 Insley and Myrone 2021, pp. 25–31
10 See Murdoch 2022
11 These terms are included in Porter 2010
12 Criticism of Rococo was published openly by the 1730s, such as in the work by Voltaire, *Le temple du goût* (1733)
13 These works were *Thoughts on the Imitation of Greek Works in Painting and Sculpture* (1755) and *History of Ancient Art* (1764)
14 Pearce 2007
15 www.vam.ac.uk/articles/the-wedgwood-anti-slavery-medallion (accessed 13 January 2025)
16 Heard 2019

Nicholas Sprimont (1716–1771)

1 Murdoch and Robinson 2023, pp. 602–3
2 Girouard 1966, pp. 58–61
3 *Daily Advertiser*, 5 March 1745
4 Most notably by Mallet 1984, p. 237. This is based on an observation by Rouquet describing the modelling at the factory being directed by 'an able French artist' in its opening years: Roquet 1755, p. 143
5 Mallet 1977, pp. 223–5
6 The notice appeared in the *Gazeteer* and the *New Daily Advertiser*: see Adams 2001, p. 176

Thomas Chippendale (1718–1779)

1 Heckscher 2018, p. 28
2 Term used by Chippendale to designate genuine Chinese and Japanese lacquer, simulated lacquer as well as painted finishes.
3 Bowett and Lomax 2018, p. 10
4 According to Bowett and Lomax, Chippendale's very first recorded appearance in London was a year prior, when he received a payment of £6 10s for commission work from the 3rd Earl of Burlington (1694–1753).
5 Gilbert 1978, p. 8
6 Heckscher 2018, p. 4
7 Stacey Sloboda, 'St. Martin's Lane: Neighborhood as Art World', *Journal18*, no. 15, 'Cities' (Spring 2023)
8 Goodison 2017, p. 13
9 Gilbert 1978, p. 157
10 Bowett and Lomax 2018, p. 90
11 The clothes press and its pair (W.23-1917) are listed in the 1779 inventory of the contents of David Garrick's villa at Hampton. Other japanned pieces which Thomas Chippendale Sr supplied for the villa, now in the V&A's collections, include a four-poster bed (W.70-1916), a corner cupboard (W.24-1917) and a bookcase (W.14- 1994).
12 There is some question as to whether the japanned suite of furniture for the Garrick villa was made by Chippendale or whether his firm only altered some of the existing furniture by redecorating it. See Gilbert 1978, pp. 238–9
13 Bowett and Lomax 2018, p. 96
14 Christopher Gilbert, 'Chippendale's Harewood Commission', *Furniture History*, vol. 9 (1973), p. 1
15 An example of such misattributions can be found in the ribband-back chair (W.65-1935) in the V&A collections. Attributed to Chippendale, c.1760, the chair was in fact made almost a century later, between 1850 and 1870. See Lucy Wood, 'Tied up in Knots: Three Centuries of the Ribbon-back Chair', *Furniture History*, vol. 51 (2015), pp. 241–70
16 Megan Aldrich, 'The Shakespeare of English Furniture: Examining the Rich Mythology Surrounding Thomas Chippendale', *Furniture History*, vol. 54 (2018), p. 9

Jacob Sang (c.1720–1786)

1 Laméris 2023, p. 14, fig. 6
2 Ibid., p. 15

Thomas Johnson (1723–1799)

1 Simon 2003, pp. 1–64
2 Ibid., p. 51

Josiah Wedgwood (1730–1795)

1 Josiah Wedgwood to Thomas Bentley, February 1769. V&A Wedgwood Collection Archive: E25-18232
2 Reilly 1992, p. 3
3 Undated newspaper cutting, c.1771–4. V&A Wedgwood Collection Archive: WE/CUT/1/1/1
4 Harwood A. Johnson, 'Books Belonging to Wedgwood & Bentley, the 10th Augt 1770', Ars Ceramica, 7 (1990)
5 Neil McKendrick, 'Josiah Wedgwood and Factory Discipline', Historical Journal, vol. 4, no. 1 (1961)
6 Josiah Wedgwood to Sir William Hamilton, 16 June 1787. V&A Wedgwood Collection Archive: E26-19090
7 Josiah Wedgwood to Thomas Bentley, 2 January 1766. V&A Wedgwood Collection Archive: E25-18058

Johann Christian Neuber (1736–1808)

1 Camillo Count Marcolini-Ferretti (1739–1814) was a minister and general director of the fine arts for the Electorate of Saxony.
2 Its first instance is recorded in print on the title page of the unfinished book on minerals written in Latin by the Jesuit Bernardo Cesi (Bernardus Caesius Mutinensis: 1581–1630), edited by the Modena Jesuit College and published posthumously in Lyon (France) in 1636.
3 Advertisement in the Weimar Journal des Luxus und der Moden, May 1786, transcribed in Kugel 2012, p. 384
4 In total, Neuber employed 11 apprentices between 1762 and 1798. Ibid., p. 109
5 Advertisement in the Weimar Journal des Luxus und der Moden, May 1786, transcribed in ibid., p. 384

William Kilburn (1745–1818)

1 Clayton and Oakes 1954, p. 136
2 Curtis et al. c.1777–98, vol. 1, v–vi
3 Nelson 2008, p. 363
4 Patent of Inventions. Index 1617–1853, quoted in Clayton and Oakes 1954, p. 136
5 Longfield 1953, p. 230
6 O'Brien 1795
7 Eaton et al. 2014, p. 29

Paul Storr (1770–1844)

1 Hartop 2015, p. 21
2 British Museum, no. 1986,0403.1
3 Royal Museums Greenwich, no. PLT0095
4 Hartop 2005, pp. 21–6
5 Hartop 2015, p. 14
6 Ibid., pp. 54–5
7 Patterson 2021, pp. 12–31; 'The Manor House Sale' 1911, auction catalogue
8 Oman 1966, pp. 174–83
9 Culme 1977, p. 60
10 V&A: E.70-1964 (design), 473 to B-1864 (tureen)

Fortunato Pio (1794–1865), Alessandro (1823–1883), Augusto (1829–1914) and Alfredo Castellani (1856–1930)

1 V&A: M.63-1921
2 V&A: M.62-1921
3 V&A: M.64&A-1921
4 V&A: 48-1868
5 The Times, 17 May 1862
6 V&A: M.7:1,2-2011
7 V&A: 5995-1859 and 5996-1859

3: Art & Industry

1 Furniture Gazette, vol. v (1876), p. 76
2 Arrowsmith and Arrowsmith 1840, p. 111
3 Jones 1863, p. 3
4 Conway 1882, p. 34
5 Guide to the South Kensington Museum 1857, p. 1
6 Horsfall Turner 2023, p. 25
7 Ibid., p. 41
8 Findling 1990
9 Snodin and Styles 2004, p. 11
10 Britain, France, Belgium, Portugal, Spain, Germany and Italy
11 www.vam.ac.uk/blog/news/homecoming-exhibition-of-asante-gold-regalia-at-manhiya-palace-museum-kumasi (accessed 3 June 2024)
12 Prettejohn 2007
13 The Perry expedition led by Commodore Matthew Calbraith Perry was a diplomatic and military expedition in two voyages (1852–3 and 1854–5) by the United States Navy, with the goal of establishing diplomatic relations and negotiating trade agreements.
14 Popularized by Charles Locke Eastlake's Hints on Household Taste in Furniture, Upholstery and Other Details (1868), among other publications.
15 Corrigan 1997, p. 56
16 The first man-made plastic was produced from chemically modified materials found in nature: vulcanite and ebonite from rubber (1843), then celluloid from cellulose, exhibited by Alexander Parkes as 'Parkesine' at the International Exhibition in 1862 and improved by John Hyatt's 1870 US patent, and then casein from milk curds or skimmed milk, patented in 1899. For more information see Ehrman 2018, p. 128
17 Between 1816 and 1850 cotton products contributed nearly 50 per cent of the value of all British exports. Ehrman 2018, p. 71. William Perkin developed new coal-tar-based aniline dyes, the first synthetic dyes, in 1856. Hewitson, Winterbottom and Ribeyrol (eds) 2023, p. 87
18 Blakesley 2006, p. 7
19 He was also a leading supporter of the Pre-Raphaelite Brotherhood, who were heavily inspired by the art of late medieval and early Renaissance Europe.
20 William Morris, 'The Art of the People' (1879), in The Collected Works of William Morris, 1910–15, vol. 22, p. 50, and Harrod 1999, p. 16
21 Thomas 2020, p. 4
22 Livingstone and Parry (eds) 2005, p. 10
23 Tucker 2010
24 Notable exhibitions included the 1855 Paris Exhibition, the 1862 International Exhibition in London (the first to exhibit new synthetic dyes and Japanese art and design), the 1873 Vienna World Fair, the Centennial Exposition in Philadelphia in 1876 and the 1886 Colonial and Indian Exposition in London, with 50 exhibitions held between 1873 and 1915. Marshall 2021
25 Greenhalgh (ed.) 2000, p. 18
26 Bing 1902, pp. 279–85
27 Debora L. Silverman, 'Art Nouveau, Art of Darkness: African Lineages of Belgian Modernism, Part I', West 86th, vol. 18, no. 2 (2018), pp. 139–81

Augustus Welby Northmore Pugin (1812–1852)

1 Wedgwood 1985, p. 24
2 Ibid.
3 Ibid.
4 Wedgwood 1988, p. 179
5 A.W.N. Pugin, True Principles of Pointed or Christian Architecture (London 1841), p. 1
6 Ibid., p. 56
7 Sedding 1893, p. 144

Léonard Morel-Ladeuil (1820–1888)

1 Day 1888, p. 13
2 Morel 1904, p. 31
3 Pyhrr and Godoy 1998
4 Antoine Vechte, Italian Poets Shield, chased steel, Paris, 1848–51, V&A: 1482-1851
5 Catherine Granger, L'Empereur et les arts: La liste civile de Napoléon III (Paris: Écoles des Chartes, 2005), p. 150 and pp. 748–9
6 Elkington Business Archive, V&A Archive of Art and Design, AAD/179/3/1/8
7 Grant and Patterson 2018
8 Morel 1904, p. 13
9 Ibid., plate II, pp. 14–15
10 Grant 2015, p. 277
11 Morel 1904, p. 16 (translated by Alistair Grant)
12 Chapter 5, 'A Global Artwork', in Grant and Patterson 2018, pp. 88–103; 'The Milton Shield', in Patterson and Trusted (eds) 2018, pp. 62–8
13 'Unique Display of Works of Art by Messrs. Elkington and Co.', Liverpool Mercury, 21 January 1868, no. 6235, p. 5
14 Elkington & Co., Visitors' Book: Containing Names and Addresses of Visitors, together with Some Orders and Prices at the International Exhibitions in Paris in 1855 and 1878, Vienna in 1873, and Philadelphia in 1876 (Victoria and Albert Museum, National Art Library, Special Collections, Manuscript MSL/1971/707-709, Pressmark: 86.NN.33)
15 Grant and Patterson 2018, pp. 97–101
16 Lechelon 2011. See also Aurélia Lechelon, Les dessins d'orfèvrerie de Léonard Morel-Ladeuil (1820–1888), conservés au Musée d'Art Roger Quilliot de Clermont-Ferrand (un mémoire de Master, Université Blaise Pascal, Clermont II, 2007)
17 Day 1890, p. 271

Edward Burne-Jones (1833–1898)

1 Burne-Jones 1904, vol. 1, pp. 206–7
2 Quoted in Suzanne Fagence Cooper, 'Burne-Jones as a Designer', in Smith 2018, p. 197
3 Henry James, 'London Pictures and London Plays', Atlantic Monthly (August 1882), pp. 253–63
4 Burne-Jones 1904, vol. 2, p. 111
5 Frances Horner, Time Remembered (London 1933), p. 125
6 Thomas Matthews Rooke, typewritten notes of conversations with Burne-Jones, V&A Museum, NAL, 1897, p. 68
7 Julia Mary Cartwright Ady, 'The Life and Work of Sir Edward Burne-Jones', Art Journal (Christmas 1894), p. 1

William Morris (1834–1896)

1 William Morris, A Rather Long-Winded Sketch of my Very Uneventful Life (unpublished letter, 1883), quoted in Briggs (ed.) 1984, p. 29
2 William Morris, 'How I Became a Socialist', Justice (16 June 1894), quoted in Briggs (ed.) 1984, p. 36
3 William Morris, 'Preface', in Ruskin 1892, p. i
4 William Morris, The Beauty of Life (lecture, given 1880), quoted in Naylor 1988, p. 210
5 William Morris, The Lesser Arts (lecture, given 1878), quoted in Briggs (ed.) 1984, p. 93
6 Ibid., p. 36
7 William Morris, 'How I Became a Socialist', Justice (16 June 1894), quoted in Briggs (ed) 1984, p. 36
8 William Morris, A Rather Long-Winded Sketch of my Very Uneventful Life (unpublished letter, 1883), quoted in Briggs (ed.) 1984, p. 30
9 William Morris, The Lesser Arts (lecture, given 1878), quoted in Briggs (ed.) 1984, p. 85
10 Ibid., p. 99
11 Discharge printing involves removing dye to create a pattern. In this instance, plain cotton was first dyed blue in an indigo vat before being printed with a bleaching agent to remove some of the dye following a design. A blue and white patterned cloth was produced, which could then be overdyed with additional colour using natural dyes, such as madder (red) and weld (yellow). Requiring several preparatory steps and the precise use of chemicals, discharge printing was a slow process that demanded accuracy and patience – especially when producing complex, polychromatic designs such as Strawberry Thief and Wandle.

Christopher Dresser (1834–1904)

1 Christopher Dresser, 'Hindrances to the Progress of Applied Art' (lecture to the Society of Arts, London, 1872), quoted in House Furnisher and Decorator, vol. II (1 May 1872), p. 49
2 Dresser 1882, p. 319
3 Awarded in absentia by the University of Jena in Thuringia (Germany)
4 Dresser 1873, p. 94
5 Christopher Dresser, 'Ornamentation a High Art' (letter), Journal of the Society of Arts, vol. XIX, no. 956 (17 March 1871), p. 352
6 Dresser 1873, p. 107
7 Ibid., Preface, p. v
8 Darlington and Richmond Herald, 24 October 1874, p. 2
9 Dresser 1882
10 Furniture Gazette, vol. XII (August 1879), p. 124. The writer was describing metalwork designed by Dresser and made by Hukin & Heath in Birmingham
11 York Herald, 13 November 1879, p. 6
12 Dresser 1873, p. 127

William De Morgan (1839–1917)

1 Gaunt and Clayton-Stamm 1971, p. 17
2 Stirling 1922, p. 9

Émile Gallé (1846–1904)

1 Roger Marx, La Décoration et l'art industriel à l'Exposition universelle de 1889 (Paris 1890), p. 26
2 Calling card written by Émile Gallé to Takashima Hokkai, 1886, Shimonoseki City Art Museum

3 Émile Gallé, 'Le Mobilier contemporain orné d'après la nature' (1900), in *Écrits pour l'Art: Floriculture – Art Décoratif – Notices d'Exposition* (Paris 1908), p. 239
4 Émile Gallé, 'Le Décor symbolique' (1900), in ibid., p. 217
5 Le Tacon 2004, p. 201

Louis Comfort Tiffany (1848–1933)

1 McKean 1980, pp. 2–3
2 Koch 1966, p. 8
3 Ibid., p. 7
4 Ibid., p. 8
5 Ibid., p. 3
6 Ibid., p. 54
7 Ibid., p. 5
8 Joppien 2009, p. 207
9 Koch 1966, p. 1
10 McKean 1980, p. 186

Phoebe Anna Traquair (1852–1936)

1 Margaret Bartholomew was the adopted daughter of Mrs Napier, Phoebe Anna Traquair's daughter. Cumming 1993 and Cumming 2022
2 Letter of 23 June 1887 from Ruskin to Traquair. In the late 1890s Traquair had this letter incorporated into the binding of *The Dream* in the V&A collection: MSL/1936/1765
3 These were given to the Museum by Traquair's granddaughter Margaret Bartholomew in 1965 and 1976. V&A: Circ.318-321-1965 and T.422-1976
4 Caw 1900, pp. 143–8
5 Carruthers 2013, p. 164
6 In 1903 she became a member of the Arts and Crafts Exhibition Society and sent more than 20 enamels, embroidery panels and illuminated pages of D.G. Rossetti's *The House of Life* to the exhibition. *Arts & Crafts Exhibition Society: Catalogue of the Seventh Exhibition*, the New Gallery, 121 Regent Street (London, 1903)
7 V&A: M.404-1977

May Morris (1862–1938)

1 Morris 1973, vol. 1, p. 233
2 V&A: 83-1864
3 Morris 1893, p. 17
4 Morris, Marshall, Faulkner & Co. became Morris & Co. in 1875.
5 V&A: MSL/1939/2636 (Day Book)
6 George Bernard Shaw (1888), quoted in Marsh 1986, p. 220
7 Morris 1973, vol. 1, p. 143
8 V&A: M.34-1939
9 V&A: M.19A-1939
10 Morris 1973, vol. 2, p. 432
11 V&A: MA/1/L1755
12 V&A: MA/1/L1755

Charles Robert Ashbee (1863–1942)

1 Ashbee 1890, p. 19
2 Ibid., p. 21
3 Ibid., p. 22
4 Ashbee 1898, p. 337
5 Janet Ashbee, *Essex House Alphabet*, quoted in MacCarthy 1981, p. 30
6 Charles Robert Ashbee, letter to Janet Forbes, 2 September 1887, quoted in F. Ashbee 2022, p. 25

4: Modernism & the Post-War Craft Revival

1 Britton 2013, p. 95
2 Schwarz 1996, p. 3
3 Benton, Benton and Wood (eds) 2003, p. 13
4 Harrod 1999, p. 20
5 Omega Workshops Ltd, Artist Decorators, 33 Fitzroy Square, *c*.1915
6 In his 1937 survey book *An Enquiry into Industrial Art in England*, the German émigré art historian Nikolaus Pevsner notes that this was largely due to the unadventurous attitudes of British industrialists.
7 Harrod 1999, p. 26
8 Ibid., p. 29
9 Kardon (ed.) 1995, p. 62
10 The Council of Industrial Design was founded to 'promote by all practicable means the improvement of design in the products of British industry' and organized the *Britain Can Make It* exhibition at the V&A in 1946, intended to reinvigorate Britain's manufacturing industry and promote public design consciousness. In 1951 the Festival of Britain on London's South Bank showcased the best of British manufacturing and design.
11 Harrod 1999, p. 256
12 Adamson 2007, p. 3
13 *Objects: USA* 1972
14 He taught at the Otis Art Institute and at the University of California, Berkeley.
15 Britton 2013, p. 9
16 Ibid., p. 95
17 It was renamed the Crafts Council in 1979. For more information, see Harrod 1999, p. 369, and Graves 2023, p. 21
18 www.craftscouncil.org.uk/about/history (accessed 3 June 2024)
19 *The Maker's Eye* 1981
20 Victor Margrie, 'Introduction', in ibid.
21 Ralph Turner, 'The Maker's Eye', *Crafts*, vol. 54 (January/February 1982), p. 27
22 In 2021 the Crafts Council hosted the exhibition *Maker's Eye: Stories of Craft* and invited a new group of makers to reflect on the breadth, qualities and diversity of craft today.
23 Adamson 2007, p. 3

René Jules Lalique (1860–1945)

1 V&A: M.140-2007
2 'The variety that gives movement, movement, which is Life.' Quote taken from the 1905 exhibition catalogue of Lalique's work at Agnew & Sons, London: *Works of René Lalique* (London 1905)

Eileen Gray (1878–1976)

1 Eileen Gray's notebook pertaining to lacquering techniques contains multiple recipes obtained from Dean Charles: V&A: AAD/1980/9/3
2 V&A: AAD/1980/9/11
3 Exerpt from Jean Badovici and Eileen Gray's preface to the Winter 1929 special issue of *L'Architecture Vivante* entitled E.1027: *Maison en Bord de Mer*, in Adam 1987, p. 236
4 Ibid.
5 Recent studies include the work of Jasmine Rault, Jane Stevenson and Despina Stratigakos.
6 Rault 2010, p. 30
7 Rykwert 1968

Aino Marsio-Aalto (1894–1949) and Alvar Aalto (1898–1976)

1 Ailson and Mallsard (eds) 2018
2 Alvar Aalto, 'Rationalism and Man', in Schildt 1997, pp. 80–93
3 See Gerrit Rietveld's *Red Blue Chair*
4 Wilk 1996, p. 207
5 Nina Stritzler-Levine, 'Research, Archives and Interpretations', in Stritzler-Levine and Riekko (eds) 2022, pp. 19–37

Gunta Stölzl (1897–1983)

1 Stadler 2009, p. 13
2 Müller 2009, pp. 52, 63
3 Radewaldt (ed.) 1997, p. 122
4 Wortman Weltge 1993, p. 58
5 Müller 2009, p. 35
6 Stölzl refers to her title in the masculine form in letters protesting her wage as *Werkmeister*, and writes 'Meister' on her ID card when she's made *Jungmeister*, rather than using the feminine form, 'Meisterin'.
7 Gunta Stölzl, 'Weaving at the Bauhaus', *Handweaving Today: Traditions and Changes*, in Mairet 1939, p. 113
8 Ibid.
9 Smith 2014
10 Stölzl 1926, p. 109
11 Ibid.
12 Stölzl, 'Weaving at the Bauhaus', p. 114
13 Wortman Weltge 1993, p. 112
14 Stölzl 1926, p. 110
15 Radewaldt (ed.) 1997, p. 180
15 Radewaldt (ed.) 1997, p. 180
16 Müller 2009, p. 49
17 Droste and Ellwanger 1987, p. 34

Lucie Rie (1902–1995)

1 Rie said: 'He did excavations there in his vineyard, and there were fantastic Roman bowls which were floating. I always tried to copy those floating bowls.' Quoted in David Sexton, 'Floating towards Freedom', *Sunday Telegraph*, 1 May 1988
2 Ibid.
3 Robert Melville, 'Pots in Rows', *Architectural Review*, vol. 112 (November 1952), p. 344
4 Cooper 2021, p. 5
5 Ibid., p. 253

Ruth Duckworth (1919–2009)

1 Tony Birks, *Art of the Modern Potter* (2nd edn, London 1976), p. 23
2 Lauria and Birks 2004, p. 15
3 Tony Birks, *The Art of the Modern Potter* (London 1967), p. 11
4 Ruth Duckworth, 'My History in Ceramics', in Ruthin 2009, p. 19

Althea McNish (1924–2020)

1 Personal statement, given on Althea McNish's CV, as captured in an undated photograph from a private collection
2 Althea McNish, interview with Christine Checinska, in Checinska 2018, p. 197
3 Ibid.

Marjorie Schick (1941–2017)

1 Oral history interview with Marjorie Schick 2004
2 Rosolowski (ed.) 2007
3 Turner 1996
4 Oral history interview with Marjorie Schick 2004
5 Ibid.
6 Ibid.
7 Letter to Clare Phillips in Victoria and Albert Museum maker's file dated 16 May 1997

Dale Chihuly (b.1941)

1 Oldknow 1996, p. 38
2 *The Times*, 13 August 1999, quoted in Hawkins Opie (ed.) 2001, p. 21
3 Hawkins Opie (ed.) 2001, p. 137
4 Chihuly 2006, p. 70
5 Chihuly et al. 2000, pp. 29–30

Albert Paley (b.1944)

1 Lucie-Smith 1996, p. 10
2 Letter to Marian Campbell from Albert Paley, 5 July 1994, File Number 94/829, V&A Registry
3 *Towards a New Iron Age* 1982
4 Quote by Albert Paley from conversations with the author, 24 June and 30 October 1993, in Mildred F. Schmertz, 'From Lines in Pencil to Forms in Space', in Paley et al. 1994, p. 4
5 Letter to Marian Campbell and Victoria Timberlake, 16 September 1997, File number 2005/105, V&A Registry
6 Paley and Corcoran Gallery 2014

Charlotte de Syllas (b.1946)

1 De Syllas quoted in Phillips 1999/2000
2 For the shell necklace (fig. 5) there are wooden models, V&A: M.4C-F-1990, and an accompanying paper design, V&A: E.345-1985, that show this process.
3 Coates (ed.) 2016, p. 33
4 V&A: M.17-2008
5 de Syllas, personal correspondence (6 January 1992)
6 V&A: M.215-2011

Alison Britton (b.1948)

1 *The Work of Alison Britton* 1979, p. 25
2 *The Maker's Eye* 1981, p. 16
3 Britton 2022, p. 10
4 Alison Britton, 'The Story So Far', *Ceramic Review* (May/June 1991), pp. 20–2
5 Alison Britton, 'Past and Present', *Crafts* (March/April 2016), p. 14
6 Alison Britton, unpublished notes, 2013
7 Alison Britton, 'Past and Present', *Crafts* (March/April 2016), p. 15
8 Alison Britton, Introduction, in Martina Margetts, *International Crafts* (London 1991), p. 9

BIBLIOGRAPHY

1: The Emergence of the Celebrated Maker

John Cherry, *Goldsmiths* (London 1992)
Glyn Davies, 'Embroiderers and the Embroidery Trade', in Clare Brown et al. (eds), *English Medieval Embroidery: Opus Anglicanum* (New Haven 2016)
Robin Hildyard, *European Ceramics* (London 1999)
———, *English Pottery 1620–1840* (London 2005)
Arthur Mayger Hind, *Catalogue of Early Italian Engravings* (London 1910)
Bernard Pallisey, *Admirable Discourses*, 1580, trans. Aurèle La Rocque 1909 (Urbana 1957)

Léonard Limosin (c.1505– c.1576/7)

Sophie Baratte, *Léonard Limosin au musée du Louvre* (Paris 1993)
Françoise Barbe and Véronique Notin, *La rencontre des Héros* (Limoges 2002)
Maryvonne Beyssi-Cassan, *Le métier d'émailleur à Limoges, xvie–xviie siècles* (Limoges 2006)
Thierry Crépin-Leblond et al., *Marie Stuart: Le destin français d'une reine d'Écosse*, exh. cat., Musée national de la Renaissance (Écouen 2008)
Thierry Crépin-Leblond and Stéphanie Deprouw, *De la lettre à l'émail: Léonard Limosin interprète Ovide*, exh. cat., Musée national de la Renaissance (Écouen 2010)
Thierry Crépin-Leblond and M. Barbier (eds), *Une reine sans couronne? Louise de Savoie, mère de François Ier*, exh. cat., Musée national de la Renaissance (Écouen 2015)
Stéphanie Deprouw-Augustin, 'Léonard Limosin: l'apogée de l'émail peint (1 & 2)', *Apprendre à voir* (https://deprouw.fr/blog/), 6 November and 28 December 2013
Irmgard Müsch et al., *New Research on Limoges Painted Enamels*, International Colloquium 18–20 April 2002, Herzog Anton Ulrich-Museum, Braunschweig 2004
Philippe Verdier, *Catalogue of the Painted Enamels of the Renaissance*, Walters Art Gallery (Baltimore 1967)
———, *Limoges Painted Enamels, in The Frick Collection: An Illustrated Catalogue, Vol. VIII: Enamels, Rugs, Silver* (New York 1977)

André-Charles Boulle (1642–1732)

Frédéric Dassas, 'Trois siècles de passion pour le mobilier Boulle', *Dossier de l'Art*, no. 224 (2014), 'André-Charles Boulle, ébéniste de Louis XIV'
Mathieu Deldicque (ed.), *André Charles Boulle*, exh. cat., Musée Condé de Chantilly (San-Rémy-en-l'Eau, 2024)
Călin Demetrescu, *Les ébénistes de la Couronne sous le règne de Louis XIV* (Lausanne 2021)
Mia Jackson, 'Boulle, auteur, éditeur et revendeur d'estampes', *Dossier de l'Art*, no. 224 (2014), 'André-Charles Boulle, ébéniste de Louis XIV'
Wolfram Koeppe and William Rieder (eds), *European Furniture in The Metropolitan Museum of Art: Highlights of the Collection* (New York 2006)
Alexandre Pradère, *French Furniture Makers: The Art of the Ébéniste from Louis XIV to the Revolution* (London 1990)
Pierre Ramond, *André-Charles Boulle: Ébéniste, Ciseleur & Marqueteur ordinaire du Roy* (Paris 2011)
Jean Nérée Ronfort, *André Charles Boulle (1642–1732): Un nouveau style pour l'Europe* (Paris 2009)
Jean-Pierre Samoyault, *André-Charles Boulle et sa famille* (Geneva 1979)
Gillian Wilson et al., *French Furniture and Gilt Bronzes. Baroque and Régence. Catalogue of the J. Paul Getty Museum Collection* (Los Angeles 2008)

Grinling Gibbons (1648–1721)

Geoffrey Beard, *The Work of Grinling Gibbons* (London 1989)
E.S. De Beer (ed.), *The Diary of John Evelyn*, vol. III (Oxford 1955)

Ada de Wit, *Grinling Gibbons and his Contemporaries (1650–1700): The Golden Age of Woodcarving in the Netherlands and Britain* (Turnhout 2021)
David Esterly, *Grinling Gibbons and the Art of Carving* (London 1998)
Frederick Oughton, *Grinling Gibbons & the English Woodcarving Tradition* (London 1979)
H. Avray Tipping, *Grinling Gibbons and the Woodwork of his Age (1648–1720)* (London 1914)
'Vertue Note Books, IV', *Walpole Society*, vol. XXIV (1936)

Ignaz Preissler (1676–1741)

Helena Brožková (ed.), *Daniel a Ignác Preisslerové: Barokní malíři skla a porcelánu* (Prague 2009)
——— (ed.), *Gleam of Gold, Blaze of Colours: The Art of Reverse Glass Painting in the Collection of the Museum of Decorative Arts in Prague* (Prague 2020)
Maureen Cassidy-Geiger, 'Two Pieces of Porcelain Decorated by Ignaz Preissler in the J. Paul Getty Museum', *J. Paul Getty Museum Journal*, vol. 15 (1987
F.X. Jiřík, 'K dějinám porculánu v Čechách. Domácký malíř skla a porculánu v Kunštátě Ignatius Preissler (1728–1732)', in *Zpráva kuratoria za správní rok 1923* (Prague 1924)
Sebastian Kuhn, 'The Hausmaler', in Meredith Chilton and Claudia Lehner-Jobst (eds), *Fired by Passion: Vienna Baroque Porcelain of Claudius Innocentius Du Paquier*, vol. I (Stuttgart 2009), pp. 498–545
Reino Liefkes (ed.), *Glass* (London 1997)
E. and H. Manners, *Decorators of Ceramics in Europe, Independent, Itinerant and the Hausmaler* (London 2024)
Gustav Pazaurek, *Deutsche Fayence- und Porzellan-Hausmaler* (Leipzig 1925)
Rudolf von Strasser, 'Twelve Preissler Glasses', *Journal of Glass Studies*, vol. 15 (1973)

Paul de Lamerie (1688–1751)

E.M. Alcorn, *Beyond the Maker's Mark: Paul de Lamerie Silver in the Cahn Collection* (Cambridge 2006)
A. Grimwade, *Rococo Silver 1727–1765* (London 1974)
S. Hare et al., *Paul de Lamerie: At the Sign of the Golden Ball. An Exhibition of the Work of England's Master Silversmith (1688–1751)*, exh. cat., Goldsmiths' Hall (London 1990)
C. Hartop, *The Huguenot Legacy: English Silver 1680–1760, from the Alan and Simone Hartman Collection* (London 1996)
J.F. Hayward, *Huguenot Silver in England 1688–1727* (London 1959)
T. Murdoch, *Europe Divided: Huguenot Refugee Art and Culture* (London 2021)
P.A.S. Phillips, *Paul de Lamerie, Citizen and Goldsmith of London: A Study of his Life and Work, A.D. 1688–1751* (London 1935; repr. London 1968)
T. Schroder, 'Paul de Lamerie: Businessman or Craftsman?', *The Silver Society Journal*, vol. 6 (Winter 1994)
———, 'Evidence without Documents: Patterns of Ornament in Rococo and Régence Silver', *Rococo Silver in England and its Colonies. Papers from a Symposium at Virginia Museum of Fine Arts Richmond, in 2004, Silver Studies, the Journal of the Silver Society*, special issue, vol. 20 (2006)

Anna Maria Garthwaite (1690–1763)

Zara Anishanslin, *Portrait of a Woman in Silk: Hidden Histories of the British Atlantic World* (New Haven 2016)
Anon. (Anna Maria Garthwaite?), 'Of Designing and Drawing of Ornaments, Models, and Patterns, with Foliages, Flowers, &c. for the Use of the Flowered Silk Manufactory, Embroidery, and Printing (of the Various Kinds of Flower'd Silks)', in Godfrey Smith, *The Laboratory; or, School of Arts* (London 1756)
Natalie Rothstein, *Silk Designs of the Eighteenth Century in the Collection of the Victoria and Albert Museum, London: With a Complete Catalogue* (London 1990)

———, 'Taste and Technique: The Work of an 18th Century Silk Designer', *Bulletin du CIETA*, no. 70 (1992)
———, *The Victoria & Albert Museum's Textile Collection: Woven Textile Design in Britain to 1750* (London 1994)
———, *The Victoria & Albert Museum's Textile Collection: Woven Textile Design in Britain from 1750 to 1850* (London 1994)
———, 'Garthwaite, Anna Maria, British Textile Designer', in Delia Gaze (ed.), *Dictionary of Women Artists*, Vol. I (London 1997)
———, 'Woven Textile Design in Britain: Late 17th Century to 1750', in *British Textiles: 1700 to the Present* (London 2010)
Peter Thornton, 'A Silk Designer's Manual', *Bulletin of the Needle and Bobbin Club*, vol. 42, nos 1 and 2 (1958)
Alicia K. Weisberg-Roberts, *Variety, Simplicity, Intricacy, and Quantity: Reading the Life and Work of Anna Maria Garthwaite*, Courtauld Institute of Art, MA Report (1998)

Johann Joachim Kändler (1706–1775)

Sarah-Katharina Andres-Acevedo and Hans Ottomeyer, *From Invention to Perfection: Masterpieces of Eighteenth-century Porcelain* (Stuttgart 2016)
Reino Liefkes and Hilary Young, *Masterpieces of World Ceramics* (London 2008)
Ulrich Pietsch, *Meissener Porzellanplastik von Gottlieb Kirchner und Johann Joachim Kaendler* (Munich 2006)
Ulrich Pietsch, Anette Loeschm and Eva Strober, *The Dresden Porcelain Collection, China, Japan, Meissen* (Berlin and Munich 2006)
Ulrich Pietsch and Theresa Witting, *Fascination of Fragility, Masterpieces of European Porcelain* (Leipzig 2010)
Vanessa Sigalas and Meredith Chilton, *All Walks of Life: A Journey with the Alan Shimmerman Collection: Meissen Porcelain Figures of the Eighteenth Century* (Stuttgart 2023)
Angela Gräfin von Wallwitz, *Celebrating Kaendler 1706–1775* (Munich 2006)
Samuel Wittwer, *The Gallery of Meissen Animals: Augustus the Strong's Menagerie for the Japanese Palace in Dresden* (Munich 2006)

2: Enlightenment & Empire

Jennifer L. Anderson, *Mahogany: The Costs of Luxury in Early America* (Cambridge 2012)
Victoria Avery, Melissa Calaresu and Mary Laven (eds), *Treasured Possessions from the Renaissance to the Enlightenment* (Cambridge 2015)
Maxine Berg, 'In Pursuit of Luxury: Global History and British Consumer Goods in the Eighteenth Century', *Past & Present*, vol. 182 (2004)
———, *Luxury and Pleasure in Eighteenth-Century Britain* (Oxford 2005)
Viccy Coltman, *Fabricating the Antique: Neoclassicism in Britain, 1760–1800* (London 2006)
Janet Gleeson, *The Arcanum: The Extraordinary True Story of the Invention of European Porcelain* (London 1998)
Kate Heard (ed.), *George IV: Art & Spectacle* (London 2019)
David Hume, *Essays, Moral, Political and Literary*, ed. Eugene Miller (Indianapolis 1985)
Oliver Impey and Arthur MacGregor, *The Origins of Museums: The Cabinet of Curiosities in 16th- and 17th-century Europe* (Oxford 1985)
Alice Insley and Martin Myrone, *Hogarth and Europe* (London 2021)
Fiske Kimball, *Creation of the Rococo* (Philadelphia 1943)
Paul E. Lovejoy, 'The "Middle Passage": The Enforced Migration of Africans across the Atlantic' (2007), https://api.semanticscholar.org/CorpusID:44009485
Tessa Murdoch, *Europe Divided: Huguenot Refugee Art and Culture* (London 2022)
Susan Pearce, *Visions of Antiquity: The Society of Antiquaries of London, 1707–2007* (London 2007)

David Porter, *The Chinese Taste in Eighteenth-Century England* (Cambridge 2010)

Larry Silver, *Europe Views the World, c.1500–1700* (London 2022)

Michael Snodin (ed.), *Rococo: Art and Design in Hogarth's England* (London 1984)

John Styles and Amanda Vickery (eds), *Gender, Taste and Material Culture in Britain and North America, 1700–1830* (London 2006)

Peter Thornton, *Form & Decoration: Innovation in the Decorative Arts 1470–1870* (New York 1998)

James Walvin, *Slavery in Small Things: Slavery and Modern Cultural Habits* (Hoboken 2017)

Nicholas Sprimont (1716–1771)

Elizabeth Adams, *Chelsea Porcelain* (London 2001)

Malcolm Baker, 'Roubiliac and Chelsea in 1745', *Transactions of the English Ceramic Circle*, vol. 16, no. 2 (1997)

Mark Girouard, 'Coffee at Slaughter's: English Art and the Rococo I', *Country Life* (January 1966)

Arthur Lane, *English Porcelain Figures of the 18th Century* (London 1961)

J.V.G. Mallet, 'A Chelsea Greyhound and Retrieving Setter: Some Early Chelsea Figure Models perhaps by Sprimont', *The Connoisseur* (1977)

———, 'Rococo in English Ceramics', in M. Snodin (ed.), *Rococo: Art and Design in Hogarth's England* (London 1984)

———, 'A Painting of Nicholas Sprimont, his Family and his Chelsea Vases', *Les Cahiers de Mariemont* (1993)

Tessa Murdoch and Sandra Robinson, 'Roubiliac and Sprimont: A Friendship Revisited', *Burlington Magazine* (June 2023)

J.E. Nightingale, *Contributions towards the History of Early English Porcelain* (Salisbury 1881)

Jean André Rouquet, *L'Etat des Arts, En Angleterre* (Paris 1755)

Hilary Young, *English Porcelain, 1745–95: Its Makers, Design, Marketing and Consumption* (London 1999)

Thomas Chippendale (1718–1779)

Adam Bowett and James Lomax, *Thomas Chippendale 1718–1779: A Celebration of British Craftsmanship*, The Chippendale Society (2018)

Thomas Chippendale, *The Gentleman and Cabinet Maker's Director: A Reprint of the Third Edition* (Mineola 1966)

Christopher Gilbert, *The Life and Work of Thomas Chippendale* (London 1978)

Judith Goodison, *The Life and Work of Thomas Chippendale Junior* (London 2017)

Morrison H. Heckscher, 'Chippendale's *Director*: A Manifesto of Furniture Design', *Metropolitan Museum of Art Bulletin*, vol. 75, no. 4 (Spring 2018)

John Kenworthy-Browne, *Chippendale and his Contemporaries* (London 1975)

Jane Sellars (ed.), *The Art of Thomas Chippendale: Master Furniture Maker* (London 2000)

Jacob Sang (c.1720–1786)

Anna Laméris, 'Pur Sang', *Annales du 13e Congrès de l'Association Internationale pour l'Histoire du Verre: Pays Bas 1995* (Lochum 1996)

———, 'De Amsterdamse glasgraveur Jacob Sang', *Glas in het Amsterdams Historisch Museum en Museum Willet-Holthuysen* (Amsterdam and Zwolle 1998)

———, 'Jacob Sang – Radgraveur in Amsterdam: De definitieve oplossing van het raadsel Jacob Sang en Simon Jacob Sang', *Vormen uit Vuur*, vol. 252 (June 2023)

Pieter C. Ritsema van Eck, *Glass in the Rijksmuseum*, vol. II (Zwolle 1995), pp. 174–5, 196–213, cats 208–226

Thomas Johnson (1723–1799)

Adam Bowett, *Early Georgian Furniture 1715–1740*, Antique Collectors' Club (2009)

Morrison H. Heckscher, 'Gideon Saint: An Eighteenth-Century Carver and his Scrap Book', *Metropolitan Museum of Art Bulletin*, vol. 27, no. 6 (1996)

Anne Puetz, 'Design Instruction for Artisans in Eighteenth Century Britain', *Journal of Design History*, vol. 12, no. 3 (1999)

Jacob Simon, 'Thomas Johnson's *The Life of the Author*', *Furniture History*, vol. XXXIX (2003)

Taking Shape: Finding Sculpture in the Decorative Arts, exh. cat., Henry Moore Institute and J. Paul Getty Museum (Leeds and Los Angeles 2009)

Lucy Wood, *Upholstered Furniture in the Lady Lever Art Gallery* (New Haven and London 2009)

Josiah Wedgwood (1730–1795)

Aileen Dawson, *Masterpieces of Wedgwood in the British Museum* (London 1984)

Brian Dolan, *Josiah Wedgwood: Entrepreneur to the Enlightenment* (London 2004)

Tristram Hunt, *The Radical Potter: Josiah Wedgwood and the Transformation of Britain* (London 2021)

Catrin Jones, *Wedgwood: Craft & Design* (London 2023)

Iris Moon, *Melancholy Wedgwood* (Cambridge, MA 2024)

Robin Reilly, *Josiah Wedgwood 1730–1795* (London 1992)

Jenny Uglow, *The Lunar Men: The Friends who Made the Future* (London 2002)

Hilary Young (ed.), *The Genius of Wedgwood* (London 1995)

Johann Christian Neuber (1736–1808)

L'art de la paix: Trésors et secrets de la diplomatie, Petit Palais – Musée des Beaux Arts de la Ville de Paris, 19 October 2016–15 January 2017 (Paris 2016)

Serge Grandjean, *Les tabatières du musée du Louvre* (Paris 1981)

Jutta Kappel, 'Taddel, Stiehl and Neuber in Dresden', in Tessa Murdoch and Heike Zech (eds), *Going for Gold: Craftsmanship and Collecting of Gold Boxes* (London 2012)

Alexis Kugel (ed.), *Gold, Jasper and Carnelian: Johann Christian Neuber at the Saxon Court* (Paris and New York 2012)

Kenneth Snowman, *Eighteenth Century Gold Boxes of Europe* (London 1966)

William Kilburn (1745–1818)

Patricia Butler, 'Designers of Distinction', *Irish Arts Review Yearbook* (Dublin 1990–1)

——— (with a foreword by Shirley Sherwood), *Drawn from Nature: The Flowering of Irish Botanical Art* (Woodbridge 2023)

Ann Christie, 'A Taste for Seaweed: William Kilburn's Late Eighteenth-Century Designs for Printed Cottons', *Journal of Design History*, vol. 24, no. 4 (2011)

Muriel Clayton and Alma Oakes, 'Early Calico Printers around London', *Burlington Magazine*, vol. 96, no. 614 (1954)

William Curtis et al., *Flora Londinensis: Or, Plates and Descriptions of Such Plants as Grow Wild in the Environs of London* (London 1777–98)

Linda Eaton et al., *Printed Textiles: British and American Cottons and Linens 1700–1850* (New York 2014)

I.H., 'William Kilburn', *The Dublin Penny Journal*, vol. 1, no. 23 (1 Dec. 1832)

Ada K. Longfield, 'Linen and Cotton Printing in the Eighteenth Century at Ballsbridge, Dublin', *Burlington Magazine*, vol. 89, no. 531 (1947)

———, 'William Kilburn and the Earliest Copyright Acts for Cotton Printing Designs', *Burlington Magazine*, vol. 95, no. 604 (1953)

Charles E. Nelson, 'William Kilburn's Calico Patterns, Copyright and *Curtis's Botanical Magazine*', *Curtis's Botanical Magazine*, vol. 25, no. 4 (2008)

Charles O'Brien, *The British Manufacturers Companion, and Callico Printers Assistant* (London 1795)

Linda Parry, *British Textiles: 1700 to the Present* (London 2010)

Paul Storr (1770–1844)

Shirley Bury, 'The Lengthening Shadow of Rundell's', *Connoisseur Magazine*, vol. CLXI (1966)

John Culme, *Nineteenth-Century Silver* (London 1977)

Christopher Hartop, *Royal Goldsmiths: The Art of Rundell & Bridge, 1797–1843*, exh. cat., Koopman Rare Art (London 2005)

———, *Art in Industry: The Silver of Paul Storr* (Cambridge 2015)

Charles Oman, 'A Problem of Artistic Responsibility: The Firm of Rundell, Bridge and Rundell', *Apollo Magazine* (March 1966)

Angus Patterson, 'From London to Upton via Piddletrenthide and Copenhagen: Building a Biography for Jan Gadd's Metal Cast of the Lomellini Basin', *Journal of the Antique Metalware Society*, vol. 26 (2021)

Norman M. Penzer, *Paul Storr 1771–1844: Silversmith and Goldsmith* (London 1954)

Timothy Schroder, *The Gilbert Collection of Gold and Silver* (Los Angeles 1988)

'The Manor House Sale, Piddletrenthide, near Dorchester … Highly Interesting and Valuable Collection of Works of Art, Historical and Royal Relics formed by J. Bridge and J. Gawler Bridge', Waring & Gillow, 20–22 September 1911, National Art Library, Sales Catalogues, 23.P.19110920

Fortunato Pio (1794–1865), Alessandro (1823–1883), Augusto (1829–1914) and Alfredo Castellani (1856–1930)

Shirley Bury, 'Alessandro Castellani and the Survival of Granulation', *Burlington Magazine*, vol. 117 (October 1975)

Denise Di Castro, *The Castellani Jewelry Workshop: An Approach under the Lens of Archival Material* (Anzio 2019)

Charlotte Gere and Judy Rudoe, *Jewellery in the Age of Queen Victoria: A Mirror to the World* (London 2010)

Jeannette Hanisee Gabriel, *Micromosaics* (London 2000)

Geoffrey Munn, *Castellani and Giuliano: Revivalist Jewellers of the 19th Century* (London 1984)

Jack Ogden, *Ancient Jewellery* (London 1992)

Susan Weber Soros and Stefanie Walker (eds), *Castellani and Italian Archaeological Jewellery* (New Haven and London 2004)

3: Art & Industry

H.W. Arrowsmith and A. Arrowsmith, *The House Decorator and Painter's Guide; containing a Series of Designs for Decorating Apartments, suited to the Various Styles of Architecture* (London 1840)

Samuel Bing, 'L'Art Nouveau', *Architectural Record*, vol. XII (1902)

Rosalind Blakesley, *The Arts and Crafts Movement* (London 2006)

Julius Bryant, *Creating the V&A: Victoria and Albert's Museum (1851–1861)* (London 2019)

———, *Enriching the V&A: A Collection of Collections (1862–1914)* (London 2022)

S. Calloway and L. Federle Orr (eds), *The Cult of Beauty: The Victorian Avant-garde 1860–1900* (London, San Francisco, New York 2011)

Moncure Daniel Conway, *Travels in South Kensington with Notes on Decorative Art and Architecture in England* (London 1882)

Peter Corrigan, *The Sociology of Consumption: An Introduction* (London 1997)

Charles Locke Eastlake, *Hints on Household Taste in Furniture, Upholstery and Other Details* (London 1868)

Edwina Ehrman (ed.), *Fashioned from Nature* (London 2018)

John Findling, *Historical Dictionary of Worlds Fairs and Expositions, 1851–1988* (New York 1990)

C. Gere and L. Hoskins, *The House Beautiful: Oscar Wilde and the Aesthetic Interior* (London 2000)

A. Grant and A. Patterson, *The Museum and the Factory: The V&A, Elkington and the Electrical Revolution* (London 2018)

Paul Greenhalgh (ed.), *Art Nouveau, 1890–1914* (New York 2000)

Guide to the South Kensington Museum (London 1857)

Tanya Harrod, *The Crafts in Britain in the Twentieth Century* (London 1999)

M. Hewitson, M. Winterbottom and C. Ribeyrol (eds), *Colour Revolution: Victorian Art, Fashion & Design* (Oxford 2023)

Olivia Horsfall Turner, *Owen Jones and the V&A: Ornament for a Modern Age* (London 2023)

Owen Jones, 'An Attempt to Define the Principles which Should Regulate the Employment of Colour in the Decorative Arts', read before the Society of Arts, 28 April 1852, in Owen Jones, *Lectures on Architecture and the Decorative Arts* (London 1863)

Lara Kriegel, *Grand Designs: Labor, Empire, and the Museum in Victorian Culture* (Durham, NC 2007)

Lionel Lambourne, *The Aesthetic Movement* (London 1996)

Karen Livingstone and L. Parry (eds), *International Arts and Crafts* (London 2005)

N.R. Marshall (ed.), *Victorian Science & Imagery: Representation and Knowledge in Nineteenth-century Visual Culture* (Pittsburgh 2021)

William Morris, *The Collected Works of William Morris, 1910–15* (reproduced New York 1966)

———, 'The Beauty of Life' (1880 lecture), in *The Collected Works of William Morris, 1910–15*, vol. 22

E. Prettejohn, *Art for Art's Sake: Aestheticism in Victorian Painting* (New Haven 2007)

M. Snodin and J. Styles, *Design & the Decorative Arts: Victorian Britain 1837–1901* (London 2004)

Zoe Thomas, *Women Art Workers and the Arts and Crafts Movement* (Manchester 2020)

Kevin W. Tucker, *Gustav Stickley and the American Arts and Crafts Movement* (New Haven 2010)

Augustus Welby Northmore Pugin (1812–1852)

Michael Fisher, *'Gothic For Ever': A.W.N. Pugin, Lord Shrewsbury, and the Rebuilding of Catholic England* (Salisbury 2017)

Rosemary Hill, *God's Architect: Pugin and the Building of Romantic Britain* (London 2007)

A.W.N. Pugin, *Contrasts, or, A Parallel between the Noble Edifices of the Fourteenth and Fifteenth Centuries, and Similar Buildings of the Present Day: Shewing the Present Decay of Taste: Accompanied by Appropriate Text* (London 1836)

John Dando Sedding, *Art and Handicrafts* (London 1893)

Clive Wainwright, *Pugin: A Gothic Passion* (New Haven 1994)

Alexandra Wedgwood, *A.W.N. Pugin and the Pugin Family (Catalogues of Architectural Drawings in the Victoria and Albert Museum)* (London 1985)

———, '"Pugin in his Home": A Memoir by J.H. Powell', *Architectural History*, vol. 31 (1988)

Léonard Morel-Ladeuil (1820–1888)

Lewis F. Day, 'The Late Mr Morel Ladeuil', *The Watchmaker, Jeweller and Silversmith*, vol. XIV, no. 1 (2 July 1888)

———, 'The Work of Morel-Ladeuil', *Magazine of Art*, vol. 13 (1890)

Alistair Grant, *Elkington & Co. and the Art of Electro-metallurgy, circa 1840–1900* (University of Sussex 2015), https://hdl.handle.net/10779/uos.23416799.v1

Alistair Grant and Angus Patterson, *The Museum and the Factory: The V&A, Elkington and the Electrical Revolution* (London 2018)

Aurélia Lechelon, 'Léonard Morel-Ladeuil: L'orfèvre oublié', *Bulletin historique et scientifique de l'Auvergne*, vol. 112/1, no. 788–9 (January 2011)

Léon Morel, *L'œuvre de Morel-Ladeuil: sculpteur-ciseleur, 1820–1888* (Paris 1904)

Angus Patterson and Marjorie Trusted (eds), *The Cast Courts* (London 2018)

Stuart W. Pyhrr and José Godoy, *Heroic Armor of the Italian Renaissance: Filippo Negroli and his Contemporaries* (New York 1998)

Edward Burne-Jones (1833–1898)

Georgiana Burne-Jones, *Memorials of Edward Burne-Jones* (London 1904)

Stephen Calloway and Lynn Federle Orr (eds), *The Cult of Beauty: The Aesthetic Movement 1860–1900* (London 2011)

Suzanne Fagence Cooper, *Pre-Raphaelite Art in the Victoria and Albert Museum* (London 2003)

Fiona MacCarthy, *The Last Pre-Raphaelite: Edward Burne-Jones and the Victorian Imagination* (Cambridge, MA 2012)

Alison Smith (ed.), *Edward Burne-Jones* (London 2018)

Stephen Wildman and John Christian, *Edward Burne-Jones: Victorian Artist-Dreamer* (New York 1998)

Andrea Wolk Rager, *The Radical Vision of Edward Burne-Jones* (London 2022)

William Morris (1834–1896)

Asa Briggs (ed.), *William Morris: News from Nowhere and Selected Writings and Designs* (Harmondsworth 1984)

J.W. Mackail, *The Life of William Morris* (London 1912)

Anna Mason (ed.), *William Morris* (London 2021)

Gill Naylor (ed.), *William Morris by Himself* (London 1988)

John Ruskin, *The Nature of Gothic: A Chapter of The Stones of Venice* (London 1892)

Linda Parry, *Textiles of the Arts and Crafts Movement* (London 1997)

E.P. Thompson, *William Morris: Romantic to Revolutionary* (London 1955)

Christopher Dresser (1834–1904)

Max Donnelly, *Christopher Dresser: Design Pioneer* (London 2021)

Christopher Dresser, *Principles of Decorative Design* (London, Paris and New York 1873)

———, *Studies in Design* (London 1874–6)

———, *Japan: Its Architecture, Art, and Art Manufactures* (London and New York 1882)

Stuart Durant, *Christopher Dresser* (London and Berlin 1993)

Widar Halén, *Christopher Dresser* (Oxford 1990)

Harry Lyons and Christopher Morley, *Christopher Dresser: The People's Designer, 1834–1904* (Woodbridge 2005)

Michael Whiteway (ed.), *Christopher Dresser: A Design Revolution / Shock of the Old: Christopher Dresser's Design Revolution* exh. cat., Victoria and Albert Museum and Cooper Hewitt, National Design Museum (London and New York 2004)

William De Morgan (1839–1917)

Jon Catleugh, *William De Morgan Tiles* (New York 1983)

William Gaunt and M.D.E. Clayton-Stamm, *William De Morgan* (London 1971)

Martin Greenwood, *The Designs of William De Morgan: A Catalogue* (London 1989)

Roger Pinkham, *Catalogue of Pottery by William De Morgan* (London 1973)

A.M.W. Stirling, *William De Morgan and his Wife* (New York 1922)

Émile Gallé (1846–1904)

Janine Bloch-Dermant, *The Art of French Glass 1860–1914* (London 1980)

Jessica M. Dandona, *Nature and the Nation in Fin-de-Siècle France: The Art of Emile Gallé and the Ecole de Nancy* (London 2017)

S. Kiyoshi (ed.), *Emile Gallé* (Hokkaido 2000)

François Le Tacon, *Émile Gallé: Maître de l'Art Nouveau* (Nancy 2004)

R. Tschuchida, M. Igaki and K. Seki (eds), *Gallé and Japonisme* (Osaka 2008)

R. Tschuchida, Y. Yasukouchi and D. Shibahashi (eds), *Emile Gallé, 170th Anniversary, with the exceptional support from the Musée d'Orsay* (Tokyo 2016)

Louis Comfort Tiffany (1848–1933)

J.B. Bullen, 'Louis Comfort Tiffany and the Romano-Byzantine Design', *Burlington Magazine*, vol. 147, no. 1227, 'Furniture, Decorative Arts, Sculpture' (June 2005)

Alice Cooney Frelinghuysen, *Louis Comfort Tiffany at the Metropolitan Museum of Art* (New Haven 2000)

———, *Louis Comfort Tiffany and Laurelton Hall: An Artist's Country Estate* (New Haven 2006)

Paul E. Doros, *The Art Glass of Louis Comfort Tiffany* (London 2013)

Richard H. Driehaus, *Louis Comfort Tiffany: Treasures from the Driehaus Collection* (New York 2013)

Martin Eidelberg and Alice Cooney Frelinghuysen, *The Lamps of Louis Comfort Tiffany* (London and New York 2005)

Martin Eidelberg and Margi Hofer, *A New Light on Tiffany: Clara Driscoll and the Tiffany Girls* (London 2007)

Rüdiger Joppien, 'Tiffany and Europe', in Rosalind M. Pepall (ed.), *Tiffany Glass: A Passion for Colour* (Paris 2009)

Robert Koch, *Louis C. Tiffany 1848–1933*, exh. cat., Museum of Contemporary Crafts of the American Craftsmen's Council (New York 1958)

———, *Rebel in Glass* (New York 1966)

———, *Louis C. Tiffany's Glass – Bronzes – Lamps: A Complete Collector's Guide* (New York 1971)

———, *Louis C. Tiffany's Art Glass* (New York 1977)

Roberta A. Mayer and Carolyn K. Lane, *Disassociating the 'Associated Artists': The Early Business Ventures of Louis C. Tiffany, Candace T. Wheeler and Lockwood de Forest, Studies in the Decorative Arts*, Spring–Summer 2001, vol. 8, no. 2 (University Chicago Press on behalf of the Bard Graduate Center 2001)

Hugh F. McKean, *The Lost Treasures of Louis Comfort Tiffany* (New York 1980)

Lindsy Riepma Parrott, 'Sheets and Shards, Gems and Jewels: The Glass Archive of the Neustadt Collection of Tiffany Glass', *Journal of Glass Studies*, vol. 51 (2009)

Phoebe Anna Traquair (1852–1936)

Nicola Gordon Bowe and Elizabeth Cumming, *The Arts & Crafts Movements in Dublin & Edinburgh 1885–1925* (Dublin 1998)

Annette Carruthers, *The Arts and Crafts Movement in Scotland* (New Haven 2013)

J.L. Caw, 'The Artwork of Mrs Traquair', *Art Journal*, vol. 62 (1900)

Elizabeth Cumming, *Phoebe Anna Traquair* (Edinburgh 1993)

———, *Hand, Heart and Soul: The Arts and Crafts Movement in Scotland* (Edinburgh 2006)

———, *Phoebe Anna Traquair* (rev. edn, Edinburgh 2022)

Bridget Elliott and Janice Helland (eds), *Women Artists and the Decorative Arts, 1880–1935: The Gender of Ornament* (Vermont 2003)

Peter Floud (ed.), *Victorian and Edwardian Decorative Arts* (London 1952)

May Morris (1862–1938)

Lynn Hulse (ed.), *May Morris: Art & Life, New Perspectives* (London 2017)

Karen Livingstone (ed.), *Women Pioneers of the Arts and Crafts Movement* (London 2024)

Jan Marsh, *Jane and May Morris: A Biographical Story 1839–1939* (London 1986)

———, 'Morris, Mary [May] (1862–1938)', Oxford Dictionary of National Biography, https://doi.org/10.1093/ref:odnb/37787 (accessed 27 March 2024)

Anna Mason et al., *May Morris: Arts & Crafts Designer* (London 2017)

May Morris, *Decorative Needlework* (London 1893)

———, *William Morris: Artist, Writer, Socialist*, 2 vols (Oxford 1936)

———, *The Introductions to The Collected Works of William Morris*, 2 vols (New York 1973)

Linda Parry, *William Morris Textiles* (London 2013)

Zoë Thomas, *Women Art Workers and the Arts and Crafts Movement* (Manchester 2020)

Charles Robert Ashbee (1863–1942)

Steven Adams, *The Arts and Crafts Movement* (London 1996), pp. 67–71

C. R. Ashbee, *Transactions of the Guild & School of Handicraft* (London 1890)

———, 'On Table Service', *Art Journal*, vol. 60 (1898)

———, *Modern English Silverwork: An Essay* (London 1974)

Felicity Ashbee, *Janet Ashbee: Love, Marriage, and the Arts & Crafts Movement* (New York 2002)

Cheltenham Art Gallery and Museum, *C.R. Ashbee & the Guild of Handicraft* (Cheltenham 1981)

Alan Crawford, *C.R. Ashbee: Architect, Designer & Romantic Socialist* (New Haven 1985)

Peter Davey, *Arts and Crafts Architecture* (London 1995), pp. 155–8

Fiona MacCarthy, *The Simple Life: C.R. Ashbee in the Cotswolds* (London 1981)

4: Modernism & the Post-War Craft Revival

Glenn Adamson, *Thinking Through Craft* (Oxford 2007)

———, *The Invention of Craft* (London 2013)

Glenn Adamson and Jane Pavitt (eds), *Postmodernism: Style and Subversion, 1970–90* (London 2011)

Charlotte Benton, Tim Benton and Ghislaine Wood (eds), *Art Deco 1910–1939* (London 2003)

Alison Britton, *Seeing Things: Collected Writings on Art, Craft and Design* (London 2013)

Craft Today USA, exh. cat., American Craft Museum (New York 1989)

Peter Dormer, *The Culture of Craft: Status and Future* (Manchester 1997)

Alun Graves, *Studio Ceramics: British Studio Pottery 1900 to Now* (London 2023)

Paul Greenhalgh (ed.), *The Persistence of Craft: The Applied Arts Today* (New Brunswick 2002)

Tanya Harrod, *The Crafts in Britain in the 20th Century* (New Haven 1999)

Lloyd E. Herman, *Art That Works: The Decorative Arts of the Eighties* (Seattle 1990)

Janet Kardon (ed.), *Craft in the Machine Age, 1920–1945* (New York 1995)

Janet Koplos and Bruce Metcalf, *Makers: A History of American Studio Craft* (Chapel Hill 2010)

Martina Margetts, *International Crafts* (London 1991)

Objects: USA, The Johnson Collection of Contemporary Craft, exh. cat., American Crafts Council, Museum of Contemporary Crafts (New York 1972)

Omega Workshops Ltd, Artist Decorators, 33 Fitzroy Square (*c.* 1915; photocopy in the National Art Library, V&A)

Frederic J. Schwarz, *The Werkbund: Design Theory and Mass Culture before the First World War* (New Haven 1996)

Jewel Stern, *Modernism in American Silver: 20th-Century Design* (Dallas 2005)

The Maker's Eye, exh. cat., Crafts Council (London 1981)

Christoph Thun-Hohenstein, Matthias Boeckl, Rainald Franz and Christian Witt-Dörring (eds), *Josef Hoffmann, 1870–1956: Progress through Beauty* (Vienna 2021)

Gerald W.R. Ward, Nonie Gadsden, Kelly H. L'Ecuyer and Melinda Talbot Nasardinov (eds), *American Decorative Arts and Sculpture* (Boston 2006)

René Jules Lalique (1860–1945)

Patricia Bayer and Mark Waller, *The Art of René Lalique* (London 1988)

Yvonne Brunhammer (ed.), *The Jewels of Lalique* (Paris 1998)

———, *René Lalique: Exceptional Jewellery, 1890–1912* (Milan 2007)

Nicholas M. Daes, *Lalique Glass* (Harmondsworth 1986)

Kelley Jo Elliot (ed.), *René Lalique: Enchanted by Glass* (New Haven 2014)

Tony L. Mortimer, *Lalique: Jewellery and Glassware* (London 1989)

Eileen Gray (1878–1976)

Peter Adam, *Eileen Gray: Architect, Designer: A Biography* (London 1987)

Archives of Art and Design: Eileen Gray, architect, furniture and interior designer: papers, 1913–1974; AAD/1980/9/3 and 11

Eileen Gray, exh. cat., Centre Pompidou (Paris 2013)

Jennifer Goff, *Eileen Gray: Her Life and her World* (Newbridge 2015)

Cloé Pitiot and Nina Stritzler-Levine (eds), *Eileen Gray* (New York 2020)

Jasmine Rault, 'Designing Sapphic Modernity', *Interiors*, vol. 1 (2010)

Joseph Rykwert, 'A Tribute to Eileen Gray, Design Pioneer', *Domus*, vol. 33 (December 1968)

Jane Stevenson, *Baroque between the Wars: Alternative Style in the Arts, 1918–1939* (Oxford 2018)

Despina Stratigakos, 'A Queer Analysis of Eileen Gray's E.1027', in Hilde Heynen and Gülsüm Baydar (eds), *Negotiating Domesticity: Spatial Productions of Gender in Modern Architecture* (New York 2005), pp. 162–81

Aino Marsio-Aalto (1894–1949) and Alvar Aalto (1898–1976)

Heikki Aalto-Alanen, *Aino + Alvar Aalto: A Life Together* (London 2023)

Jane Alison and Coralie Malissard (eds), *Modern Couples: Art, Intimacy and the Avant-garde* (London 2018)

Mia Hipeli and Esa Laaksonen, *Alvar Aalto Architect: Paimio Sanatorium 1929–33* (Helsinki 2014)

Göran Schildt, *Alvar Aalto in his Own Words* (New York 1997)

Nina Stritzler-Levine and Timo Riekko (eds), *Artek and the Aaltos: Creating a Modern World* (New York 2022)

Christopher Wilk, *Western Furniture 1350 to the Present Day* (London 1996)

Gunta Stölzl (1897–1983)

Magdalena Droste and Marion Ellwanger, *Gunta Stölzl Weberei am Bauhaus und aus eigener Werkstatt* (Berlin 1987)

Ethel Mairet, *Handweaving Today: Traditions and Changes* (London 1939)

Ulrika Müller, *Bauhaus Women: Art, Handicraft, Design* (Paris 2009)

Ingrid Radewaldt (ed.), *Gunta Stölzl–Meisterin am Bauhaus Dessau: Textilien, Textilentwürfe und freie Arbeiten 1915–1983* (Dessau 1997)

T'ai Smith, *Bauhaus Weaving Theory: From Feminine Craft to Mode of Design* (London and Minneapolis 2014)

Monika Stadler, *Gunta Stölzl: Bauhaus Master* (New York 2009)

Gunta Stölzl, 'Weberei am Bauhaus', *Offset: Buch und Werbekunst*, vol. 7 (1926)

Sigrid Wortman Weltge, *Women's Work: Textile Art from the Bauhaus* (San Francisco 1993)

Lucie Rie (1902–1995)

Margot Coatts (ed.), *Lucie Rie and Hans Coper: Potters in Parallel* (London 1997)

Emmanuel Cooper, *Lucie Rie: Modern Potter* (London 2021)

Alun Graves, *Studio Ceramics: British Studio Pottery 1900 to Now* (London 2023)

John Houston (ed.), *Lucie Rie: A Survey of her Life and Work* (London 1981)

Andrew Nairne and Eliza Spindel (eds), *Lucie Rie: The Adventure of Pottery* (Cambridge 2022)

Ruth Duckworth (1919–2009)

Ruth Duckworth and Alice Westphal, *Ruth Duckworth* (Evanston, IL, 1977)

Tanya Harrod, 'Free Spirit', *Crafts*, no. 85 (1987)

Jo Lauria and Tony Birks, *Ruth Duckworth: Modernist Sculptor* (Aldershot 2004)

Ruthin Craft Centre, *Ruth Duckworth: Duckworth at Ninety*, exh. cat. (Ruthin 2009)

Stanislav Libenský (1921–2002) and Jaroslava Brychtová (1924–2020)

Suzanne K. Frantz (ed.), *Stanislav Libenský and Jaroslava Brychtová: A 40 Year Collaboration in Glass* (New York 1994)

Stanislav Libenský & Jaroslava Brychtová, *Stanislav Libenský & Jaroslava Brychtová: Paintings, Drawings and Sculpture* (Seattle 1995)

Sylva Petrová, *Czech Glass* (Prague 2001)

Helmut Ricke (ed.), *Czech Glass 1945–1980: Design in an Age of Adversity* (New York and Prague 2005)

Althea McNish (1924–2020)

Christine Checinska, 'Althea McNish and the British African Diaspora', in Anne Massey and Alex Seago (eds), *British Pop Art and Design* (London 2017)

———, 'In Conversation with Althea McNish and John Weiss', in Christine Checinska (ed.), *Textile: Journal of Cloth and Culture* (London 2018)

———, Interview with Ceri Hand, 16 September 2019

Lesley Jackson, *Shirley Craven and Hull Traders, Revolutionary Fabrics and Furniture 1957–1980* (Hull 2017)

John La Rose, 'Althea McNish in Conversation with John Weiss with John La Rose in the Chair', in Roxy Harris and Sarah White (eds), *Building Britannia* (London 2022)

Anne Massey, *The Independent Group: Modernism and Mass Culture in Britain 1945–59* (Manchester 1995)

Anne Walmsley, *The Caribbean Artists Movement 1966–1972* (London 1992)

Marjorie Schick (1941–2017)

Oral history interview with Marjorie Schick, 4–6 April 2004, Archives of American Art, Smithsonian Institution (si.edu)

Tacey Rosolowski (ed.), *Sculpture to Wear: The Jewelry of Marjorie Schick* (Stuttgart 2007)

Ralph Turner, *Jewelry in Europe and America: New Times, New Thinking* (London 1996)

Dale Chihuly (b.1941)

Dale Chihuly, *Fire* (Seattle 2006)

Dale Chihuly et al., *Chihuly: Jerusalem 2000* (Seattle 2000)

———, *The Art of Dale Chihuly*, exh. cat., Museums of San Francisco (San Francisco 2008)

Jennifer Hawkins Opie (ed.), *Chihuly at the V&A* (London 2001)

Donald Kuspit, *Chihuly* (New York 2014)

Tina Oldknow, *Pilchuck: A Glass School* (Seattle 1996)

——— (ed.), *Venice and American Studio Glass* (Milan 2020)

Albert Paley (b.1944)

Edward Lucie-Smith, *The Art of Albert Paley: Iron, Bronze, Steel* (New York 1996)

Albert Paley et al., *Inspiration and Context: The Drawings of Albert Paley*, exh. cat., Memorial Art Gallery of the University of Rochester (Rochester 1994)

Albert Paley and Craig E. Adcock (eds), *Albert Paley: Sculpture, Drawings, Graphics and Decorative Arts*, exh. cat., Florida State University (Tallahassee 2001)

Albert Paley and Carter Ratcliff, *Albert Paley in the 21st Century*, exh. cat., Memorial Art Gallery of the University of Rochester (Rochester 2010)

Albert Paley and Corcoran Gallery, *American Metal: The Art of Albert Paley* (Washington DC 2014)

Towards a New Iron Age, exh. cat, Victoria and Albert Museum (London 1982)

Charlotte de Syllas (b.1946)

Jenefer Coates (ed.), *Charlotte de Syllas: Jewellery in Carved Gemstones* (UK 2016)

Joanna Hardy and Malcolm Cossons (eds), *Collect Contemporary Jewellery* (London 2012)

Clare Phillips, 'Charlotte de Syllas: A Profile', *Goldsmith's Review* (1999/2000)

Alison Britton (b.1948)

Alison Britton, *Seeing Things: Collected Writing on Art, Craft and Design* (London 2022)

Peter Dormer, *Alison Britton in Studio* (London 1985)

Tanya Harrod, *Alison Britton: Ceramics in Studio* (London 1990)

Life and Still Life: New Pots by Alison Britton shown with Objects from her Collection, exh. cat., Crafts Study Centre (Farnham 2012)

Linda Sandino, *Complexity and Ambiguity: The Ceramics of Alison Britton* (London 2000)

The Maker's Eye, exh. cat., Crafts Council (London 1981)

The Work of Alison Britton, exh. cat., Crafts Council (London 1979)

AUTHORS' BIOGRAPHIES

Claire Allen-Johnstone is an Assistant Curator in the Performance, Furniture, Textiles and Fashion Department at the V&A. She was part of the editorial team for *Silk: Fibre, Fabric and Fashion* (London 2021). Her doctoral thesis explored 'Dress, Feminism and British New Woman Novels'.

Silvija Banić is the Curator of Textiles before 1800 in the Performance, Furniture, Textiles and Fashion Department at the V&A.

Connie Karol Burks is Curator of Textiles and Fashion Since 1900 at the V&A.

Christine Checinska is the V&A's inaugural Senior Curator of Africa and Diaspora Textiles and Fashion. She is the Lead Curator of the V&A international touring exhibition *Africa Fashion* (2022–6). She is also a Research Associate at the Visual Identities in Art and Design Research Centre (VIAD), University of Johannesburg.

Emefa Cole is a Curator of Jewellery (Diaspora) at the V&A. She is also a practising jewellery artist.

Judith Crouch is Curatorial Operations Coordinator for the Department of Decorative Art and Sculpture at the V&A. She specializes in painted enamels on copper. Over many years with the Museum, she has curated displays both permanent and temporary and written on ceramics, glass and enamels subjects.

Kate Devine is Assistant Curator of Ceramics and Glass at the V&A and writes on modern craft and culture.

Max Donnelly is the Curator of Furniture and Woodwork, 1800–1915, at the V&A. He contributed to the book *C.F.A. Voysey: Arts and Crafts Designer* (2016), authored *Christopher Dresser: Design Pioneer* (2021) and curated the V&A touring exhibition, *Beyond William Morris: British Arts and Crafts 1890–1920* (China, 2023–6).

Iona Farrell is the Assistant Curator of Metalwork at the V&A. She previously worked at the Science Museum Group on a large-scale collections review project, and prior to that she curated the social history collection at Southend Museums Service.

Alistair Grant is a Lecturer in Art History at the University of Sussex. His research has shaped and informed the displays and interpretations in the refurbished Cast Courts and new Chitra Nirmal Sethia Gallery at the V&A, which has transformed the Museum's understanding and approach to presenting its unique and extensive collection of copies, especially electrotypes. With Angus Patterson he co-wrote *The Museum and the Factory: The V&A, Elkington and the Electrical Revolution* (London 2018).

Alun Graves is Senior Curator, Ceramics and Glass 1900–Now, in the Decorative Art and Sculpture Department at the V&A. He is the author of *Studio Ceramics: British Studio Pottery 1900 to Now* (London 2023) and has written widely on twentieth- and twenty-first-century British ceramics and sculpture.

Jessica Harpley is an Assistant Curator within the V&A's Department of Performance, Furniture, Textiles and Fashion. She has published on the Victorian chatelaine and contributed to the exhibitions *Bags: Inside Out* and *Africa Fashion*.

Olivia Horsfall Turner is Chief Curator at the Royal Institute of British Architects. From 2014 to 2024 she was Senior Curator of Architecture and Design at the V&A.

Nick Humphrey is Curator of Furniture and Woodwork, 1300–1700 at the V&A. He was co-curator of the Dr Susan Weber Gallery of Furniture (2012) and has published variously in relation to the Museum's galleries, covering Britain 1500–1900 (2001), Medieval and Renaissance (2009) and Europe 1600–1815 (2015).

Catrin Jones is Chief Curator of the V&A Wedgwood Collection. Her exhibitions include *Grayson Perry: The Pre-Therapy Years* (2020) and she has published widely on historic and contemporary applied arts, including the recent V&A/Thames & Hudson book *Wedgwood: Craft & Design* (2023). She is a Trustee of the Clay Foundation.

Sandy Jones is Assistant Curator of Architecture at the V&A with a special interest in graphic design and jewellery design. She was Curatorial Researcher for the exhibition *Plastic: Remaking Our World* (2021 and touring).

Kirstin Kennedy is Curator of Metalwork, 1450–1900, in the Department of Decorative Art and Sculpture at the V&A.

Rebecca Knott is Senior Curator of Metalwork, 1900–Now and V&A Dundee Scottish Design Galleries, in the Department of Decorative Art and Sculpture at the V&A. She was previously Lead Curator of the V&A East Storehouse.

Reino Liefkes is Senior Curator, Ceramics and Glass, in the Department of Decorative Art and Sculpture at the V&A. He specializes in European glass and ceramics.

Clementine Loustric is an art and craft historian, specializing in European material culture and decorative arts from 1650 to now. She was previously Assistant Curator of Metalwork, 1900–Now at the V&A, Assistant Curator of the Rosalinde and Arthur Gilbert Collection, and Curator of the Chitra Collection.

Rosalind McKever is Curator of Paintings and Drawings at the V&A and specializes in modern European art, its reception in Britain and North and South America, and its relationship with fashion and design. Her V&A publications include *Fashioning Masculinities: The Art of Menswear* (2022) and *Vanessa Bell: Modern Living* (2025).

Danilo Marques dos Reis is an Assistant Curator of Furniture, Textiles and Fashion at the V&A. He contributed to the creation of the V&A's first sustainability public programme *Make Good: Rethinking Material Futures* (2022).

Alice Minter is Senior Curator of the Rosalinde and Arthur Gilbert Collection on loan to the V&A. She specializes in European decorative arts, principally silver and gold boxes, and recently published *The Art of Stone: Masterpieces from the Rosalinde and Arthur Gilbert Collection* (2023).

PICTURE CREDITS

Sophie Morris is Curator of the Rosalinde and Arthur Gilbert Collection at the V&A. She contributed to the publications *The Art of Stone* (2023) and *La Goût de la Renaissance: Un dialogue entre collections* (2024).

Angus Patterson is Senior Curator of Metalwork at the V&A and is responsible for collections of European metalwork and arms and armour from 1450 to 1900. He has a particular interest in the impact of industrialization on metalwork and is the V&A's Trustee on the Board of Sheffield Museums. With Alistair Grant he co-wrote *The Museum and the Factory: The V&A, Elkington and the Electrical Revolution* (London 2018).

James Robinson is Keeper of Decorative Art and Sculpture at the V&A. He was formerly Director at the Burrell Collection, Glasgow; Keeper of Art and Design at the National Museum of Scotland, Edinburgh; and Senior Curator of Late Medieval Collections at the British Museum.

Jessica Rosenthal McGrath is Assistant Curator of Jewellery and Metalwork at the V&A. She has a particular interest in commemorative and *memento mori* jewellery, and her doctoral studies at Swansea University and the National Portrait Gallery in London investigated post-Reformation commemorative portraiture in English and Welsh parish churches.

Jenny Saunt, Senior Curator of Furniture and Woodwork at the V&A, specializes in furniture and interiors from 1660 to *c*.1780. She publishes and lectures on her research interests, which include histories of making, craft practices and networks, and interactions of materials, design and production in seventeenth- and eighteenth-century England.

Simon Spier is Curator of Ceramics and Glass, 1600–1800. Prior to joining the V&A he worked for other collections including Royal Collection Trust and The Bowes Museum.

Florence Tyler is Curator of Ceramics and Glass, 1800–1900, in the Department of Decorative Art and Sculpture at the V&A. She contributed to the publications *Women Pioneers of the Arts & Crafts Movement* (2024) and *Filthy Lucre: Whistler's Peacock Room Reimagined* (2020). She curated the display *The Artistic Home: British Art Pottery from the Ian and Rita Smythe Collection* (2022–3).

Ashley Weaver-Paul is Curator of Ceramics and Glass, 1800–1900, at the V&A. Her interests include European and American ceramics and glass in the eighteenth and nineteenth centuries. Prior to joining the V&A, she worked at Emery Walker's House, an Arts and Crafts house museum in west London.

Maude Willaerts is an Assistant Curator in the Performance, Furniture, Textiles and Fashion Department at the V&A, primarily working with contemporary furniture and product design. V&A projects include the new permanent gallery Design 1900–Now and the ten-year-long *Make Good: Rethinking Material Futures* programme.

INDEX

Page numbers in *italics* refer to illustrations

Cover: Lucie Rie considering an incised pot (RIE/20/1/11), c.1990s. Photographer unknown. From the collection of the Crafts Study Centre, University for the Creative Arts, Farnham.
Quarter-binding: Gunta Stölzl, Detail of *Red-Green Tapestry*, 1927–8 (illus. page 298). © DACS 2024. Photo: © Bauhaus-Archiv Berlin
Frontispiece: Josiah Wedgwood & Sons, Detail of first-edition copy of the Portland Vase, 1790 (illus. page 125). Photo: © V&A

First published in the United Kingdom in 2025 by
Thames & Hudson Ltd, 6–24 Britannia Street, London WC1X 9JD
in association with the Victoria and Albert Museum, London

First published in the United States of America in 2025 by
Thames & Hudson Inc., 500 Fifth Avenue, New York, New York 10110

Lives of the Great Makers: 500 Years of Creative Excellence © 2025
Victoria and Albert Museum, London/Thames & Hudson Ltd, London

Text and V&A photographs © 2025 Victoria and Albert Museum, London
Design © 2025 Thames & Hudson Ltd, London

Designed by Studio Noel

EU Authorized Representative: Interart S.A.R.L.
19 rue Charles Auray, 93500 Pantin, Paris
productsafety@thameshudson.co.uk
interart.fr

A CIP catalogue record for this book is available from the British Library

Library of Congress Control Number 2024951556

ISBN   978-0-500-48104-2
01

Printed and bound in China by C&C Offset Printing Co. Ltd.

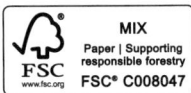

MIX
Paper | Supporting responsible forestry
FSC® C008047
www.fsc.org

Be the first to know about our new releases, exclusive content and author events by visiting
thamesandhudson.com
thamesandhudsonusa.com
thamesandhudson.com.au

V&\ Publishing
The power of creativity

Discover more at vam.ac.uk

ACKNOWLEDGMENTS

This book has been a true team effort, and the editors are extremely grateful to all the contributors who have so generously shared their expertise through their biographies. Many other colleagues supported and participated in the project in different ways, including Jenny Lister, Clare Phillips, Helen Molesworth, Victoria Bradley, Anna Bates, Christopher Wilk, Spike Sweeting, Sarah Medlam and Clarissa Ward. External specialists responded generously to queries or read the text, including Frédéric Dassas, Yannick Chastang, John Mallet, Errol and Henry Manners, Clunie Fretton, Patricia Butler, Gabriel Sempill, Eleni Bide, Eric Turner, Jack Hayes and Alison Britton. We are particularly grateful to Nick Humphrey, Reino Liefkes, Tim Barringer and Tanya Harrod for so thoughtfully and generously reviewing and providing feedback on the texts. Special thanks are also due to William, Judith, Douglas and James Bollinger for their generous loan of the *Winter Woodland* pendant to the V&A. Iona Farrell, Ashley Weaver-Paul, Sandy Jones and Danilo Marques dos Reis ably undertook the task of coordinating new photography of V&A objects, while Kira Zumkley, Sarah Duncan, George Eksts, Ed Lyon, Kieron Boyle and Kevin Percival captured the works so creatively and expertly. From V&A Publishing we are enormously grateful to Rebecca Fortey and Hannah Newell for their patience, hard work and expert guidance throughout the project, and at Thames & Hudson to Julian Honer for his support and advice, and Rosalind Horne and Julie Bosser for their careful management of the later stages of the project. Studio Noel produced an excellent design, while Robert Sargent honed the text with patient and careful copy-editing, and Amy Lewis undertook the picture research. Lastly, many thanks to friends and family for their encouragement and support throughout the development of this book.